T0214047

Lecture Notes in Computer Science   12479

Tiziana Margaria · Bernhard Steffen (Eds.)

Leveraging Applications of Formal Methods, Verification and Validation

Tools and Trends

9th International Symposium
on Leveraging Applications of Formal Methods, ISoLA 2020
Rhodes, Greece, October 20–30, 2020
Proceedings, Part IV

 Springer

Editors
Tiziana Margaria 🆔
University of Limerick and Lero
Limerick, Ireland

Bernhard Steffen 🆔
TU Dortmund
Dortmund, Germany

ISSN 0302-9743   ISSN 1611-3349   (electronic)
Lecture Notes in Computer Science
ISBN 978-3-030-83722-8   ISBN 978-3-030-83723-5   (eBook)
https://doi.org/10.1007/978-3-030-83723-5

LNCS Sublibrary: SL1 – Theoretical Computer Science and General Issues

This Springer imprint is published by the registered company Springer Nature Switzerland AG
The registered company address is: Gewerbestrasse 11, 6330 Cham, Switzerland

Introduction

It is our responsibility, as general and program chairs, to welcome the participants to the 9th International Symposium on Leveraging Applications of Formal Methods, Verification and Validation (ISoLA), planned to take place in Rhodes, Greece, during October 20–30, 2020, endorsed by the European Association of Software Science and Technology (EASST).

This year's event follows the tradition of its symposia forerunners held in Paphos, Cyprus (2004 and 2006), Chalkidiki, Greece (2008), Crete, Greece (2010 and 2012), Corfu, Greece (2014 and 2016), and most recently in Limassol, Cyprus (2018), and the series of ISoLA workshops in Greenbelt, USA (2005), Poitiers, France (2007), Potsdam, Germany (2009), Vienna, Austria (2011), and Palo Alto, USA (2013).

Considering that this year's situation is unique and unlike any previous one due to the ongoing COVID-19 pandemic, and that ISoLA's symposium touch and feel is much unlike most conventional, paper-based conferences, after much soul searching we are faced with a true dilemma. "Virtualizing" the event, as many conferences have done, violates the true spirit of the symposium, which is rooted in the gathering of communities and the discussions within and across the various communities materialized in the special tracks and satellite events. Keeping with the physical meeting and holding it in a reduced form (as many may not be able to or feel comfortable with travel) under strict social distancing rules may also end up not being feasible. At the time of writing there is a resurgence of cases in several countries, many nations are compiling "green lists" of countries with which they entertain free travel relations, and these lists are updated – most frequently shortened – at short notice, with severe consequence for the travelers. Many governments and universities are again strengthening the travel restrictions for their employees, and many of us would anyway apply caution due to our own specific individual situation.

To be able to react as flexibly as possible to this situation, we decided to split ISoLA 2020 into two parts, one this year and one in October 2021, with the track organizers deciding when their track will take place. So far both dates have promoters, but it may still happen that, in the end, the entire event needs to move. All accepted papers are published in time, but some tracks will present their papers at the 2021 event.

As in the previous editions, ISoLA 2020 provides a forum for developers, users, and researchers to discuss issues related to the adoption and use of rigorous tools and methods for the specification, analysis, verification, certification, construction, test, and maintenance of systems from the point of view of their different application domains. Thus, since 2004, the ISoLA series of events serves the purpose of bridging the gap between designers and developers of rigorous tools on one side, and users in engineering and in other disciplines on the other side. It fosters and exploits synergetic relationships among scientists, engineers, software developers, decision makers, and other critical thinkers in companies and organizations. By providing a specific, dialogue-oriented venue for the discussion of common problems, requirements, algorithms, methodologies, and practices, ISoLA aims in particular at supporting researchers in their quest to improve the usefulness, reliability, flexibility, and efficiency of tools for building systems, and users in their search for adequate solutions to their problems.

The program of the symposium consists of a collection of special tracks devoted to the following hot and emerging topics:

- Reliable Smart Contracts: State-of-the-art, Applications, Challenges and Future Directions
  (Organizers: Gordon Pace, César Sànchez, Gerardo Schneider)
- Engineering of Digital Twins for Cyber-Physical Systems
  (Organizers: John Fitzgerald, Pieter Gorm Larsen, Tiziana Margaria, Jim Woodcock)
- Verification and Validation of Concurrent and Distributed Systems
  (Organizers: Cristina Seceleanu, Marieke Huisman)
- Modularity and (De-) composition in Verification
  (Organizers: Reiner Hähnle, Eduard Kamburjan, Dilian Gurov)
- Software Verification Tools
  (Organizers: Markus Schordan, Dirk Beyer, Irena Boyanova)
- X-by-Construction: Correctness meets Probability
  (Organizers: Maurice H. ter Beek, Loek Cleophas, Axel Legay, Ina Schaefer, Bruce W. Watson)
- Rigorous Engineering of Collective Adaptive Systems
  (Organizers: Rocco De Nicola, Stefan Jähnichen, Martin Wirsing)
- Automated Verification of Embedded Control Software
  (Organizers: Dilian Gurov, Paula Herber, Ina Schaefer)
- Automating Software Re-Engineering
  (Organizers: Serge Demeyer, Reiner Hähnle, Heiko Mantel)
- 30 years of Statistical Model Checking!
  (Organizer: Kim G. Larsen, Axel Legay)
- From Verification to Explanation
  (Organizers: Holger Herrmanns, Christel Baier)
- Formal methods for DIStributed COmputing in future RAILway systems (DisCo-Rail 2020)
  (Organizers: Alessandro Fantechi, Stefania Gnesi, Anne Haxthausen)
- Programming: What is Next?
  (Organizers: Klaus Havelund, Bernhard Steffen)

With the embedded events:

- RERS: Challenge on Rigorous Examination of Reactive Systems (Falk Howar, Markus Schordan, Bernhard Steffen)
- Doctoral Symposium and Poster Session (A.L. Lamprecht)
- Industrial Day (Falk Howar, Johannes Neubauer, Andreas Rausch)

Colocated with the ISoLA symposium is:

- STRESS 2020 – 5th International School on Tool-based Rigorous Engineering of Software Systems (J. Hatcliff, T. Margaria, Robby, B. Steffen)

Altogether the ISoLA 2020 proceedings comprises four volumes, Part 1: Verification Principles, Part 2: Engineering Principles, Part 3: Applications, and Part 4: Tools and Trends, which also covers the associated events.

We thank the track organizers, the members of the Program Committee and their referees for their effort in selecting the papers to be presented, the local organization chair, Petros Stratis, and the EasyConferences team for their continuous and precious support during the entire two-year period preceding the events, and Springer for being, as usual, a very reliable partner for the proceedings production. Finally, we are grateful to Kyriakos Georgiades for his continuous support for the website and the program, and to Markus Frohme and Julia Rehder for their help with the editorial system Equinocs.

Special thanks are due to the following organization for their endorsement: EASST (European Association of Software Science and Technology) and Lero – The Irish Software Research Centre, and our own institutions – TU Dortmund University and the University of Limerick.

We wish you, as an ISoLA participant, a wonderful experience at this edition, and for you, reading the proceedings at a later occasion, valuable new insights that hopefully contribute to your research and its uptake.

August 2020   Tiziana Margaria
                                                                     Bernhard Steffen

Organization

PC Chair

Bernhard Steffen   TU Dortmund University, Germany

PC Members

Christel Baier	Technische Universität Dresden, Germany
Maurice ter Beek	ISTI-CNR, Italy
Dirk Beyer	LMU Munich, Germany
Irena Bojanova	NIST, USA
Loek Cleophas	Eindhoven University of Technology, The Netherlands
Rocco De Nicola	IMT Lucca, Italy
Serge Demeyer	Universiteit Antwerpen, Belgium
Alessandro Fantechi	University of Florence, Italy
John Fitzgerald	Newcastle University, UK
Stefania Gnesi	CNR, Italy
Kim Guldstrand Larsen	Aalborg University, Denmark
Dilian Gurov	KTH Royal Institute of Technology, Sweden
John Hatcliff	Kansas State University, USA
Klaus Havelund	Jet Propulsion Laboratory, USA
Anne E. Haxthausen	Technical University of Denmark, Denmark
Paula Herber	University of Münster, Germany
Holger Hermanns	Saarland University, Germany
Falk Howar	Dortmund University of Technology and Fraunhofer ISST, Germany
Marieke Huisman	University of Twente, The Netherlands
Reiner Hähnle	Technische Universität Darmstadt, Germany
Stefan Jähnichen	TU Berlin, Germany
Eduard Kamburjan	Technische Universität Darmstadt, Germany
Anna-Lena Lamprecht	Utrecht University, The Netherlands
Peter Gorm Larsen	Aarhus University, Denmark
Axel Legay	Universitè Catholique de Louvain, Belgium
Heiko Mantel	Technische Universität Darmstadt, Germany
Tiziana Margaria	Lero, Ireland
Johannes Neubauer	Materna, Germany
Gordon Pace	University of Malta, Malta
Cesar Sanchez	IMDEA Software Institute, Madrid, Spain
Ina Schaefer	TU Braunschweig, Germany
Gerardo Schneider	University of Gothenburg, Sweden
Markus Schordan	Lawrence Livermore National Laboratory, USA
Cristina Seceleanu	Mälardalen University, Sweden

Bernhard Steffen	TU Dortmund University, Germany
Bruce Watson	Stellenbosch University, South Africa
Martin Wirsing	Ludwig-Maximilians-Universität München, Germany
James Woodcock	University of York, UK

Reviewers

Pekka Aho
Bernhard Aichernig
Peter Backeman
Eduard Baranov
Davide Basile
Bernhard Beckert
Dirk Beyer
Ferruccio Damiani
Jean-Christophe Filliâtre
Roberto Guanciale
Bart Jacobs
Manfred Jaeger

Peter Jensen
Einar Broch Johnsen
Sung-Shik Jongmans
Sudeep Kanav
Igor Konnov
Nikolai Kosmatov
Jan Kretinsky
Bettina Könighofer
Ivan Lanese
Romain Soulat
Mattias Ulbrich

Contents – Part IV

From Verification to Explanation

From Verification to Explanation
(Track Introduction)

Christel Baier[1] and Holger Hermanns[2,3]

[1] Technische Universität Dresden, Germany
[2] Universität des Saarlandes, Saarland Informatics Campus, Germany
[3] Institute of Intelligent Software, Guangzhou, China

1 Introduction

It is becoming the norm that software artefacts participate in actions and decisions that affect humans. This trend has been catching momentum for decades, and is now amplified considerably by the remarkable abilities of machine-learnt methods.

However, our understanding of what is the cause of a specific automated decision is lagging far behind. More severe, we are lacking the scientifc basis to explain how several such applications interact in cascades of automated decisions. With the increase in cyber-physical technology impacting our lives, the consequences of this gradual loss in understanding are becoming severe.

The long-term ambition of this track of ISOLA is to explore how computer aided verification techniques can be leveraged to master the explanation challenge. Our focus are algorithmic and tool-supported approaches that aim at making the behaviour of software and CPS systems understandable.

2 Context

Scientifc work on explanations has not been an explicit focus of past research in the verification community, but nevertheless there are a number of prominent techniques that can be considered individual attack points for orchestrated efforts. We review the (according to our limited understanding) major research directions below.

Explaining negative verification results. Most model-checking tools accompany negative verification results with *counterexamples* to provide an evidence why the model violates its specification. These are finite prefixes of erroneous executions of the model. Although such counterexamples can support debugging, they often tend to be long and identifying the failure in the counterexample trace becomes a non-trivial task. This observation has motivated research on how to extract the relevant information from counterexamples that is needed for debugging purposes. Following the structural equation approach of Halpern and Pearl, the causality-based analysis of counterexamples has been first proposed by Beer et al. [2] with the intention to generate and visualise user-understandable

© Springer Nature Switzerland AG 2021
T. Margaria and B. Steffen (Eds.): ISoLA 2020, LNCS 12479, pp. 3–9, 2021.
https://doi.org/10.1007/978-3-030-83723-5_1

explanations in terms of diagrams for selected paths. This approach has been further advanced by analysing sets of counterexample traces for the purpose of extracting causal relations and representing them by logical formulas, which are then used to generate visualisable fault trees [32,31]. Other techniques aiming at explanations of negative model-checking results rely on distance metrics for program executions to support understanding and the localisation of errors [17,18]. An approach for cause consequence analysis using temporal logics has been presented in [36,20].

Explaining positive verification results. Orthogonal to the approaches for explaining negative verification results is *vacuity detection* and the *certification* of verification results. Vacuity detection [3,27,5] is motivated by the observation that positive verification results cannot rule out cases where the model is wrong or where there is no perfect match between the formal specification and the desired requirements. It relies on a stronger ("non-vacuous") satisfaction relation than in standard model checking and aims to report sufficiently informative witnesses for non-vacuously valid temporal formulas in a given model. Another direction is the *certification* of formal verification results [28,38] where the task is to accompany positive model-checking results with a certificate that serves as evidence for the successful system verification and can be checked separately to confirm that the system indeed meets its specification. Certification techniques for probabilistic models have been proposed that are based on Farkas certificates [16,23,22] and shown to be related to the construction of witnessing subsystems as in [1,40,21]. There is also recent work on certification techniques for timed automata [43,42]. One step further is the line of research that addresses the verification and certification of formal verifiers using theorem-proving techniques, see, e.g., [13,24].

Causality Reasoning. Besides the above mentioned work on the causality-based analysis of counterexamples to extract user-understandable explanations of model-checking results, combinations of causality-based reasoning and model-checking techniques have also been used by Chockler et al. [8,9,4,7] to reason about the *degree of the responsibility* of components for the satisfaction or violation of system properties as well as related coverage metrics. First steps towards compositional causality reasoning in nonprobabilistic systems and for temporal events of a simple modal logic have been presented recently in [6].

Another research direction is to exploit synergies between causality techniques and model checking. An on-the-fly approach to detect causal relationships and to classify execution traces as good or bad with respect to the property to be checked has been presented in [32] and extended in [33] for the quantitative analysis of Markov chains. The essential idea of the *causality-based model-checking* [29,30,15] is to avoid the explicit reference to states of a system model as it is the case for standard model checking. Instead it relies on a notion of concurrent traces and causal links between them and proof rules given by trace transformers. Together with sophisticated data structures, this approach can reduce the complexity of model checking for multi-threaded programs from exponential to polynomial time.

Verfication Explanations for Humans. Many forms of graphical models have been introduced to reason about causality. Examples include cause-effect graphs that have been introduced in the context of software testing [35] or Petri nets [10], or causal graphs [12] that have been used to design tractable algorithms for deciding different forms for causes in Halpern and Pearl's structural-model approach.

In the probabilistic setting, various graphical models have been proposed in the literature to represent causal dependencies. Most prominent are Bayesian networks that rely on directed acyclic graphs where the nodes represent variables and the edges indicate conditional dependencies (see, e.g., [37]). To overcome the limitations of classical Bayesian networks that assume discrete variables and do not support reasoning about time, several extensions have been proposed in the literature to formalise how the dependencies evolve over time slices (dynamic Bayesian networks) or to reason about continuous variables (e.g., hybrid or heterogeneous Bayesian networks). Another prominent visualisable model are (dynamic) fault trees [39,11], a well-established industrial standard and graphical notation to illustrate how a hazard can be caused by a combination of so called basic events. In the context of probabilistic model checking, the generation of fault trees from probabilistic counterexamples for Markov chains has been studied by Leitner-Fischer et al. [26,34,31].

Aiming at human-understandable textual explanations, the translations of minimal critical sub-MDPs (counterexamples for MDPs as in [40]) into guarded command language has been developed in [41]. The recent paper [14] proposes an alternative approach based on structural natural language sentences to describe the behaviour that leads to a violation of system requirements.

3   Contributions in this Track

For the 2020 edition of ISOLA, the track editors have selected two contribution that represent the spectrum of research on verification methods for explanations very well.

The paper by Kölbl and Leue entitled *An Algorithm to Compute a Strict Partial Orderering of Actions in Action Trees* [25] focusses on tool support for causality checking. At its core is a novel method for computing a causal explanation. This explanation here takes the form of an ordered sequences of actions that lead to a violation of a reachability property. Earlier work in this context was able to compute the unordered set of such actions, while the present contribution additionally provides them in a strictly partial ordered form, thus giving more specific axplanatory feedback to the user. The approach is implemented in the tool QuantUM and its performance and usability is discussed.

The paper by Gros et al. entitled *TraceVis: Towards Visualization for Deep Statistical Model Checking* [19] showcases a very innovative explanation component for neural network behaviour. It starts off from deep statistical model checking (DSMC), a recently proposed approach to statistically analyse the behaviour of a neural network employed as a decision entity to solve a family of two-dimensional navigation problems, known as the Racetrack. The DSMC analysis delivers a variety of estimates of numerical nature. The present paper explores the use of visualization techniques to support human analysts and domain engineers when exploringthese results. The authors present an interactive visualization tool which enables visual exploration of Racetrack crash probabilities as well as in-depth examination of the policy traces generated by DSMC. By this, the authors succesfully demonstrate how visualization can foster the effective model-checking-based analysis for the purpose of advanced explanation support for neural network behaviour.

Acknowledgments. This initiative would not have been possible without the support by the Deutsche Forschungsgemeinschaft for the Center for Perspicuous Computing (TRR 248, Grant 389792660). It furthermore has received support by the Key-Area Research and Development Program Grant 2018B010107004 of Guangdong Province.

References

1. Erika Ábrahám, Bernd Becker, Christian Dehnert, Nils Jansen, Joost-Pieter Katoen, and Ralf Wimmer. Counterexample generation for discrete-time markov models: An introductory survey. In Marco Bernardo, Ferruccio Damiani, Reiner Hähnle, Einar Broch Johnsen, and Ina Schaefer, editors, *Formal Methods for Executable Software Models - 14th International School on Formal Methods for the Design of Computer, Communication, and Software Systems (SFM)*, volume 8483 of *Lecture Notes in Computer Science*, pages 65–121. Springer, 2014.
2. Ilan Beer, Shoham Ben-David, Hana Chockler, Avigail Orni, and Richard J. Trefler. Explaining counterexamples using causality. *Formal Methods in System Design*, 40(1):20–40, 2012.
3. Ilan Beer, Shoham Ben-David, Cindy Eisner, and Yoav Rodeh. Efficient detection of vacuity in temporal model checking. *Formal Methods in System Design*, 18(2):141–163, 2001.
4. Shoham Ben-David, Hana Chockler, and Orna Kupferman. Attention-based coverage metrics. In *9th Int. Haifa Verification Conf. on Hardware and Software: Verification and Testing (HVC)*, volume 8244 of *LNCS*, pages 230–245. Springer, 2013.
5. Shoham Ben-David, Fady Copty, Dana Fisman, and Sitvanit Ruah. Vacuity in practice: temporal antecedent failure. *Formal Methods in System Design*, 46(1):81–104, 2015.
6. Georgiana Caltais, Stefan Leue, and Mohammad Reza Mousavi. (de-)composing causality in labeled transition systems. In *First Workshop on Causal Reasoning for Embedded and safety-critical Systems Technologies*, volume 224 of *EPTCS*, pages 10–24, 2016.
7. Hana Chockler, Norman E. Fenton, Jeroen Keppens, and David A. Lagnado. Causal analysis for attributing responsibility in legal cases. In *15th Int. Conf. on Artificial Intelligence and Law (ICAIL)*, pages 33–42. ACM, 2015.

8. Hana Chockler and Joseph Y. Halpern. Responsibility and blame: A structural-model approach. *Journal of Artificial Intelligence Research (JAIR)*, 22:93–115, 2004.

9. Hana Chockler, Joseph Y. Halpern, and Orna Kupferman. What causes a system to satisfy a specification? *ACM Transactions on Computational Logic*, 9(3), 2008.

10. Jörg Desel, Andreas Oberweis, Torsten Zimmer, and Gabriele Zimmermann. Validation of information system models: Petri nets and test case generation. In *IEEE Int. Conf. on Cybernetics and Simulation*, pages 3401–3406, 1997.

11. J.B. Dugan, S.J. Bavuso, and M.A. Boyd. Dyanamic fault-tree models for fault-tolerant computer systems. *IEEE Transactions on Reliability*, 41(3):363–377, 1992.

12. Thomas Eiter and Thomas Lukasiewicz. Causes and explanations in the structural-model approach: Tractable cases. *Artifical Intelligence*, 170(6-7):542–580, 2006.

13. Javier Esparza, Peter Lammich, René Neumann, Tobias Nipkow, Alexander Schimpf, and Jan-Georg Smaus. A fully verified executable LTL model checker. *Archive of Formal Proofs*, 2014.

14. Lu Feng, Mahsa Ghasemi, Kai-Wei Chang, and Ufuk Topcu. Counterexamples for robotic planning explained in structured language. *CoRR*, arXiv:1803.08966, 2018. To appear in IEEE Int. Conf. on Robotics and Automation (ICRA'18).

15. Bernd Finkbeiner, Manuel Gieseking, and Ernst-Rüdiger Olderog. Adam: Causality-based synthesis of distributed systems. In *27th Int. Conf. on Computer Aided Verification (CAV)*, volume 9206 of *LNCS*, pages 433–439. Springer, 2015.

16. Florian Funke, Simon Jantsch, and Christel Baier. Farkas certificates and minimal witnesses for probabilistic reachability constraints. In Armin Biere and David Parker, editors, *26th International Conference on Tools and Algorithms for the Construction and Analysis of Systems (TACAS)*, volume 12078 of *Lecture Notes in Computer Science*, pages 324–345. Springer, 2020.

17. Alex Groce. Error explanation with distance metrics. In *10th Int. Conf. on Tools and Algorithms for the Construction and Analysis of Systems (TACAS)*, volume 2988 of *LNCS*, pages 108–122. Springer, 2004.

18. Alex Groce, Daniel Kroening, and Flavio Lerda. Understanding counterexamples with explain. In *16th Int. Conf. on Computer Aided Verification (CAV)*, volume 3114 of *LNCS*, pages 453–456. Springer, 2004.

19. Timo P. Gros, David Groß, Stefan Gumhold, Jörg Hoffmann, Michaela Klauck, and Marcel Steinmetz. Tracevis: Towards visualization for deep statistical model checking. in this volume.

20. Axel Habermaier, Alexander Knapp, Johannes Leupolz, and Wolfgang Reif. Fault-aware modeling and specification for efficient formal safety analysis. In *Critical Systems: Formal Methods and Automated Verification (FMICS-AVoCS)*, volume 9933 of *LNCS*, pages 97–114. Springer, 2016.

21. Nils Jansen. *Counterexamples in probabilistic verification*. PhD thesis, RWTH Aachen University, Germany, 2015.

22. Simon Jantsch, Florian Funke, and Christel Baier. Minimal witnesses for probabilistic timed automata. In Dang Van Hung and Oleg Sokolsky, editors, *18th International Symposium on Automated Technology for Verification and Analysis (ATVA)*, volume 12302 of *Lecture Notes in Computer Science*, pages 501–517. Springer, 2020.

23. Simon Jantsch, Hans Harder, Florian Funke, and Christel Baier. SWITSS: computing small witnessing subsystems. In Alexander Ivrii and Ofer Strichman, editors, *20th Conference on Formal Methods in Computer-Aided Design (FMCAD)*. Academic Press TU Wien, 2020.

24. Jacques-Henri Jourdan, Vincent Laporte, Sandrine Blazy, Xavier Leroy, and David Pichardie. A formally-verified C static analyzer. In *42nd Annual ACM SIGPLAN-SIGACT Symposium on Principles of Programming Languages (POPL)*, pages 247–259. ACM, 2015.

25. Martin Kölbl and Stefan Leue. An algorithm to compute a strict partial orderering of actions in action trees. in this volume.

26. Matthias Kuntz, Florian Leitner-Fischer, and Stefan Leue. From probabilistic counterexamples via causality to fault trees. In *30th Int. Conf. on Computer Safety, Reliability, and Security*, volume 6894 of *LNCS*, pages 71–84. Springer, 2011.

27. Orna Kupferman and Moshe Y. Vardi. Vacuity detection in temporal model checking. In *10th IFIP WG 10.5 Advanced Research Working Conf. on Correct Hardware Design and Verification Methods (CHARME)*, volume 1703 of *LNCS*, pages 82–96. Springer, 1999.

28. Orna Kupferman and Moshe Y. Vardi. From complementation to certification. *Theoretical Computer Science*, 345(1):83–100, 2005.

29. Andrey Kupriyanov and Bernd Finkbeiner. Causality-based verification of multi-threaded programs. In *24th Int. Conf. on Concurrency Theory (CONCUR)*, volume 8052 of *LNCS*, pages 257–272. Springer, 2013.

30. Andrey Kupriyanov and Bernd Finkbeiner. Causal termination of multi-threaded programs. In *26th Int. Conf. on Computer Aided Verification (CAV)*, volume 8559 of *LNCS*, pages 814–830, 2014.

31. Florian Leitner-Fischer. *Causality Checking of Safety-Critical Software and Systems*. PhD thesis, University of Konstanz, Germany, 2015.

32. Florian Leitner-Fischer and Stefan Leue. Causality checking for complex system models. In *14th Int. Conf. on Verification, Model Checking, and Abstract Interpretation (VMCAI)*, volume 7737 of *LNCS*, pages 248–267. Springer, 2013.

33. Florian Leitner-Fischer and Stefan Leue. On the synergy of probabilistic causality computation and causality checking. In *20th Int. Symp. on Model Checking Software (SPIN)*, volume 7976 of *LNCS*, pages 246–263. Springer, 2013.

34. Florian Leitner-Fischer and Stefan Leue. Probabilistic fault tree synthesis using causality computation. *Int. Journal of Critical Computer-Based Systems*, 4(2):119–143, 2013.

35. Glenford J. Myers. *The Art of Software Testing*. John Wiley & Sons, 1979.

36. F. Ortmeier, W. Reif, and G. Schellhorn. Formal safety analysis of a radio-based railroad crossing using deductive cause-consequence analysis. In *5th European Dependable Computing Conf. (EDCC)*, volume 3463 of *LNCS*. Springer, 2006.

37. Judea Pearl. *Causality: Models, Reasoning and Inference*. Cambridge University Press, 2nd edition, 2009.

38. Ali Taleghani. *Using Software Model Checking for Software Certification*. PhD thesis, University of Waterloo, Ontario, Canada, 2010.

39. W.E. Vasely and F.F. Goldberg. *Fault Tree Handbook*. US Nuclear Regulatory Commission, 2014. NUREG-0492.

40. Ralf Wimmer, Nils Jansen, Erika Ábrahám, Joost-Pieter Katoen, and Bernd Becker. Minimal counterexamples for linear-time probabilistic verification. *Theoretical Computer Science*, 549:61–100, 2014.

41. Ralf Wimmer, Nils Jansen, Andreas Vorpahl, Erika Ábrahám, Joost-Pieter Katoen, and Bernd Becker. High-level counterexamples for probabilistic automata. *Logical Methods in Computer Science*, 11(1), 2015.

42. Simon Wimmer, Frédéric Herbreteau, and Jaco van de Pol. Certifying empti-
    ness of timed büchi automata. In Nathalie Bertrand and Nils Jansen, editors,
    *18th International Conference on Formal Modeling and Analysis of Timed Sys-
    tems (FORMATS)*, volume 12288 of *Lecture Notes in Computer Science*, pages
    58–75. Springer, 2020.
43. Simon Wimmer and Joshua von Mutius. Verified certification of reachability check-
    ing for timed automata. In Armin Biere and David Parker, editors, *26th Inter-
    national Conference on Tools and Algorithms for the Construction and Analysis
    of Systems (TACAS)*, volume 12078 of *Lecture Notes in Computer Science*, pages
    425–443. Springer, 2020.

An Algorithm to Compute a Strict Partial Ordering of Actions in Action Traces

Martin Kölbl[✉] and Stefan Leue[✉]

University of Konstanz, Konstanz, Germany
{martin.koelbl,Stefan.Leue}@uni-konstanz.de

Abstract. Causality Checking [LL13] computes a causal explanation in the form of minimal action traces that lead to the violations of a reachability property. Causality Checking is implemented in the tool QuantUM [LFL11] that currently only depicts in a fault tree the causal actions in the action traces that lead to a property violation, but not the possible order of these actions. We present an analysis to compute the strict partial order of actions in action traces and succinctly depict these orders by a fault tree. We implemented the analysis in the tool QuantUM. We assess the performance of our algorithm by applying it to several models of different size. The results show that the analysis can compute the action order for thousands of action traces.

1 Motivation

Model-driven development is an efficient way to deal with the complexity of modern systems. A model is a high-level abstraction of a system and can support the development of a correct system. Before the implementation of a system, a model checker can verify a model of the system to ensure that the system behaves according to its specification. For the verification, the specification of a model is given as a property. An initial design typically has shortcomings and violates the property. When a model checker finds a violation of a property, it returns a counterexample in the form of an execution that leads to the violation. An execution contains an ordered sequence of actions that we call an action trace. We proposed Causality Checking in [LL13] that analyzes the counterexamples of a model based on the counterfactual argument [Lew01] and results in a set of action traces that are considered to be causal, according to the counterfactual actual cause definition given in [LL13]. When a system execution contains one of the action traces the property will be violated. A system execution that contains none of the action traces will not violate the property.

We implemented Causality Checking in the tool *QuantUM*. The input of QuantUM is a reachability property and a model in SysML [Obj17]. QuantUM converts the SysML model into the model checking language `Spin` [Hol04] and executes Causality Checking based on a systematic state space exploration to find every causal action trace in the model. Afterwards, QuantUM pools the causal action traces with the same set of actions to a causality class.

© Springer Nature Switzerland AG 2021
T. Margaria and B. Steffen (Eds.): ISoLA 2020, LNCS 12479, pp. 10–26, 2021.
https://doi.org/10.1007/978-3-030-83723-5_2

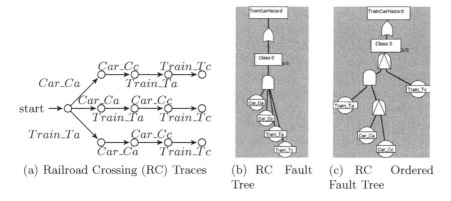

(a) Railroad Crossing (RC) Traces   (b) RC Fault Tree   (c) RC Ordered Fault Tree

Fig. 1. Railroad example

The disjunction of the different causality classes constitutes the cause of the property violation and will be displayed as a fault tree [KL19]. Currently, QuantUM depicts the set of actions in a causality class by a fault tree without indicating the order of the contained actions. In previous work, amongst others we applied Causality Checking to the architecture of a self-driving car [KL19], and showed that Causality Checking supports the safety assessment in the development of a safety-critical system.

We now illustrate the analysis performed during causality checking by applying it to the model of a railroad crossing, which we will refer to as a running example throughout the paper. In this model, a train approaches a crossing (Train_Ta), then enters the crossing (Train_Tc) and leaves the crossing (Train_Tl). A car also approaches at the crossing (Car_Ca), then enters the crossing (Car_Cc) and leaves the crossing (Car_Cl). The crossing is unguarded and has no gate. The car will not enter the crossing when the train is already in the crossing. A hazard in this system occurs when a state can be entered in which both the train and the car are in the crossing at the same time, which has the potential to lead to a fatal accident. We, therefore, state the property that such a state can not be reached.

Causality Checking computes causes for the violation of such a reachability property in case it is violated in the model. The result of this cause computation is a number of what is referred to as *causality classes*. The action traces in one causality class are all formed over the same set of actions, and only vary in the order in which these actions occur. For the railroad crossing example, Causality Checking computes just one causality class over the set {Train_Ta, Train_Tc, Car_Ca, Car_Cc} of actions. It contains 3 action traces, depicted in Fig. 1(a). Notice that for systems of realistic size, a causality class may contain a much higher number of action traces. For reasons of convenience and since QuantUM is primarily used in the area of safety-critical system analysis, causality classes are depicted as fault trees. The fault tree in Fig. 1(b) depicts the causality class computed for the Railroad Crossing example. The top-level event *TrainCarHazard* is valid when one of the causality classes is valid. Thus, an or-gate is connected to the single causality class *Class 0*. A causality class is valid when every contained basic event *Car_Ca*, *Car_Cc*, *Train_Ta* and *Train_Tc* occurred, which means that an action trace is obtained from the system that contains exactly these events in a given order. The basic events can occur in the model in different orders. These basic events are combined by an and-gate that requires all of them to occur without imposing a particular order on the occurrence. This fault tree returned by QuantUM does not currently depict these different action orders, even though the ordering information is contained in the set of action traces that form the causality class. Assume, in the example above, that the train enters the crossing before the car, then the car will never enter the crossing, as per the model definition, and the hazard state will not be reached.

We describe the necessity of an action to occur before another action to reach a property violation by a dependency relation. For this dependency relation, the following properties hold.

- An action can not depend on itself, otherwise, the action can never occur (*irreflexivity*).
- When an action b depends on another action a, then a cannot also depend on b (*antisymmetricity*). Assume two actions would mutually dependent on another, then these actions could never occur.
- When an action c depends on b and b depends on a then c depends also on a (*transitivity*).

A strict partial order has exactly these properties. It differs from a (general) partial order only in the property of irreflexivity. We use a strict partial order to describe the dependencies of the actions in action traces.

In this paper, we propose an analysis that computes the strict partial orders of actions in action traces and depicts the computed order in a fault tree. In order to depict the action orders, we introduce the ordered-and-gate into the Fault Tree notation. It is depicted as an and-gate labeled with a triangle. It is satisfied when the actions connected to the gate occur from left to right. For the running example, the analysis results in the fault tree depicted in Fig. 1(c) which represents all orders of the action traces given in Fig. 1(a) that correspond to the causality criteria defined in Causality Checking. The order in the fault tree depicts, for instance, that Tc occurs always after the other actions, and the action Ta is independent of action Ca and action Car_Cc.

Contributions. In this paper, we present an analysis that computes and depicts the order of actions in the action trace set belonging to a causality class. We also implement this analysis in QuantUM.

Structure. In Sect. 2 we discuss the foundations of our work. In Sect. 3 we present an algorithm to compute the strict partial order for the action traces of a causality class. We evaluate and compare an implementation of the algorithms in Sect. 4. In Sect. 5 we draw conclusions and suggest future developments.

Related Work. A Mazurkiewicz trace [DR95] describes a set of traces by a sequence t of actions and a dependence relation D. The D is symmetric which means when (a, b) is in D then (b, a) is in D. Two in t neighboured actions a and b can be reordered when (a, b) is not in D. In contrast, the strict partial order that our analysis computes is antisymmetric. In the context of causality, either a depends on b then b occurs before a in an action trace, or b depends on a then a occurs before b but both dependencies are not possible at once.

Lamport's happen-before describes strict partial orders for messages in an asynchronous system [Lam78]. In contrast, we compute the strict partial order of actions in a set of action traces.

A (strict) partial order is usually depicted by a Hasse diagram which is an undirected acyclic graph where lower vertices connected to vertices above have to happen first [ES13]. In the context of QuantUM, we prefer to use Fault Trees to depict causality classes and the orders that they represent since they are a notation that is well known to engineers of safety-critical systems.

We are not aware of any work that computes a strict partial order for a set of action traces.

2   Preliminaries

The model of a system is given in form of a transition system [BK08]. A transition system (TS) is a tuple $(S, Act, \rightarrow, I, AP, L)$ where S is a finite set of states, Act is a finite set of actions, $\rightarrow \subseteq S \times Act \times S$ is a transition relation, $I \subseteq S$ is a set of initial states, AP is a set of atomic propositions, and $L : S \rightarrow 2^{AP}$ is a labeling function. An execution p of the transition system TS is an alternating sequence of states $s \in S$ and actions $a \in Act : p = s_0 a_1 s_1 a_2 \ldots$ such that $(s_i, a_{i+1}, s_{i+1}) \in \rightarrow$ for all $i \geq 0$. The behavior of a system is described by the executions of the TS. For an invariant property ϕ, a finite execution $s_0 a_0 s_1 \ldots s_{n-1} a_{n-1} s_n$ where $s_n \not\models \phi$ is called a counterexample.

An action trace $a_0 a_1 \ldots$ is the projection of an execution $s_0 a_0 s_1 a_1 \ldots$ on Act. An action trace set is a set of action traces T where every action trace t in T has the same alphabet $A \subseteq Act$ and every action of the alphabet occurs in t exactly once. Thus, every action trace in an action trace set has the same length $n = |A|$. Notice that a causality class is an action trace set. An action trace t of a TS can contain an action a several times. In this case, we substitute every occurrence a in t with a_i where the index i is the number of occurrences of a up to the current action in t, and add a_i to the alphabet.

A *directed graph* G is a pair (V, E) of a set of vertices V and a set of edges $E \subseteq V \times V$ where $V \cap E = \emptyset$ [CLF05]. A *walk* of G is a finite sequence of states $u_0, u_1, \ldots, u_n$ where for $0 \leq i \leq n$, $u_i \in V$ and for $0 \leq i \leq n - 1$, $(u_i, u_{i+1}) \in E$. A cycle is a nontrivial walk $u_0 \ldots u_n$ with $u_0 = u_n$. A vertex v is connected in G to a vertex u when a walk $v..u$ exists. A graph is connected when for every two vertices v and u in V either a walk $v..u$ or a walk $u..v$ exists. A *directed acyclic graph* (DAG) is a directed graph without a cycle. A tree is an acyclic connected graph [CLF05]. The transitive closure (V, E^*) of a directed graph (V, E) contains an edge (v, u) in E^* for every walk $v...u$ in (V, E).

In concurrent systems, the order in which events can occur is often determined by a *partial order* relation.

Definition 1 (Partial Order [SRH18]**).** *A homogeneous relation $\preceq \subseteq A \times A$ is called a partial order over set A if, and only if*

- $\forall a \in A.a \preceq a$ *(reflexive)*
- $\forall a, b \in A.a \preceq b$ *and* $b \preceq a$ *then* $a = b$ *(antisymmetric)*
- $\forall a, b, c \in A.a \preceq b$ *and* $b \preceq c$ *then* $a \preceq c$ *(transitive).*

A *strict partial order* is a partial order that is irreflexive, which means that $\forall a \in A.a \npreceq a$ holds. We use the sign $\prec$ to denote a strict partial order.

The function $i_t(a)$ returns the index of an action a in an action trace t. For an action trace set T, we say that an action b depends on a when in every action trace $t \in T$ the index of a is smaller than the index of b. Formally, a depends on b if $\forall t \in T.i_t(a) < i_t(b)$ holds. We express dependencies by a strict partial order. A dependency of action a on action b is denoted by $a \prec b$. When $a \prec b$ holds, we say that a is a precondition for b. When neither $a \prec b$ nor $b \prec a$ holds, we say a and b are independent.

The action set A has a number $|A|$ of actions. For some given causality class over an action set A, we represent the dependencies of the actions in this causality class in a Boolean matrix M of dimension $|A| \times |A|$. An entry (a, b) in M has the value *true* when b depends on a in the corresponding causality class.

3   Algorithm to Analyze Action Orders in Action Traces

In this section, we present an algorithm that we refer to as Algorithm 1, which is designed to compute the strict partial order of the actions in a set of action traces. We also define an algorithm called Algorithm 2, which translates this strict partial order into a fault tree.

The input to Algorithm 1 is an action trace set defining a causality class. For instance, in the railroad example the action trace set in Fig. 1(a) is the action trace set forming the causality class computed for the railroad model. This action trace set is built over the action set {Car_Ca, Car_Cc, Train_Ta, Train_Tc}. Algorithm 1 computes the strict partial order of the actions in an action trace set and stores it in a DAG which is accomplished in the following way. The strict partial order $a \prec b$ holds for an action trace in which an action a occurs before an action b. In the railroad model, for instance, Train_Tc occurs in every action trace after Car_Cc and Car_Ca. Thus, Car_Cc $\prec$ Train_Tc and Car_Ca $\prec$ Car_Cc holds in every action trace. Since Car_Cc $\prec$ Train_Tc holds in every action trace in Fig. 1(a), we deduce that Train_Tc depends on Car_Cc occurring first in order to reach a property violation. In the same way, Car_Cc also depends on Car_Ca and Train_Tc depends on Car_Ca. In the DAG for the railroad example, the algorithm only needs to store the information that Train_Tc depends on Car_Cc and that Car_Cc depends on action Car_Ca because Train_Tc also transitively depends on Car_Ca. We define the direct dependency relation in Definition 2 that removes transitive dependency relations.

Definition 2 (Direct Dependency Relation $\hat{\prec}$). *An action b directly depends on action a, written as $a \hat{\prec} b$, in an action trace set T with an action set A when $a \prec b$ holds and $\neg \exists a' \in A.a \prec a' \wedge a' \prec b$.*

For instance, in the running example, the direct dependency relations Car_Ca $\hat{\prec}$ Car_Cc and Car_Cc $\hat{\prec}$ Train_Tc holds and imply the dependency relation Car_Ca $\prec$ Train_Tc but Car_Ca $\hat{\nprec}$ Train_Tc because Car_Cc has a direct dependency with Car_Ca and Train_Tc.

The DAG in which the algorithm stores the dependencies is a DDAG G defined in Definition 3. A DDAG has no superfluous edge e that can be implied by transitivity, formally $(E \backslash e)^* = E^*$, and stores this transitive reduction of the strict partial order.

Definition 3 (Dependency DAG (DDAG)). *A dependency DAG (DDAG) is a DAG (V, E) that stores a strict partial order $\prec$ over a set A with $V = A$ and $(a, b) \in E$ for any actions $a, b \in A$ where $a \hat{\prec} b$ holds.*

An action trace $t = a_0 \ldots a_n$ satisfies G when for every vertex $v \in V$ there exists an action $a_i \in t$, and any two vertices a_i and a_j in t with a walk $a_i...a_j$ in G satisfy $0 \leq i < j \leq n$.

G is the input for Algorithm 2, which computes a causal tree as defined in Definition 4. The causal tree represents the strict partial order in G. In the context of Causality Checking, a causal tree is the part of a fault tree that represents a single causality class. A causal tree consists of basic events that represent the actions in a causality class, ordered-and-gates where a connected event on the right side depends on every event on the left side, and and-gates where the connected events are independent. The fault tree in Fig. 1(c) depicts the basic events Car_Ca, Car_Cc, Train_Ta and Train_Tc. In the fault tree, an ordered-and-gate specifies that Car_Cc depends on Car_Ca to occur first, and a regular and-gate specifies that Train_Ta and Car_Cc are independent.

Definition 4 (Causal Tree). *A causal tree CT is a connected DAG where a vertex v is a basic event for an action, or is a gate. Any vertex v can have an edge (v, g) to a gate g. A gate g is either an ordered-and-gate, where the vertices $v_0...v_j$ with edges (v_i, g) are ordered by increasing index i from left to right, or is an and-gate that does not impose an order of the vertices attached to it.*

An action trace $t = a_0...a_n$ satisfies the action order imposed by a causal tree CT when every vertex of CT is valid as defined in the following:

- *A basic event v for an action a is valid by t when $\exists 0 \leq i \leq n.t[i] = a$ exists and the validity of v at index i does not contradict the order of an ordered-and-gate in CT.*
- *An order-and-gate og is valid when the vertices $v_0...v_j$ become valid in the order $\forall 0 \leq i < i' \leq j.v_i \prec v_{i'}$.*
- *An and-gate g is valid when every vertex v with an edge (v, g) to g is valid.*

In order to compute a fault tree, we compute a causal tree for every causality class and combine the obtained causal trees with an or-gate. For the railroad example, the result of these computations is the fault tree depicted in Fig. 1(c). It contains one causal tree which is the subgraph below and including the ordered-and-gate, denoted by the and-gate symbol labeled with a triangle.

Algorithm 1 computes the strict partial order of the actions in an action trace set and stores the resulting strict partial order relation in a DDAG. The functions given in Listing 1 compute a DDAG with the strict partial order for a given action trace set T built from an action set A. The function createPreconditionMap preprocesses the action trace set and returns for any two actions a and b whether the relation $i_t(a) < i_t(b)$ holds in an action trace $t \in T$. These relations are stored in a map aM that returns for every action b in A the set of actions that occurred in an action trace directly before b. The function iterates in lines 3 to 5 through every action t[i] in every action trace t and adds the action t[i-1] occurring before t[i] to the set of t[i] in aM.

The function createDAG obtains the map aM as an input and computes a DDAG representing the strict partial order of a given action trace set T. The algorithm uses aM as an input in line 8 to create a dependency matrix m of size $|A| \times |A|$. For any actions a and b, an entry (a, b) in m is true when $i_t(a) < i_t(b)$ holds in an action trace t of T. Hence, (a, b) is true when an action a is in aM[b]. Next, the algorithm ensures that the properties of a strict partial order hold for the relation stored in m. In line 10, the algorithm computes the transitive closure of m and stores it in m. In line 12, the algorithm removes symmetries in m by setting (a, b) and (b, a) to false since, as we argue above, symmetrically ordered actions cannot be dependent on each other. In line 13, the algorithm removes reflexive transitions when for an action a the relation $a \prec a$ holds.

```
1   Map<Action, Set<Action>> aM;
2   function createPreconditionMap(Set<ActionTrace> T)
3     for ActionTrace t in T
4       for i: 1 ... t.length - 1
5             aM.get(t[i]).add(t[i-1]);
6
7   function createDAG(Map<Action, List<Action>> aM)
8     Matrix m = createDependencyMatrix(aM);
9     //transitive closure: a1 < a2 && a2 < a3 => a1<a3
10    m = ensureTransitivity(m);
11    //antisymmetric: a1<a2 && a2<a1 => independent(a1, a2)
12    m = ensureAntisymmetricity(m);
13    m = removeReflexivity(m);
14    m = removeTransitiveDependencies(m);
15    return getDAG(m);
```

Listing 1. Pseudocode of Algorithm 1 to Compute DAG.

m now contains a strict partial order for T. In line 14, the algorithm removes the transitive relations from m in order to compute a DDAG that contains only direct dependencies. The algorithm removes transitive relations starting with an action that has the most precondition actions and then iterating in decreasing order over the other actions in A. In order to remove the transitive relations for an action c, the algorithm checks for any actions b and a whether valid entries (b, c) and (a, b) exists in m, in which case it sets the entry (a, c) to false.

In line 15, m is converted into a DDAG G. Every action is a vertex in G. For any two actions a and b where the entry (a, b) is valid in m, the algorithm adds an edge (a, b) to the DDAG. This DDAG is returned by the function getDAG.

Algorithm 2 uses the DDAG G returned by function getDAG as an input and computes a causal tree. In lines 4 to 6 in Listing 2, the algorithm first iterates through every action p in G where p is a precondition of another action a. It stores this property of p using a Boolean variable Used for p in a map m. In lines 7 to 9, we search for every action that is not a precondition of another action. These actions are independent of any other action. For every independent action a, we call the recursive function createTree in line 10 in order to create a tree that represents the dependencies of a. The function createTree creates a tree

```
1   Map<Action, (Tree, Used)> m;
2   Set<Tree> indep;
3   function createCausalTree(DDAG G)
4     for Action a in G
5       for p in a.getPre()
6         m(p).Used = true
7     for Action a in G
8       if m(a).Used
9           continue;
10      indep.add(createTree(a));
11    return and(indep);
12
13  function createTree(Action a)
14    if(m(a).Tree)
15      return m(a).Tree;
16    Tree t, t';
17    Tree e = createBasicEvent(a);
18    Set<Action> pL = a.getPre();
19    if pL.size() = 0 then t = e;
20    else
21      if pL.size() = 1
22        t' = createTree(pL[0]);
23      else //combine set of preconditions
24        t' = and(foreach p in pL : createTree(p))
25      t = orderedAnd(t', e); //preconditions before e
26    m.put(a, t);
27    return t;
```

Listing 2. Pseudocode of Algorithm 2 to Compute Causal Tree.

for the dependencies of an action a. In line 14, the algorithm checks whether the tree of an action a was previously created. In case, this tree for a is stored in m, the function `createTree` returns this tree. Otherwise, the algorithm creates the tree for a and stores it in variable t. The algorithm first creates a basic event e for a in line 17. In line 18, the algorithm gets the set pL of actions on which a depends. In case a depends on no other action, e is the tree with the dependencies of a and the algorithm stores e in t. In case pL contains only a single action stored in pL[0], the algorithm creates the tree t' with the dependencies for the action in pL[0] in line 22. In case pL has several actions, the algorithm creates a tree for every action in pL in line 24 and combines these trees with an and-gate t'. g' depicts the precondition actions for a, thus, the algorithm combines g' and a in line 25 in this sequence with an ordered-and-gate. This ordered-and gate is stored in t. t is stored in m for the action a in line 26 and in line 27 returned by the function. The function `createTree` is called in line 10 for every independent action. The trees of these actions are stored in a set `indep`. After all trees are created, they are combined by an and-gate in line 11 and this and-gate is the causal tree that we wanted to compute.

It is possible to optimize the algorithm in the following way. An ordered-and gate in the causal tree can be connected to another ordered-and gate. For instance, when a_1 occurs before a_2 and a_2 occurs before a_3 then the presented algorithm creates two ordered-and-gates instead of one with all three actions. The implementation of line 22 and 25 in Listing 2 combines several ordered-and-gates to a single one when possible and returns it.

Correctness of the Algorithms. We now prove that the presented algorithms to compute a causal tree that depicts a strict partial order for an action trace set T is correct with respect to completeness and soundness.

A DDAG G computed by Algorithm 1 is complete according to Definition 5 when every action trace in T corresponds to a valid ordering of the actions according to the dependencies stored in G.

Definition 5 (Completeness DDAG Construction). *Assume a DDAG G computed for an action set T. G is complete when any action trace $t \in T$ is an action trace satisfying G.*

Theorem 1 (Completeness of Algorithm 1). *Algorithm 1 computes a complete DDAG according to Definition 5.*

Proof. Assume a DDAG G computed by Algorithm 1 for an action trace set T and an action trace t in T that is not satisfying G. Since t is not satisfying G two actions a and b exist that satisfy $i_t(b) < i_t(a)$ but in G the dependency relation $a \prec b$ holds. Since $a \prec b$ holds in G by construction of G another trace t' in T exists that satisfies $i_{t'}(a) < i_{t'}(b)$. For t and t', Algorithm 1 would store the relations $i_t(b) < i_t(a)$ and $i_{t'}(a) < i_{t'}(b)$ in matrix m (line 8) and removes them (line 12) afterwards since these relations contradict antisymmetricity. Thus, either $a \prec b$ cannot hold in G or $t \notin T$. Both cases contradict our assumptions.   □

A DDAG G computed by Algorithm 1 could be considered sound when any action trace that satisfies G is in T. However, as we shall see, this definition of soundness is too strict. Assume, a set with two action traces a, b, c and c, a, b. Then, Algorithm 1 computes a strict partial order $a \prec b$. This strict partial order allows the action trace $t_3 = a$, c, b but t_3 is not in the original action trace set. This observation was considered further in [Wei19]. For G, we therefore use a different soundness criterium based on pairs of actions. Notice that in an action trace that satisfies G, only the order of independent actions can be changed while preserving its satisfaction of G. As mentioned above, two actions a and b are independent when neither $a \prec b$ nor $b \prec a$ holds in G. $a \prec b$ does not hold when a trace t with $i_t(b) < i_t(a)$ exists, and $b \prec a$ does not hold when a trace t' with $i_{t'}(a) < i_{t'}(b)$ exists. G is sound according to Definition 6 when for any two independent action in G the action traces t and t' exist.

Definition 6 (Soundness DDAG Construction). *Assume a DDAG G computed for an action set T. G is sound when for any two independent action a and b in G, an action trace $t \in T$ satisfying $i_t(b) < i_t(a)$ exists and another action trace $t' \in T$ satisfying $i_{t'}(a) < i_{t'}(b)$ exists.*

Theorem 2 (Soundness of the Algorithm 1). *Algorithm 1 computes a sound DDAG according to Definition 6.*

Proof. Assume a DDAG G computed by Algorithm 1 for an action trace set T and two actions a and b that are independent in G and $a \neq b$. Two actions are independent in G when no walk $a...b$ and no walk $b..a$ exists. By construction of G, a walk $a...b$ does not exist when a trace t with $i_t(b) < i_t(a)$ and a walk $b...a$ does not exist when a trace t' with $i_{t'}(a) < i_{t'}(b)$ exists. We now show by contradiction that the action traces t and t' are in T.

In a first case, we assume that no action trace t exists that satisfies $i_t(b) < i_t(a)$. Thus, the relation $a \prec b$ is not removed in line 12 in Listing 1. In this case, either $a \hat{\prec} b$ and the algorithm creates an edge (a, b) (line 15) or actions a_1, ..., a_n with $a \prec a_1 \prec ... \prec a_n \prec b$ exists and the algorithm creates edges $(a, a_1)(a_1, a_2)...(a_n, b)$ in G. Both, the single edge and the sequence of edges represents a walk $a...b$. This walk contradicts the assumption that a and b are independent.

In a second case, we assume that no action trace t' exists that satisfies $i_t(b) < i_t(a)$. This case is equivalent to the first case since a and b are only substituted with another. Thus, the reasoning that t' has to exist is similar to the argumentation for t.

We see that every case contradicts its assumption. Thus, when a and b are independent then t and t' have to exists. □

We now discuss whether Algorithm 1 terminates. Algorithm 1 iterates over actions and their relations. Since the number of action traces in T is finite, the actions and the action relation are also finite. We conclude that Algorithm 1 terminates.

Assume that Algorithm 2 computes a causal tree CT for a DDAG G. Algorithm 2 is sound when for any two actions a and b where $a \prec b$ holds in CT, $a \prec b$ holds in G, and the algorithm is complete when $a \prec b$ holds in G then $a \prec b$ holds in CT. Remember that action b depends on a does not imply that b directly depends on a, formally $\neg \forall a, b.\ a \prec b \Rightarrow a \stackrel{\cdot}{\prec} b$. In G, $a \prec b$ holds when a walk $a \ldots b$ exists. In CT, the dependencies of actions are depicted by ordered-and-gates. $a \prec b$ holds in CT when an ordered-and-gate g_b with edges (v_x, g_b) and (b, g_b), where $v_x \prec b$, and a walk $a...v_x g_b$ exist. Definition 7 ensures that an action b depends on an action a in G iff b depends on a in CT.

Definition 7 (Correctness of Causal Tree Construction). *Assume a causal tree CT computed for a DDAG G with an action set A. CT is sound when any two action $a, b \in A$ that satisfy $a \prec b$ in CT also satisfy $a \prec b$ in G. CT is complete when any two action $a, b \in A$ that satisfy $a \prec b$ in G also satisfy $a \prec b$ in CT. CT is correct when it is sound and complete.*

Theorem 3 (Correctness of Algorithm 2). *Algorithm 2 computes a correct causal tree according to Definition 7.*

Proof Assume a causal tree CT computed by the Algorithm 2 for a DDAG G, and two actions a and b in G. In a first case $\Rightarrow$, we assume that $a \prec b$ holds in G and will show that $a \prec b$ holds in CT, and in a second case $\Leftarrow$, we assume that $a \prec b$ holds in CT and will show that $a \prec b$ holds in G. In line 25 of Listing 2, an ordered-and-gate g_b is created for b when b directly depends on at least one other action in G. Thus, when b depends on another action, g_b exists and when g_b exists, b depends on another action. By the construction of g_b, b is its most right vertex and so for any walk $a..v_x g_b$ in CT, $v_x \prec b$ holds.

$\Rightarrow$ We assume that $a \prec b$ holds in G but not in CT. Because $a \prec b$ holds in G, a walk $a_0...a_n$ with $a_0 = a$ and $a_n = b$ in G has to exist. This walk witnesses that every action a_i with $0 < i \leq n$ has a precondition. Thus, Algorithm 2 creates an ordered-and-gate for every a_i with $i \geq 1$ (line 25 in Listing 2), and for $i > 1$ either an edge (g_{i-1}, g_i) when a_i has a single precondition (line 22), or creates an and-gate g_i' and the edges (g_{i-1}, g_i') and (g_i', g_i) (line 24). We see a walk $g_1...g_n$ has to exist in CT. Action a can also have a precondition then similar to the other actions a walk $a g_0 g_1...g_n$ exists in CT. Otherwise, a has no precondition (line 19) and a walk $a g_1...g_n$ exists. Since $g_n = g_b$ both walks $a g_0 g_1...g_n$ and $a g_1...g_n$ witness that a walk $a..g_b$ exists in CT. We conclude that $a \prec b$ holds in CT. This contradicts the assumption that $a \prec b$ does not hold in CT.

$\Leftarrow$ We assume that $a \prec b$ holds in CT. Thus, an ordered-and-gate g_b with edge (b, g_b) and a walk $a...g_b$ exists in CT. We now construct a walk $a...b$ in G. In CT, an edge (a, g) is either an edge from a basic event to a gate or from a gate to another gate. Hence, a is the only basic event in the walk $a...g_b$ and we know that the other vertices g_0, ..., g_b are gates. Every gate g_i in $g_0...g_b$ is an and-gate or an ordered-and-gate. By construction (line 25 and 17), every ordered-and-gate g_i is created for an action a_x in G and has an edge (g_i, a_x) in CT. An and-gate g_i is created (line 24) when a_x has several preconditions and depicts independence. We can remove every and-gate and substitute every ordered-and-gate g_i with its action a_x in $a g_0...g_b$ and result in a walk $aa_1...b$. Thus, we found a walk $a...b$ in G that ensures $a \prec b$ in G.

Since both cases hold, we conclude that $a \prec b$ holds in G iff $a \prec b$ holds in CT. ☐

Algorithm 2 executes only finite loops over the actions in G in the function *createCausalTree* and creates at most once a dependency tree for every action in G. Since the actions in G are finite, Algorithm 2 will terminate.

Theorem 1 and Theorem 2 show that according to our correctness criteria, Algorithm 1 computes a DDAG G with the dependencies contained in an action trace set T. Theorem 3 shows that Algorithm 2 computes a causal tree CT for G that depicts the action dependencies in G. In summary, a causal tree CT computed by Algorithm 1 and Algorithm 2 correctly depicts the action dependencies in T.

Complexity. In the following, we analyze the worst-case complexity of Algorithm 1 and Algorithm 2.

The worst-case complexity of Algorithm 1 is determined by the size $|T|$ of the action trace set T and the size $|A|$ of its alphabet A. Algorithm 1 has several computation steps of different complexity. First, Algorithm 1 iterates over every action trace in T and every action in an action trace (line 3–5), which has a complexity in $O(|A| \cdot |T|)$. In the next computation step in line 8, a lookup is executed for every tuple of two actions in $A \times A$ to create the dependency matrix m. Thus, the complexity to create m is in $O(|A|^2)$. The worst-case-complexity to compute the transitive closure is in $O(|A|^3)$ [OO73]. For every action in A, irreflexivity is ensured in line 13 and this has a complexity in $O(|A|)$. Next, the transitive dependencies are removed in line 14. Therefore, the actions are ordered by the number of their preconditions, which has a complexity in $O(|A|^2)$ to count the number of preconditions, and a lookup happens for every triple of three different actions in $A \times A \times A$ which results in a complexity of $O(|A|^3)$. In summary, the most complex computation steps are in $O(|A|^3 + |A| \cdot |T|)$ and this is the worst-case complexity of Algorithm 1.

Algorithm 2 first determines the independent actions in G in $O(|A|^2)$. Afterwards, function `CreateTree` is called for every action a in G to depict the dependencies of a. Notice that a depends on at most $|A| - 1$ other actions. For every a, `CreateTree` creates at most one and-gate (line 24), one ordered-and-gate (line 25), and $|A| + 1$ edges. One edge starts in every action on which a depends and one edge starts in every gate that is created. This computation to depict the dependencies of a is executed at most once since the result is stored in the map m. We see, `CreateTree` is called $|A|$ times where every call is in $O(|A|)$) which results in an overall worst-case complexity in $O(|A|^2)$. In summary, the worst-case-complexity of Algorithm 2 is in $O(|A|^2)$.

Table 1. Quantitative experimental results.

Model	States	Transitions	#Causality Classes	#Traces	#Actions	Time	Memory
Railroad	92	231	1	3	4	4 ms	0.605 MB
Railroad_gate	143	373	4	20	10	28 ms	2.438 MB
Airbag	3,456	14,257	5	252	9	28 ms	2.622 MB
TrainOdometer	4,032	19,624	3	5	5	34 ms	2.590 MB
FFU_ECU	9,728	30,209	19	80	6	40 ms	9.660 MB
FFU_Star	207,052	964,695	16	80	6	27 ms	17.038 MB
ASR	680,897	3,745,635	2	61,920	29	4 ms	14.864 MB

4   Case Study

We implemented Algorithm 1 and Algorithm 2 in the tool QuantUM. We qualitatively evaluate the algorithms in that we assess whether they can jointly analyze the strict partial order in a given set of action traces. In the quantitative assessment, we measure the computing resources needed by the algorithms when analyzing a set of models. All experiments were performed on a computer with an i7-6700K CPU (4.00 GHz), 60 GB of RAM and a Linux operation system.

Qualitative Results and Interpretation. The resulting fault tree of the running example is given in Fig. 1(c). In [KL19], we analyzed a slightly different model of the railroad crossing example which includes the functionality of a gate. Without the use of the algorithms proposed in the current paper, QuantUM computes the fault tree in Fig. 2 in [KL19] that does not depict the order of the actions. When using the proposed algorithms, QuantUM computes the fault tree in Fig. 3. It depicts the order of the actions in a causality class as we defined it above. Both fault trees contain the causality classes Class0 to Class3. In both fault trees, all actions of Class0 are contained in Class2 and all actions of Class1 are contained in Class3. It is not clear from the fault tree in [KL19] why Class2 and Class3 contain minimal counterexamples which would contradict the conditions of a cause [KL19]. In the fault tree in Fig. 3, we see that in Class0 and Class2 the gate has a failure caused by event Gate_fail. In Class0, the gate is stuck open and in Class2 the gate first closes and then opens in error. Thus, both times the train and the car can be in the crossing at the same time, and therefore incur an accident. In the fault tree in Fig. 3, we see the difference between Class0 and Class2 in the order of the actions. This fault tree also depicts the difference between Class1 and Class3. In Class1, the car crosses the railroad and meanwhile, the gate closes and the train enters the crossing. In Class3, two trains enter the crossing subsequently, but the signal gate_open to open the gate is late. Thus, the gate opens when the second train is already in the crossing. The car can then enter, leading to the hazard. In Class1 and Class3 the system behaves without a failure of the system but the order of the actions causes the hazard. We conclude

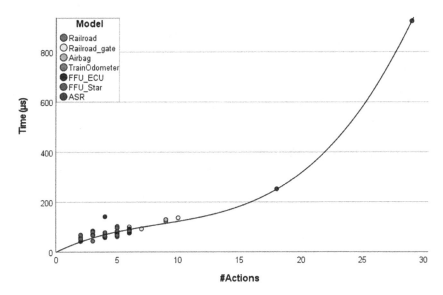

Fig. 2. Time to compute a causal tree in relation to #Actions in a causality class.

that the ordering of the actions helps to understand causes for the occurrence of the hazards.

Quantitative Results and Interpretation. We now want to analyze the performance of the causal tree computation by Algorithm 1 and Algorithm 2. Therefore, we applied the algorithms to several models of different size, in terms of the number of states and transitions that they encompass, taken from [Lei15]. The quantitative results are given in Table 1. The complexity of a model is given in terms of the number of its states and transitions. For every model, we indicate the number of causality classes and the maximal number of traces and actions in one of the causality classes. The columns Time and Memory indicate the maximal computation time and memory consumption that the analysis required in order to compute a fault tree of a model including the action order as per the proposed algorithms.

For every model, QuantUM produces a fault tree where the causality classes are depicted with the strict partial order of the actions. We had a detailed look at all the fault trees and according to this manual inspection, every fault tree depicts the strict partial orders of its causality classes.

The diagram in Fig. 2 gives the time in microseconds (μs) that is necessary to compute a causal tree for every causality class in every model. For a model with several causality classes, the diagram depicts several data-points. The worst-case complexity to compute a causality class is the combined worst-case complexity of Algorithm 1 and Algorithm 2 and is in $O(|A|^3)$. We let IBM SPSS [IBM20] analyzed the cubic relation between the time to compute a causality class and the number of actions and IBM SPSS automatically fits the function $31.583 +$

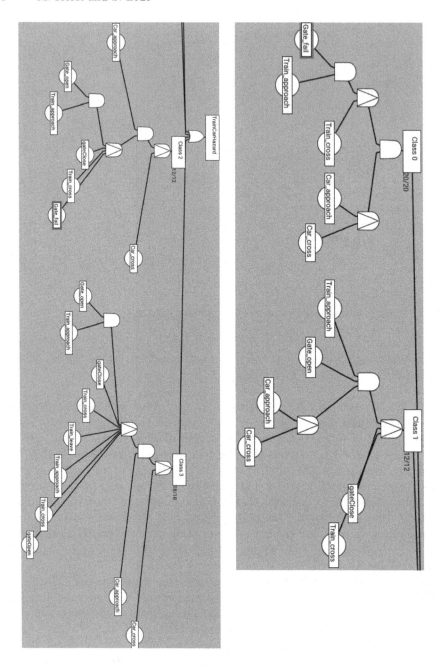

Fig. 3. Fault tree of railroad crossing with gate with action order

$13.583x - 1.057x^2 + 0.057x^3$ which is depicted as a black in line in the diagram. The distance of the points to the function can be measured by the coefficient of determination R^2 which is the quadrate of the correlation. The value range of R^2 is $[0, 1]$ where $R^2 = 1$ would be a perfect fit. The function in the diagram has a $R^2 = 0.985$. This function fits nearly perfectly to the data points, which supports that the runtime of the proposed order analysis has a cubic complexity.

While the time to compute a causal tree is given in Fig. 2 in microseconds, the overall time to compute a fault tree is in Table 1 in the area of milliseconds. We wondered about this gap of factor 100 and detected that Java, which was used for the implementation of QuantUM and the proposed algorithms, has an offset time in the area of milliseconds to load and create a class when the class is instantiated the first time. This implies that the overall computation times given in Table 1 consists primarily of the time for loading classes and not of the time for computing the causal trees.

Our proposed algorithms computed the strict partial orders within at most 40 ms and at most 17.038 MB of memory. This seems reasonable and is acceptable for QuantUM since a causality class in the analyzed models contains up to $61, 920$ traces of 29 actions.

5   Conclusion

In this work, we present an algorithm that computes a strict partial order of the actions occurring in an action traces set and represents this strict partial order as a fault tree. We implemented the algorithm in the tool QuantUM and computed fault trees for several models. We showed that a representation of the action order can be computed using a reasonable amount of computing resources, and that the computed results provide helpful insight into the causes for a reachability property violation.

In future research, we plan to further explore the considerations in [Wei19] and to integrate the rewrite-logic based approach pursued in that work with the algorithm described here. Another direction of research is to extend causality checking as well as the computation of event orders in causality classes to the violation of general $\omega-$regular temporal properties.

References

[BK08]   Baier, C., Katoen, J.-P.: Principles of Model Checking. MIT Press, Cambridge (2008)

[CLF05] Chartrand, G., Lesniak-Foster, L.: Graphs & Digraphs, 4th edn. Chapman and Hall/CRC, Boca Raton [u.a.] (2005)

[DR95]   Diekert, V., Rozenberg, G. (eds.): The Book of Traces. World Scientific, Singapore (1995)

[ES13]   Eppstein, D., Simons, J.A.: Confluent Hasse diagrams. J. Graph Algorithms Appl. **17**(7), 689–710 (2013)

[Hol04] Holzmann, G.J.: The SPIN Model Checker - Primer and Reference Manual. Addison-Wesley, Boston (2004)

[IBM20] IBM Corp.: IBM SPSS Statistics for Windows, Version 27 (2020). https://www.ibm.com/analytics/spss-statistics-software

[KL19] Kölbl, M., Leue, S.: An efficient algorithm for computing causal trace sets in causality checking. In: Chen, Y.-F., Cheng, C.-H., Esparza, J. (eds.) ATVA 2019. LNCS, vol. 11781, pp. 171–186. Springer, Cham (2019). https://doi.org/10.1007/978-3-030-31784-3_10

[Lam78] Lamport, L.: Time, clocks, and the ordering of events in a distributed system. Commun. ACM **21**(7), 558–565 (1978)

[Lei15] Leitner-Fischer, F.: Causality checking of safety-critical software and systems. Ph.D. thesis, University of Konstanz, Germany (2015)

[Lew01] Lewis, D.: Counterfactuals. Wiley-Blackwell, London (2001)

[LFL11] Leitner-Fischer, F., Leue, S.: Quantum: quantitative safety analysis of UML models. In: Massink, M., Norman, G. (eds.) QAPL, volume 57 of EPTCS, pp. 16–30 (2011)

[LL13] Leitner-Fischer, F., Leue, S.: Causality checking for complex system models. In: Giacobazzi, R., Berdine, J., Mastroeni, I. (eds.) VMCAI 2013. LNCS, vol. 7737, pp. 248–267. Springer, Heidelberg (2013). https://doi.org/10.1007/978-3-642-35873-9_16

[Obj17] Object Management Group: OMG Systems Modeling Language, Specification 1.5 (2017). http://www.omg.org/spec/SysML

[OO73] O'Neil, P.E., O'Neil, E.J.: A fast expected time algorithm for Boolean matrix multiplication and transitive closure. Inf. Control **22**(2), 132–138 (1973)

[SRH18] Steffen, B., Rüthing, O., Huth, M.: Mathematical Foundations of Advanced Informatics, Volume 1: Inductive Approaches. Springer, Cham (2018). https://doi.org/10.1007/978-3-319-68397-3

[Wei19] Weiser, J.: Derivation of a minimal representation of incomplete partial orders from event sequences. Master's thesis, University of Konstanz (2019)

TraceVis: Towards Visualization for Deep Statistical Model Checking

Timo P. Gros[2(✉)], David Groß[1(✉)], Stefan Gumhold[1(✉)], Jörg Hoffmann[2(✉)],
Michaela Klauck[2(✉)], and Marcel Steinmetz[2(✉)]

[1] Technical University Dresden, Dresden, Germany
{david.gross1,stefan.gumhold}@tu-dresden.de
[2] Saarland University, Saarland Informatics Campus, Saarbrücken, Germany
{timopgros,hoffmann,klauck,steinmetz}@cs.uni-saarland.de

Abstract. With the proliferation of neural networks (NN), the need to analyze, and ideally verify, their behavior becomes more and more pressing. Significant progress has been made in the analysis of individual NN decision episodes, but the verification of NNs as part of larger systems remains a grand challenge. Deep statistical model checking (DSMC) is a recent approach addressing that challenge in the context of Markov decision processes (MDP) where a NN represents a policy taking action decisions. The NN determinizes the MDP, resulting in a Markov chain which is analyzed by statistical model checking. Initial results in a Racetrack case study (a simple abstract encoding of driving control) suggest that such a DSMC analysis can be useful for quality assurance in system approval or certification.

Here we explore the use of visualization to support DSMC users (human analysts, domain engineers). We implement an interactive visualization tool, TraceVis, for the Racetrack case study. The tool allows to explore crash probabilities into particular wall segments as a function of start position and velocity. It furthermore supports the in-depth examination of the policy traces generated by DSMC, in aggregate form as well as individually. This demonstrates how visualization can foster the effective analysis of DSMC results, and it forms a first step in combining model checking and visualization in the analysis of NN behavior.

Keywords: Statistical Model Checking · Neural Networks · Visualization

1 Introduction

Neural networks (NN), in particular deep neural networks, have led to astounding advances in many areas of computer science [21, 26, 36]. NNs are more and more at the core of *intelligent systems*, taking decisions traditionally taken by humans.

Authors are listed alphabetically.

© Springer Nature Switzerland AG 2021
T. Margaria and B. Steffen (Eds.): ISoLA 2020, LNCS 12479, pp. 27–46, 2021.
https://doi.org/10.1007/978-3-030-83723-5_3

For such systems, the need to analyze, and ideally verify, NN behavior becomes more and more pressing. This constitutes a grand challenge as it combines (1) the complexity of analyzing NN function representations with (2) the state space explosion problem (analyzing large system behavior state spaces). Remarkable progress is being made on (1), through SAT modulo theories [8,23,25], abstract interpretation [12,29], and quantitative analysis [6,42]. This pertains to the verification of individual NN decision episodes, i.e., the behavior of a single input/output function call. Yet the verification of decision-taking NNs in intelligent systems requires the analysis of all possible situations that may result from sequences of NN decisions.

Many intelligent systems using NN, e.g., the control of various forms of cyber-physical systems, can be cast as discrete decision-making in the presence of random phenomena. Hence a natural framework within which to start addressing the problem are Markov decision processes [35] (MDP), and specifically the model families considered in probabilistic model checking [28]. Assume a decision-making problem for which a NN has been trained, and assume that the problem can be formally cast as a MDP. Then we may use this MDP as a context to study properties of the NN. The NN is perceived as an action *policy* in the MDP, determinizing the non-deterministic choices. This yields a Markov chain which can be analyzed by probabilistic model checking techniques.

Recent work [14], henceforth referred to as *DSMC20*, proposed so-called *deep statistical model checking (DSMC)* as a scalable approach of this kind. The idea is to apply statistical model checking [20,43] to the Markov chain resulting from the use of a NN policy in an MDP. DSMC20 realize this idea in the context of MDPs represented in JANI [5], a language interfacing with leading probabilistic model checking tools. They implement a generic connection between NNs and the state-of-the-art statistical model checker MODES [2,4], part of THE MODEST TOOLSET [19].

DSMC20 perform practical experiments in a Racetrack case study (adopted from benchmarks in AI autonomous decision-making [1,34]), where a vehicle needs to choose accelerate/decelerate actions on a discrete map so as to reach a goal line without bumping into a wall. We adopt this case study here. While the problem is simple, it is suited as a starting point in the grand challenge of intelligent system verification. It can be readily extended to include traffic, sensing, fuel consumption, etc., ultimately up to models reflecting important challenges in autonomous driving.

DSMC20 propose DSMC as a tool for quality assurance by human analysts or domain engineers in system approval or certification. Clearly, given the complexity of problem parameter spaces and the need to understand what is going wrong and how, visualization methods are potentially very useful for that purpose. DSMC20 illustrate this with simple heat maps localizing safety issues. In the present paper, we begin to address the full scope of this visualization problem.

We design a new highly immersive visual exploration tool, that we baptize *TraceVis*, for the data space in DSMC on Racetrack. TraceVis exploits 3D visualization for mapping probabilities to height, stacking of trajectories and mapping of time. We develop a hierarchical navigation concept to avoid multiple views, such that all visualizations are integrated into a single 3D scene (which will ease a future extension to a virtual reality setup). Besides TraceVis itself, our contributions are:

- An interactive overview and context visualization of the goal and crash probabilities computed by DSMC, where we can inspect for all start positions p of the track either a single start velocity v or all start velocities at the same time.
- An aggregate view of all trajectories for a given start configuration (p, v) that visualizes the velocity distribution over the whole track in a concise and comprehensible way. Optionally, we allow disaggregation of time providing more details into the data space.
- An efficient hierarchical navigation approach, from an overview over the whole track to a trajectory ensemble for a selected start configuration, and over two levels of trajectory clusters down to individual trajectories.
- A replay mode that animates policy traces, which can be used in the stacked as well as in the aggregate trajectory visualization mode.
- A case study illustrating the analysis power of the new visual exploration tool in Racetrack.

Our endeavor differs from previous work on visualization techniques for NNs (e.g. [22,40,44]) in its focus on DSMC and Racetrack. We draw on established techniques in visualization, in particular in ensemble visualization (e.g. [9,31,38]).

Overall, we initiate a connection between DSMC and visualization research, laying the groundwork for long-term synergy between model checking and visualization in this context. In particular, we believe that some of the key ideas in TraceVis will carry over to more faithful representations of autonomous driving, and to other domains involving cyber-physical systems where position and velocity in physical space are key dimensions.

The paper is organized as follows. Section 2 discusses related work. Section 3 briefly summarizes DSMC20 as relevant to understand our work and contribution. Section 4 outlines our data space and visualization concept, followed by Sects. 5 and 6 which describe our visualization techniques for crash probabilities and policy traces respectively. Section 7 exemplifies the use of TraceVis for DSMC result analysis in Racetrack. Section 8 closes the paper with an outlook on future challenges.

A video demonstrating TraceVis as well as its source code is available at DOI 10.5281/zenodo.3961196 [13].

2   Related Work

In the context of explainable AI research, a lot of recent research has been devoted to interactive visualization of NN [22]. Goals for such techniques include interpretability, explainability, NN debugging, as well as model comparison and selection. Most of the work has been dedicated to NNs for image analysis tasks. Only few recent works address the debugging and interpretation of deep networks used in reinforcement learning [40,44]. These are dedicated to Deep Q-Learning of agents playing Atari Retro Games, where high state-space dimensionality is the core problem addressed. In [44] the authors embed the state space based on the last layer of the NN with t-SNE into two dimensions and colorize the 2D points with handcrafted features. Their main contribution is an analysis of the MDP through spacetime clustering of the state space. The resulting hierarchical decomposition into skills allows for a better interpretation of the strategy of the learned agents. Wang et al. [40] developed a visual analysis tool with multiple coordinated views supporting a hierarchical navigation from an overview of the learning process down to individual traces of gameplays. Their main contribution is a scalable visualization of these traces that visualizes the position of the paddle together with the actions taken.

One of our contributions pertains to the visual analysis of large collections of traces. So our work relates to ensemble visualization, which is an active research area. Wang et al. [41] survey sixty recent ensemble visualization papers and found that all visualization techniques are based on aggregation over ensemble members before the visualization, and on composition of ensemble members after the visualization. For the case of trace or trajectory ensembles, prominent aggregation techniques generalize 1D boxplots [39]. Mirzargar et al. [31] use the concept of data depth to define a band which encloses a given percentile of the curves in a curve ensemble. Due to the high computational complexity of curve boxplots, Etienne et al. [9] propose trajectory box plots, which are based on per frame oriented boxes that are fast to compute but introduce more visual clutter. With respect to composition of 2D trajectory ensembles, the stacking of the trajectories in 3D has shown to be a versatile solution [38]. Here, we develop a new aggregation technique specifically designed for Racetrack, and also support the stacking of trajectory ensembles.

3   Background: DSMC20 and Racetrack

This paper is a direct follow-up on DSMC20 [14], so we give the background in terms of a summary of that work, as relevant to understand our study and contribution.

Deep Statistical Model Checking (DSMC). The models considered in DSMC20, and here, are discrete-state MDPs. For any nonempty set S let $\mathcal{D}(S)$ denote the set of probability distributions over S.

Definition 1 (Markov Decision Process). *A Markov Decision Process (MDP) is a tuple $\mathcal{M} = \langle S, A, T, s_0 \rangle$ consisting of a finite set of states S, a finite set of actions A, a partial transition probability function $T : S \times A \nrightarrow \mathcal{D}(S)$, and an initial state $s_0 \in S$. We say that action $a \in A$ is applicable in state $s \in S$ if $T(s, a)$ is defined. We denote by $A(s) \subseteq A$ the set of actions applicable in s. We assume that $A(s)$ is nonempty for each s (which is no restriction).*

An action policy resolves the non-deterministic choices in a state, determining which applicable action to apply as a function of the state history so far. We represent histories as finite sequences of states, hence elements of S^+. We use $last(w)$ to denote the last state in $w \in S^+$.

Definition 2 (Action Policy). *A (deterministic, history-dependent) action policy is a function* $\sigma: \mathcal{S}^+ \to \mathcal{A}$ *such that* $\forall w \in \mathcal{S}^+ : \sigma(w) \in \mathcal{A}(last(w))$.

An MDP together with an action policy defines a Markov chain:

Definition 3 (Markov Chain). *A Markov Chain is a tuple* $\mathcal{C} = \langle \mathcal{S}, \mathcal{T}, s_0 \rangle$ *consisting of a set of states* $\mathcal{S}$, *a transition probability function* $\mathcal{T}: \mathcal{S} \to \mathcal{D}(\mathcal{S})$ *and an initial state* $s_0 \in \mathcal{S}$.

Given an MDP $\mathcal{M} = \langle \mathcal{S}, \mathcal{A}, \mathcal{T}, s_0 \rangle$, an action policy $\sigma: \mathcal{S}^+ \to \mathcal{A}$ induces a countable-state Markov chain $\langle \mathcal{S}^+, \mathcal{T}', s_0 \rangle$ over state histories in the obvious way: For any $w \in S^+$ with $\mathcal{T}(last(w), \sigma(w)) = \mu$, set $\mathcal{T}'(w) = \rho$ where $\rho(ws) = \mu(s)$ for all $s \in \mathcal{S}$.

The idea in DSMC is to analyze this Markov chain for an action policy represented as a neural network (NN). The NN is assumed to be trained externally prior to the DSMC analysis, but is assumed to operate on the same state space as a given MDP $\mathcal{M}$ (i.e., the NN's inputs are states and its outputs are actions). The NN policy σ together with $\mathcal{M}$ then induces a Markov chain $\mathcal{C}$ as described. Statistical model checking is a promising approach to analyze $\mathcal{C}$, as it merely requires to evaluate the NN on input states, otherwise treating it like a blackbox. DSMC20 implemented this approach for MODES [4] in THE MODEST TOOLSET [19].

Observe that, for DSMC to work in this form, the MDP and the NN need to operate on the same level of system abstraction. This is a simplification (relative to, e.g., NNs whose input are camera images) that renders the model checking problem crisp. Another subtlety is that the NN may return inapplicable actions (giving guarantees on NN outputs is notoriously hard), and in that sense may not actually fit the definition of an action policy. DSMC20 handle this through a more permissive definition of *action oracle*, transitioning to a new stalled state in the induced Markov chain $\mathcal{C}$ if the NN oracle's chosen action is inapplicable.

Racetrack Benchmark and JANI *Model.* Racetrack is originally a pen and paper game [10]. It was adopted as a benchmark for MDP algorithms in the AI community [1,3,15,30,33,34]. The track is a two-dimensional grid, where each cell of the grid can be a starting position, a goal position, a free position, or a wall. The vehicle starts with velocity 0 at any of the starting positions, and the objective is to reach the goal as fast as possible without crashing into a wall. The actions modify the velocity vector by one unit in the eight discrete directions; one can also choose to keep the current velocity. We consider noise emulating slippery road conditions: actions may *fail* with a given probability, in which case the velocity remains unchanged. Here we use two Racetrack benchmarks, i.e., track shapes, originally introduced by Barto et al. [1]. They are illustrated in Fig. 1.

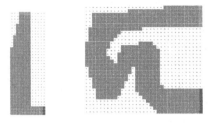

Fig. 1. The maps of our Racetrack benchmarks: Barto-small (left) and Barto-big (right). Starting positions green, goal positions red. (Color figure online)

DSMC20 encode these Racetrack benchmarks in JANI [5,24]. Many tools offer direct support for JANI, including ePMC, Storm and THE MODEST TOOLSET [7,18,19]; an automatic translation from JANI to PRISM [27] is available too.

DSMC20's JANI model represents the grid as a two-dimensional array. Vehicle movements and collision checks are represented by separate automata that synchronize using shared actions. This is straightforward except for the collision checks, i.e., checking whether the vehicle's move – represented through horizontal and vertical speed (dx, dy) – hits a wall. This is done by generating a (discrete approximation of) a straight line from the vehicle position (x, y) to $(x + dx, y + dy)$, and checking whether any position on that line contains a wall segment.

Neural Networks. NNs consist of neurons that apply a non-linear function to a weighted sum of their inputs. DSMC20 use feed-forward NNs, where neurons are arranged in a sequence from an input layer via several hidden layers to an output layer. So-called "deep" neural networks consist of many layers. Feed-forward NNs are comparatively simple, yet are wide-spread [11] (and anyway our visualization techniques are independent of the NN architecture).

To learn NN action policies in Racetrack, DSMC20 employ *deep Q-learning* [32], where the NN is trained by iterative execution and refinement steps. Each step executes the current policy until a terminal state is reached (goal or crash), and updates the NN weights using gradient descent. NNs are learnt for a specific map (cf. Fig. 1). The NNs have two hidden layers each of size 64.

Case Study and Heat Maps. DSMC20 use Racetrack as a case study to highlight the use of DSMC for quality assurance. They use simple heat maps for a limited visualization of the DSMC outcome. Here we advance way beyond this, to interactive visualization of a much richer data space. To give the comparison to DSMC20, in what follows we briefly show a representative result from their case study.

Fig. 2. DSMC20 heat maps, showing aggregated crash probability as a function of start position when fixing start velocity to 0. (Color figure online)

Figure 2 shows aggregated crash probability – the probability of crashing into any wall – as a function of start position when fixing start velocity to 0. The heat maps use a simple color scheme as indicated in the figure. From this simple visualization, quality assurance analysts can conclude that the NN policies are fairly safe, to different degrees depending on the map region. What the heat maps don't show is, for example, how the shown probabilities depend on initial velocity, *where* unsuccessful policy runs tend to crash into the wall, and to what degree such crashes are due to noise or bad policy decisions. We show in what follows how to make all these details accessible through interactive visualization methods.

4   Visualization Concept

Before we go into the details of our visualization techniques, let us outline our concept in terms of the data space we visualize, and the principles behind our visualization approach.

Data Collection. We collect extensive information about the to-be-analyzed action policy from MODES, allowing to analyze policy behavior as a function of start position p *and* start velocity v, and showing not only whether the policy succeeded or crashed but also *where*. To this end, we run separate model checks with MODES for every pair (v, p), with properties representing every possible terminal (goal/crash) position. The number of runs is thus quadratic in map size, with a constant factor of 25 for the start velocities (in $\{-2, -1, 0, 1, 2\}^2$). We ignore start velocities that directly lead to a crash in the first step.

We furthermore collect all policy traces generated by MODES during DSMC, with detailed per-step information: position, velocity, action taken by policy, and a Boolean indicating whether the action succeeded or failed (i.e., whether noise occurred). In Barto-big, to keep computation times reasonable, we generated this data only for 7 of the 25 possible start velocities.

We want to highlight that the information about the policies we extracted from MODES are not specific to DSMC. We only used state and action information of the MDP under investigation. These trace information can be obtained with every statistical model checker independent of the mechanism used to resolve nondeterminism which in our case was DSMC.

Computation and export of this data for Barto-small/Barto-big took 17/20 h on 25 virtual machines having an AMD EPYC Processor at approximately 2.5 GHz using Ubuntu 18.04 with 8vCPUs and 16 GB RAM. The data comprises 5473/3826 start configurations consuming 1.25 MB/1.18 MB for probabilities and 15.3 GB/13.4 GB for traces/reduced traces on disk, in a concise text file format organized in two folders for probabilities and traces with one file per start configuration. The largest trace file has 13 MB on disk and contains 18270 traces of average/max length 44/65. The data is publicly available at DOI 10.5281/zenodo.3961196 [13].

Visualization Principles and Rationales. Neither the probabilities nor the traces can be visualized in their entirety in a single visualization. We therefore opted for the development of a highly interactive visual analysis tool, TraceVis. As Racetrack is 2-dimensional, we chose a 3-dimensional visualization space to be able to exploit the 3rd dimension to map additional features. We implemented TraceVis as a plugin to the CGV-Framework [16], which allows rapid prototyping of interactive 3D tools in C++ with OpenGL. The CGV-Framework supports efficient high-quality rendering of large amounts of primitive shapes like boxes, spheres and rounded cones based on the concept of GPU based raycasting [17, 37]. All primitives allow color mapping.

Figure 3 illustrates the design of TraceVis. For each track position we render a box whose type is color coded: start/goal locations in green/blue, walls in red, other track locations in light gray or color-mapped, and an additional row of dark grey boundary cells added around the track.

To keep the tool as clear as possible, we completely abstained from multiple views, incorporating all visualizations and interactions within a single 3D scene built on top of the Racetrack map. The view onto the 3D scene can be adjusted with the mouse based on an adjustable focus point with the typical navigation commands for translate, zoom and orbiting around the focus. Mode switches are used to navigate through different visualizations, and mouse pointer and wheel are used for direct selection and ergonomic configuration. All selections and configurations can also be adjusted through a classical user interface, which shows the current status of TraceVis and serves as manual by providing help on mouse interaction and hotkeys through tooltips. For fast navigation and to foster comprehension, an important design goal was the support for high frame rates even when visualizing a large number of traces at the same time.

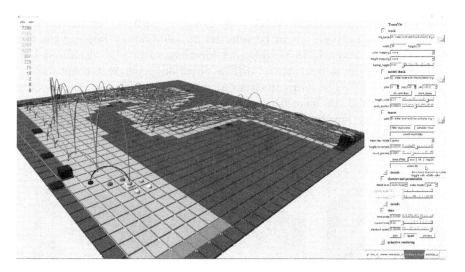

Fig. 3. Screenshot to illustrate the design of TraceVis. Highly interactive 3D view, accompanied by classical UI showing current tool state and providing tooltip based help. (Color figure online)

In accordance to Schneiderman's mantra – "Overview first, zoom and filter, then details-on-demand" – we designed a hierarchical navigation scheme. A heatmap visualization similar to the one in DSMC20 serves as overview over all start configurations. The user can select individual start configurations to view crash and goal probabilities (as described in Sect. 5). The user can dive into more detail by switching to trace visualization mode where the corresponding trace file is read on the fly; the traces can further be navigated from main clusters down to single traces (as described in Sect. 6). To navigate to a different start configuration, the user first needs to navigate back up the hierarchy to the probability visualization mode. This allows for the reuse of the same hotkeys on different hierarchy levels, reducing the number of hotkeys to be learned for fast interaction.

5   Visualizing Probabilities

We next describe our techniques for visualizing crash/goal probabilities as a function of start position p and start velocity v.

Start Configuration Selector. DSMC20 provides for each start configuration (p, v) and each wall, boundary and goal location q the probability that traces from (p, v) end in q. Visualizing the entire probability mapping $P(p, v, q)$ in a single image or 3D-scene seems futile. Our approach is to instead leverage interactive visualization, based on selection and aggregation of arguments to $P(p, v, q)$. TraceVis supports selection of a single p and/or a single v at a time. We indicate these user-fixed parameters notationally as $\hat{p}$ and $\hat{v}$.

The user can interactively select $\hat{p}$ by hovering with the mouse over the track while pressing Shift. $\hat{v}$ can be selected by additionally holding the Ctrl modifier key and hovering to neighboring locations of $\hat{p}$. $\hat{p}$ is visualized by a yellow box and $\hat{v}$ by a bent arrow with a direction dependent color scale as shown in Fig. 4 (left). The user can either focus on $\hat{v}$, or on all possible velocities v for which probabilities have been precomputed. The latter *all velocity* mode is auto-selected by hovering over the track with the Ctrl modifier pressed as illustrated in Fig. 4 (right).

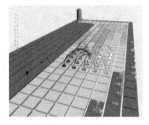

Fig. 4. Start configuration selection and different probability visualization approaches. Left: selected start configuration $(\hat{p}, \hat{v})$ shown as yellow box and pink arrow. Summed crash probabilities $\sum_{\tilde{q}} P(p, \hat{v}, \tilde{q})$ mapped to color of valid track locations p. Pink bar charts show crash and goal probabilities for start configuration $(\hat{p}, \hat{v})$. Middle: Same as left, with additional mapping of summed crash probabilities to height of track boxes. Right: *All velocity* mode shows summed probabilities aggregated over all start velocities – here the maximum of the summed crash probabilities. Colored charts show crash and goal probabilities for all start configurations $(\hat{p}, v)$. (Color figure online)

Heat Map Overview. We extend the DSMC20 heat map overview by the option to adjust the height of the track boxes, as shown in Fig. 4 (middle). The user can select the probability type with hotkeys. In *all velocity mode* the summed probabilities are aggregated per start location over all start velocities with one of the user-selectable aggregation operators min, max or range = min − max. In this way we can visualize $\sum_{\tilde{q}} P(p, \hat{v}, \tilde{q})$ and $\text{agg}_{\tilde{v}} \sum_{\tilde{q}} P(p, \tilde{v}, \tilde{q})$, where agg denotes the selected aggregation operator. These visualizations can be used as a guidance to finding start configurations of interest and continuing further investigation from there.

Bar Chart Details. While the heat maps allow to efficiently determine start positions with a high rate of crashing, they do not show the crash positions q. TraceVis supports the latter through track boxes in the form of bar charts, visible e.g. in Fig. 4 (left) in the back on the left-hand side (pink bar). The bar heights indicate the probability of crashing/reaching the goal, thus visualizing $P(\hat{p}, \hat{v}, q)$. In *all velocity* mode, an individual bar is included for each possible start velocity, i.e. we visualize $P(\hat{p}, v, q)$. To this end, we use the visual metaphor of spatial and color coding: the thin bars have the same color and positional offset as the start velocity vectors, as can be seen in Fig. 4 (right).

6   Visualizing Policy Traces

Once a start configuration $(\hat{p}, \hat{v})$ of interest is found, a natural means to investigate further is to inspect the actual policy traces generated by DSMC starting from $(\hat{p}, \hat{v})$. TraceVis supports this in depth, through the techniques we describe next.

Trace Visualization Modes. To initiate trace inspection, the user presses the Enter key. TraceVis reads the trace file, and by default filters out duplicates of the traces while keeping track of the number of duplicates per trace. Figure 5 illustrates our three distinct modes to visualize traces: *Stacked, spatial* and *spacetime.*

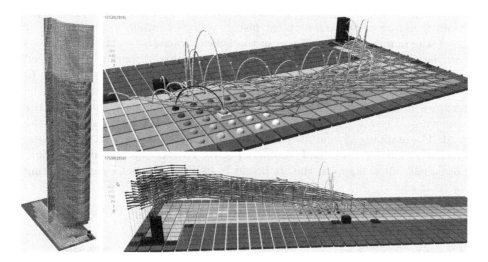

Fig. 5. Comparison of different trace rendering modes for a start configuration with 17530 traces of which 2856 remain after duplicate filtering. Left: *stacked* rendering of 2856 traces, sorted and color coded by end location. Top right: *spatial* aggregation showing segments as arcs with appearance counts mapped to height and luminance. Bottom right: *spacetime* mode disaggregates segments over time, mapping time to height. (Color figure online)

Traces are visualized as colored 3D tubes or, in the case of an aggregated view, bent arrows. While the direction of traces is towards the goal positions in general, there are exceptions (e.g. when the agent needs to turn around first given a particular start velocity). Using tubes alone is not sufficient to show the direction of movement, hence we map an arrow texture onto the tubes.

Stacked Trace Visualization. In *stacked* mode, all traces that were calculated for a specific start configuration are shown stacked vertically above the track. Traces are sorted by their end location, and are arranged into two main clusters:

one for traces that end at a goal position and one for those that crash. A sub-cluster is formed for each end position. As shown in Fig. 5 (left), the goal (crash) clusters are colored with a blue to cyan (red to orange) color scale. Stacking in the order of the sub clusters and with cluster based coloring reduces visual cluttering significantly. The stacking offset in z direction can be adjusted with the mouse wheel.

Spatial Aggregation. Given the number of traces, simply visualizing the set of all traces is often not helpful. We design a more comprehensible visualization in terms of the velocity distribution over the track. To this end, we leverage the discrete nature of the underlying MDP, aggregating over discrete time and space. Specifically, we consider the possible move segments that action applications result in on the map. Each segment is defined by a start position p_s and end position p_e. Multiple segments of different traces share the same p_s and p_e. We can therefore compute a segment histogram by counting, for each segment (p_s, p_e), the number of appearances in the DSMC traces.

In the *spatial* mode shown in Fig. 5 (top right) this histogram is visualized by mapping the appearance counts to bent arcs with height proportional to the appearance count. Additionally, the appearance count is mapped to the luminance of the bent arc with a gamma correction that can be adjusted with the mouse wheel. The absolute values of the appearance counts can be read from the legend. The mapping to bent arcs has the additional advantage that overlapping segments get visually separated (compare Fig. 6). To maximize visual separation, we optionally allow mapping the arc height to half the segment length, resulting in circular arcs.

Fig. 6. Variants of segment rendering. From left to right: straight tube segments; added arrow texture; arcs with height equal to half step size; tilted arcs; arcs with height proportional to appearance counts. (Color figure online)

For starting configurations where the agent needs to reverse its direction, overlapping inverse movements can be observed, see Fig. 6 (middle). This prevents the visual separation of oppositely pointing arrows. We overcome this issue by slightly tilting the arcs sideways to visually separate them again as shown in Fig. 6 (2nd from right).

Spacetime Visualization. The aggregation of segments characterized by start and end position (p_s, p_e) can be extended to also incorporate time information. Due to the noise influencing the successful application of a policy action, it is possible that no agent movement occurs in a given time step. Since we do not consider time in the other visualization modes, this is hard to notice. Furthermore, different traces might run along segments with equal start and end position but at different times. For exploration scenarios where this is important, we therefore implemented the *spacetime* mode as shown in Fig. 5 (bottom right). Given the discrete-time nature of the MDP, the time t of a segment is simply defined by its position in the trace.

To calculate the aggregated segments for the *spacetime* mode we calculate the appearance count histogram over the triples (p_s, p_e, t). While rendering the segments, appearance counts are again mapped to luminance and optionally to arc height. We map time to an increasing height offset. This allows to efficiently identify faster and slower runs, as well as showing track points where the agent temporarily stops. A thin yellow stick is rendered to visually link trace vertices to their corresponding track locations.

To support the analysis of local behavior at a given position, we added another mouse hovering mode (activated by the Alt modifier), that restricts the view to the outgoing arcs at the current mouse pointer position. The height scale for arcs and the time offset can be adapted with the mouse wheel with different modifier keys.

Cluster Navigation. To reduce visual clutter in the aggregated trace visualization modes further, the user can navigate hierarchically through clusters and individual traces as illustrated in Fig. 7. The Enter key goes down the hierarchy from all traces to main clusters, then to sub-clusters and finally to individual traces. Sub-clusters can also be selected by hovering over a trace end position. At each level, the Up and Down arrow keys allow to navigate through the respective clusters/traces. Backspace is used to back up one hierarchy level. Pressing Backspace on the all-trace level terminates the trace mode, and brings the user back to probability mode.

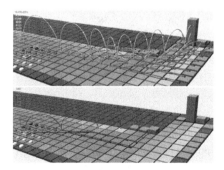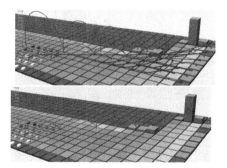

Fig. 7. Illustration of four cluster hierarchy levels in *spatial* mode: top level (top left), main cluster level (top right), sub-cluster level (bottom left), individual trace (bottom right). (Color figure online)

Noise Visualization. All visualization modes make use of spheres placed at the track points where two segments are connected. The color coding of these spheres correlates to the amount of noise which influenced the agent during the DSMC runs. Red color indicates the appearance of noise, while green color states the successful movement according to the action chosen by the NN. This is especially useful for the in-depth examination of individual traces, visualizing the policy reacting to action failures at difficult track locations and configurations. For aggregated views, the color is interpolated between red and green according to the noise frequency.

Animation. To illustrate synchronicity in time across traces, we added an animation of spherical probe particles moving along the traces synchronously with adjustable speed. The animation is supported in all trace visualization modes. Space allows to toggle the animation, and with the Left and Right arrow keys one can step back and forth over individual time steps.

7   Case Study

To illustrate the use of TraceVis for policy behavior analysis, we now consider TraceVis from a user's (rather than a visualization researcher's) perspective. We highlight some interesting observations supported by TraceVis in analyzing the NN policies trained by DSMC20 in Racetrack.

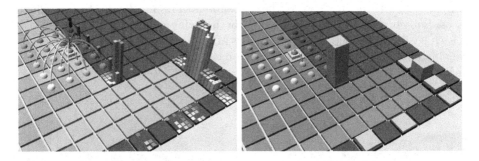

Fig. 8. Unsafe behavior near goal line. Overview of crash/goal probabilities across start velocities (left), and individual view for particularly problematic start velocity (right). (Color figure online)

Figure 8 shows our first observation, for a position just before the goal curve in Barto-small. We can see in Fig. 8 (left) that, overall, the policy has a high chance of reaching the goal line as one would expect. However there are two start velocities not directed into the wall for which that is not so. Such problematic cases can very conveniently be located simply by dragging this overview presentation over the map. Selecting the most problematic start velocity in Fig. 8 (right), it becomes evident that policy behavior is highly, and unnecessarily, unsafe here. One can reach the goal with high probability simply by keeping the velocity and turning once the wall is cleared. Yet the policy tends to "cut the corner" and crash.

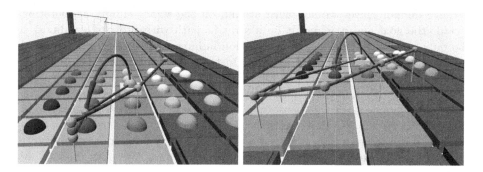

Fig. 9. Unsafe turning between walls: Successful (left) vs. crashed (right) trace. (Color figure online)

Figure 9 shows another instance of curious policy behavior, also needlessly unsafe but less obviously so. Here the start position is in a tight spot between walls on the left and right, with a start velocity away from the goal and to the left. The safest decision would be to "turn around on the spot", i.e., decelerate, get left-right velocity down to 0, accelerate to the goal. Instead, as we see in the successful policy trace in Fig. 9 (left), the policy over-accelerates to the right, going for a curve that only just avoids the right-hand side wall. Yet that curve relies on action success (green balls at move arcs in the visualization), and is brittle to action failure (red balls) as we see in the crashing trace in Fig. 9 (right).

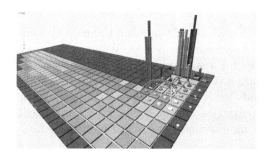
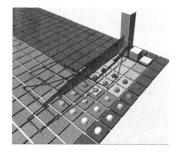

Fig. 10. Counterintuitive turning near goal: Overview of crash/goal probabilities across start velocities (left), and policy-trace overview for one particular start velocity (right). (Color figure online)

Consider finally Fig. 10. Here the agent is placed in front of the goal near the corner, and the overview (left) shows that the start velocities going towards the corner have a tendency to crash. This is not surprising given the actual risk of crashing here when actions fail, plus our previous observations in Fig. 8. A more surprising insight is obtained when choosing a harmless start velocity, away from the goal at speed 1. Here we again get a counterintuitive turning behavior. Like above, a human player would "turn around on the spot", simply accelerating towards the goal and reaching it on a straight path with probability almost 1 (the only possibility to crash being 7 action failures in a row). Yet the trained neural network policy does not do that. Instead, it travels along a potentially large de-tour towards the start line, curving back to reach the goal on a trajectory scraping along the wall. This does work out with a high probability here, but nevertheless points to a weakness in policy behavior. Together with the odd behavior observed in Fig. 9, it seems the policy generally has issues in situations requiring a full turn-around – giving a strong hint for possible re-training.

Note that TraceVis is key to all these observations. We miss them if we aggregate over start velocities (or fix these to 0 as DSMC20 does), if we aggregate over crash positions, if we have no in-depth visualization of policy traces.

Interestingly, TraceVis enabled us to find bugs in our own technology stack. Apart from initial data discrepancies due to bugs in cross-tool communication, this pertained also to a bug in our JANI model introduced when modifying it for this paper. Examining crash probabilities as a function of start velocity as illustrated above, we observed unintuitive results where start velocities heading directly into a wall did not lead to a crash. This behavior prompted us to re-examine the JANI model, identifying a bug in the vehicle automaton (where an initialization value was set incorrectly). Such a faulty behavior would not have been visible in DSMC20's heat maps as these ignore start velocities. The bug would be exceedingly hard (if not impossible) to identify based solely on MODES, given the overwhelming amount of log data. Hence TraceVis can be useful also for debugging the model itself, arguably a crucial part of model checking.

8   Conclusion

Deep statistical model checking (DSMC) is a natural approach to quality assurance of MDP action policies represented by neural networks. We have designed and implemented a new tool, TraceVis, for visualizing and navigating DSMC results, as well as for deeply understanding the underlying causes by examining the actual policy traces. Our case study and own debugging experience with TraceVis suggests that interactive visualization can be useful for the practical application of DSMC, and potentially more general statistical model checking contexts as well.

We believe that the combination of formal methods with visualization is a key instrument to address the problem of NN action policy analysis (by DSMC or other methods). First, in contrast to traditional software artefacts, NN defy direct human inspection. Second, in many cases, full verification will be prohibitively complex or bound to fail (an autonomous car will hardly guarantee to avoid all possible accidents). Therefore, third, to gain trust in an action policy, human quality assurance analysts will have to understand its behavior and inspect its reactions against a large space of possible environment behaviors. The combination of formal analysis tools with human-accessible data and results presentation seems predestined for that purpose. We view our work as one initial piece of this big puzzle.

Our contribution at this point is, of course, limited to the simple Racetrack benchmark, and it remains to be seen which ideas will carry over to other and more complex domains. That said, we believe that the Racetrack case study was useful, and remains useful, to focus on key aspects of many cyber-physical systems: position and velocity in physical space. This is different from the focus on visualizing complex strategy patterns, naturally entailed by the study of policies for computer games as done by the aforementioned previous works [40, 44].

Our envisioned research trajectory thus is to stick to Racetrack-like case studies, incrementally extending these to reflect more aspects of, and ultimately approach, autonomous driving. Fuel consumption for example seems easy to integrate, Lidar sensing can be integrated by additional views, similarly for simple camera images showing a grey-scale view of what's ahead. In 3-dimensional extensions like drone control, most of TraceVis's current features will be applicable.

In the longer term, a major challenge will be multi-dimensional state spaces, in particular multi-agent behavior like traffic in autonomous driving/drones, or collaborative agents in cyber-physical production. We envision to extend TraceVis by dimension reduction techniques, providing an abstract visualization of the state space, where we can morph back to 3D space in order to focus on the behavior of individual agents or the 3D relationship between the agents at certain instances of time. It may also be possible to leverage prior insights from computer games, not as much to elicit strategy patterns, but to elicit environment patterns, like typical traffic scenarios of special cases of particular interest. We expect to still stick to physical space as the main organization paradigm for the visualization.

Acknowledgements. This work was partially supported by the ERC Advanced Investigators Grant 695614 (POWVER), by DFG grant 389792660 as part of TRR 248 (see https://perspicuous-computing.science) and by the two Clusters of Excellence CeTI (EXC 2050/1, grant 390696704) and PoL (EXC-2068, grant 390729961) of TU Dresden.

References

1. Barto, A.G., Bradtke, S.J., Singh, S.P.: Learning to act using real-time dynamic programming. Artif. Intell. **72**(1–2), 81–138 (1995)
2. Bogdoll, J., Ferrer Fioriti, L.M., Hartmanns, A., Hermanns, H.: Partial order methods for statistical model checking and simulation. In: Bruni, R., Dingel, J. (eds.) FMOODS/FORTE 2011. LNCS, vol. 6722, pp. 59–74. Springer, Heidelberg (2011). https://doi.org/10.1007/978-3-642-21461-5_4
3. Bonet, B., Geffner, H.: Labeled RTDP: improving the convergence of real-time dynamic programming. In: ICAPS, pp. 12–21 (2003)

4. Budde, C.E., D'Argenio, P.R., Hartmanns, A., Sedwards, S.: A statistical model checker for nondeterminism and rare events. In: Beyer, D., Huisman, M. (eds.) TACAS 2018. LNCS, vol. 10806, pp. 340–358. Springer, Cham (2018). https://doi.org/10.1007/978-3-319-89963-3_20

5. Budde, C.E., Dehnert, C., Hahn, E.M., Hartmanns, A., Junges, S., Turrini, A.: JANI: quantitative model and tool interaction. In: Legay, A., Margaria, T. (eds.) TACAS 2017. LNCS, vol. 10206, pp. 151–168. Springer, Heidelberg (2017). https://doi.org/10.1007/978-3-662-54580-5_9

6. Croce, F., Andriushchenko, M., Hein, M.: Provable robustness of ReLU networks via maximization of linear regions. In: AISTATS, PMLR 89, pp. 2057–2066 (2019)

7. Dehnert, C., Junges, S., Katoen, J.-P., Volk, M.: A STORM is coming: a modern probabilistic model checker. In: Majumdar, R., Kunčak, V. (eds.) CAV 2017. LNCS, vol. 10427, pp. 592–600. Springer, Cham (2017). https://doi.org/10.1007/978-3-319-63390-9_31

8. Ehlers, R.: Formal verification of piece-wise linear feed-forward neural networks. In: D'Souza, D., Narayan Kumar, K. (eds.) ATVA 2017. LNCS, vol. 10482, pp. 269–286. Springer, Cham (2017). https://doi.org/10.1007/978-3-319-68167-2_19

9. Etienne, L., Devogele, T., Buchin, M., McArdle, G.: Trajectory Box Plot: a new pattern to summarize movements. Int. J. Geograph. Inf. Sci. 30(5), 835–853 (2016). https://doi.org/10.1080/13658816.2015.1081205

10. Gardner, M.: Mathematical games. Sci. Am. 229, 118–121 (1973)

11. Gardner, M., Dorling, S.: Artificial neural networks (the multilayer perceptron)–a review of applications in the atmospheric sciences. Atmos. Environ. 32(14), 2627–2636 (1998)

12. Gehr, T., Mirman, M., Drachsler-Cohen, D., Tsankov, P., Chaudhuri, S., Vechev, M.T.: AI2: safety and robustness certification of neural networks with abstract interpretation. In: IEEE Symposium on Security and Privacy 2018, pp. 3–18 (2018)

13. Gros, T.P., Groß, D., Gumhold, S., Hoffmann, J., Klauck, M., Steinmetz, M.: TraceVis: Visualization for DSMC: tool, demonstration video, data (2020). https://doi.org/10.5281/zenodo.3961196

14. Gros, T.P., Hermanns, H., Hoffmann, J., Klauck, M., Steinmetz, M.: Deep statistical model checking. In: Gotsman, A., Sokolova, A. (eds.) FORTE 2020. LNCS, vol. 12136, pp. 96–114. Springer, Cham (2020). https://doi.org/10.1007/978-3-030-50086-3_6

15. Gros, T.P., Höller, D., Hoffmann, J., Wolf, V.: Tracking the race between deep reinforcement learning and imitation learning. In: Gribaudo M., Jansen, D.N., Remke, A. (eds.) Proceedings of the 17th International Conference on Quantitative Evaluation of SysTems (QEST). Springer, Cham (2020). https://doi.org/10.1007/978-3-030-59854-9

16. Gumhold, S.: The computer graphics and visualization framework. https://github.com/sgumhold/cgv. Accessed 18 May 2020

17. Gumhold, S.: Splatting illuminated ellipsoids with depth correction. In: Ertl, T. (ed.) Proceedings of the Vision, Modeling, and Visualization Conference 2003 (VMV 2003), München, Germany, 19–21 November 2003, pp. 245–252. Aka GmbH (2003)

18. Hahn, E.M., Li, Y., Schewe, S., Turrini, A., Zhang, L.: ISCASMC: a web-based probabilistic model checker. In: Jones, C., Pihlajasaari, P., Sun, J. (eds.) FM 2014. LNCS, vol. 8442, pp. 312–317. Springer, Cham (2014). https://doi.org/10.1007/978-3-319-06410-9_22

19. Hartmanns, A., Hermanns, H.: The modest toolset: an integrated environment for quantitative modelling and verification. In: Ábrahám, E., Havelund, K. (eds.) TACAS 2014. LNCS, vol. 8413, pp. 593–598. Springer, Heidelberg (2014). https://doi.org/10.1007/978-3-642-54862-8_51

20. Hérault, T., Lassaigne, R., Magniette, F., Peyronnet, S.: Approximate probabilistic model checking. In: Steffen, B., Levi, G. (eds.) VMCAI 2004. LNCS, vol. 2937, pp. 73–84. Springer, Heidelberg (2004). https://doi.org/10.1007/978-3-540-24622-0_8

21. Hinton, G., et al.: Deep neural networks for acoustic modeling in speech recognition: the shared views of four research groups. IEEE Signal Process. Mag. **29**(6), 82–97 (2012)

22. Hohman, F., Kahng, M., Pienta, R., Chau, D.H.: Visual Analytics in Deep Learning: An Interrogative Survey for the Next Frontiers. arXiv:1801.06889 [cs, stat], May 2018

23. Huang, X., Kwiatkowska, M., Wang, S., Wu, M.: Safety verification of deep neural networks. In: Majumdar, R., Kunčak, V. (eds.) CAV 2017. LNCS, vol. 10426, pp. 3–29. Springer, Cham (2017). https://doi.org/10.1007/978-3-319-63387-9_1

24. The JANI specification. http://www.jani-spec.org/. Accessed 28 Feb 2020

25. Katz, G., Barrett, C., Dill, D.L., Julian, K., Kochenderfer, M.J.: Reluplex: an efficient SMT solver for verifying deep neural networks. In: Majumdar, R., Kunčak, V. (eds.) CAV 2017. LNCS, vol. 10426, pp. 97–117. Springer, Cham (2017). https://doi.org/10.1007/978-3-319-63387-9_5

26. Krizhevsky, A., Sutskever, I., Hinton, G.E.: ImageNet classification with deep convolutional neural networks. In: NIPS, pp. 1097–1105 (2012)

27. Kwiatkowska, M., Norman, G., Parker, D.: PRISM 4.0: verification of probabilistic real-time systems. In: Gopalakrishnan, G., Qadeer, S. (eds.) CAV 2011. LNCS, vol. 6806, pp. 585–591. Springer, Heidelberg (2011). https://doi.org/10.1007/978-3-642-22110-1_47

28. Kwiatkowska, M., Norman, G., Parker, D.: Stochastic model checking. In: Bernardo, M., Hillston, J. (eds.) SFM 2007. LNCS, vol. 4486, pp. 220–270. Springer, Heidelberg (2007). https://doi.org/10.1007/978-3-540-72522-0_6

29. Li, J., Liu, J., Yang, P., Chen, L., Huang, X., Zhang, L.: Analyzing deep neural networks with symbolic propagation: towards higher precision and faster verification. In: Chang, B.-Y.E. (ed.) SAS 2019. LNCS, vol. 11822, pp. 296–319. Springer, Cham (2019). https://doi.org/10.1007/978-3-030-32304-2_15

30. McMahan, H.B., Gordon, G.J.: Fast exact planning in Markov decision processes. In: ICAPS, pp. 151–160 (2005)

31. Mirzargar, M., Whitaker, R.T., Kirby, R.M.: Curve Boxplot: generalization of boxplot for ensembles of curves. IEEE Trans. Vis. Comput. Graph. **20**(12), 2654–2663 (2014). https://doi.org/10.1109/TVCG.2014.2346455. Conference Name: IEEE Transactions on Visualization and Computer Graphics

32. Mnih, V., et al.: Human-level control through deep reinforcement learning. Nature **518**, 529–533 (2015)

33. Pineda, L.E., Lu, Y., Zilberstein, S., Goldman, C.V.: Fault-tolerant planning under uncertainty. In: IJCAI, pp. 2350–2356 (2013)

34. Pineda, L.E., Zilberstein, S.: Planning under uncertainty using reduced models: revisiting determinization. In: ICAPS, pp. 217–225 (2014)

35. Puterman, M.L.: Markov Decision Processes: Discrete Stochastic Dynamic Programming. Wiley, New York (1994)

36. Silver, D., et al.: A general reinforcement learning algorithm that masters chess, shogi, and Go through self-play. Science **362**(6419), 1140–1144 (2018)

37. Stoll, C., Gumhold, S., Seidel, H.P.: Incremental raycasting of piecewise quadratic surfaces on the GPU. In: 2006 IEEE Symposium on Interactive Ray Tracing, pp. 141–150. IEEE. https://doi.org/10.1109/RT.2006.280225. http://ieeexplore.ieee.org/document/4061556/

38. Tominski, C., Schumann, H., Andrienko, G., Andrienko, N.: Stacking-based visualization of trajectory attribute data. IEEE Trans. Vis. Comput. Graph. **18**(12), 2565–2574 (2012). https://doi.org/10.1109/TVCG.2012.265. Conference Name: IEEE Transactions on Visualization and Computer Graphics

39. Tukey, J.W.: Mathematics and the picturing of data. In: Proceedings of the International Congress of Mathematicians, Vancouver, 1975, vol. 2, pp. 523–531 (1975)

40. Wang, J., Gou, L., Shen, H.W., Yang, H.: DQNViz: a visual analytics approach to understand deep Q-networks. IEEE Trans. Vis. Comput. Graph. **25**(1), 288–298 (2019). https://doi.org/10.1109/TVCG.2018.2864504. https://ieeexplore.ieee.org/document/8454905/

41. Wang, J., Hazarika, S., Li, C., Shen, H.W.: Visualization and visual analysis of ensemble data: a survey. IEEE Trans. Vis. Comput. Graph. **25**(9), 2853–2872 (2019). https://doi.org/10.1109/TVCG.2018.2853721. Conference Name: IEEE Transactions on Visualization and Computer Graphics

42. Wicker, M., Huang, X., Kwiatkowska, M.: Feature-guided black-box safety testing of deep neural networks. In: Beyer, D., Huisman, M. (eds.) TACAS 2018. LNCS, vol. 10805, pp. 408–426. Springer, Cham (2018). https://doi.org/10.1007/978-3-319-89960-2_22

43. Younes, H.L.S., Simmons, R.G.: Probabilistic verification of discrete event systems using acceptance sampling. In: Brinksma, E., Larsen, K.G. (eds.) CAV 2002. LNCS, vol. 2404, pp. 223–235. Springer, Heidelberg (2002). https://doi.org/10.1007/3-540-45657-0_17

44. Zahavy, T., Zrihem, N.B., Mannor, S.: Graying the black box: understanding DQNs. arXiv:1602.02658 [cs], April 2017

Engineering of Digital Twins
for Cyber-Physical Systems

Engineering of Digital Twins
for Cyber-Physical Systems

John Fitzgerald[1]([⊠]), Peter Gorm Larsen[2], Tiziana Margaria[3],
and Jim Woodcock[2,4]

[1] School of Computing, Newcastle University, Newcastle upon Tyne, UK
John.Fitzgerald@ncl.ac.uk
[2] DIGIT, Department of Electrical and Computer Engineering, Aarhus University,
Aarhus, Denmark
{pgl,jcpw}@ece.au.dk
[3] University of Limerick and Lero, Limerick, Ireland
Tiziana.Margaria@lero.ie
[4] Department of Computer Science, University of York, York, UK
jim.woodcock@york.ac.uk

Abstract. Advances in sensing, communications and data analytics have made it possible to construct virtual replicas of Cyber-Physical Systems (CPSs). Such replicas, known as digital twins, can in principle inform decision making during operation and evolution of the systems they model. This short paper introduces the ISoLA 2020/21 series of papers on the technology and practice of engineering digital twins for CPSs. The focus is on the relationship between model-based design, machine learning, digital twins and CPSs.

1 Introduction

Ensuring the dependability of Cyber-Physical Systems (CPSs) poses challenges for model-based engineering, stemming from the semantic heterogeneity of the models of computational, physical and human processes, and from the range of stakeholders involved. Delivering such dependability may thus be expected to require the coordinated use of multi-disciplinary models developed during design alongside models derived from data gathered from the operational system. Together, these have the potential to form the basis of a learning *digital twin*, able to inform decision making both in redesign and in operation.

There is an extensive and diverse literature on digital twins. The Gartner group put the concept among its 10 strategically most important technologies in 2019 because of the many potential benefits by establishing digital twins[1]. The benefits claimed for digital twins include the ability to:

1. reduce time to market,
2. establish preventive maintenance possibilities,

---

[1] https://tinyurl.com/y5wkfewe.

© Springer Nature Switzerland AG 2021
T. Margaria and B. Steffen (Eds.): ISoLA 2020, LNCS 12479, pp. 49–53, 2021.
https://doi.org/10.1007/978-3-030-83723-5_4

3. enable additional services for the users,
4. visualise the physical twin,
5. enable fault detection and possibly fault diagnosis,
6. increase autonomy, and
7. provide decision support capabilities.

Although there is considerable hype around the potential for digital twins, the technology poses many open research questions, particularly when one considers twins of CPSs and the need for dependability in order that decisions based on twins are sound. The foundations, processes, techniques and tools for engineering digital twins have not so far been the subject of large-scale and systematic study.

– What foundations are needed for a dependable digital twin of a CPS?
– What are the key concepts to be captured in understanding the requirements for a digital twin?
– Where are the limits for a digital twin? When is it 'good enough'?
– What value can be expected from a digital twin, and when it is worthwhile constructing one?

The dependable operation of CPSs requires both the ability to address the consequences of evolving system components, and the ability to explore and identify optimal changes that do not unduly compromise overall dependability. This combination of prediction and response alongside support for informed decision-making and redesign by humans requires both the data derived from operations and the models developed in design. Tackling the challenges of CPS design thus requires a marriage of both descriptive multi-models of the type that might be developed in a design process, and inductive models derived from data acquired during operation. This combination of models, cutting across formalisms as well as across design and operation, has the potential to form a learning digital twin for a CPS, enabling off-line and on-line decision-making.

The goal of the track on the Engineering of Digital twins for CPSs at ISoLA 2020 is to discuss how one can enable the well-founded engineering of digital twins for dependable CPSs. In order to make the benefits listed above a reality there are important challenges to overcome. These range from the creation of a common basis for discourse in what is inherently a mulitdisciplinary field, through design methodology in the face of the uncertainties that arise when computational process interact with the physical environment, through system architecture to verification. The papers selected for this track address some of these issues from the perspective of formal and model-based approaches, seeking to leverage advances in modelling and verification to address the dependability of digital twins for CPSs.

2   Contributions

In the context of a diverse and rapidly growing literature on digital twins, Yue et al. recognise the need for a conceptual framework to underpin discourse [7]. The framework includes characterisations of digital and physical twins and their environments, and also the critical properties of systems that contain twins, such as notions of fidelity. Central to the benefits claimed for digital twin technology is the ability to manage change, and this in turn requires careful conceptualisation of evolution and life-cycle events in both the digital and physical twins. Further, there is a need to clarify the role of uncertainty in many contemporary CPSs, especially where autonomy is present.

Woodcock et al. [6] consider some of the sources of uncertainty alluded to by Yue et al. In particular, they consider the challenge of handling discrepancies between the values of observed data – which may be subject to noise and delays – and the values predicted in the digital twin. Following an example in agricultural robotics, they consider the description of tolerable deviations the generation of runtime monitors that enforce the identified tolerances. They also consider the use of the digital twin to perform what-if analysis in order to identify optimal system configurations.

Modern CPSs are decentralised, distributed structures. As Kamburjan et al. [2] point out, it may be unrealistic to expect that such CPSs will be captured adequately as physical twins by single models; the architecture of the digital twin will be more heterogeneous and layered. To support such a view, the authors develop a formalised hybrid active object model and demonstrate the expressiveness of the approach. An interesting trade-off is identified between ease of composition and support for simulation: two properties that are needed together to support both analysis and prediction in the digital twin.

Four of the contributed papers examine the potential and the challenges of model-based and formal techniques in realising the potential of digital twins in specific industry sectors: construction, rail transportation, manufacturing and agricultural robotics.

In the construction sector, model-based methods are beginning to bring real benefits, through the use of Building Information Models (BIM). In [4], Li et al. examine the potential of 4-dimensional BIM (BIM updated with real-time sensor data from a construction site or building) as a basis for digital twins. In particular, the paper illustrates how abductive reasoning can provide a basis for checking conformance to construction safety codes. The authors note how a consideration of the digital twin from a formal perspective leads to a need for precision in often tangled concepts, such as building code formalisation and building code execution. As with [7], codification of core concepts via an ontology forms a key part of their approach.

Lecomte [3] reviews the classes of model and modelling activity in the rail sector, pointing out that the heterogeneity of models in the industry results from the diverse purposes for which models are constructed (such as specification, validation, and certification) or the diversity of subjects being modelled (such as signalling and rolling stock). Given the characteristics of the sector, Lecomte concludes that a universal model or digital twin is unlikely to arise, but that new analyses (such as performance improvement) or threats (such as that of infrastructure cyber attack) might provide a motivator to develop digital twins in the future.

Matei et al. [5] recount experience in developing a digital twin for a manufacturing system with computational, physical and human elements. A notable feature of this study is the combination of Virtual Reality with machine learning in a manufacturing scenario where a human is collaborating with an assembly workstation (usually a cobot). This includes quite advanced sensors enabling detailed feedback from the human live.

In [1] Foldager et al. have taken the first steps towards exploiting multi-modelling as the basis for a digital twin of an agricultural robot. The paper demonstrates the co-simulation of dynamics using a multi-physics modelling framework that allows modelling of comparatively low-level features such as soil/surface interaction. In such an application, the discrepancies (in time as well as value) between data reaching the twin and the twin's predictions becomes a significant aspect of the twin's design.

3   Concluding Remarks

The contributions in this track make it clear that realising the considerable potential benefits of digital twins for CPSs presents many challenges and opportunities for research and innovation. It is evidently not simply a matter of taking heterogeneous design models and streaming data from a physical twin to identify discrepancies. Many other factors that have a significant impact on the interaction between the physical and digital twins must be taken into account systematically before one can consider the digital twin's predictive functionality to be sufficiently dependable. We look forward to the interdisciplinary research that will be conducted over at least the next decade as digital twin technology comes to deliver its promise in many fully independent domains.

Acknowledgements. We acknowledge the support of the Poul Due Jensen Foundation for research towards the engineering of digital twins; the European Union's funding of HUBCAP (Grant Agreement 872698) and DIGITbrain (Grant Agreement 952071); the Innovation Foundation Denmark for funding MADE FAST; AgroRobottiFleet and ITEA3 for funding the UPSIM project (19006).

References

1. Foldager, F.F., Thule, C., Balling, O., Larsen, P.G.: Towards a digital twin - modelling an agricultural vehicle. In: Margaria, T., Steffen, B. (eds.) ISoLA 2020, Part IV. LNCS, vol. 12479, pp. 109–123. Springer, Cham (2021)
2. Kamburjan, E., Schlatte, R., Johnsen, E.B., Tarifa, S.L.T.: Designing distributed control with hybrid active objects. Margaria, T., Steffen, B. (eds.) ISoLA 2020, Part IV. LNCS, vol. 12479, pp. 88–108. Springer, Cham (2021)
3. Lecomte, T.: Digital modelling in the railways. In: Margaria, T., Steffen, B. (eds.) ISoLA 2020, Part IV. LNCS, vol. 12479, pp. 124–139. Springer, Cham (2021)
4. Li, B., Neilsen, R.O., Johnasen, K.W., Teizer, J., Larsen, P.G., Schultz, C.: Towards digital twins for knowledge-driven construction progress and predictive safety analysis on a construction site. In: Margaria, T., Steffen, B. (eds.) ISoLA 2020, Part IV. LNCS, vol. 12479, pp. 153–174. Springer, Cham (2021)

5. Matei, A., Tocu, N.A., Zamfirescu, C.B., Gellert, A., Neghină, M.: Engineering a digital twin for manual assembling. In: Margaria, T., Steffen, B. (eds.) ISoLA 2020, Part IV. LNCS, vol. 12479, pp. 140–152. Springer, Cham (2021)
6. Woodcock, J., Gomes, C., Macedo, H.D., Larsen, P.G.: Uncertainty quantification and runtime monitoring using environment-aware digital twins. In: Margaria, T., Steffen, B. (eds.) ISoLA 2020, Part IV. LNCS, vol. 12479, pp. 72–87. Springer, Cham (2021)
7. Yue, T., Arcaini, P., Ali, S.: Understanding digital twins for cyber-physical systems: a conceptual model. In: Margaria, T., Steffen, B. (eds.) ISoLA 2020, Part IV. LNCS, vol. 12479, pp. 54–71. Springer, Cham (2021)

Understanding Digital Twins for Cyber-Physical Systems: A Conceptual Model

Tao Yue[1,2]([⊠])[iD], Paolo Arcaini[3]([⊠])[iD], and Shaukat Ali[2]([⊠])[iD]

[1] Nanjing University of Aeronautics and Astronautics, Nanjing, China
taoyue@ieee.org
[2] Simula Research Laboratory, Oslo, Norway
shaukat@simula.no
[3] National Institute of Informatics, Tokyo, Japan
arcaini@nii.ac.jp

Abstract. Digital Twins (DTs) are revolutionizing Cyber-Physical Systems (CPSs) in many ways, including their development and operation. The significant interest of industry and academia in DTs has led to various definitions of DTs and related concepts, as seen in many recently published papers. Thus, there is a need for precisely defining different DT concepts and their relationships. To this end, we present a conceptual model that captures various DT concepts and their relationships, some of which are from the published literature, to provide a unified understanding of these concepts in the context of CPSs. The conceptual model is implemented as a set of Unified Modeling Language (UML) class diagrams and the concepts in the conceptual model are explained with a running example of an automated warehouse case study from published literature and based on the authors' experience of working with the real CPS case study in previous projects.

Keywords: Cyber-physical systems · Digital twins · Conceptual model

1 Introduction

Cyber-Physical Systems (CPSs) are complex interdisciplinary systems present in many domains. With time, these systems are getting even more complicated due to, e.g., ever-changing hardware, software updates, protocols, the increased use of advanced artificial intelligence (AI) techniques, and highly uncertain operating environments. As a result, advanced technologies such as digital twins (DTs)

The work is supported by the National Natural Science Foundation of China under Grant No. 61872182. The work is also partially supported by the Co-evolver project (No. 286898/F20) funded by the Research Council of Norway under the FRIPRO program. Paolo Arcaini is supported by ERATO HASUO Metamathematics for Systems Design Project (No. JPMJER1603), JST; Funding Reference number: 10.13039/501100009024 ERATO.

T. Margaria and B. Steffen (Eds.): ISoLA 2020, LNCS 12479, pp. 54–71, 2021.
https://doi.org/10.1007/978-3-030-83723-5_5

have been proposed to ensure correct development and dependable operation throughout lifetimes of such CPSs.

However, DTs are not specific to CPSs and can be built for any living or non-living thing. For example, there exists an initiative in the European Union about building digital twins for life sciences[1] and even building a digital twin of the Earth (i.e., the Destination Earth (DestinE) initiative)[2]. In the context of this paper, we focus only on DTs for CPSs. DTs for CPSs may share similarities with DTs for other things, but may also differ. For instance, a DT built for an ocean may be reused for various CPSs operating in the ocean such as subsea oil production systems [6] and autonomous vessels [11].

DTs for CPSs have attracted huge interests in industrial and academic circles, as it can be seen by major companies promoting their digital twin platforms (e.g., ANSYS[3], Siemens[4]), and an increased number of scholarly publications [16,21,25]. Due to the increasing interest in DTs for CPSs, DTs and their concepts have been emerging with various definitions. Though some recent papers have started to unify the meaning of such concepts (e.g., [16,22,25]), due to several similar publications appearing close to each other, they have resulted in another set of definitions of DTs and their concepts. To this end, we present a conceptual model for the purpose of unifying various DT concepts. In addition, in our conceptual model, we made the effort to establish relationships among the concepts and characterize important concepts such as DTs with their functionalities, maturity level, and quality requirements. We developed our conceptual model as a set of UML class diagrams. To explain the concepts, we used a running example of a CPS case study from the logistics domain.

The rest of the paper is organized as follows. Section 2 presents the description of our running example. Section 3 introduces core concepts, while Sect. 4 describes more detailed concepts of a DT and its CPS. We discuss evolution and uncertainty of DTs and their CPSs in Sect. 5 and their life-cycles in Sect. 6. Finally, we present related work in Sect. 7 and draw conclusions in Sect. 8.

2 Running Example

To explain various concepts, we will use the running example of a CPS case study, i.e., Automated Warehouse System (AWS), all throughout the paper to explain the conceptual model. This AWS CPS case study has been used in our previous works for assessing the definition of: a conceptual model for uncertainty in CPSs [30], a UML state machine based methodology for modeling uncertainty [29], a model-based testing framework for CPS testing under uncertainty [28], a CPS product line modeling methodology [23], and an approach for monitoring CPSs [15].

---

[1] https://euroocs.eu/funding-opportunities/eu-fet-proact-eic-07-2020-digital-twins-for-the-life-sciences/.

[2] https://ec.europa.eu/digital-single-market/en/destination-earth-destine/.

[3] https://www.ansys.com/products/systems/digital-twin.

[4] https://www.plm.automation.siemens.com/global/en/our-story/glossary/digital-twin/24465.

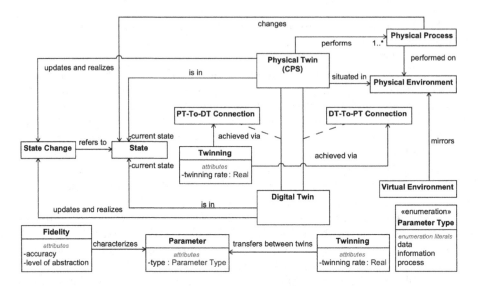

Fig. 1. Physical twin, digital twin, their connections and environments

AWSs can be used for diverse applications, such as in food industry for automatically producing orders for supermarkets. An AWS system typically consists of many different physical systems such as conveyor belts, sorting systems, and cranes. An AWS usually has an accompanying supervision system, which is often deployed on a cloud. This supervision system performs various operations such as monitoring warehouses, taking actions in case of emergency situations, and performing advanced analyses based on data collected from various warehouses. This can be considered as the initial version of a DT for the AWS. We can imagine that the DT can be extended with additional functionalities to reach a higher level of maturity (see Sect. 4.2). In this paper, we describe our vision towards this direction, and illustrate it with this running example.

3   Overview

In this section, we introduce basic concepts related to DTs. We introduce common concepts that have been used in different papers, as reported in the systematic literature review in [16]. Note that sometimes different terms have been used in different papers to refer to the same concept. We will report the most common term or, in any case, the one that we think is more representative. Figure 1 reports the concepts we identified.

A central concept is *Physical Twin* (also called *physical entity*), representing the physical artifact for which a DT has been built or is to be built. Examples of physical twins include buildings, vessels, farms, and vehicles. In our context, we particularly focus on CPSs, and we use the example of an AWS in this paper. Various concepts related to the DT of AWS are listed in Table 1.

A physical twin (PT) is characterized by a list of *physical processes* that it performs (see Fig. 1). Different processes require different considerations by a DT. Some are critical processes required to be monitored by the DT, while others are non-critical and no attention is needed from the DT. Usually, the execution of a monitored process produces a state change, which should be observed and dealt with accordingly by the DT. A PT exists and lives/operates in a *PT environment* that encompasses all the elements that can affect, in some way, its operation. Examples are environmental conditions of the AWS such as temperature and humidity in the warehouse. More detailed discussions about PTs are provided in Sect. 4.1.

Digital Twin (also named *virtual twin*) is the central concept of the conceptual model we propose in this paper. A DT of a PT represents the digital and live replica of the PT. The DT synchronizes with its PT, and performs different functionalities. More detailed discussions about *DT Functionalities* are provided in Sect. 4.2.

A DT interacts with a *virtual environment* (see Fig. 1), which is a replica of the physical environment of its counterpart PT. Note that some of the aspects of the physical environment may be unknown, and so the view provided by the virtual environment is, by definition, partial. Please refer to Sect. 5 for more detailed discussions on this. Having the virtual environment separated from the DT is convenient, as this could be reused over different DTs (e.g., the virtual environment of the warehouse could be used for the DT of a food production and retail). Moreover, variations of the virtual environment could also be used for prediction activities, to predict what could happen to the PT under possible future (probably uncertain) environmental conditions.

Both the PT and the DT are characterized, at any given time point, by their *State* (see Fig. 1). The twins operate by changing their states. The concept of *state change* is particular relevant in this context, as the modification of the current state of the PT could be used to trigger analyses implemented in the DT.

An important concept for the operation of the DT is the connection between the twins. This is actually achieved through two different types of connections: *PT-To-DT-connection* and *DT-To-PT-connection* (see Fig. 1). PT-To-DT-connection allows the DT to update its view of the state of the PT (e.g., the positioning of stock and number of shelving units), i.e., transmitting such information through the connection from the PT to the DT. In the opposite direction, the DT-To-PT-connection allows the DT to trigger the evolution of the operating PT for, e.g., applying some mitigation actions. For instance, the DT of an AWS might send a request to reboot one or more programmable logic controller (PLCs) of an AWS system. Another example could be that the DT of a smart building [10] could request its Heating, Ventilation, and Air Conditioning (HVAC) system to turn down the temperature of some empty rooms, as a shortage of electricity has been forecasted by a prediction model of the DT. The connection can be established with the same connection means used in the PT-To-DT-Connection. Additionally, the DT-To-PT-connection requires that the PT provides actuators to apply changes decided by the DT. Note that the DT-To-PT-Connection could also be performed by a human operator who, on the basis of the outcomes of the analyses performed by the DT, manually modifies the PT. This is necessary when no digital connection can be established, and/or the PT does not provide a way to be digitally controlled. For instance, an operator of the DT of an AWS system might directly talk to an onsite AWS operator to inspect a malfunctioning PLC in the warehouse. Alternatively, when the DT observes an anomaly of a PLC, the DT sends a signal directly to the computer that a specific AWS operator is interacting with and requests for manual inspection of the PLC.

The overall process of synchronization (in both directions) between the PT and the DT is referred to as *Twinning* (see Fig. 1). The twinning is characterized by the *twinning rate*, i.e., how often the synchronization takes place. In case of (almost) real-time synchronization, the twins are always aligned. However, if the twinning rate is non-negligible, there could be moments in which, for example, the DT has an outdated view of the PT.

The type of information that is exchanged between the twins can be described in terms of *parameters*, each characterized by a *parameter type* (see Fig. 1). The number and the accuracy of these parameters define the *fidelity* of the virtual representation. Indeed, despite the name *twin*, the DT is by definition an *abstraction* of the PT. Increasing the number and accuracy of the parameters allows to lower down the abstraction and, therefore, increase the fidelity of the representation.

The running case study illustrating this part of the conceptual model is shown in Table 1.

4   Physical Twin and Digital Twin

In this section, we present the conceptual models for characterizing PTs and DTs.

4.1   Physical Twin

PTs, i.e., CPSs in our context, appear in many diverse domains, such as communication, energy, healthcare, robotics, and transportation, as shown in enumeration *CPS Application Domain* in Fig. 2.

This classification was borrowed from the concept map of CPSs developed by Lee et al. [2]. Also, based on the concept map, we characterize a CPS with a list of *properties* such as being networked and/or distributed, being adaptive (responding to its changing *Physical Environment* and requests from its DT) and predictive (predicting changes in its *Physical Environment*), being intelligent in terms of self-learning, understanding and perception, and/or being real-time. Additionally, there are two other properties that are interleaved with these properties: uncertainty and evolution, which will be discussed separately in Sect. 5.

We would also like to acknowledge that there exist many conceptual models for characterizing CPSs in the literature. In this paper, we tried to characterize

Table 1. Running example for conceptual model – overview

Concept(s)	Explanation
Physical Twin	An AWS and its constituent systems such as sorters, cranes, and conveyor belts
Physical Process	A process to automatically create an order requested by a supermarket, including various quantities of various items such as breads and soda
Physical Environment	Everything included in the operating environment of an AWS (including humans), characterized with factors such as the warehouse temperature
DT and DT Environment	A digital replica of an AWS and its operating environment. Such a replica may consist of several simulators integrated with each other with the FMI standard [1] simulating the physical environment of the AWS
DT Functionality	Examples include monitoring an AWS, raising alarms in case of emergencies, and predicting the time for the next warehouse maintenance
DT-To-PT Connection/PT-to-DT Connection	Communication interfaces defined for transferring information from sensors of the AWS to its DT. The DT feeds back insights to the PT via actuators to intervene with the physical processes of the AWS
Twinning	The DT is synchronized with its AWS every half an hour, for instance
State	The current values of all the state variables of an AWS, its constituent systems, and environment
State Change	The change in the current values of all the state variables of an AWS
Parameter	Examples include values of the state variables of the sorter system in an AWS being transferred from the AWS and its DT

Table 2. Running example for conceptual model – physical twin

Concept(s)	Explanation
CPS Application Domain	The AWS CPS belongs to the manufacturing domain
CPS Property	The AWS CPS is a networked, adaptive, and real-time system

CPSs at the minimum level as readers can refer to many available descriptions of CPSs at the conceptual level such as the concept map presented by Lee et al. [2] and the survey presented in [14].

The running case study illustrating this part of the conceptual model is shown in Table 2.

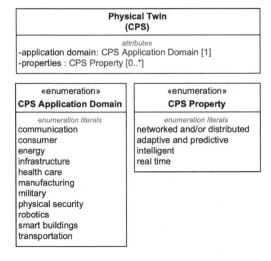

Fig. 2. Characterizing cyber-physical systems (CPSs)

4.2   Digital Twin

We first like to acknowledge that, in this section, we make the effort to characterize DTs from several aspects that we think are important. Therefore, it is, by no means, comprehensive. This part of the conceptual model is presented in Fig. 3.

As shown in Fig. 3, a *Digital Twin* can be operated by human operators, developed with specific DT platforms (e.g., GE Digital Twin[5]), supported by a diverse set of technologies such as machine learning and artificial intelligence (ML/AI), modeling and simulation techniques belonging to different paradigms (e.g., numerical modeling, software and system modeling, co-simulation supported with Simulink and SysML), as shown in the enumeration *Technology Type* of Fig. 3.

A DT is situated in its *DT Environment* (as discussed in Sect. 3), which naturally requires a *Data Management Infrastructure*, as the DT needs to obtain data from the PT at real time, analyze the data received at real time and also historical data collected in the past, manage the data in terms of storing, sharing, authorizing the access of data, and so on.

The essential component of a DT is its *DT Model*, which aims to virtually represent a diverse set of aspects of its counterpart, i.e., the PT. As suggested by Solomon W. Golomb in [12] decades ago: 'Don't limit yourself to a single model, more than one may be useful for understanding different aspects of the same phenomenon'. Considering that engineering a CPS is inherently multi-disciplinary, a DT model, therefore, needs to be developed with modeling languages (e.g., SysML, Simulink, Modelica), methodologies and tools belonging

---

[5] https://www.ge.com/digital/applications/digital-twin.

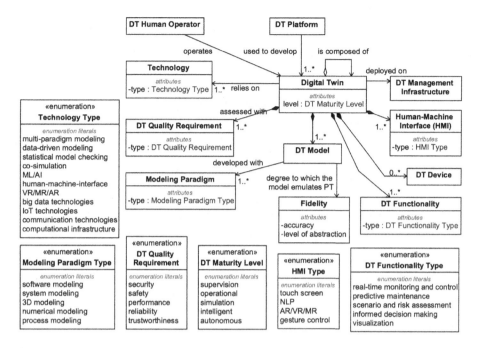

Fig. 3. Characterizing digital twins

to different modeling paradigms, some of which are shown in the enumeration *Modeling Paradigm Type* of Fig. 3.

Fidelity is often used to characterize the degree to which a DT model imitates the PT. High fidelity models are often required to infer properties of real systems in the context of scientific modeling and simulations from the perspective of physics, for instance [18]. However, when a model already clearly serves its purpose in an engineering context, it is often unrealistic and even meaningless to pursue a higher fidelity, which often requires significant amount of effort and might result in low efficient models. Therefore, selecting suitable modeling paradigms and capturing different modeling aspects at suitable levels of abstractions will lead to multi-fidelity DT models, as also discussed in [5].

A DT is intended for achieving one or more specific functionalities such as real-time monitoring and control, predictive maintenance, scenario and risk assessment (e.g., unknown or uncertain scenarios, what-if analyses), efficient and informed decision making, and data/information visualization, as shown in the enumeration *DT Functionality Type* in Fig. 3. Achieving these functionalities requires the support of various technologies (shown in enumeration *Technology Type*) and the achieved functionalities determine the maturity level of a DT. We borrow the different DT maturity levels defined in [26] and present them as enumeration *DT Maturity Level* in Fig. 3. The first two levels offer *supervision* via monitoring and manual control of the *operation* of the PT, respectively. At the third level, the DT can *simulate* the PT's behavior to provide a stronger decision support for the design and operation of the PT. Such decision support is further enhanced by benefiting from machine learning (ML) and advanced artificial intelligence (AI) techniques to automate decision support with minimal human intervention, to achieve the *intelligent* and *autonomous* maturity levels.

Same as for other software systems, a developed DT should be verified against a list of quality requirements such as security, safety, performance, reliability, and trustworthiness, as shown in the enumeration *DT Quality Requirement* in Fig. 3. For example, as shown in Fig. 1, a DT is bidirectionally connected with its corresponding PT to support *Twinning*, i.e., transferring data of parameters between twins at runtime through the established connections. Therefore, in certain application contexts (e.g., healthcare), a particular care should be taken to ensure no leaking of sensitive information (e.g., patient personal medical profiles).

A DT may be composed of a set of other DTs of the same or different types (*DT Aggregation* in Fig. 3). This is because a complex CPS might be composed of different components, which are developed or operated with their own DTs. For example, an AWS might have a set of aggregated DTs corresponding to various subsystems (e.g., automated material handling systems, warehouse management and execution systems) for dealing with different physical processes. A better example is presented in [9], where two connected digital twins are suggested for the trauma management: managing the physical process of the pre-hospital phase with one DT, and the physical process of managing the trauma inside the hospital with another DT, as reported in [9].

A DT often needs a *Human-Machine Interface (HMI)*, which can be of various types and developed with different technologies such as Augmented Reality (AR)/Virtual Reality (VR), Natural Language Processing (NLP) enabled communication between humans and machine via voice, hand gesture-based control, or simply a control panel with or without a touch screen, as represented in enumeration *HMI Type* in Fig. 3. HMI is important for DTs because being fully autonomous (without human intervention, having the *DT Maturity Level* being the highest, i.e., *autonomous*) is not realistic in a lot of application contexts; therefore, operating DTs will be highly dependent on human interactions and, consequently, their designs need to take care of the human-in-the-loop aspect by selecting and applying appropriate HMI techniques. Dependent on the design of HMI, additional devices might need to be introduced to DTs, represented as concept *DT Device* in Fig. 3. A relevant work is presented in [13], where the authors proposed to enhance the capability of DTs with VR in the context of manufacturing Cyber-Physical Production System.

The running case study illustrating this part of the conceptual model is shown in Table 3.

Table 3. Running example for conceptual model – digital twin

Concept(s)	Explanation
Human-Machine Interface	The HMI of the DT of an AWS can come in different shapes, for instance, designed to have a touch screen
Data Management Infrastructure	The DT can use various data management infrastructures which can be cloud-based solutions or in-house data centers
DT Aggregation	It is realistic to develop a DT that is an aggregation of a set of DTs, which corresponds to various subsystems of an AWS such as automated material handling systems and warehouse management and execution systems
DT Platform	Existing platforms for developing DTs can be used
DT Human Operator	DT operators monitor the operation of the AWS through the provided HMI, identify potential improvements to the AWS operation, and intervene with its operation when needed, with the help of data analytic of the DT
Technology	Different sensors attached to monitor the surface of conveyor belts in an AWS. Such sensors help to determine when to clean the surface of the conveyor belts
DT Quality Requirement	The DT and the AWS are connected through internet; therefore, any unauthorized access to the DT should be prevented
DT Maturity Level	The DT of the AWS provides supervision facility and allows running simulations to assess the performance of the operational AWS
DT Model and Modeling Paradigm	The DT of an AWS can consist of various hardware models of various systems (e.g., sorters), in Simulink for instance. In addition, the environment of the DT of the AWS can be modeled with numerical models. Moreover, the warehouse management process can be modeled with Petri Nets
Fidelity	Depending on what functionalities a DT implements, the DT model might have different fidelity levels. For instance, 3D model of high fidelity is often used to allow users to visualize certain pallets in the warehouse and help operators to have an overview of the warehouse such that the operators might identify opportunities to improve stock placement and picking processes. Such a high fidelity model is however inappropriate for visualizing goods quantities, and data visualization techniques such as customizable charts and tables might better serve the purpose

5   Evolution and Uncertainty

As previously discussed, we consider evolution and uncertainty as two important aspects to be considered when developing, operating and maintaining DTs and CPSs. Therefore, in this section, we provide our vision and call for contributions on these two aspects.

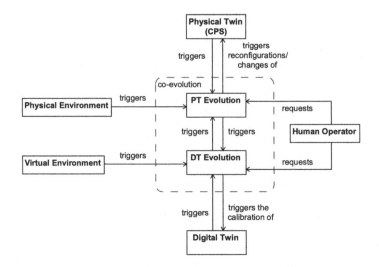

Fig. 4. PT and DT evolution

5.1   Evolution

An intelligent PT naturally evolves during its operation by constantly interacting with its physical environment (probably partially known at a given time point), humans and its DT, which we call *PT Evolution* (Fig. 4).

Consequently, a DT also naturally evolves when it interacts with the virtual environment (probably presenting a partial view of the physical environment as this is partially known at a given time point), and continuously receives data from its PT, i.e., *DT Evolution*. As shown in Fig. 4, *PT Evolution* triggers *DT Evolution*, and vice versa.

Specifically, *DT Evolution* is often triggered in the following situations:

- The PT evolves as a result of a software update or replacement of a hardware component, etc., which consequently triggers the evolution of the DT;
- The DT needs to be evolved to accommodate a new *DT Functionality*;
- The DT needs to be evolved to refine the *DT Model* when more data from the PT becomes available and more information becomes available during its interactions with the virtual environment and human operators via HMI;
- An adaptive and autonomous DT self-evolves when its operating environment changes, through its implemented self-configuration mechanism for instance.

PT Evolution is often triggered in three situations:

- The upgrade or replacement of its own software and hardware components;
- Configurations from human operators or the DT received during its operation and maintenance;
- Self-adaptation or self-configuration implemented in an adaptive and/or autonomous physical twin.

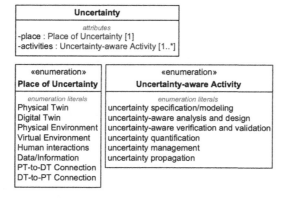

Fig. 5. Characterizing uncertainty

Therefore, this situation is an instance of *co-evolution* of two intelligent systems. Particular designs of the twins themselves and the twinning between them are needed to cost-effectively accommodate such co-evolution, which, to the best of our knowledge, has not received sufficient attention probably because applying DTs to empower CPSs is still at its early stage.

5.2 Uncertainty

In the last decade, uncertainty, especially external uncertainty in the open and operational environment in CPSs (e.g., [3, 29]) and self-adaptive systems (e.g., [19, 20]), has attracted a lot of attention because uncertainty is an unavoidable feature of such systems. Properly dealing with uncertainty in DTs and CPSs is especially critical, considering the increasing complexity in terms of the scales of the digital and physical twins, network communications within and between the twins, and/or deployed ML/AI algorithms in both of the twins, and their ever-changing and open operating environment. Therefore, as presented in enumeration *Place of Uncertainty* in Fig. 5, different places of the digital and physical twins, the twinning between them, their respective environments, interactions with humans, and even data/information transferred collected by the twins and transferred across the twins, all possibly contain uncertain information. Therefore, uncertainty is yet another dimension that significantly increases the complexity of engineering both DTs and CPSs.

There exist related works on specifying, modeling and measuring/quantifying uncertainty in the context of CPSs. For example, Zhang et al. [30] proposed a conceptual model (named *U-Model*) to understand and characterize uncertainty and its associated concepts from the angle of software engineering and especially model-based engineering. Later on, Zhang et al. also instantiated U-Model for specifying system requirements as use case models [31] and for modeling uncertainty by extending standard UML state machine notations [29]. Along the same line, in the context of dynamically adaptive systems, Betty et al. [8]

Table 4. Running example for conceptual model – evolution and uncertainty

Concept(s)	Explanation
PT Evolution	The introduction of a new sorter hardware to the AWS
DT Evolution	New and high quality sensors are added to monitor the surface of the sorter systems
Uncertainty	The AWS system sometimes stops without any obvious reason, which requires manual restart of the AWS. This is an example of uncertainty in the PT. The network connection between the DT and PT might get lost occasionally, which should be considered as a kind of uncertainty in the connections between the DT and the PT. There might be uncertainty in DT-recommended warehouse maintenance strategies

proposed RELAX [8] to support uncertainty specification and analysis. Later on, FLAGS [4] was proposed for enabling the specification of adaptive goals. To support decision making under uncertainty, various methodologies have been proposed for testing CPSs under uncertainty [7,28], etc.

Though these related works have built the foundation for developing uncertainty-aware solutions in the context of engineering DTs for CPSs, it lacks systematic solutions going from uncertainty specification, modeling and analysis, design and development of solutions to support decision making under uncertainty, all the way down to uncertainty-wise verification and validation, as shown in enumeration *Uncertainty-aware Activity* in Fig. 5. Especially during its operation, the DT constantly receives data from its corresponding PT, which can be used to discover (previously) unknown information from these received data and, consequently, make more informed decisions. It is expected that specific DT functionalities are hence needed to elegantly deal with uncertainties that may exist or occur in different places (enumeration *Place of Uncertainty* in Fig. 5).

An instantiation of the running case study for these conceptual models is shown in Table 4.

6   Life-Cycle

A DT co-exists with its counterpart and it is expected to support the full life-cycle of its PT. As a complex system itself, a DT has its own development life-cycle. As shown in Fig. 6, inspired by the concept model developed by Lee et al. [2], we consider that both the life-cycles of a DT and its PT are composed of a list of essential activities, captured in enumeration *Essential Activity Type*. We acknowledge that there exist standards and methodologies (e.g., ISO/IEC/IEEE 15288) for developing CPSs, but we are not aware of any standard or methodology for developing DTs.

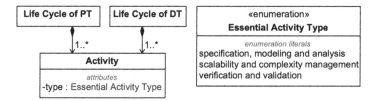

Fig. 6. DT and PT life-cycles and essential activities

In addition, to support a CPS development and operation through a DT, a fundamental research question is: how to coordinate the life-cycle of the DT with the life-cycle of its counterpart CPS? Below, we list three such DT and CPS dual life-cycle options (with in total five different settings):

Option 1: CPS and DT do not exist. This is the typical case when a very complex and safety-critical CPS (e.g., an entirely new smart hospital) need to be built, and the usage of a DT is chosen to strengthen, for instance, the safety and the performance of the CPS. There are three settings for this option: 1) Building a CPS and its DT together right from scratch; 2) Starting with building a CPS, and, at a later point in time, starting the development of the DT and aligning its development with its CPS); 3) Starting with building a DT for a CPS, and later introducing the development of the CPS itself, with the DT that has been (partially) developed as the basis.

Option 2: DT exists. It starts developing a CPS from an existing DT. This is the typical case that can occur in product lines, i.e., a DT DT_1 has been developed in the past for a product p_1, and the DT DT_2 for another new product p_2 is derived by extending DT_1 (reasoning on the similarities and differences between p_1 and p_2).

Option 3: CPS exists. It builds a DT for an operational CPS to better support its operation and maintenance. This case happens when the CPS has been developed in the past, but further requirements on its operation have emerged. If its re-engineering is not feasible, the development of a DT can be a cost-effective solution.

Rigorous methodologies are needed to guide the development of a DT and coordinate with the development life-cycle of the counterpart CPS. Also, the *Twining Process* (see Fig. 1) brings another layer of complexity to the *dual* development life-cycles of the twins. We also acknowledge that developing the twins is naturally a highly iterative process due to their complex nature.

The running case study illustrating this part of the conceptual model is shown in Table 5.

7   Related Work

Jones et al. [16] presented a systematic literature review of 92 digital twin publications and identified a list of concepts such as physical entity, virtual entity,

Table 5. Running example for conceptual model – life-cycle

Concept(s)	Explanation
Life-cycle of PT	The AWS system is in the operational phase
Life-cycle of DT	The DT is in the operational phase
Activity	The development of an AWS and its corresponding DT often requires to go through some of the phases defined in enumeration *Essential Activity Type* shown in Fig. 6

fidelity, and twining. In our paper, we constructed the conceptual model presented in Fig. 1 based on the review results of this paper. The authors of the paper also presented a list of future directions and research gaps. For example, they discovered that the majority of the works studies have put their focuses on the implementation phase of the DT life-cycle and insufficient attention has been given to the early phases of the DT life-cycle. In addition, the majority of identified use cases of DTs are manufacturing-related, and talk about simulation modeling, optimization, and data management. Similarly, another literature review was presented by Josifovska et al. in [17], which defines concepts similar to those of Jones et al. [16].

Negri et al. [21] conducted a literature review of 26 publications to answer two questions: how DTs are defined in the literature and what is the role of a DT in Industry 4.0. The authors concluded that: (1) the scientific literature is still immature as the studied literature mostly refers to different definitions of DTs; and (2) in the manufacturing industry, it is relevant to define a DT as a virtual counterpart (a digital representation) of a physical device, which is augmented/updated/synchronized with data continuously from the physical object, to support decision making and predictive maintenance.

Tao et al. [24] presented their vision of engineering DTs for CPSs of the manufacturing domain, by providing a mapping between the physical and digital worlds, and a hierarchical structure that divides CPSs and DTs into three levels: the unit, system, and system of systems (SoS) levels. In this structure, DTs are connected to their corresponding CPSs at every single level. For instance, a unit-level DT is actually a model of a physical object specifying its geometric shape, identity, operating status, and even its high-fidelity visual simulation. A system-level DT is an integration of the models constructed at the unit level. In addition, the system-level CPS and DT share the same architecture. For instance, an aircraft is composed of various components (e.g., engines, wings), each of which has a DT. An SoS-level DT is simply the integration of the system-level DTs. This structure naturally implies the development life-cycle of going from the unit-level to the SoS-level, which is the same for both CPSs and DTs. The authors also explicitly say that they consider CPSs and DTs as conceptually similar in smart manufacturing, and the key difference is that DTs are more concerned about models and data.

Rasheed et al. [22] also presented a literature review of methodologies and techniques for constructing DTs with the aim of identifying values of applying DTs (e.g., supporting what-if analysis and informed decision making), their application domains (e.g., health, meteorology, and manufacturing), and current challenges (e.g., large-scale data fusion, data security, and real-time simulations). In addition, the paper also discussed enabling technologies such as physics-based modeling, data-driven modeling, big data and IoT technologies, and human-machine interface.

Xiaodong et al. [27] reviewed the use of DTs for Prognostics and Health Management (PHM) in the literature. They identified that, in this context, the main functionalities of a DT are (i) keeping historical data about the PT, (ii) monitoring its health and performing fault diagnosis, (iii) devising an efficient maintenance schedule for the PT, and (iv) allowing testing in a virtual environment to avoid damages to the PT occurring from destructive tests. The concepts are illustrated with a high-speed train electric multiple unit.

Boschert and Rosen [5] focused on the simulation aspects of the DT. Apart from common concepts also presented in other papers, the authors underline the importance of selecting the suitable abstraction of the model for the problem to be solved, as having unnecessarily too-detailed models can lead to scalability issues. Moreover, they underline that the simulation facilities of the DT make it suitable to be used along all the life-cycle of the physical twin, not only in operation. In the design phase, for example, the models that are created for building the system are a first foundation of the DT itself.

8   Conclusion

Digital twins (DTs) for Cyber-Physical Systems (CPSs) aim to improve the current practice of developing and operating CPSs. The increased interest in DTs for CPSs have resulted in various definitions of DTs and their associated concepts. Thus, in this paper, we presented a conceptual model of different DTs concepts and their relationships based on the published literature. Moreover, concepts are also explained with a running example. The conceptual model serves as the first step towards providing a unified meaning of various DT concepts in the CPS community. In addition, we acknowledge the needs of developing systematic solutions for dealing various uncertainties in the development and operation of both CPSs and their DTs, and their co-evolution. We also encourage more research activities on designing dual lifecycles of engineering DTs and CPSs.

References

1. The FMI Standard. https://fmi-standard.org/
2. Asare, P., et al.: Cyber-Physical Systems - A Concept Map. http://cyberphysicalsystems.org/

3. Bandyszak, T., Daun, M., Tenbergen, B., Weyer, T.: Model-based documentation of context uncertainty for cyber-physical systems. In: 2018 IEEE 14th International Conference on Automation Science and Engineering (CASE), pp. 1087–1092. IEEE (2018)

4. Baresi, L., Pasquale, L., Spoletini, P.: Fuzzy goals for requirements-driven adaptation. In: 2010 18th IEEE International Requirements Engineering Conference, pp. 125–134. IEEE (2010)

5. Boschert, S., Rosen, R.: Digital twin—the simulation aspect. In: Hehenberger, P., Bradley, D. (eds.) Mechatronic Futures, pp. 59–74. Springer, Cham (2016). https://doi.org/10.1007/978-3-319-32156-1_5

6. Cameron, D.B., Waaler, A., Komulainen, T.M.: Oil and gas digital twins after twenty years. How can they be made sustainable, maintainable and useful? In: Proceedings of the 59th Conference on Simulation and Modelling (SIMS 59), 26–28 September 2018, Oslo Metropolitan University, Norway, pp. 9–16. Linköping University Electronic Press (2018)

7. Camilli, M., Bellettini, C., Gargantini, A., Scandurra, P.: Online model-based testing under uncertainty. In: 2018 IEEE 29th International Symposium on Software Reliability Engineering (ISSRE), pp. 36–46. IEEE (2018)

8. Cheng, B.H.C., Sawyer, P., Bencomo, N., Whittle, J.: A goal-based modeling approach to develop requirements of an adaptive system with environmental uncertainty. In: Schürr, A., Selic, B. (eds.) MODELS 2009. LNCS, vol. 5795, pp. 468–483. Springer, Heidelberg (2009). https://doi.org/10.1007/978-3-642-04425-0_36

9. Croatti, A., Gabellini, M., Montagna, S., Ricci, A.: On the integration of agents and digital twins in healthcare. J. Med. Syst. **44**(9), 1–8 (2020)

10. Dembski, F., Wössner, U., Letzgus, M., Ruddat, M., Yamu, C.: Urban digital twins for smart cities and citizens: the case study of Herrenberg, Germany. Sustainability **12**(6), 2307 (2020). https://doi.org/10.3390/su12062307

11. Fonseca, Í.A., Gaspar, H.M.: Challenges when creating a cohesive digital twin ship: a data modelling perspective. In: Ship Technology Research, pp. 1–14 (2020)

12. Golomb, S.W.: Mathematical models: uses and limitations. IEEE Trans. Reliab. **R-20**(3), 130–131 (1971)

13. Havard, V., Jeanne, B., Lacomblez, M., Baudry, D.: Digital twin and virtual reality: a co-simulation environment for design and assessment of industrial workstations. Prod. Manuf. Res. **7**(1), 472–489 (2019)

14. Hehenberger, P., Vogel-Heuser, B., Bradley, D., Eynard, B., Tomiyama, T., Achiche, S.: Design, modelling, simulation and integration of cyber physical systems: methods and applications. Comput. Ind. **82**, 273–289 (2016). https://doi.org/10.1016/j.compind.2016.05.006

15. Iglesias, A., Lu, H., Arellano, C., Yue, T., Ali, S., Sagardui, G.: Product line engineering of monitoring functionality in industrial cyber-physical systems: a domain analysis. In: Proceedings of the 21st International Systems and Software Product Line Conference - Volume A, SPLC 2017, pp. 195–204. Association for Computing Machinery, New York (2017). https://doi.org/10.1145/3106195.3106223

16. Jones, D., Snider, C., Nassehi, A., Yon, J., Hicks, B.: Characterising the digital twin: a systematic literature review. CIRP J. Manuf. Sci. Technol. (2020). https://doi.org/10.1016/j.cirpj.2020.02.002

17. Josifovska, K., Yigitbas, E., Engels, G.: Reference framework for digital twins within cyber-physical systems. In: Proceedings of the 5th International Workshop on Software Engineering for Smart Cyber-Physical Systems, SEsCPS 2019, pp. 25–31. IEEE Press (2019). https://doi.org/10.1109/SEsCPS.2019.00012

18. Lee, E.: The past, present and future of cyber-physical systems: a focus on models. Sensors (Basel, Switzerland) **15**, 4837–4869 (2015). https://doi.org/10.3390/s150304837
19. Ma, T., Ali, S., Yue, T., Elaasar, M.: Testing self-healing cyber-physical systems under uncertainty: a fragility-oriented approach. Softw. Qual. J. **27**(2), 615–649 (2019)
20. Moreno, G.A., Cámara, J., Garlan, D., Klein, M.: Uncertainty reduction in self-adaptive systems. In: Proceedings of the 13th International Conference on Software Engineering for Adaptive and Self-Managing Systems, pp. 51–57 (2018)
21. Negri, E., Fumagalli, L., Macchi, M.: A review of the roles of digital twin in CPS-based production systems. Procedia Manuf. **11**, 939–948 (2017). https://doi.org/10.1016/j.promfg.2017.07.198
22. Rasheed, A., San, O., Kvamsdal, T.: Digital twin: values, challenges and enablers from a modeling perspective. IEEE Access **8**, 21980–22012 (2020)
23. Safdar, S.A., Yue, T., Ali, S., Lu, H.: Evaluating variability modeling techniques for supporting cyber-physical system product line engineering. In: Grabowski, J., Herbold, S. (eds.) SAM 2016. LNCS, vol. 9959, pp. 1–19. Springer, Cham (2016). https://doi.org/10.1007/978-3-319-46613-2_1
24. Tao, F., Qi, Q., Wang, L., Nee, A.: Digital twins and cyber–physical systems toward smart manufacturing and Industry 4.0: correlation and comparison. Engineering **5**(4), 653–661 (2019). https://doi.org/10.1016/j.eng.2019.01.014
25. Tao, F., Zhang, H., Liu, A., Nee, A.Y.: Digital twin in industry: state-of-the-art. IEEE Trans. Ind. Inform. **15**(4), 2405–2415 (2018)
26. Wagg, D.: Asset Management using the Digital Twin concept. https://www.thefuturefactory.com/blog/26. Accessed 4 Sept 2020
27. Xiaodong, W., Feng, L., Junhua, R., Rongyu, L.: A survey of digital twin technology for PHM. In: Jain, V., Patnaik, S., Popentiu Vlădicescu, F., Sethi, I.K. (eds.) Recent Trends in Intelligent Computing, Communication and Devices. AISC, vol. 1006, pp. 397–403. Springer, Singapore (2020). https://doi.org/10.1007/978-981-13-9406-5_48
28. Zhang, M., Ali, S., Yue, T.: Uncertainty-wise test case generation and minimization for cyber-physical systems. J. Syst. Softw. **153**, 1–21 (2019). https://doi.org/10.1016/j.jss.2019.03.011
29. Zhang, M., Ali, S., Yue, T., Norgren, R., Okariz, O.: Uncertainty-wise cyber-physical system test modeling. Softw. Syst. Model. **18**(2), 1379–1418 (2019). https://doi.org/10.1007/s10270-017-0609-6
30. Zhang, M., Selic, B., Ali, S., Yue, T., Okariz, O., Norgren, R.: Understanding uncertainty in cyber-physical systems: a conceptual model. In: Wąsowski, A., Lönn, H. (eds.) ECMFA 2016. LNCS, vol. 9764, pp. 247–264. Springer, Cham (2016). https://doi.org/10.1007/978-3-319-42061-5_16
31. Zhang, M., et al.: Specifying uncertainty in use case models. J. Syst. Softw. **144**, 573–603 (2018)

Uncertainty Quantification and Runtime Monitoring Using Environment-Aware Digital Twins

Jim Woodcock[1,2]([✉]), Cláudio Gomes[2]([✉]), Hugo Daniel Macedo[2],
and Peter Gorm Larsen[2]

[1] Department of Computer Science, University of York, York, UK
jim.woodcock@york.ac.uk
[2] DIGIT, Department of Electrical and Computer Engineering, Aarhus University,
Aarhus, Denmark
{claudio.gomes,hdm,pgl}@ece.au.dk

Abstract. A digital twin for a Cyber-Physical System includes a simulation model that predicts how a physical system should behave. We show how to quantify and characterise violation events for a given safety property for the physical system. The analysis uses the digital twin to inform a runtime monitor that checks whether the noise and violations observed fall within expected statistical distributions. The results allow engineers to determine the best system configuration through what-if analysis. We illustrate our approach with a case study of an agricultural vehicle.

1 Introduction

We engineer a Cyber-Physical System (CPS) using separate models for its different parts [9,13,16,27,32]. If we use different formalisms, then this is a multi-model and we must use the corresponding support tools in coordination. In particular, we must connect the different simulation tools in a co-simulation. A co-simulation is a generalised form of simulation where different simulation tools are coupled together (see [14,19] for an introduction to the topic).

Typically, we use multi-models only in the engineering phase of the CPS in question (e.g., as in the V-process [31]). Recently, we have been reusing multi-models as digital twins after deploying the CPS (see [10]). We stream sensor and actuation signals from the CPS (the physical twin) to the multi-model co-simulation (the digital twin). We then predict how the physical twin should behave. However, the predictions can never be 100% accurate. This is because the multi-models cannot capture the full detail of physical reality: the sensor data is noisy and sampled at a finite frequency; the numerical solution of the multi-models is an approximation; and the environment for the physical twin may be different from the one used for prototyping.

An important practical question is: how large can these discrepancies be before we judge that the CPS is no longer behaving as we intended? We cannot

© Springer Nature Switzerland AG 2021
T. Margaria and B. Steffen (Eds.): ISoLA 2020, LNCS 12479, pp. 72–87, 2021.
https://doi.org/10.1007/978-3-030-83723-5_6

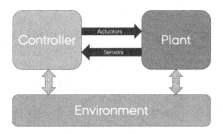

Fig. 1. The necessary components of a CPS operating in its environment.

hope to answer this question in general, as it depends on the CPS, the level of detail of the multi-models, and the properties of the CPS that we are interested in. However, we can provide tools and methods that make it easier to specify allowed discrepancies.

In this paper, we try to answer the above question based on a case study representing an agricultural vehicle. The data used is simulated data, but representative of the real system. The reproducibility code for the results can be found in [15]. This work is a stepping stone towards bridging numerical and statistical simulation techniques with the runtime monitoring and verification field, where important techniques have been developed to synthesise monitoring algorithms [2,5,8]. We show how, by embedding noise into the model of the system, we may understand how that noise impacts the system's behaviour (e.g., are safety boundaries still respected?), and devise a runtime monitor that checks whether the noise observed in practice still corresponds to the modelled noise. When this condition is not observed, actions need to be taken to ensure that the system continues to operate correctly.

After this introduction, Sect. 2 motivates the need to operate with tolerances in a digital twin context. Afterwards Sect. 3 presents a case study with an agricultural vehicle. Finally Sect. 4 discusses how it is possible to talk about safety in the presence of statistical inaccuracies and provides a few concluding remarks and points towards the future work we wish to carry out.

2   The Need for Digital Twins and Tolerance

A simplified[1] representation of a CPS is depicted in Fig. 1. It comprises a digital component that controls a physical asset operating in some environment. In order to study the behaviour of the CPS, having a good model of the environment is as important as having a model of both the digital and the physical component, as the environment affects the behaviour of both.

As stated in Kritzinger et al. [18] and Tao et al. [30], a digital twin can be used to monitor the conformance of the real CPS to these models, and possibly affect the real CPS when such conformance is violated.

---

[1] In practice, there may be many sub-components of each of the controller, plant, and environment, elements, and they may have complex interactions.

Here we define the digital twin as the system that ensures the correct functioning of the system, aptly named the physical twin. For some systems, the digital twin can be realised with sensory data directly. For more complex systems, a combination of state estimators, data fusion algorithms, and numerical simulation, might be required to get a more comprehensive state of the system. As a simple example, suppose we want to monitor the torque acting on an electrical agricultural vehicle's wheels. The digital twin can read the current on the motor of each wheel. It measures this from sensory data. If the digital twin has a well-calibrated torque constant, then the torque is just the multiplication of the torque constant by the current measured.

Discrepancies between the values observed from the system and the values computed by the digital twin may occur for the following reasons:

1. Sensor data represent delayed discrete samples of the system;
2. Sensors (and actuators) have inaccurate and noisy readings.
3. The models used by the digital twin (e.g., used to derive data) do not fully represent the physical twin.
4. There are processing delays in the digital twin.

The statistician George Box is famous for the quote: "All models are wrong, but some are useful" [3]. This is sometimes used as an excuse for bad models, but that is not what Box meant. Box clarifies this: "Remember that all models are wrong; the practical question is how wrong do they have to be to not be useful?" [4]. The same question applies to discrepancies between digital twin and the system.

To give an example, suppose we need to check whether the physical twin satisfies some safety property. In the face of uncertainty of noisy sampled sensor data, how do we know that a violation is not a false positive? Or that a non-violation is a real non-violation? These questions highlight the need to incorporate noise models, which can be considered environment models, into the digital twin, and monitor whether those noise models correspond to the noise observed in practice.

If we successfully address the above questions, we can use the detection of violations for:

– Switching system operation to a fail-safe mode (as in Mitsch et al. [24]).
– Alerting human operators.
– Triggering a recalibration of the digital twin in a tracking simulator (e.g., [20,23,25]) (if the violation represents a change in the environment).
– Triggering maintenance activities (if the violation represents a change in the system's components, e.g., due to wear and tear).
– Triggering root-cause analysis [28] (e.g., by running multiple simulations with varying parameters that try to explain the violation observed).

3   The Agricultural Vehicle Case Study

Autonomous agricultural systems are a prime application domain for digital twin technology. They are complex systems working in remote environments with a high degree of intrinsic uncertainty.

As example of the need to monitor these vehicles, consider the following.

Example 1. The speed controllers on the wheels of an agricultural vehicle are tuned such that, for a particular static and viscous friction profile, they quickly settle on the speed that is commanded by the user. This is highly beneficial not just from a safety point of view, but also because it enables the use of path planning and job scheduling algorithms that rely only on kinematic[2] models. With wear and tear, manufacturing variability, unexpected operating temperatures, etc., the friction profile used to tune the speed controller becomes outdated. This makes the controllers perform poorly, and may invalidate the kinematic models used for planning.

Monitoring alleviates the problem highlighted in Example 1 by, e.g., measuring the current drawn and speed of the motors to detect when the controllers have deviated from the original behaviour (obtained through simulations and initial experimentation with the system). We must tolerate certain deviations because they might be due to noisy current measurements. We can specify a threshold as a function of the uncertainty in current measurements. Deviations that exceed the threshold trigger one of the following actions:

1. Alert human operators to lubricate the joints of the vehicle (i.e., change the physical system to match the kinematics).
2. Alert human operators to re-tune the controller parameters (i.e., calibrate the controller's models of friction).
3. Recalibrate the kinematic models, finding new acceleration and speed profiles.

Each of the above actions has a different impact in the operations of the vehicle. For instance, option (3) invalidates all prior path planning and optimisation results.

We now show two analyses to quantify the uncertainty in the measurements of the physical system. The first analysis is a well known Montecarlo simulation, which consists of running several simulations, with noise drawn from statistical distributions that characterise the environment of the system. The second consists of combining what-if analysis with Montecarlo co-simulations. It enables designers to understand which noise sources have the biggest impact in the safety of the vehicle. Both analyses use models of the system environment (in this case, the noise).

We introduce a simple agricultural vehicle and derive its kinematic and controller equations. We can generalise the analysis described here to the more complex system described in Foldager et al. [11] and Macedo et al. [22].

---

[2] Some terminology. *Kinematics* is the space of all possible configurations of a system at one time without considering the forces acting on the system. For example, invariants between state variables that follow from conservation laws. *Dynamics* is how configurations change as a function of time, due to the forces acting on the system.

3.1   Vehicle Kinematics

We derive simple kinematic equations for the agricultural vehicle. We consider it to be a bicycle model[3] with front steering and centre of gravity at the centre of the rear axis. For a more general derivation see Rajamani [26, Section 2.2].

Figure 2 gives a diagram of the agricultural vehicle, inspired by Alur [1]. The vehicle has four wheels, two at the back that have a fixed direction and two at the front that the driver can steer towards the left or the right. We define the vehicle's current position to be the centre of the rear axle (x, y). The distance between the front and back axles is L m. The vehicle is moving forward at a speed of v ms^{-1}. The front wheels are at an angle of $\theta°$ to the frame of reference (the x-y axes in the diagram). The driver has turned the front wheels to the right by an angle of $\delta°$. Because of its steering geometry, this is causing the vehicle to follow a circle with the origin at point C. We determine the centre of the turning circle by producing two lines, one following the rear axle and the other following the front axle rotated clockwise by the steering angle δ.[4]

We deduce some facts about the vehicle's motion. The geometric interpretation of the derivative of a function $f(x)$ at $x = x_0$ is the slope of the graph of f at that point. This is defined to be the slope of the tangent line to the graph at x_0.[5] Thus, by definition we have:

$$\frac{dy}{dx} = \tan\theta$$

$$= \quad \left\{ \text{by the chain rule of differentiation: } \frac{dy}{dt} = \frac{dy}{dx} \cdot \frac{dx}{dt} \right\}$$

$$\frac{dy/dt}{dx/dt} = \tan\theta$$

$$= \quad \{ \text{changing from Leibniz's notation to Newton's for conciseness} \}$$

$$\dot{y}/\dot{x} = \tan\theta$$

---

[3] The term "bicycle model" is used because the equations assume that the angle of each front wheel is the same, as happens with vehicles that have only one front wheel. In practice, the angle between the two front wheels differs and the difference is proportional to the distance between them (as in Ackermann steering geometry).

[4] We assume that the vehicle moving at a constant speed describes a circle about its forward travelling frame of reference. In reality, steering is more complicated than this. It depends on whether the vehicle is front or rear-wheel driven; whether the front or rear-wheels steer the vehicle; what particular steering geometry is present; what the tyre characteristics are; and whether there are differential axles. A standard configuration is for the vehicle to have front-wheel steered driving wheels with Ackermann steering geometry (Zhao et al. show how to derive this geometry in a mechanical engineering setting [33]). This approximates idealised steering along a circular arc.

[5] More formally, it is the limit of the secant lines through $(x_0, f(x_0))$ and nearby points $(x, f(x))$ as x approaches x_0. For the tangent line to be well-defined, the graph of f at x_0 must be continuous. The tangent line must not be vertical: a vertical line is not a function and so does not have a slope.

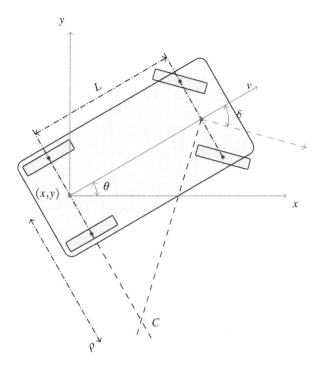

Fig. 2. Agricultural vehicle.

$$= \quad \{\,\text{trigonometry: } \tan\theta = \sin\theta/\cos\theta\,\}$$
$$\dot{y}/\dot{x} = \sin\theta/\cos\theta$$
$$= \quad \{\,\text{arithmetic}\,\}$$
$$\dot{y}\cos\theta = \dot{x}\sin\theta$$

This equation is satisfied by $\dot{x} = \cos\theta$ and $\dot{y} = \sin\theta$ and their scalar multiples, which correspond to the vehicle's velocity v. That means $\dot{x} = v\cos\theta$ and $\dot{y} = v\sin\theta$.

Now we want to find the angular speed of the vehicle. The angle between the lines that meet at C is also δ. The distance between the centre of the axle and C is ρ (see Fig. 2). Therefore,

$$\tan\delta = L/\rho$$
$$= \quad \rho = L/(\tan\delta)$$

The vehicle follows a circular path. Suppose that the vehicle travels s metres along its circular trajectory and s is half the distance it takes to intersect the $y = x$ axis again. Given that θ is the angle subtended by this arc, identical to the one measured at the centre of the rear axle, and ρ is the radius of this circular trajectory, then we have $s = \rho\,\theta$. This comes directly from the formula that relates degrees of arc and radians: angle $\theta = \dfrac{s}{\rho}$ radians. Now calculate:

$$s = \rho\,\theta$$
$$\Rightarrow \quad \{\text{ differentiate both sides (assumption: monotonic functions) }\}$$
$$\frac{ds}{dt} = \frac{d(\rho\,\theta)}{dt}$$
$$= \quad \{\text{ constant circle radius } \rho\,\}$$
$$\frac{ds}{dt} = \rho\,\frac{d\theta}{dt}$$
$$= \quad \left\{\text{ replacing linear velocity } \frac{ds}{dt} = v \text{ and angular velocity } \frac{d\theta}{dt} = \dot{\theta}\,\right\}$$
$$v = \rho\,\dot{\theta}$$

To summarise, the kinematic equations of our simplified vehicle are:

$$\dot{x}(t) = v(t)\cos\theta(t)$$
$$\dot{y}(t) = v(t)\sin\theta(t) \tag{1}$$
$$\dot{\theta}(t) = (v/L)\tan\delta(t)$$

where the controlled inputs are t and $\delta(t)$, and the initial values for the states x, y, θ are known.

3.2 Controller

To keep the explanation simple, we develop a controller whose purpose is to drive the vehicle in a straight line, in the x direction with a constant speed.

Given a position (x, y) and orientation of the vehicle θ, the controller computes δ and v that get the vehicle closer to the intended y coordinate $y_{target} = 0$ and orientation $\theta_{target} = 0$, as follows:

$$\delta_{error}(t) = -(k_t\theta(t) + k_p y(t))$$

$$\delta(t) = \begin{cases} \delta_{max} & \text{if } \delta_{error}(t) > \delta_{max} \\ -\delta_{max} & \text{if } \delta_{error}(t) < -\delta_{max} \\ \delta_{error}(t) & \text{otherwise} \end{cases} \tag{2}$$

$$v(t) = 1$$

where $k_t > 0$ and $k_p > 0$ are tunable constants and δ represents the steering angle limited by the maximum steering wheel angle, represented by δ_{max}. Figure 3 shows an example solution of the closed (no inputs) system formed by putting together Eqs. (1) and (2).

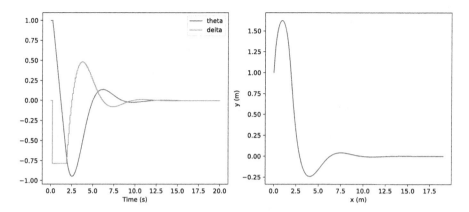

Fig. 3. Example simulation where vehicle starts 1 m away from the straight line (right), and with wrong orientation (left). As can be seen, the controller corrects this (saturating δ initially) and settles the vehicle in the straight line after a few seconds. Here, the parameters $k_t = k_p = 1$, and theta and delta correspond to θ and δ.

3.3 Deployed System

The system of equations derived so far in Eqs. (1) and (2) does not reflect the actual deployment of the system. This is because: (i) the deployed controller will sample the position and orientation of the vehicle every $H > 0$ seconds; and (ii) there is noise in the sensor measurements of x, y, θ and in the actuators v, δ.

To represent the sampled system, we note that, between samples, the actuation of the controller is constant, and the only continuous behaviour is the vehicle's. In the time interval $\tau \leq t < \tau + H$, the system's motion is given by Eqs. (1) and (2) with the difference that the vehicle speed and steering angle are kept constant throughout the interval, and are computed according to the orientation and position of the vehicle at the beginning of the interval:

$$
\begin{aligned}
\dot{x}(t) &= v(\tau) \cos \theta(t) \\
\dot{y}(t) &= v(\tau) \sin \theta(t) \\
\dot{\theta}(t) &= (v(\tau)/L) \tan \delta(\tau)
\end{aligned}
\tag{3}
$$

where the initial state values $x(\tau), y(\tau), \theta(\tau)$, are given, and $\delta(\tau), v(\tau)$ are computed as in Eq. (2) (or Eq. (4) if there's noise) from the initial state values. Note that throughout the interval, $\dot{\theta}(t)$ is constant.

The behaviour of the system is computed in a co-simulation involving the controller and the vehicle kinematics as follows:

1. At time $t = \tau$, the controller gets the values for position and orientation from the sensors, calculates the steering wheel angle and speed, and sets those values through the actuators.
2. We use a numerical solver to solve Eq. (3) in the interval $\tau \leq t \leq \tau + H$.

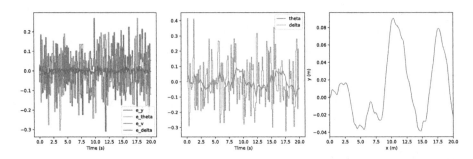

Fig. 4. Results of the co-simulation using the controller with noise (Eq. (4)) and the system dynamics in Eq. (3). The noise terms are drawn from statistical distributions. The communication step size $H = 0.1$ seconds.

3. At the end of the interval, when $t = \tau + H$, the controller gets new values for position and orientation from the sensors, recalculates the steering wheel angle and speed, and sets those values through the actuators (this is Step 1 for the new interval $\tau + H \leq t \leq \tau + 2H$), and the cycle is repeated.

To account for noise, we introduce noise terms by reformulating Eq. (2) as follows:

$$\delta_{error} = -(k_t(\theta + \epsilon_\theta) + k_p(y + \epsilon_y)) + \epsilon_\delta$$

$$\delta = \begin{cases} \delta_{max} & \text{if } \delta_{error} > \delta_{max} \\ -\delta_{max} & \text{if } \delta_{error} < -\delta_{max} \\ \delta_{error} & \text{otherwise} \end{cases} \tag{4}$$

$$v = 1 + \epsilon_v$$

We assume that the noise terms introduced are constant during the continuous evolution of the system's kinematics, but may change at each control execution cycle. The system behaviour is computed by the same co-simulation algorithm as described above, except when the controller computes δ, v, it does so using new values for the noise terms. The values for these terms can be taken from a statistical distribution. They will perturb the system and cause deviations on its correct behaviour, even when the vehicle starts in the target position and orientation. The simulation results in Fig. 4 illustrate an example.

3.4 Statistical Analysis

In the previous subsections, we derived a simple model of how the deployed agricultural vehicle behaves. In the following subsections, we introduce the statistical analysis used to quantify the uncertainty of the vehicle's behaviour with respect to the uncertainty in the environment of the vehicle. The methods we introduce here can be applied automatically for different parametrisations of the system, and therefore they can be used to guide design choices and parameter tuning.

To illustrate the importance of these analyses with respect to safety, suppose that we wish the system to always stay within a maximum distance of the center of road.

$$\forall \, t, \, Y(t) < y_{max} \tag{5}$$

where Y denotes the trace of y coordinates of the system, and y_{max} is a constant reflecting, for example, the half-width of the road where the vehicle will drive. The more general property $\forall \, t, |Y(t)| < y_{max}$ could be used, but the analyses are analogous.

Assuming that the noise in the system can be characterised as a statistical distribution, then running Montecarlo co-simulations may help us determine the expected system's behaviour with respect to its safety properties.

For instance, suppose that each time the controller computes the velocity and steering angle, in Eq. (4), the noise values are drawn from a Normal distribution with zero mean and standard deviation that's been estimated from real measurements:

$$\epsilon_p \sim \mathcal{N}(0, \sigma_p) \text{ for } p \in \{\theta, y, \delta, v\} \tag{6}$$

Then running many simulations, as Fig. 5 exemplifies, will yield estimates on important measures of expected violations. Those measures can then be used in a runtime monitor that checks whether the violations of the real system agree with the simulation data. To exemplify this, we first need to define the quantities of interest for the case study used.

Definition 1 (Violation Events, Peak, and Duration). *Given a trajectory of the vehicle $Y(t)$, the i-th violation event, denoted as a tuple with the start time and end time $[\underline{t}_i, \overline{t}_i]$, represents the interval during which the vehicle is violating that property. Formally, $\forall \, t \in [\underline{t}_i, \overline{t}_i], \, Y(t) \geq y_{max}$. The peak of the i-th violation event is given by $\max\{Y(t) - y_{max} : t \in [\underline{t}_i, \overline{t}_i]\}$. The maximum peak of a trace is the maximum of the peak of each violation event.*

Figure 6 illustrates these concepts.

Within the same trace, violation events are not Independent and Identically Distributed (i.i.d.), because of the dynamics of the vehicle. To see why, note that, right after a violation event, the probability of another event occurring depends on the dynamics of the control system. In particular, the control system is steering the vehicle towards the line $y = 0$, regardless of the values that the noise terms may take (the noise terms are i.i.d.). The further the vehicle is from the line, the stronger the control action, and the smaller the set of possible noise terms that will make the vehicle violate the property. This set gets bigger as

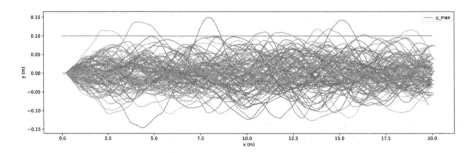

Fig. 5. Results of 100 co-simulations using the controller with noise (Eq. (4)) and the system kinematics in Eq. (3). The noise terms are drawn from statistical distributions with the following standard deviations: $\sigma_\theta = \sigma_y = \sigma_v = 0.1, \sigma_\delta = 0.01$. The communication step size matches the controller execution cycle $H = 0.1$ seconds. The straight line represents the property limit $y_{max} = 0.1$. As can be seen, there are a few violations.

the control action gets weaker, e.g., as the vehicle gets closer to the line $y = 0$, affecting the probability of a subsequent violation event.

However, between two traces, the violation events are i.i.d.. Hence, we can compute statistics between traces for:

- Maximum violation peak within the same trace.
- Maximum violation duration.

Figure 7 shows the results of these quantities, computed from simulations like the ones in Fig. 5.

3.5   Runtime Monitoring

Having estimated the quantities in Fig. 7, a run-time monitor can be synthesised that will perform the following, at each monitoring step:

1. Compute moving average of each sensor and actuation signal.
2. Compute moving standard deviation of each sensor and actuation signals (such standard deviations represent the noise standard deviations observed).
3. Compare each observed noise standard deviation with the noise standard deviation used to obtain the simulation results.
4. If the observed noise parameters are too different from the noise parameters used to create the simulations, give an alert to the user (because the simulation results used the wrong assumptions and should be repeated).
5. Quantify how safe the system is (e.g., evaluate Eq. (5), compute for how long it does not hold, maximum violation, etc.).
6. If such quantification does not match what was observed with the simulation data (in Fig. 7), then alert the user that the system is unsafe.

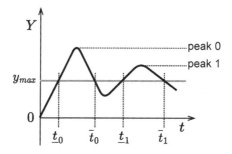

Fig. 6. Illustration of the concepts in Definition 1. There are two violation events. The peak of each violation event is the maximum distance between the trace and the safety line y_{max}. The maximum peak is peak 0.

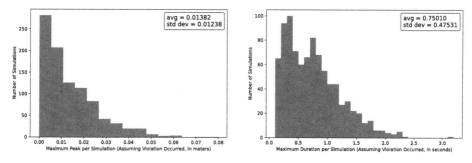

Fig. 7. Statistics of quantities of interest for runtime monitoring, computed from 10000 co-simulations. The parameters are the same as in Fig. 5.

3.6 What-If Analysis

The property in Eq. (5) reflects a characteristic of the road in which the vehicle operates. These properties may come from industrial regulations, etc., and are independent of the way the vehicle is designed. The previous subsection shows how to characterise and quantify the violation events caused by the vehicle and control system characteristics, in particular, the noise in the sensors and actuators. This subsection shows how the same technique can be used to identify which noise sources have a bigger impact in the system operation.

Suppose we are trying to decide whether to upgrade the vehicle with a better GPS receiver, or a better servomotor for the steering wheel. With only enough budget for one purchase, we would like to know which makes the system safer. Repeating the statistical analysis with the new noise characteristics provides estimates on the impact of each configuration.

For brevity, we show the results and conclusions of the statistical for both new GPS configuration and new servo, in Fig. 8.

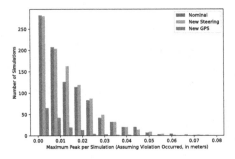 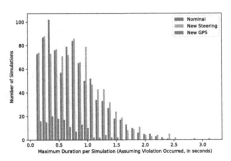

Fig. 8. What-if analysis results. The nominal standard deviations for the noise terms are as in Fig. 5: $\sigma_\theta = \sigma_y = \sigma_v = 0.1, \sigma_\delta = 0.01$. As can be seen, the new GPS configuration reduces both the mean and standard deviation of the violation events more than the new servo configuration.

4 Conclusion

We set out to describe some of the techniques that can be used to measure discrepancies between a CPS and a digital twin. We have shown how, for a given safety property Eq. (5), to quantify and characterise the violation events of that property. The analysis is based on a model of the system, and can then inform a runtime monitor that checks whether the noise and violations observed fall within the expected statistical distributions. For this analysis, we assume that the noise, initial states, and inputs to the system must be such that violation events can occur. If the system is already safe with respect to the property, regardless of the noise, then the analyses presented here confirm that and there's nothing to be tolerated.

Additionally, the results presented here allow the engineers to determine the best system configuration through what-if analysis. For instance, the statistical analysis could be used to calculate the minimum accuracy of the GPS signal, so that the probability of a violation event occurring is below some threshold.

We now summarise the limitations and assumptions of this case study:

1. The statistical analysis can be computationally expensive (even though the simulations can be run in parallel).
2. The analyses presume that the standard deviations of the noise can be obtained from empirical data. They are supposed to make use of the models to relieve but not eliminate the need for some physical experimentation with the real vehicle.
3. In each simulation, we assume that the noise terms are constant in between controller samples. In practice, noise may affect the physical system in between those samples.
4. The performance of the co-simulation plays a fundamental role in enabling the Montecarlo co-simulations.

Additionally, we have assumed that it is possible to quantify the violation degree of a safety property. Signal Temporal Logic (STL) is a formalism for specifying the requirements of CPSs [7]. It mixes models of discrete and analogue components and a continuous environment. STL has a quantitative semantics and is a natural candidate to quantify safety. Algorithms exist for offline computation of quantitative semantics and methods for online analysis monitoring satisfaction during simulation [6].

Our work is related to the field of run-time verification. These techniques checks that a run of a system satisfies or violates a given correctness property [21]. This is the natural technology for checking behavioural deviations between a physical asset and its digital twin. Techniques exist for robust online monitoring of properties described in STL [6].

Regarding the performance of the co-simulation, if the example is sufficiently complex, it won't be feasible to run the 10 000 co-simulations. To this end, researchers have employed many system identification [17], grey-box modelling [29], and surrogate modelling techniques [12], to create faster simulation models that can be used for the analysis.

Ongoing work is focusing on generalising this method into a framework that allows user to describe the safety properties, described tolerable violations, and generate runtime monitors that enforce such tolerances. In particular, we will develop an ontology based on multiple case studies, which will in turn inform us of the most common tolerable violations for safety properties.

Acknowledgements. We acknowledge the European Union for funding the INTO-CPS project (Grant Agreement 644047), which developed the open tool chain and the INTO-CPS Application; the Poul Due Jensen Foundation that funded subsequent work on taking this forward towards the engineering of digital twins; and the European Union for funding the HUBCAP project (Grant Agreement 872698). We acknowledge support from the UK EPSRC for funding for the RoboCalc (EP/M025756/1) and RoboTest projects (EP/R025479/1). Finally, we acknowledge support from the Royal Society and National Natural Science Foundation of China for funding for the project Requirements Modelling for Cyber-Physical Systems IEC/NSFC/170319. Early versions of the ideas in this paper were presented to the Digital Twin Centre in Aarhus in December 2019 (twice) and to the RoboStar team in York in January 2020. We are grateful for their feedback.

References

1. Alur, R.: Principles of Cyber-Physical Systems. The MIT Press, Cambridge (2015)
2. Bartocci, E., Falcone, Y., Francalanza, A., Reger, G.: Introduction to runtime verification. In: Bartocci, E., Falcone, Y. (eds.) Lectures on Runtime Verification. LNCS, vol. 10457, pp. 1–33. Springer, Cham (2018). https://doi.org/10.1007/978-3-319-75632-5_1
3. Box, G.E.P.: Robustness in the strategy of scientific model building. In: Launer, R.L., Wilkinson, G.N. (eds.) Robustness in Statistics, pp. 201–236. Academic Press (1979)

4. Box, G.E.P., Draper, N.R.: Empirical Model-Building and Response Surfaces. Wiley, Hoboken (1987)
5. Cassar, I., Francalanza, A., Aceto, L., Ingólfsdóttir, A.: A survey of runtime monitoring instrumentation techniques. Electron. Proc. Theor. Comput. Sci. **254**, 15–28 (2017)
6. Deshmukh, J.V., Donzé, A., Ghosh, S., Jin, X., Juniwal, G., Seshia, S.A.: Robust online monitoring of signal temporal logic. Formal Methods Syst. Des. **51**(1), 5–30 (2017). https://doi.org/10.1007/s10703-017-0286-7
7. Donzé, A.: On signal temporal logic. In: Legay, A., Bensalem, S. (eds.) RV 2013. LNCS, vol. 8174, pp. 382–383. Springer, Heidelberg (2013). https://doi.org/10.1007/978-3-642-40787-1_27
8. Falcone, Y., Krstić, S., Reger, G., Traytel, D.: A taxonomy for classifying runtime verification tools. In: Colombo, C., Leucker, M. (eds.) RV 2018. LNCS, vol. 11237, pp. 241–262. Springer, Cham (2018). https://doi.org/10.1007/978-3-030-03769-7_14
9. Fitzgerald, J., Gamble, C., Larsen, P.G., Pierce, K., Woodcock, J.: Cyber-physical systems design: formal foundations, methods and integrated tool chains. In: 2015 IEEE/ACM 3rd FME Workshop on Formal Methods in Software Engineering (FormaliSE), pp. 40–46 (2015)
10. Fitzgerald, J., Larsen, P.G., Pierce, K.: Multi-modelling and co-simulation in the engineering of cyber-physical systems: towards the digital twin. In: ter Beek, M.H., Fantechi, A., Semini, L. (eds.) From Software Engineering to Formal Methods and Tools, and Back. LNCS, vol. 11865, pp. 40–55. Springer, Cham (2019). https://doi.org/10.1007/978-3-030-30985-5_4
11. Foldager, F.F., Larsen, P.G., Green, O.: Development of a driverless lawn mower using co-simulation. In: Cerone, A., Roveri, M. (eds.) SEFM 2017. LNCS, vol. 10729, pp. 330–344. Springer, Cham (2018). https://doi.org/10.1007/978-3-319-74781-1_23
12. Forrester, A., Sobester, A., Keane, A.: Engineering Design via Surrogate Modelling: A Practical Guide. Wiley, Hoboken (2008)
13. Gibson, J.P., Larsen, P.G., Pantel, M., Fitzgerald, J., Woodcock, J.: Cyber-physical systems engineering: an introduction. In: Margaria, T., Steffen, B. (eds.) ISoLA 2018, Part III. LNCS, vol. 11246, pp. 407–410. Springer, Cham (2018). https://doi.org/10.1007/978-3-030-03424-5_27
14. Gomes, C., Thule, C., Broman, D., Larsen, P.G., Vangheluwe, H.: Co-simulation: a survey. ACM Comput. Surv. **51**(3), 49:1–49:33 (2018)
15. INTOCPS Association: Uncertainty quantification repository (2020). https://gitlab.au.dk/clagms/2020.isola.uncertaintyquantification. Accessed 21 Dec 2020
16. Jantsch, A., Sander, I.: Models of computation and languages for embedded system design. IEE Proc. Comput. Digit. Tech. **152**(2), 114–129 (2005)
17. Keesman, K.J.: System Identification: An Introduction. Springer, London (2011). https://doi.org/10.1007/978-0-85729-522-4
18. Kritzinger, W., Karner, M., Traar, G., Henjes, J., Sihn, W.: Digital twin in manufacturing: a categorical literature review and classification. IFAC-PapersOnLine **51**, 1016–1022 (2018)
19. Larsen, P.G., Fitzgerald, J., Woodcock, J., Gamble, C., Payne, R., Pierce, K.: Features of integrated model-based co-modelling and co-simulation technology. In: Cerone, A., Roveri, M. (eds.) SEFM 2017. LNCS, vol. 10729, pp. 377–390. Springer, Cham (2018). https://doi.org/10.1007/978-3-319-74781-1_26

20. Legaard, C.M., Gomes, C., Larsen, P.G., Foldager, F.F.: Rapid prototyping of self-adaptive-systems using python functional mockup units. In: SummerSim 2020. ACM, New York (2020)
21. Leucker, M., Schallhart, C.: A brief account of runtime verification. J. Log. Algebraic Program. **78**(5), 293–303 (2009)
22. Macedo, H., Nilsson, R., Larsen, P.: The harvest coach architecture: embedding deviation-tolerance in a harvest logistic solution. Computers **8**(2), 31 (2019)
23. Martínez, G.S., Karhela, T., Vyatkin, V., Miettinen, T., Pang, C.: An OPC UA based architecture for testing tracking simulation methods. In: 2015 IEEE Trustcom/BigDataSE/ISPA, vol. 3, pp. 275–280 (2015)
24. Mitsch, S., Platzer, A.: ModelPlex: verified runtime validation of verified cyber-physical system models. Formal Methods Syst. Des. **49**(1–2), 33–74 (2016). https://doi.org/10.1007/s10703-016-0241-z
25. Nakaya, M., Li, X.: On-line tracking simulator with a hybrid of physical and Just-In-Time models. J. Process Control **23**(2), 171–178 (2013)
26. Rajamani, R.: Vehicle Dynamics and Control. Springer, Boston (2012). https://doi.org/10.1007/978-1-4614-1433-9
27. Rajhans, A., et al.: Supporting heterogeneity in cyber-physical systems architectures. IEEE Trans. Autom. Control **59**(12), 3178–3193 (2014)
28. Rooney, J.J., Heuvel, L.N.V.: Root cause analysis for beginners. Qual. Prog. **37**(7), 45–56 (2004)
29. Sohlberg, B., Jacobsen, E.: Grey box modelling – branches and experiences. IFAC Proc. Vol. **41**(2), 11415–11420 (2008)
30. Tao, F., Zhang, H., Liu, A., Nee, A.Y.C.: Digital twin in industry: state-of-the-art. IEEE Trans. Ind. Inf. **15**(4), 2405–2415 (2019)
31. Van der Auweraer, H., Anthonis, J., De Bruyne, S., Leuridan, J.: Virtual engineering at work: the challenges for designing mechatronic products. Eng. Comput. **29**(3), 389–408 (2013). https://doi.org/10.1007/s00366-012-0286-6
32. Vangheluwe, H.: Foundations of modelling and simulation of complex systems. Electron. Commun. EASST **10** (2008)
33. Zhao, J.S., Liu, Z.J., Dai, J.: Design of an Ackermann type steering mechanism. J. Mech. Eng. Sci. **227**, 2549–2562 (2013)

Designing Distributed Control
with Hybrid Active Objects

Eduard Kamburjan[1,2]([✉]) [iD], Rudolf Schlatte[1]([✉]) [iD], Einar Broch Johnsen[1]([✉]) [iD],
and Silvia Lizeth Tapia Tarifa[1]([✉]) [iD]

[1] University of Oslo, Oslo, Norway
{eduard,rudi,einarj,sltarifa}@ifi.uio.no
[2] Technische Universität Darmstadt, Darmstadt, Germany

Abstract. Models of distributed software systems extend naturally to
cyber-physical systems "in the large"; i.e., systems of loosely coupled software components which interact with models of physical processes. But
how do we model such combined systems? This paper discusses this problem from the perspective of active object systems. We attach different
active objects to models of physical systems, but maintain the objects'
actor-like decoupling of communication and synchronization. The result
is a model of hybrid active objects. In this setting, we discuss different
ways of modeling and controlling time advance and value propagation
between components, which may be inside the model, controlled by the
model, or controlling the model as a simulation unit. The patterns of
on-demand value propagation as well as fixed- and variable-step time
advance arise naturally from the semantics of hybrid active object models in HABS, a hybrid extension of the formal specification language
ABS.

1 Introduction

Models of distributed systems extend naturally to cyber-physical systems "in
the large"; i.e., loosely coupled distributed systems which include one or more
cyber-physical components. Cyber-physical systems in the large describe both
applications building on the Internet of Things and for Digital Twins in which
various models of physical systems interact with a distributed software system.
It is today a challenge to verify and even to validate such hybrid distributed
system models [11].

This paper discusses a compositional approach to this challenge, based on
formal semantics and executable models of loosely coupled distributed systems
of so-called *hybrid active objects*. Hybrid active objects are a hybrid extension of
active objects for modeling distributed cyber-physical systems. Active objects [5]
are object-oriented systems based on the actor concurrency model [12] which
decouple communication and synchronization through asynchronous message
passing, allowing very flexible decentralized systems to be easily expressed. ABS
[13] is a formally defined, executable modelling language based on active object

© Springer Nature Switzerland AG 2021
T. Margaria and B. Steffen (Eds.): ISoLA 2020, LNCS 12479, pp. 88–108, 2021.
https://doi.org/10.1007/978-3-030-83723-5_7

concepts that has proven to be suited for intuitive and natural modeling, and formal verification of complex systems in an industrial context and a multitude of domains, ranging from railway operations [17] to cloud-based systems [27]. Timed ABS adds a dense-time discrete event semantics to active objects. ABS also includes an interface for data acquisition from outside sources via http requests, called the Model API. To model hybrid active object systems, the *Hybrid Abstract Behavioral Specification language* (HABS) [14,18] is designed to combine simulation and verification as a hybrid extension of the modeling language ABS.

In this paper, we explore concepts of *distributed control* in the setting of HABS. We discuss these concepts in the context of two simple water tank examples, the first one targeting distributed controllers and the second one targeting prediction capabilities. We examine their components to discuss the runtime structure of the HABS models. In particular, we distinguish between implicit (or declarative) and explicit (or operational) components of a model, and between messages needed for time advance and value-passing. A central consideration is the level of control in the HABS models. HABS differentiates between *control over time advance* and *control over value passing*. Time advance is specified by the active objects and regulated by a central orchestrator that computes the maximal possible time advance. This time-orchestrator cannot rewind time and can only send time advance messages to the objects. Control over value passing does not involve the time orchestrator; it is distributed and explicitly modeled in the active objects. This allows flexible and complex communication patterns to be expressed, that capture communication as it is happening in the modeled system. This decoupling may also make the system simulation more performant, because the time-orchestrator is no bottleneck for communication of values. This is critical if the modeled system itself is distributed and communication is more complex than simple value propagation, but triggers complex behavior in the hybrid active objects.

HABS relies on a white-box model of discrete controllers as well as continuous dynamics for verification. To bridge between HABS and possible white- and black-box components of a model, we explore how interfacing to the continuous dynamics can be used to integrate implemented systems with recreated live data, as functional mock-ups or complex simulators for simulation (as a white-box) while retaining the ability of formal reasoning. We also explore how to integrate recorded data (as a black-box), via the Model API, a REST interface, to explore what-if scenarios for predictions, in this case formal analysis can still be done using, e.g., runtime monitoring and assertion checking. These integrations provide two ways to link between HABS models and Digital Twins.

Related Work. Digital Twins are a very interesting application area for formal methods because the basis for Digital Twins is model-based analysis. To cover an asset life-cycle, a digital twin need to combine a declarative model of the design of the asset with an inductive model derived from data observations of the system in operation [8]. However, the richness of the models makes it hard to do full verification and analysis in a digital twin setting, particularly for hybrid models with discrete and dynamic components. Such analysis is often based on simulation [22] or co-simulation [11]. A prominent example of work in this direction is INTO-CPS [30], which is pushing a co-simulation platform in the direction of Digital Twins based on FMI [3], an emerging standard for connecting simulators. In the case of ABS, the Model API allows data to be fed into a running model, thus integrating snapshots of industrial data with simulations in real time [27]. We have also used ABS to model a digital twin triggering software upgrades of connecting cars by sensor data [21,26].

Digital Twins are closely related to cyber-physical systems, but typically consider only distributed cyber-physical systems which connect various cyber-physical components into a distributed system, which is a major challenge for formal methods [28]. We do not attempt to cover that large area here, but mention Platzer's work on verification of cyber-physical systems using differential dynamic logic $d\mathcal{L}$ [25], which has been a source of inspiration for our work on HABS as a hybrid extension of ABS. HABS is a formally defined, executable modeling language with a proof theory building on $d\mathcal{L}$. Formal support for co-simulation algorithms has been done by means of model checking [29] and verification of the simulation itself by means of basic contracts [10]. The use of Hybrid Active Objects complements this work by offering a rich toolkit for the analysis of expressive properties for distributed and hybrid systems, which hopefully suffice to verify models of distributed control. Whereas this paper hints at verification for such models, the verification of such algorithms is not attempted here.

Structure. In Sect. 2 we describe active objects and the ABS modelling language for distributed active objects, and in Sect. 3 the hybrid extension HABS. In Sect. 4 we give two water tank models to illustrate modeling with HABS showcasing different notions of distributed control. In Sect. 5 we relate these notions to co-simulation and digital twins. We conclude the paper in Sect. 6 and present future work.

2   A Short Overview of ABS

ABS [13] is an actor-based, object-oriented language for modeling concurrent and distributed systems and supporting the design, verification, and execution of such systems. ABS has a purely *functional layer* of functions and algebraic datatypes, and an *object-oriented layer* for modeling Java-like objects and interfaces. Communication between objects is implemented via *asynchronous method calls*, which produce a *future* at the caller and a *new process* at the callee object. The caller continues execution immediately and only synchronizes with the future when the result of the call is needed. The callee schedules one of its pending processes; that process runs without preemption until it either finishes or *suspends*, e.g., when waiting for a future, at which point the object schedules another waiting process. These cooperative, explicit scheduling points are the foundation of the compositional proof system of distributed ABS models [6] and of its timed semantics which is explained later in this section.

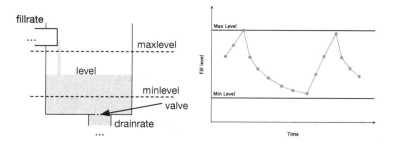

Fig. 1. The discrete-event watertank model and its behavior

Example 1. Consider a simple model of a WaterTank, which is filled from the top at a fixed fillrate and is drained (if the valve is open) from the bottom at a fixed drainrate (see Fig. 1 left for a basic sketch and Fig. 2 for its ABS implementation). We explain the basic concepts of asynchronous method calls and cooperative scheduling in ABS using an example from class Controller (Fig. 2, Line 27), which controls the water level of such tank. The execution of an asynchronous call statement like tank!valvecontrol(Open) (Line 33) creates a new process in the object tank which will execute the method valvecontrol but *does not release the control* at the caller object, where the current process continues its execution. Since we do not store the return value of the call, this corresponds to a "pure" message sending operation.

If we want to synchronize and/or receive the result of a method call, we store its future (f=o!m();). This future f can be used to both *suspend* the current process until the callee process has finished (Syntax: **await** f?;) and to read the future's value (Syntax: f.**get**). Suspending the current process means that the object running the calling process can schedule another process from its own pool or stay idle; when awaiting on a future, the suspended process becomes eligible for scheduling once the future f contains a value (i.e., when its process has finished).

As a shorthand, the statement level = **await** tank!getLevel() (Fig. 2 Line 31) creates a new process in the object tank, suspends the calling process until the return value of that method has been received, and then assigns the value to the variable level. Figure 1 shows a sketch of the physical setup (left) and its expected behavior (during "a kind of" discrete event simulation) in terms of how the level of the water changes as time progress (right).

2.1 The Time Model of Timed ABS

The previous section has already hinted that an object in ABS can be either running or idle; the latter case occurs when its process queue is empty or all processes are waiting on some condition. Timed ABS, an extension of ABS, adds a global logical clock, which acts as a time orchestrator that advances once all

```
1  data ValveCommand = Open | Close;
2
3  interface WaterTank {
4      Float getLevel();
5      Unit valvecontrol(ValveCommand command);
6  }
7
8  class WaterTank(Float fillrate, Float drainrate)
9  implements WaterTank {
10  Float level = 0.0;
11  Bool valve_open = False;
12
13  Float getLevel() { return level; }
14  Unit valvecontrol(ValveCommand command) {
15   valve_open = when command == Open then True else False;
16  }
17  Unit run() {
18   while (True) {
19    await duration(1, 1);
20    level = level + fillrate;
21    if (valve_open)
22     level = max(0.0, level - drainrate * level);
23   }
24  }
25 }
26
27 class Controller(WaterTank tank, Float minlevel,
28                  Float maxlevel) implements Controller {
29   Unit run() {
30     while (True) {
31       Float level = await tank!getLevel();
32       if (level >= maxlevel) {
33         tank!valvecontrol(Open);
34       } else if (level <= minlevel) {
35         tank!valvecontrol(Close);
36       }
37       await duration(1, 1);
38     }
39   }
40 }
```

Fig. 2. ABS (Non-hybrid) model of a water tank and controller

objects are idle. All objects can specify their own time advance interval; the clock
will advance by the maximum amount that satisfies all these conditions. Since
the time domain is the rational numbers, dense time and thus Zeno behavior is
supported.

For example, In Lines 19 and 37 of Fig. 2, we see statements **await duration** (1, 1);. These statements suspend the running process until the global clock has advanced by 1 (which is both the minimum and maximum advance given in the statement).

Timed ABS thus allows models to incorporate explicit manipulation of time from a dense time domain, which can be used to represent execution time inside methods, which either block an object, using **duration**(min, max); or suspend a thread, using **await duration**(min, max); for a certain amount of time between min and max. This way of modelling timed behavior is well-known from, e.g., timed automata in UPPAAL [20]. By using this modelling of the passage of time, we abstract from the actual execution time and execution context of a thread (i.e., the computation time of the thread is independent of the cpu speed and the load on the server where it is executed).

2.2   The Model API

The Model API of ABS is a way to call methods on objects of a running model from the outside via http requests. The model annotates the objects and methods that should be callable, i.e., the model is not completely open via the Model API. In addition, the Model API provides some measure of control over the model time advance: As explained in Sect. 2.1, the clock advances by the maximum possible amount. The Model API can set a limit for the clock and then raise it, again controlled by a http request from an agent on the outside of the model.

Using the Model API transforms a model into an *open system*, where the behavior cannot be determined statically, although class invariants and method contracts hold as before. The Model API is *reactive*, i.e., it receives method calls and time advance triggers as external stimuli but cannot send stimuli to the outside of the model.

3   Hybrid Abstract Behavioral Specification Language

The Hybrid ABS (HABS) [18] language is an extension of Timed ABS for modeling Cyber-Physical systems. In this section we introduce the main features of HABS: (1) integrated continuous behavior declared in a special block in the class that contains ODEs, (2) special **await** statements to react to changes caused by this continuous behavior and (3) a transparent extension of the time model.

3.1   Syntax and Semantics

HABS extends ABS by two new constructs:

– A **physical** block in class definitions contains *physical fields* which define the continuous behavior over time of a part of the object state via (autonomous) ordinary first-order differential equations (ODE). In the definition of a physical field f, the notation f' is used for the first derivative of f. All physical fields have the type Real, while non-physical fields can have any type.

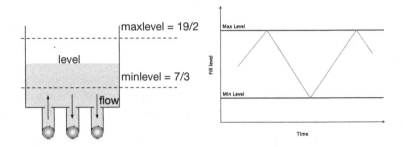

Fig. 3. The multi-controller watertank and its behavior

– A new suspension statement **await diff** g which suspends the running thread until g holds. The guard g is a quantifier-free formula over the object's physical fields and the local variables of the process. This statement plays a similar role as transition guards in hybrid automata [2] and allows one to model reaction to state change.

In HABS, an object that has a **physical** block is a *hybrid* object. If the object has no physical block, but uses **duration** statements in its methods, then it is a *timed* object. Otherwise it is a *discrete* object. Note that HABS does not model evolution domains (e.g., level ≥ 0, sometimes called mode invariants) directly, to give the user the possibility to implement how leaving the evolution domain shall influence the behavior of the object upon time advance of the system.

Example 2. Consider a model of a water tank, depicted in Fig. 3 left, and coded in Fig. 4. It declares an object with a physical field level to describe the water level of the tank, and three normal fields flowA, flowB, flowC that hold the status of three different valves of the tank, which let water either fill or drain depending on the direction of the flow. The field declaration in the physical block, in addition to specifying an initial value inVal, describes the dynamics of the level field via an ODE. We use level' = flowA+flowB+flowC to denote that the derivative of level (seen as a function over time) is equal to the sum of the three flows. The setFlow method, when called, sets any of the valves, and the outLevel method returns the current water level. Finally, the acqLevel method suspends until the water level falls below a certain level r.

The acqLevel method shows how continuous behavior in the **physical** block and discrete program in the rest of the object interact, by using a differential suspension **await diff** g. Semantically, this statement suspends the running process P until the earliest time t_d where g holds for the physical block. The solution F of the physical block can be computed over the time interval within now() and t_d, with the initial values (with underscore 0) provided by the current state. Upon reactivation, the values of the physical fields are updated according to $F(t_d)$. In our example, F for the variable level is the solution defined by:

$$F(t_d) = \texttt{level}_0 + \texttt{flowA}_0 \times t_d + \texttt{flowB}_0 \times t_d + \texttt{flowC}_0 \times t_d$$

```
1  class Tank(Rat inVal, Rat dIVal) implements ITank {
2      Real flowA = dIVal;
3      Real flowB = dIVal;
4      Real flowC = dIVal;
5      physical{
6          Real level = inVal : level' = flowA+flowB+flowC;
7      }
8      Unit setFlow(Real newFlow, Int id){
9          if(id == 0) flowA = newFlow;
10         if(id == 1) flowB = newFlow;
11         if(id == 2) flowC = newFlow;
12     }
13     Real outLevel(){ return level; }
14     Unit acqLevel(Real r){ await diff level <= r; }
15 }
```

Fig. 4. A water tank with three controllers in Hybrid ABS.

such that the solution over the time interval keeps the current values of `level`, `flowA`, `flowB` and `flowC` as constants.

Any other process that runs between `now()` and t_d, and thereby modifies the object state and the state of the physical variables, will cause the solution for `g` to be recomputed and the waiting time for P to be extended or shortened according to the new object state. For every blocking statement that might cause time to advance, such as **get** or **duration**, we similarly compute the solution to the continuous behavior in the current state and update the state once the passed time is known.

This is transparent to the time model of Timed ABS because the messages for suspension, possible time advance and reactivation do not change for HABS.

For simulation, HABS uses maxima [23] to (1) compute the solution to the initial value problem stated by the physical block and the current heap and (2) to compute t_d by minimization of time for the solution, constrained by the guard. For the scheduler of the active object in ABS, the extension is transparent: Processes in hybrid active objects are scheduled in the same way as for normal active objects and the time orchestrator handles t_d in the same way as timed duration statements. HABS and the tools in its backend, can handle differential equations beyond ODEs and linear dynamics.

3.2 Analyzability

The semantics of HABS take care of the problems that naturally occur in hybrid systems: solving ODEs and computing the next time advance, and keeping the state updated after discrete time steps. The model in Example 2 is, thus, more concise and natural than its discretized counterpart in Example 1. The update of state is crucial for modeling distributed systems, as a hybrid object must be reactive to calls from the outside at any point in time.

Formal analysis and verification is also more simple than in the discrete case: the continuous behavior of each object is described directly and centralized in the physical block with a well-established mechanism. The physical block is an *abstraction* of the numerical and symbolic operations performed by the runtime (in HABS) or the explicit discretization (in ABS). Verification of Example 2 can use the ODEs to reason about continuous dynamics, while Example 1 requires an analysis of the implemented simulator. There are established tools for ODEs and the code in Example 2 can be automatically translated in proof obligations in differential dynamic logic [24] which can be checked with the KeYmaera X theorem prover [9].

A hybrid system in HABS contains hybrid objects and non-hybrid (timed and discrete) objects. Due to the strong encapsulation of the language semantics, properties of distributed systems that are not dependent on the hybrid objects can be analyzed by the rich toolkits [1] and logics [15] for discrete objects.

However, execution (simulation) becomes more complex, as the abstraction provided by the physical block does not help with simulation. While simulation is not an analysis per se, it plays an important role during development by using testing as a complement to verification. HABS uses **assert** statements for runtime verification. HABS can be executed using a simple simulator, but increasing its performance by connecting it to external tools is an open challenge.

The Model API and HABS. The model API allows one to connect a HABS model to external tools at runtime. This makes the model open and has two main consequences: On one hand, continuous behavior which is too complex to be described in the **physical** block can interact with the model. On the other hand, static analysis becomes difficult and must possibly be mixed with runtime monitoring with **assert** statements. The reason for this are two-fold: (1) there is no abstraction of the external continuous behavior that can be used for verification and (2) the order of send messages cannot be analyzed a priori.

4   Models for Distributed Control

This section explores the design of modular cyber-physical systems in HABS. Two HABS models of distributed water tanks show different possible runtime structures, showing in particular the issue of *control*: which parts of the HABS code are models of physical devices and which parts are modeling their control.

- The first HABS model has a tank with three controllers that must coordinate the three valves, as in Fig. 3, to keep the tank level in a safe zone. The three controllers read the level of the tank and use a simple round-robin leader election mechanism to make decisions. The behavior of the water tank model is passive.
- The second HABS model has a different scenario: the model API is used to communicate the current level to the HABS model and the water tanks are used to *predict* the optimal control of a single valve.

```
1  class FlowCtrl(ITank tt, Real tick, Int id)
2          implements FlowCtrl{
3  // We elide details on initialization of these attributes
4  Bool isLeader = False;
5  FlowCtrl ctrlA; FlowCtrl ctrlB;
6
7  Unit ctrlFlow(){
8    while True {
9     await duration(tick,tick);
10    if (isLeader) {
11     Real level = tt.outLevel();
12     if(level <= 7/2 ){
13      tt!setFlow(-1/2,id); ctrlA!act(1/2); ctrlB!act(1/2);
14     }
15     if (level >= 19/2) {
16      tt!setFlow(1/2,id); ctrlA!act(-1/2); ctrlB!act(-1/2);
17     }
18     ctrlA!makeLeader();
19     isLeader = False;
20    }
21   }
22 }
23 Unit makeLeader() { isLeader = True; }
24 Unit act(Rat flow) { tt!setFlow(flow, id); }
25 }
```

Fig. 5. Distributed control with *pull* communication from physical device to controllers.

4.1   Internal Control

The first model uses the tank from Fig. 4 and adds three controllers, one for each valve. The controllers read the value of the current level and coordinate the new state of the valves accordingly. Time advances in constant intervals of size tick via an **await duration**(tick,tick); statement in each controller.

Example 3. Consider the tank in Fig. 4, with its three controllers. Each controller can control the flow of up to $0.5\frac{l}{s}$ water in or out of the tank, but the tank is only considered safe if the total flow is between $-1\frac{l}{s}$ and $1\frac{l}{s}$, hence the controllers need to coordinate.

The code in Fig. 5 shows one controller implementing the following behavior: After every tick seconds (Line 9), the controller checks whether it is the current leader (Line 10) and if so, reads the current water level (Line 11). If the level is below a certain threshold, it sets its own valve to $-0.5\frac{l}{s}$ and orders the other controllers to set theirs to $0.5\frac{l}{s}$ (Line 13). This realizes the requirement above that it is not safe to add/remove water with more than $1\frac{l}{s}$ at every valve. The inverse happens if the water level is above a certain threshold (Line 16). Finally, the controller passes leadership to its left controller (Lines 18–19). Figure 3 shows

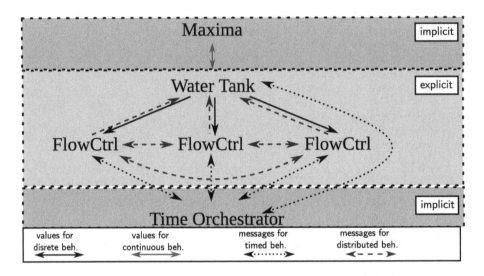

Fig. 6. Structure of the compiled HABS model of Fig. 5.

a sketch of the physical setup (left) and its expected behavior (right) in terms of how the level of the water changes as time progress (during "a kind of" continuous time simulation). In the sketch we are depicting a state in which the first controller has a positive flow (filling water into the tank), while the other two have a negative flow (draining water from the tank).

Runtime Structure. The structure of the compiled model of Example 3 has the following components:

Water Tank Object. This object is hybrid, because it has a **physical** block.

Three Valve Controller Objects. These objects are timed, because they have a **duration** guard but no **physical** block. The messages send around in the distributed system are *only* between the three controller and the water tank objects.

Maxima. A maxima instance computes the continuous dynamics of the physical block of the water tank instance on-demand when asked by it.

Time Orchestrator. The global scheduler of ABS coordinates the global time advance over all objects. It is not responsible for passing values and scheduling messages. Maxima, in essence the "main" simulator in this system, is controlled by its hybrid object.

The communication is pictured in Fig. 6. Communication here is pull communication, because the valve controllers pull the values of the tank object, which is passive otherwise. The main control lies with the three controllers, which also execute the leader election.

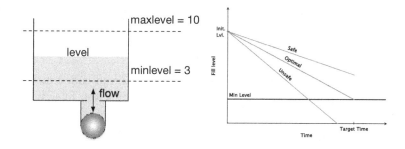

Fig. 7. The predictive watertank and its behavior

As for modeling, each object is a representation of a real world structure, while the implicit components (time orchestrator, maxima) are not exposed in the model. The model is more intuitive, as it requires no knowledge about the details of time advance or synchronization and, thus, is more easy to validate with domain experts. Having the implicit components fixed in the language also simplifies analysis.

We discussed the water tank from the modeling point of view. From a co-simulation point of view we make three observations.

Observation 1. *The maxima instance for a* **physical** *block of the water tank object is essentially a simulation unit, controlled by the* **ABS** *water tank object (for values) and the orchestrator (for time). Its ODEs can be seen twofold: as configuration of the simulation unit or as the behavioral interface of the continuous behavior used for verification.*

Observation 2. *The* **ABS** *objects without the* **physical** *block can be seen as a (value and time) orchestrator that propagates and computes values of the sole continuous simulation unit.*

Observation 3. *The controllers can be seen as simulation units themselves.*

From the model and the observations we can derive three points to connect HABS with co-simulation:

1. One can connect the co-simulation engine to the **physical** block, i.e., extend the **physical** block with a more generic interface to the outside. The enveloping object would play the role of an orchestrator. From this view, the water tank object is a co-simulation engine with one simulator (a maxima script).
2. One can connect the HABS-orchestrator with the orchestrator of a co-simulation engine as a sub-orchestrator. However, this would require that the orchestrator can propagate values to the objects.
3. One can connect a co-simulation engine with a designated object, that shares values with other objects and time advances with the HABS-orchestrator, but is transparent to the time semantics of HABS.

We examine these possibilities in detail in Sect. 5.

4.2   Predictive Control

The second model illustrates the use a physical tank model to simulate "what-if" scenarios in order to optimize a model parameter.

Example 4. Consider the water tank depicted in Fig. 7 and coded in Fig. 8. Its outResult methods simulates the water tank, returning the final water level by adjusting the flow at the given rate flowrate for wait time units. The initial water level is always reset to inVal. This model can therefore be used for *predictive* control by simulating possible settings for adjusting the flow and choosing an appropriate one.

```
1  class Tank(Rat inVal) implements ITank {
2      Real flow = 0;
3      physical{ Real level = inVal : level' = flow; }
4      Real outResult(Real flowrate, Real wait) {
5        level = inVal; flow = flowrate;
6        await duration(wait, wait);
7        flow = 0;
8        return level;
9      }
10 }
```

Fig. 8. Water tank for predictive control.

Figure 9 shows a controller that calculates the largest flow rate that keeps the tank level within bounds for 1 time unit. A call to go returns the maximal or minimal setting (depending on whether the water should rise or fall depending on the negative or positive value) for flow. To do so, starting from the most extreme setting (determined by pivot), the potential flow is changed by $1/10$ until the simulated water level is within bounds for 1 time units. Figure 7 shows a sketch of the physical setup (left) and its expected predicted behavior (right) in terms of how the chosen value for the flow can predict an optimal level in the water for a targeted time.

For the sake of brevity, we refrain from using the three-valve model of Sect. 4.1 here. In brief, extending the model with these cooperating controllers can be done by extending the method outResult to take three objects as parameters and simulating, e.g., pull control for one iteration.

Note that in Fig. 9, the controller itself is exposed via the model API. This means that the main control and the parallelism lie *outside* the model. Since this model simulates alternative scenarios, it will typically run under a temporary time orchestrator that does not influence the surrounding model.

Observation 4. *The previous model discussed the HABS runtime as a co-simulation framework. This model exposes that we can see the HABS model as a simulation unit in itself.*

```
1  interface FlowCtrl{
2      [HTTPCallable] Pair<Bool, Rat>  go(Int level);
3  }
4  class FlowCtrl(Real pivot) implements FlowCtrl{
5   Pair<Bool, Rat>  go(Int level){
6     Bool stop = False;
7     Pair<Bool, Rat> lastDecision = Pair(False,0);
8     ITank predict = new Tank(level);
9     Real flow = 0;
10    if(level <= pivot){
11       flow = -2;
12       while(!stop && flow <= 2){
13          Real sim = await predict!outResult(flow, 1);
14          if(sim <= 3) flow = flow + 1/10;
15          else          stop = True;
16       }
17    } else if(level > pivot){
18       flow = 2;
19       while(!stop && flow >= -2){
20          Real sim = await predict!outResult(flow, 1);
21          if(sim >= 10) flow = flow -1/10;
22          else          stop = True;
23       }
24    }
25    return Pair(stop,flow);
26  }
27 }
```

Fig. 9. Predictive controller.

Thus, we can connect co-simulation to HABS at a forth point:

4. One can connect the co-simulation engine via the model API with a special object (here: the FlowCtrl instance) as the interface.

Compared to the first model, predictive control is more easy to connect to techniques like co-simulation and digital twins, especially since the model API can be integrated into a live system, but less *natural*: the parts of the water tank do no longer correspond directly to some physical equivalent in the physical system. The outResult method, with its discrete change of the water level, is only relevant for simulation. Naturalness is a critical property of models because it influences the communication with domain experts [19].

Observation 5. *If the data is input from a live system, then the overall model is a predictive model of a digital twin.*

From an analysis point of view there are 3 challenges: 1. The model is open and thus harder to analyze statically. 2. The model is harder to specify because some properties (here: whether the water tank empties completely) are violated by design *without consequence*. 3. The model is harder to specify as parts of the system are outside the model, yet influence its behavior.

5   Discussion: Hybrid Active Objects in Relation to Co-simulation and Digital Twins

As we have shown in the last section, HABS models have some similarities to co-simulation and digital twins. This raises some questions on the relation between these concepts and how they would benefit from an integration.

5.1   Relation to Co-simulation

The distributed control patterns discussed for HABS models have some similarity with co-simulation frameworks. Co-simulation consists of techniques to enable global simulation of a coupled system via the composition of simulators [11]. Each simulator can be seen as a black-box capable of exhibiting behavior, consuming inputs, and producing outputs. In discrete event simulations, a simulation unit synchronizes with the environment at some specific timestamps to exchange values. If two events happen at the same time, both are processed before the simulated time progresses. In continuous time simulation (e.g., for cyber-physical systems), state evolves continuously, which introduces flexibility in the step size of the time synchronization. For co-simulation with hybrid simulation units, the units cannot be coupled together by simply connecting input to output ports. Instead the orchestrator needs to reconcile the different assumptions about the inputs and output of each unit, to make sure that the properties of the constituent systems are retained. In the large majority of co-simulators which couple such hybrid simulation units, the coupling is done ad-hoc [11], which makes the co-simulation systems increasingly complex and error-prone.

HABS is expressive enough to model a (distributed) co-simulation framework and reason about the correctness of the framework. We have seen that loosely coupled orchestration can be modeled, separating data exchange from time synchronization. More tightly coupled orchestration can be modeled as a special case in which, e.g., all data pass through a central object. ABS has a developed, tool-supported theory of reproducibility [31] and search through reachable states, which may be used to reason about determinism and confluence for parallel orchestrators, a recognized challenge in discrete event simulation [11]. The hybrid extension of HABS does not affect the semantics of parallelism underlying this theory. In a hybrid co-simulation, the orchestrator needs to ensure the validity of the simulation in terms of the assumptions about parameter values to the different simulation units. Although the time semantics of HABS makes it difficult to directly model roll-back and similar direct manipulation of time inside the executable model, but we believe HABS can be used to reason about such time manipulation by branching executions.

Table 1. Connection between internal and external components.

Aspect	Physical block	Orchestrator	Model API	Interface objects
Runtime	−	+	+	+
Naturalness	+	+	−	−/+
Analyzability	+	−	−−	−/+
Relevant example	Sect. 4.1	Sect. 4.1	Sect. 4.2	Sect. 4.2

HABS models can also be part of a co-simulation framework. Section 4.1 illustrates a HABS model as a decentralized orchestrator, which needs to obtain consensus on the actions of the different pumps. Section 4.2 illustrates a HABS model as a simulation unit in a co-simulation setting, which receives parameter values from the outside. Our work so far does not point to a clear "best way" to connect HABS to a co-simulation framework, as this depends on the modeling style used for a system.

The observations made in Sect. 4 suggest what we can expect from the different integration concepts we have considered between HABS and a co-simulation framework. The benefit of such an integration would be an enhancement of simulation capabilities for HABS and an enhancement of analyzability of the co-simulation framework. Such an integration would be an important step to simulate large and hybrid HABS systems. There are three main questions, which we now discuss in more detail:

I Runtime: how to technically connect external units to HABS entities?

II Naturalness: how to preserve the naturalness of a HABS model when connecting external units?

III Analyzability: how to keep parallelism analyzable and retain tools developed for closed HABS/ABS systems?

Table 1 summarizes the expected consequences of using a particular connection method with respect to runtime integration (i.e., how easy is it to exchange data with external entities), naturalness of the model and model analyzability. We discuss the table from left to right.

- Interfacing to external components using the **physical** block preserves the naturalness of the model and, if a proper abstraction can be provided, we expect the model to be analyzable in the sense that the semantics of parallelism does not change and the system is still closed (because the object containing the **physical** block retains control). However, this control over the **physical** block limits the kind of simulation one can do at runtime because the semantics do not allow for complex message exchanges.
- Using the orchestrator, we expect a better connection at runtime but a worse analyzability, because the control is now *outside* of the formal semantics. Naturalness again depends on how the interface is modeled, but as the connection is to an implicit runtime component, we expect only limited effects.

- Using the model API moves more control to the outside of the formal semantics. This gives one most freedom about the connection to an external orchestrator, but will lead to less natural models and lower analyzability.
- We can, however, internalize the model API to retain its benefits of easy integration while limiting its impact on analyzability and naturalness. This can be done by means of *designated interface objects.* which are the only objects exposed in the model API. These objects could extend the current Model API to support not only receiving messages but may also sending messages to the outside. In future work, we intend to define the design space for interface objects such that they comply with the compositional time semantics of HABS, to preserve the analyzability. Both timed and functional behavior should be specifiable, e.g., by behavioral types that specify communication, time and state [4,16]. This would allow specified assumptions about external behavior to be monitored at runtime, such that static checking of internal behavior remains feasible. We expect such specifications to improve the naturalness of models with interface objects.

In summary, the model API appears as a difficult choice because we lose the benefits of using a formal modeling language, but it gives the best prospect for simulation. The other discussed options give possible trade-offs between simulation, naturalness and analyzability. Using a special interface object that serve to control the external interface may be the best compromise if external behavior can then be encapsulated with specifications which allow static intra-model reasoning combined with runtime monitoring of the interface behavior. However, this approach does impose restrictions on the control of an external orchestrator.

5.2   Relation to Digital Twins

A digital twin (DT) is a digital replica of an underlying system, often called the physical twin (PT). The digital twin is connected to its physical twin in real-time through sensor measurements at different locations and by other ways of collecting data. This turns the DT into a *live replica* of the PT, with the purpose of providing insights into its behavior, and clearly distinguishes a DT from, e.g., a standard simulation model.

A DT is commonly seen as an architecture with three layers: the *data layer* with, e.g., CAD drawings and sensor data, an *information layer*, which turns these raw data into structures, and an *insight layer*, which applies different analysis and visualization techniques to these data structures. The analysis techniques of the insight layer can be classified as follows: The DT is typically able to compute an approximation of how the PT acts in a given scenario (**simulation** or "what-happened" scenarios), or to estimate how the PT will behave in the future based on historical and current data (**prediction** or "what-may-happen" scenarios). By configuring the parameters of the different models, the DT may analyze the consequence of different options on future behavior (**prescription** or "what-if" scenarios).

When modeling human-built artifacts, the physical twin can be divided into a *cyber-physical system* (CPS) and its *physical environment*. The latter is a mix of physical conditions (e.g., temperature or fluid pressure) and modeled conditions (e.g., motion tracking devices or computerized decision rules). In the DT, the CPS model may consist of several sub-models reflecting the different parts of the CPS. Similarly, the environment model comprises many models capturing the relevant dynamics of the operational environment. These smaller, targeted models are typically created by experts in the respective fields.

HABS is an expressive modeling language, which includes abstractions of cyber-physical systems. Although in theory an entire physical twin can be captured in a huge model, we do not think this is the way to go for complex, industrial cases. The digital twin as a "stack of models" seems more realistic, and a HABS model could be situated at many layers of such a stack. The compositional treatment of time in HABS suggests that models can contain components at different levels of abstraction, synchronized through the timed semantics. The information layer of a digital twin may quickly become very large and contain a lot of unnecessary information for a given analysis. HABS is not made for modeling complex data relations and large sets of data, and we propose to use complementary techniques to connect the executable models to static data (see, e.g., recent work on combining semantic ontologies with formal models [7]). We have shown how HABS models may both receive such data from the outside (Sect. 4.2) and call external simulators such as maxima (Sect. 4.1). Section 4.2 has shown by example how HABS models can integrate real-time data series through the Model API [27], which enables real-time simulation in a DT context of sensor data. This example also suggests through a simple example how different, alternative parameter settings can be used to explore what-if scenarios for prescriptive analysis.

6 Conclusion

This paper considers decentralized orchestration of cyber-physical systems "in the large". We have explored different ways of connecting a model of distributed active objects with cyber-physical components to model different forms of orchestration.

We did so from an active object perspective, a concurrency model that decouples communication from synchronization. This makes control-flow of active object systems flexible and enables complex orchestration patterns which depend on the exchange of values between different active objects. Our hybrid active object model HABS, a hybrid extension of ABS, is executable, which makes the language well-suited for model simulation, yet it has a formal, compositional semantics which makes the language well-suited for verification and validation.

We discuss different solutions to the modeling of distributed cyber-physical systems which combine a HABS model with external simulators for natural systems from the perspective of both analysis, simulation and naturalness. The resulting hybrid multi-models give rise to a co-simulation problem. Our examples show that it is challenging to preserve both support for simulation and for compositional reasoning which relies on the formal language semantics of HABS. The examples allow us to observe that we profit from built-in time orchestration in HABS which facilitates composition, but that we suffer from external simulation units which reduce that value of a composition formal semantics for reasoning about the orchestration model.

Despite the challenges, we identify interface objects with formal specifications as a promising solution that may provide a reasonable compromise between flexible simulation and orchestration, and restricting on the level of control to which an external unit may subject the HABS model. The work reported in this paper points to several interesting directions for further work.

Formally Analyzable Co-Simulation. By implementing orchestrators as models in HABS that interact with the external simulation units through (possibly extended) physical blocks, we plan to study correctness properties for orchestration algorithms through formal analysis, including safety proofs for value propagation.

Formally Analyzable Digital Twins. By implementing designated interface objects, we plan to study the combination of compositional reasoning and simulation for predictive and prescriptive analysis in a digital twin setting.

References

1. Albert, E., et al.: SACO: static analyzer for concurrent objects. In: Ábrahám, E., Havelund, K. (eds.) TACAS 2014. LNCS, vol. 8413, pp. 562–567. Springer, Heidelberg (2014). https://doi.org/10.1007/978-3-642-54862-8_46
2. Alur, R., et al.: The algorithmic analysis of hybrid systems. Theor. Comput. Sci. **138**(1), 3–34 (1995)
3. Blochwitz, T., et al.: Functional mockup interface 2.0: the standard for tool independent exchange of simulation models. In: Proceedings of the 9th International Modelica Conference, pp. 173–184. The Modelica Association (2012)
4. Bocchi, L., Murgia, M., Vasconcelos, V.T., Yoshida, N.: Asynchronous timed session types. In: Caires, L. (ed.) ESOP 2019. LNCS, vol. 11423, pp. 583–610. Springer, Cham (2019). https://doi.org/10.1007/978-3-030-17184-1_21
5. Boer, F.D., et al.: A survey of active object languages. ACM Comput. Surv. **50**(5), 76:1–76:39 (2017)
6. Din, C.C., Owe, O.: Compositional reasoning about active objects with shared futures. Formal Aspects Comput. **27**(3), 551–572 (2014). https://doi.org/10.1007/s00165-014-0322-y
7. Dubslaff, C., Koopmann, P., Turhan, A.-Y.: Ontology-mediated probabilistic model checking. In: Ahrendt, W., Tapia Tarifa, S.L. (eds.) IFM 2019. LNCS, vol. 11918, pp. 194–211. Springer, Cham (2019). https://doi.org/10.1007/978-3-030-34968-4_11
8. Fitzgerald, J., Larsen, P.G., Pierce, K.: Multi-modelling and co-simulation in the engineering of cyber-physical systems: towards the digital twin. In: ter Beek, M.H., Fantechi, A., Semini, L. (eds.) From Software Engineering to Formal Methods and Tools, and Back. LNCS, vol. 11865, pp. 40–55. Springer, Cham (2019). https://doi.org/10.1007/978-3-030-30985-5_4

9. Fulton, N., Mitsch, S., Quesel, J.-D., Völp, M., Platzer, A.: KeYmaera X: an axiomatic tactical theorem prover for hybrid systems. In: Felty, A.P., Middeldorp, A. (eds.) CADE 2015. LNCS (LNAI), vol. 9195, pp. 527–538. Springer, Cham (2015). https://doi.org/10.1007/978-3-319-21401-6_36

10. Gomes, C., Lúcio, L., Vangheluwe, H.: Semantics of co-simulation algorithms with simulator contracts. In: MODELS Companion, pp. 784–789. IEEE (2019)

11. Gomes, C., Thule, C., Broman, D., Larsen, P.G., Vangheluwe, H.: Co-simulation: a survey. ACM Comput. Surv. **51**(3), 49:1–49:33 (2018)

12. Hewitt, C., Bishop, P., Steiger, R.: A universal modular ACTOR formalism for artificial intelligence. In: Proceedings of the 3rd International Joint Conference on Artificial Intelligence, IJCAI 1973, San Francisco, CA, USA, pp. 235–245. Morgan Kaufmann Publishers Inc. (1973)

13. Johnsen, E.B., Hähnle, R., Schäfer, J., Schlatte, R., Steffen, M.: ABS: a core language for abstract behavioral specification. In: Aichernig, B.K., de Boer, F.S., Bonsangue, M.M. (eds.) FMCO 2010. LNCS, vol. 6957, pp. 142–164. Springer, Heidelberg (2011). https://doi.org/10.1007/978-3-642-25271-6_8

14. Kamburjan, E.: From post-conditions to post-region invariants: deductive verification of hybrid objects. In: HSCC 2021 (2021, to appear)

15. Kamburjan, E.: Behavioral program logic. In: Cerrito, S., Popescu, A. (eds.) TABLEAUX 2019. LNCS (LNAI), vol. 11714, pp. 391–408. Springer, Cham (2019). https://doi.org/10.1007/978-3-030-29026-9_22

16. Kamburjan, E., Chen, T.-C.: Stateful behavioral types for active objects. In: Furia, C.A., Winter, K. (eds.) IFM 2018. LNCS, vol. 11023, pp. 214–235. Springer, Cham (2018). https://doi.org/10.1007/978-3-319-98938-9_13

17. Kamburjan, E., Hähnle, R., Schön, S.: Formal modeling and analysis of railway operations with active objects. Sci. Comput. Program. **166**, 167–193 (2018)

18. Kamburjan, E., Mitsch, S., Kettenbach, M., Hähnle, R.: Modeling and verifying cyber-physical systems with hybrid active objects. CoRR abs/1906.05704 (2019)

19. Kamburjan, E., Stromberg, J.: Tool support for validation of formal system models: interactive visualization and requirements traceability. In: Monahan, R., Prevosto, V., Proença, J. (eds.) Proceedings of the Fifth Workshop on Formal Integrated Development Environment, F-IDE@FM 2019, Volume 310 of EPTCS, Porto, Portugal, 7 October 2019, pp. 70–85 (2019)

20. Larsen, K.G., Pettersson, P., Yi, W.: UPPAAL in a nutshell. Int. J. Softw. Tools Technol. Transfer **1**(1–2), 134–152 (1997)

21. Lin, J., Mauro, J., Røst, T.B., Yu, I.C.: A model-based scalability optimization methodology for cloud applications. In: 2017 IEEE 7th International Symposium on Cloud and Service Computing (SC² 2017), pp. 163–170. IEEE Computer Society (2017)

22. Margaria, T., Schieweck, A.: The digital thread in industry 4.0. In: Ahrendt, W., Tapia Tarifa, S.L. (eds.) IFM 2019. LNCS, vol. 11918, pp. 3–24. Springer, Cham (2019). https://doi.org/10.1007/978-3-030-34968-4_1

23. Maxima Development Group: Maxima Manual, 5.43.0 ed. (2019). maxima.sourceforge.net

24. Platzer, A.: The complete proof theory of hybrid systems. In: LICS, pp. 541–550. IEEE (2012)

25. Platzer, A.: Logical Foundations of Cyber-Physical Systems. LNCS, Springer, Cham (2018). https://doi.org/10.1007/978-3-319-63588-0

26. Røst, T.B., Seidl, C., Yu, I.C., Damiani, F., Johnsen, E.B., Chesta, C.: HyVar. In: Mann, Z.Á., Stolz, V. (eds.) ESOCC 2017. CCIS, vol. 824, pp. 159–163. Springer, Cham (2018). https://doi.org/10.1007/978-3-319-79090-9_12

27. Schlatte, R., Johnsen, E.B., Mauro, J., Tapia Tarifa, S.L., Yu, I.C.: Release the beasts: when formal methods meet real world data. In: de Boer, F., Bonsangue, M., Rutten, J. (eds.) It's All About Coordination. LNCS, vol. 10865, pp. 107–121. Springer, Cham (2018). https://doi.org/10.1007/978-3-319-90089-6_8
28. Seshia, S.A.: New frontiers in formal methods: learning, cyber-physical systems, education, and beyond. CSI J. Comput. **2**(4), R1:3–R1:13 (2015)
29. Thule, C., Gomes, C., Deantoni, J., Larsen, P.G., Brauer, J., Vangheluwe, H.: Towards the verification of hybrid co-simulation algorithms. In: Mazzara, M., Ober, I., Salaün, G. (eds.) STAF 2018. LNCS, vol. 11176, pp. 5–20. Springer, Cham (2018). https://doi.org/10.1007/978-3-030-04771-9_1
30. Thule, C., Lausdahl, K., Gomes, C., Meisl, G., Larsen, P.G.: Maestro: the INTO-CPS co-simulation framework. Simul. Model. Pract. Theory **92**, 45–61 (2019)
31. Tveito, L., Johnsen, E.B., Schlatte, R.: Global reproducibility through local control for distributed active objects. In: FASE 2020. LNCS, vol. 12076, pp. 140–160. Springer, Cham (2020). https://doi.org/10.1007/978-3-030-45234-6_7

Towards a Digital Twin - Modelling an Agricultural Vehicle

Frederik F. Foldager[1,3](✉), Casper Thule[2], Ole Balling[1],
and Peter Gorm Larsen[2]

[1] Department of Mechanical and Production Engineering, Aarhus University,
Inge Lehmanns Gade 10, 8000 Aarhus C, Denmark
{ffo,oba}@mpe.au.dk
[2] DIGIT, Department of Electrical and Computer Engineering, Aarhus University,
Finlandsgade 22, 8200 Aarhus N, Denmark
{casper.thule,pgl}@ece.au.dk
[3] Agro Intelligence ApS, Agro Food Park 13, 8200 Aarhus N, Denmark

Abstract. In this work, we present the initial steps in the development of a digital twin of the agricultural autonomous vehicle, Robotti. A model of the vehicle dynamics is initially developed in the open-source multi-physics code, Chrono, and then wrapped as a Functional Mock-up Unit. We provide an overview of the envisioned digital twin system and a description of currently implemented features. The dynamic system of the vehicle chassis is characterised by the implementation of a revolute joint that ensures wheel–surface contact in uneven terrain. The vehicle dynamics model is applied for testing two scenarios describing the loads on the vehicle as a consequence of this mechanism. Finally, we give pointers to future work on modelling the Robotti and the establishment of a digital twin.

Keywords: Modelling and Simulation · Vehicle dynamics · Chrono · Functional mock-up interface · Digital twin · Agricultural robot · Robotti

1 Introduction

Model-based approaches are commonly applied to simulate and understand the behaviour of physical or cyber-physical systems in various fields of engineering. In this work, we describe the initial steps towards establishing a digital twin of the autonomous agricultural vehicle, Robotti (Agrointelli, Denmark).

Within the last decade, various autonomous farming robots have emerged [12], including the Robotti. It is designed for applications such as seeding, weeding and spraying. The robotic system consists of a number of main components including: navigation, steering control, safety systems, and a modular mechanical system that can be configured with different track widths and different tools can be mounted. A photo of the vehicle is shown in Fig. 1. When operating in

© Springer Nature Switzerland AG 2021
T. Margaria and B. Steffen (Eds.): ISoLA 2020, LNCS 12479, pp. 109–123, 2021.
https://doi.org/10.1007/978-3-030-83723-5_8

field conditions, the effects of terrain needs to be considered. To comply with uneven terrain, the chassis of the vehicle is designed such that the two main-modules can move independently. The left module is connected to the mainframe with a revolute joint whereas the right module and the mainframe has a fixed connection.

To obtain a digital representation of the vehicle, models of the sub-components such as the mechanical and the control systems are required. Co-simulation [11] allow for combining models of such components in simulation. Previously, co-simulations have been conducted of a simple two-dimensional version of the Robotti [9] and the steering controller [10] using the Functional Mock-up Interface 2.0 (FMI) [2] and the co-simulation engine, Maestro [23]. In this work, a three-dimensional model of the dynamics is developed and FMI-enabled by generating a Functional Mock-up Unit (FMU) of the model. The FMU will serve as one of the components leading towards a digital twin [7]. The dynamic system is modelled using the open-source multi-physics code Chrono[1] [21]. It is a mature tool for simulating dynamic systems and a suitable choice for modelling the mechanical framework of the vehicle. Chrono has support for simulating various advanced features such as soft-soil surface interaction. Such capability is particularly relevant in the future work of modelling the Robotti operating in field conditions. Additional applications of Chrono [21] count granular dynamics [16], solid–fluid interaction [15] and others. A part of this work is to produce an FMU of such model developed using Chrono.

We demonstrate a single component of the digital twin, a Chrono-based multibody dynamics and the corresponding FMU. Using the model of the mechanical system of the vehicle in three dimensions, the static and dynamic loads as a consequence of driving across an uneven surface can be computed.

Our objectives are:

(i) To develop a model in Chrono of the agricultural vehicle, Robotti and produce an FMU of the model.
(ii) To take the initial steps towards a digital twin system with FMI as the simulation interface.

The rest of this paper is structured such that Sect. 2 introduces the materials and methods used in the research presented here. Afterwards, Sect. 3 presents the results produced so far from our research. Finally, Sect. 4 discusses the results achieved and look ahead for the future work planned.

2   Materials and Methods

In the following section, the fundamentals of the Chrono-based Robotti model and its relation to a digital twin tool-chain and case study is described. Simulations using FMI will become a central part of the future work on establishing a digital twin setup of the Robotti.

---

[1] https://projectchrono.org/.

Fig. 1. Robotti performing a seeding operation. Photo credit: Agrointelli.

2.1   Functional Mockup Interface

The FMI 2.0 standard [2][2], describes how to represent a component, such that it can participate in an FMI-based simulation. The FMI standard contains both FMI for Model Exchange and Co-Simulation, where the contributions of this manuscript are restricted to the latter. A component adhering to the FMI standard is referred to as an FMU and is treated as a 'black box' in the context of a simulation, thereby supporting the separation of Intellectual Property (IP). In practical terms, an FMU implements a C-interface, offers a static description file of its interface in terms of inputs, outputs and parameters along with offered functionality, i.e. the possibility of setting and getting state and is packaged in a particular fashion. This enables a *FMI master* to set inputs, compute over simulation intervals, and get outputs from FMUs that may represent different formalisms, i.e. discrete-event or continuous-time systems. The coordination of multiple FMUs is done through an orchestration engine [23], which acts as an FMI master. Such FMI masters have not been standardised, and offer challenges in both research and practice [18]. However, there is a long list of modelling and simulation tools that are able to export their functionality as independent FMUs[3]. It is even possible to enable easy-to-produce FMUs from popular programming languages such as Python as presented in [14].

2.2   Digital Twin Tool-Chain

We envision an open platform for creating *digital twins* that integrate multi-models (digital system configurations) with data derived from CPS operations. The platform should also include inductive models learned from such operational data. The goal of our current work is to create and evaluate such a digital twin, using platforms that admit, as far as possible, open integration of a wide range of tools. FMI plays a central role as interfacing technology in the realisation of such a tool-chain, which is revisited in Sect. 4.

---

[2] http://fmi-standard.org/.
[3] https://fmi-standard.org/tools/.

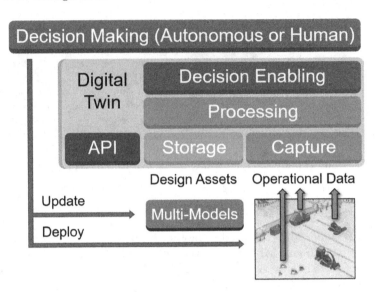

Fig. 2. Functionality of a digital twin (from [7])

Figure 2 shows the main features of a digital twin of the kind we envisage. In operation, the CPS will be interacting with the physical world and human users, generating additional data related to system commissioning, configuration or tuning from the administrator side. The twin receives data from the real CPS, and multi-models developed within design activities. It supports decision-making, either by having an autonomous supervisory system that automatically take action in case of irregularities, or having a human operator taking decisions. This may result in updates to both the operational CPS and consistent updates to multi-models. Within the digital twin, the following levels of functionality are delivered:

- **Multi-model and Data Storage** include the basic handling of multi-models covering the architecture and interaction between the operational CPS and the digital twin, recording and maintaining time series data acquired from sensors, correlating it to existing multi-models. The operational data may for example be transferred to the digital twin using a message broker as presented in [22].
- **Model and Data Processing** turns data into information. It includes static and dynamic analysis on multi-models, via a range of tools, including co-simulation and model checking. Data Analytics includes the analysis of time-series data and in particular the use of Machine Learning (ML) techniques to derive models based on the CPS 'as built', as well as incident prediction. Specific ML techniques can be selected depending on the application and data characteristics.

- **Decision Enabling** presents information to decision-makers based on the model and data processing analyses done on operational data and multi-models. This will include decision support through possibilities to carry out trials, visualisation and Design Space Exploration (DSE).
- **The API** enables interaction between the digital twin and externals, including (potentially) other digital twins.

The tooling to support the different levels outlined above are in development. Figure 3 gives an impression of the current state and is as follows: The hardware and logging of time-series data to a database (DB) are in development for a scaled replica of the realised Robotti (expanded upon in Sect. 4. The realised Robotti contains these features). Data via RabbitMQ is an off-the-shelf component[4]. An FMU capable of subscribing to such a message broker and making data available in an FMI-based co-simulation has been developed [22][5]. The FMI interface of the Robotti model has been developed as part of the work carried out in the context of this manuscript[6]. A controller FMU has been developed for other models of Robotti and is expected to be applicable to this case with minor modifications [3]. The Monitor FMU capability and methodology are under development as part of a project called AgroRobottiFleet[7]. FMI-based co-simulation is expected to be carried out with the open-source orchestration engine called Maestro [23]. Finally, an example of an open-source Digital Twin Master to connect the above-mentioned constituents of a digital twin is under development[8].

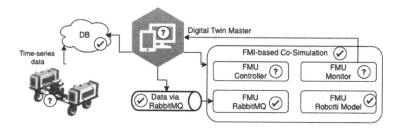

Fig. 3. Digital Twin functionality realised (checkmark) and in development (question-mark)

2.3   The Robotti Model

The Robotti is compatible with existing and third-party tools through a standard three-point linkage positioned on the centre frame. Two modules carry

---

[4] Available at https://www.rabbitmq.com/, visited December 14, 2020.

[5] Available at https://github.com/INTO-CPS-Association/fmu-rabbitmq, visited December 14, 2020.

[6] Available at https://gitlab.au.dk/software-engineering/chronofmu_isola along with a demonstration, visited January 7, 2021.

[7] See https://projects.au.dk/agrorobottifleet/, visited December 14, 2020.

[8] One such tool is being developed at the Centre for Digital Twins of Aarhus University: https://digit.au.dk/centre-for-digital-twins/, visited December 14, 2020.

the propulsion engines and additional hardware. The Robotti can be configured with different track widths up to 3.5 m. The configurations of different tools and widths add up to a number of scenarios that affect the dynamic and static loads on the vehicle which are important both in the design and during operation. Two scenarios are presented. Using a three-dimensional multi-body dynamics model of the vehicle, the forces in the system can be computed. The model is developed using Chrono [4].

The model consists of 13 bodies and 12 constraints including four driving constraints. A sketch of the model abstraction is shown in Fig. 4. The bodies are: four wheels (a-d), four wheel fixtures (e-h), a centre frame (i), two main modules (j-k), a three-point linkage (l) and a payload (m). Four kinematic drivers are applied as motors positioned at the wheels for imposing kinematic propulsion. Two drivers are implemented for steering the front wheels. The model is constrained such that only the revolute joint (Joint A in Fig. 4) is free to move. Masses and inertia are estimated based on a 3D CAD representation of the individual bodies. The static wheel loads of the unloaded machine are verified by weighing the actual vehicle. The simulations are conducted using undeformable solid surface and tyres. An FMU is generated of the model with an interface as shown in Fig. 5. The inputs to the model configuration are the track width of the Robotti, payload of the tool and steering properties. The outputs are time series of wheel normal loads, the joint forces, positions and orientation. All constraint forces, constraint torques and contact forces are available in the model.

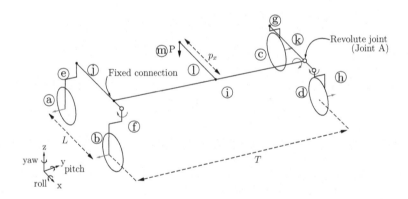

Fig. 4. Illustration of the Robotti model, bodies and joints. T is track width, L is the wheelbase and P is payload. Green arrows indicate hydraulic motors for propulsion. Dots (•) indicate fixed joints and circles (○) indicate revolute joints. (Color figure online)

The mechanical configuration affects the dynamic and static loads on the vehicle which are examined in two scenarios. A test-track is included in the model for inducing roll motion and hereby relative motion in the revolute joint. The track is designed to induce both positive and negative roll of the vehicle.

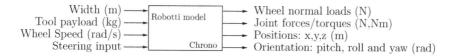

Fig. 5. Model interface.

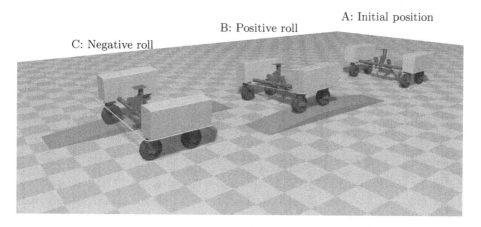

Fig. 6. Visualisation of the simulated Robotti driving from (A) to (C) across the test track. (A) is the initial position. Position (B) corresponds to the maximum negative roll. Position (C) corresponds to maximum positive roll motion. The green box illustrate the payload. (Color figure online)

A visualisation of the simulated vehicle on the track is shown in Fig. 6. To compensate for lateral motion, a simple controller is implemented to maintain the orientation of the vehicle.

3   Results

The kinematic and dynamic effects of the terrain-following mechanism are examined in two scenarios. Initially, we describe the effects of configuring the Robotti with different track widths. Secondly the effects of loading and unloading are described.

3.1   Scenario 1: Changing Track Width

The first scenario examine how the pitch, roll, and yaw motion of the vehicle are affected when changing track width T of the Robotti. By changing the width, the mass and inertia of the body describing the centre frame are adjusted accordingly.

Two simulations are conducted to investigate the kinematic response to changing the track width of the vehicle using the minimum and maximum possible track widths, 1.25 m and 3.5 m respectively. The pitch, roll and yaw are computed during the simulation at the three-point linkage as the result of passing across the track as shown in Fig. 6. The vehicle initiate at point A and passes through points B and C.

By reducing the width of the vehicle, the roll angle increased consequently as shown in Fig. 7. Similar results could have been obtained by simple kinematics. However, using the dynamics model we can examine the response of complex topographical surfaces as a function of time. Additionally, it is observed that the pitch of the three-point linkage is only introduced in the case of negative roll for both the wide and narrow configuration. This is an effect of the rotational joint on the centre frame.

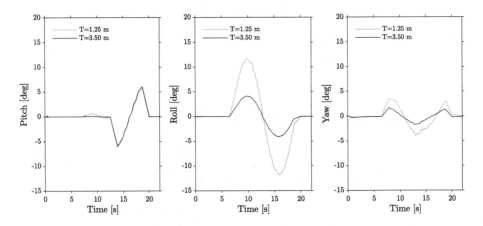

Fig. 7. Pitch, roll and yaw characteristics at the minimum and maximum track width T.

The pitch angle is relevant to compute since this affects the distance between the tool and the surface for lift mounted applications. Such kinematic considerations become increasingly important in applications of precision agriculture.

3.2   Scenario 2: Loading the Three-Point Linkage

In the second scenario, a static load, P, is introduced in the model correspondingly to the load of a carried tool e.g. a sprayer. In this example, the load is applied at a distance $p_x = 1$ m from the centre frame.

The revolute joint at the centre frame changes the normal loads on the wheels when loaded. The load shift is caused by the moment generated by the payload which can only be obtained through the fixed connection between the centre frame and the right module. Contrary to the fixed connection, the revolute joint can only obtain forces in x and z directions and no moment. The normal loads on the wheels are coupled to the ability to generate the lateral and longitudinal forces on the wheel-surface interface needed to manoeuvre the vehicle in both on-road and off-road applications.

A simulation of the Robotti in a static scenario is conducted. The vehicle is positioned stationary on a horizontal surface and at steady state, the contact forces on the wheels are monitored and interpreted as the static normal loads. To evaluate the influence of the revolute joint on the centre-frame, the vertical point load P is increased. We normalised the normal loads N by the mean wheel normal load at $P = 0$ kg using Eq. (1). In Fig. 8, the normalised loads n on each wheel k are shown as a function of increasing P.

$$n_k(P) = \frac{N_k(P)}{\sum_{k=1}^{4}(N_k(P=0))/4} \tag{1}$$

The subscript k represent each wheel: front left wheel, front right wheel, rear left wheel, and rear right wheel. N is the simulated normal load at each wheel and n is the normalised value.

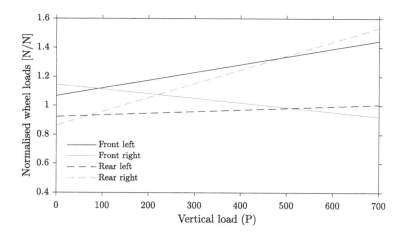

Fig. 8. Normalized wheel loads at $p_x = 1$ m from the centre frame.

By loading the vehicle at the three-point linkage changes the load distribution. The load shifts from the right front wheel to the right rear wheel and will consequently increase with the weight of the tool. However, in an unloaded situation ($P = 0$), the normal loads are close to evenly distributed. The wheel loads are important to the steering and driving performance of the vehicle. The model can be applied to investigate how a given tool or payload at a given track width configuration will affect the loads and the overall performance of the vehicle.

In a moving scenario, e.g. driving across an uneven field or in this case the test track, the contact forces on each body and the constraint forces/torques in each link are computed. By simulating the dynamic system, such values become available as a consequence of the dynamic loads from both the applied tool and the configuration of the machine.

4   Discussion and Future Work

Using the dynamics model of the Robotti, the static effects of loading the vehicle is computed. A load shift from the front right wheel to the rear right wheel is identified. However, by recognising this effect it can be compensated for in the design and operation. Similarly, a load shift would also appear on a conventional tractor by vertically loading the three-point hitch behind the rear wheels. The distribution of normal load and stress is not only a relevant topic in understanding the mobility of a vehicle but also important to the soil function and for minimising the risk of compaction [6].

The pitch, roll and yaw-response corresponding to driving across a test track are computed. Such considerations become important in applications where the distance to the ground is of importance since a pitch of the three point link will impact the distance and angle to the ground of a given tool. Such applications include camera-based detection of plants [19] or LiDAR-based soil surface detection [8]. Using co-simulation of FMUs that describe such tools or sensors combined with the Robotti FMU could elaborate on effects of the interaction between the tool and the robot.

An FMU is generated of the dynamics model to be compatible with the digital twin tool chain. However, Chrono has already interfaces to MATLAB, Simulink (MathWorks, Massachusetts, USA) and a Python-based module PyChrono [1] that alternatively could have been applied for the integration with the digital twin tool chain. FMI-enabling Chrono models allow for taking advantage of both the 3D dynamics capabilities in Chrono and the co-simulation capabilities through FMI-related tools. By wrapping the model in an FMU, we can co-simulate our physics-based models with e.g. controllers developed in dedicated tools such as 20sim (Controllab Products, The Netherlands) or in the VDM-RT notation [24].

There are several future activities related to modelling the Robotti. Especially the machine–soil interaction and modelling the control system for future fleet operations are relevant. Using the model, alternative solutions to the surface contact mechanisms or suspension systems can be examined. Furthermore, the results presented here are purely based on simulations. Experimental calibration and validation are needed in future studies. Calibration and validation of the model can be conducted using different methods depending on the scope.

To evaluate the driving performance, a model of the propulsion system needs to be calibrated via dedicated tests to relate driving torque wheel speed and hydraulic pressure in the system. Also the steering controller can be calibrated by performing a series of tests to match the measured and modelled response [3].

4.1   Soil–Machine Interaction

In the current model of the Robotti, the tyres and the surface are rigid. However, a future task involves modelling the performance in soft soil conditions. Chrono already has support for simulating soft soil using the Soil Contact Model (SCM)

[20]. The SCM is semi-empirical and based on inputs that relates the contact patch pressure and deformation of the soil. The SCM origins in the classical terramechanics by [25] and [13].

A so-called *drawbar pull test* can be conducted to quantify the performance in off road conditions by measuring corresponding values of pulling force, wheel torques and slip. Such considerations are often applied to research the mobility of off-road applications. Another relevant method for including soft soil is the use of the discrete element method (DEM) [5] where the soil is composed of distinct, often spherical, bodies that interact via friction and adhesion. The DEM is an appealing approach in agricultural research since it allows for simulating soil disturbance and reaction forces [17]. However, the results obtained using the DEM comes with a high computational cost. We intend to apply these capabilities within agricultural research to better understand the soil–machine interaction and predict the performance of the Robotti under different soil conditions.

4.2   Co-simulation and Digital Twins

The FMI is the main simulation interface of the envisioned co-simulation and digital-twin system. Thus, several tools have been/are being developed with FMI as an underlying technology, some of which are mentioned next.

So far, we have carried out initial tests in which we have aligned a physical twin with co-simulation inside a digital twin where the live data is streamed from the physical twin. For the streaming technologies, we wish to use a number of different alternatives. Currently, we have FMI-enabled a message queuing technology using the open-source message broker software RabbitMQ [22]. Additionally, research is ongoing into self-adaptive systems, also related to the Robotti, where [14] considers a self-adapting tracking model to match the trajectory of a 2D reference model (mentioned in Sect. 1). The self-adaption was carried out when the discrepancy between the models has reached a certain point, at which a re-calibration of the tracking model is issued. This research also uses FMI as the simulation interface. An ongoing research topic surrounds how to best approximate a global state at a specific point in time as sensor data arrives at different points in time. The use of Kalman filtering in conjunction with the tracking model mentioned above if currently under analysis.

We also expect that it will be necessary to have an additional layer to the INTO-CPS Application, which acts as a user interface to our co-simulation efforts, such that it enables users of the digital twin to define precisely what discrepancies can be tolerated between the values measured from the physical twin and the corresponding predictions made by the co-simulation inside the digital twin before raising the issue to a higher-level or a human [26].

4.3   Desktop-Version of Robotti

The next phase of agricultural robotics contains fleets of robots and control that can handle multiple cooperating units in a single field. Future research related to this topic will be conducted through a project called AgroRobottiFleet. In order

Fig. 9. Photo of the *Desktop-Robotti*. Dimensions: $0.7\,\mathrm{m} \times 0.4\,\mathrm{m} \times 0.2\,\mathrm{m}$ (w × l × h). (Photo: Søren Bak, Agrointelli)

to research and develop both digital twin systems and the fleet control management system, a light-weight scaled version of the Robotti called *Desktop-Robotti* is developed to accommodate indoor tests. The dynamics model presented here is parameterised such that a corresponding model of the Desktop-Robotti can be configured. A photo of the Desktop-Robotti is shown in Fig. 9. It is equipped with sensors and actuators such that it can function as the physical version of the Robotti in related digital twin case studies. Furthermore, an indoor positioning system capable of detecting the position of the Desktop-Robotti is in development. Two contemplated case studies are a part of the future work on the Desktop-Robotti:

1. The Desktop-Robotti manoeuvres around an untested, yet predefined path. The steering-controller does not perform satisfactorily for the task. To identify the updates needed to make the Desktop-Robotti capable of manoeuvring around the path, the digital representation within the digital twin is aligned to exhibit the same behaviour as the physical twin. At this stage, the steering-controller within the digital twin is updated to accommodate the desired trajectory. Once this is achieved, the steering-controller of the Desktop-Robotti is updated similarly, and the motion of the physical twin is verified.
2. The Desktop-Robotti manoeuvres around a predefined path, yet a monitor detects discrepancies between the behaviour of the Desktop-Robotti and the Robotti within the digital twin. In an attempt to identify the cause of the discrepancy, the digital twin is subjected to a number of co-simulation scenarios. One of these scenarios match the trajectory of the physical Desktop-Robotti and a possible cause is identified.

4.4   Concluding Remarks

In this work, the current state of model-developments concerning the agricultural vehicle Robotti is presented. A model of the 3D dynamics is constructed in Chrono and enabled in the context of FMI 2.0 for co-simulation. Based on the simulation results, we were able to (i) compute the normal loads as a consequence of loading the vehicle, and (ii) compute the resulting pitch, roll, and yaw response as a consequence of driving across a virtual test track designed to induce motion in the revolute joint. We presented two digital twin-related case studies that employ the Robotti model and a related physical realisation called Desktop-Robotti along with an overview of the current status of the digital twin support.

Acknowledgments. This research was supported by the Innovation Fund Denmark under grant number 7038-00231B. We acknowledge the European Union for funding the INTO-CPS project (Grant Agreement 644047), which developed the open tool chain and the INTO-CPS Application; the Poul Due Jensen Foundation that funded subsequent work on taking this forward towards the engineering of digital twins; and the European Union for funding the HUBCAP project (Grant Agreement 872698). The authors would like to acknowledge the developers of Project Chrono. We would also like to acknowledge Zachary Gasick from the University of Wisconsin for inputs to the Chrono model. And finally a great thanks to Prof. Dan Negrut and Dr. Radu Serban from University of Wisconsin for valuable discussions and inputs.

References

1. Benatti, S., Tasora, A., Fusai, D., Mangoni, D.: A modular simulation platform for training robots via deep reinforcement learning and multibody dynamics. In: ACM International Conference Proceeding Series (2019). https://doi.org/10.1145/3365265.3365274
2. Blochwitz, T., et al.: Functional mockup Interface 2.0: the standard for tool independent exchange of simulation models. In: 9th International Modelica Conference, Munich, Germany, pp. 173–184. Linköping University Electronic Press, November 2012. https://doi.org/10.3384/ecp12076173
3. Bogomolov, S., et al.: Tuning Robotti: the machine-assisted exploration of parameter spaces in multi-models of a cyber-physical system. In: Oda, T., Fitzgerald, J. (eds.) 18th Overture Workshop, 7 December 2020 (online) (2020)
4. Chrono: An open source framework for the physics-based simulation of dynamic systems (2020). https://projectchrono.org. Accessed 25 June 2020
5. Cundall, P.A., Strack, O.D.L.: A discrete numerical model for granular assemblies. Géotechnique **29**(1), 47–65 (1979)
6. ten Damme, L., et al.: Construction of modern wide, low-inflation pressure tyres per se does not affect soil stress. Soil Tillage Res. **204**, 104708 (2020). https://doi.org/10.1016/j.still.2020.104708
7. Fitzgerald, J., Larsen, P.G., Pierce, K.: Multi-modelling and co-simulation in the engineering of cyber-physical systems: towards the digital twin. In: ter Beek, M.H., Fantechi, A., Semini, L. (eds.) From Software Engineering to Formal Methods and Tools, and Back. LNCS, vol. 11865, pp. 40–55. Springer, Cham (2019). https://doi.org/10.1007/978-3-030-30985-5_4

8. Foldager, F., Pedersen, J., Skov, E., Evgrafova, A., Green, O.: Lidar-based 3D scans of soil surfaces and furrows in two soil types. Sensors (Switzerland) **19**(3), 34 (2019). https://doi.org/10.3390/s19030661

9. Foldager, F.F., Balling, O., Gamble, C., Larsen, P.G., Boel, M., Green, O.: Design space exploration in the development of agricultural robots. In: Proceedings of the AgEng2018 Conference (2018)

10. Foldager, F.F., Larsen, P.G., Green, O.: Development of a driverless lawn mower using co-simulation. In: Cerone, A., Roveri, M. (eds.) SEFM 2017. LNCS, vol. 10729, pp. 330–344. Springer, Cham (2018). https://doi.org/10.1007/978-3-319-74781-1_23

11. Gomes, C., Thule, C., Broman, D., Larsen, P.G., Vangheluwe, H.: Co-simulation: a survey. ACM Comput. Surv. **51**(3), 49:1–49:33 (2018)

12. Grimstad, L., From, P.J.: The Thorvald II agricultural robotic system. Robotics **6**(4), 45 (2017). https://doi.org/10.3390/robotics6040024,http://www.mdpi.com/2218-6581/6/4/24

13. Janosi, Z., Hanamoto, B.: The analytical determination of drawbar pull as a function of slip for tracked vehicles in deformable soils. In: Proceedings of 1st International Conference of ISTVS, Turin (1961)

14. Legaard, C.M., Gomes, C., Larsen, P.G., Foldager, F.F.: Rapid prototyping of self-adaptive-systems using Python functional mockup units. In: SummerSim 2020. ACM, New York, NY, USA (2020)

15. Rakhsha, M., Pazouki, A., Serban, R., Negrut, D.: Using a half-implicit integration scheme for the SPH-based solution of fluid-solid interaction problems. Comput. Methods Appl. Mech. Eng. **345**, 100–122 (2019)

16. Recuero, A., Serban, R., Peterson, B., Sugiyama, H., Jayakumar, P., Negrut, D.: A high-fidelity approach for vehicle mobility simulation: nonlinear finite element tires operating on granular material. J. Terramechanics **72**, 39–54 (2017). https://doi.org/10.1016/j.jterra.2017.04.002

17. Saunders, C., Ucgul, M., Godwin, R.J.: Discrete element method (DEM) simulation to improve performance of a mouldboard skimmer. Soil Tillage Res. **205**, 104764 (2021). https://doi.org/10.1016/j.still.2020.104764

18. Schweiger, G., et al.: Functional mock-up interface: an empirical survey identifies research challenges and current barriers. In: The American Modelica Conference, Cambridge, MA, USA (2018)

19. Skovsen, S., et al.: Estimation of the botanical composition of clover-grass leys from RGB images using data simulation and fully convolutional neural networks. Sensors (Switzerland) **17**(12), 56 (2017). https://doi.org/10.3390/s17122930

20. Tasora, A., Mangoni, D., Negrut, D., Serban, R., Jayakumar, P.: Deformable soil with adaptive level of detail for tracked and wheeled vehicles **5**(1), 60–76 (2019). https://doi.org/10.1504/IJVP.2019.097098

21. Tasora, A., et al.: Chrono: an open source multi-physics dynamics engine. In: Kozubek, T., Blaheta, R., Šístek, J., Rozložník, M., Čermák, M. (eds.) HPCSE 2015. LNCS, vol. 9611, pp. 19–49. Springer, Cham (2016). https://doi.org/10.1007/978-3-319-40361-8_2

22. Thule, C., Gomes, C., Lausdahl, K.G.: Formally Verified FMI Enabled External Data Broker: Rabbitmq FMU. Society for Computer Simulation International, San Diego (2020)

23. Thule, C., Lausdahl, K., Gomes, C., Meisl, G., Larsen, P.G.: Maestro: the INTO-CPS co-simulation framework. Simul. Model. Pract. Theory **92**, 45–61 (2019)

24. Verhoef, M., Larsen, P.G.: Enhancing VDM++ for Modeling Distributed Embedded Real-time Systems. Technical Report (to appear), Radboud University Nijmegen, a preliminary version of this report, (March 2006). https://www.cs.ru.nl/marcelv/vdm/

25. Wong, J.Y., Reece, A.R.: Prediction of rigid wheel performance based on the analysis of soil-wheel stresses: part II. Performance of towed rigid wheels. J. Terramechanics 4(2), 7–25 (1967)

26. Woodcock, J., Gomes, C., Macedo, H.D., Larsen, P.G.: Uncertainty quantification and runtime monitoring using environment-aware digital twins. In: Isola 2021 (2021)

Digital Modelling in the Railways

Thierry Lecomte[(⊠)]

ClearSy, 320 avenue Archimède, Aix en Provence, France
thierry.lecomte@clearsy.com

Abstract. The railways have a quite long modelling history, covering many technical aspects from infrastructure to rolling stock, train movement, maintenance, etc. These models are mostly separate and operated independently by various stakeholders and with diverse objectives. This article presents some of the various digital modelling activities, including formal ones, that are undertaken by the railway industry, for design, development, validation, qualification, and exploitation. It also introduces trends toward regrouping models to obtain more significant results together with a larger scope, prefiguring digital twins.

Keywords: Railways · Digital modelling · Formal methods

1 Introduction

Modelling activities are central to the railways, mainly in the form of separate models of diverse natures. Very early in a development, train manufacturers and operators need to assess and verify that a metro line or a main line will fulfil expectations in term of performance, number of passengers transported, operation costs, power consumed, etc. Most of these models (data and related tooling) are often developed to cover one verification activity, for historical reasons, for regulation reasons (qualification model should be independent from design model), for organisational/political reasons (different services of a same company prefer to develop their own solution), or for technical reasons (models reconciliation/connection requires excessive investment). Initiating a new product line is a good occasion to initiate a new model, distinct from the existing ones, and to contribute to increase their population. Of course, the situation depends on the company developing/operating trains but it is common trend observed during the last decades. However, with the increasing complexity of the systems developed and the competition on the railway market, modelling is going global, including more aspects to obtain more effective results.

Based on a non-exhaustive picture of the use of models for the trains/metros manufacture and operation, this article tentatively outlines what could be the integration of the digital twin concept in the railways. It presents some of the current digital modelling activities, including formal ones, that are undertaken by the railway industry, for design, development, validation, qualification, and

T. Margaria and B. Steffen (Eds.): ISoLA 2020, LNCS 12479, pp. 124–139, 2021.
https://doi.org/10.1007/978-3-030-83723-5_9

exploitation. It also introduces trends toward regrouping models to obtain more significant results together with a larger scope, prefiguring digital twins.

This paper is structured in 6 parts. Section 2 introduces the terminology. Section 3 presents how the infrastructure is modelled. Modelling safety is exposed in Sect. 4. Section 5 presents some new modelling directions in relation with emerging paradigms. Section 6 sketches some pros and cons arguments concerning the adoption of the digital twin concept in the railways before concluding.

2   Terminology

This section contains specific definitions, concepts, and abbreviations used throughout this paper.

Formal methods refers to mathematically rigorous techniques for the specification, development and verification of software and hardware systems. [9] identifies a collection of formal methods and tools to be applied in railways.

PLC put for programmable logic controller [21], is an industrial digital computer which has been ruggedized and adapted for the control of any activity that requires high reliability control and ease of programming and process fault diagnosis.

Safety refers to the control of recognised hazards in order to achieve an acceptable level of risk.

Reliability is the ability of a system to perform its required functions under stated conditions for a specified time.

3   Modelling Infrastructure

This section introduces some important notions about the railway elements subject to modelling.

3.1   Categories

Railways are divided into two main areas: metro lines and main lines. Below is a summary of the main differences between the two kinds:

– **metro lines**: installed in and around cities, the lines are tens of kilometres long. Except if the line is circular, trains are operated on a carousel: when they reach the end of a line (forward movement), they fallback using another set of rails associated to the back movement. Metro stations are usually close to the next one (around 500 m in Paris): the train spends the same time in station and travelling between stations. The interval between trains is a key performance factor: at rush hour, when a train leaves a platform, another one is going to enter. Only trains from a line are operated on this line, even if the number of trains is likely to vary to match passengers flow. One signalling system is installed on board and on the tracks. The train order is fixed as all trains stop to all successive stations.

– **main lines**: they cover large areas, possibly several countries. Lines are up to thousands of kilometres long. Trains move from point A to point B, with zero/some stops/all stops. Trains may gain/lose cars in station. Additional trains may be injected in the flow, coming from other countries/operated by different companies. Signalling systems change when crossing national borders.

3.2 Rails

Rails are common equipment among metros and main lines. As such they are first class citizens: they are the first elements modelled in a project. The network is called scheme plan or track plan (Fig. 1). These plans contain mainly:

– rails or tracks, made of connected circuits,
– switches, to guide the train from one track to another,
– optical signals, that display instruction or warning to the driver,
– balises/beacons: signals could be duplicated/replaced by electronic equipment in case of (partial) automation.
– axle counters, track circuits to detect the presence of a train,
– interlocking,
– rail crossings.

Modelling items have attributes like position, length, gradient (slope), maximum speed.

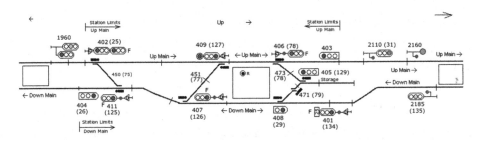

Fig. 1. Scheme plan of the Taita metro station, New Zealand.

Many track plan editor tools are available. Some examples are given below. They are either developed by:

– train manufacturers (SIGART by Alstom, TMDS by Wabtec),
– software/services companies (ERSA traffic simulator, iFrank by iRFP, Ferrovia by CGS Labs, Anylogic, Track Editor Tool by SA Transurb, OpenRail by Bentley, OpenTrack),
– or universities (SafeCap by University of Newcastle).

These tools have specific GUIs with different graphical representations. For data persistence/exchange, they rely on either:

- RailML [5]: based on XML to describe tracks and signalling equipment, timetables, vehicles (rolling stock) and signalling routes (interlocking),
- RailTopoModel [13]: promoted by the International Union of Railways, is a systemic, general, standard model for describing the topology-based railway infrastructure, able to take into account many non-standard descriptions needed for addressing specific needs.

Other proprietary formats (mostly closed specification) are also available like Siemens Infrastructure Format, Infraspeed Infrastructure Format, Bentley Rail Track, or OpenTrack.

The modelling of the tracks and related equipment is central as it provides a basis for forthcoming engineering activities. An overall system deployment is in five steps:

- capture of the railway environment and infrastructure,
- develop railway infrastructure data and generate track plan,
- prepare and compile data necessary for configuration of equipment (beacons, telecommunication, PLCs, interlocking, etc.),
- validation of data by check or automatic methods (Sect. 4.3),
- validation by simulation including train environment.

The drawing of the track and the positioning of the equipment have to comply with rules (issued from the train manufacturer, from the train operator, and from regulations). Engineering also includes the design of the technical rooms (where equipment is installed), the cable layout and its estimated length.

3.3 Dynamics

Modelling the rails and related equipment provides a static view of the network. The dynamic view is obtained with:

- **a model of the driver.** The driver is able to accelerate, decelerate, and brake (as well as open and close doors). The driving behaviour has to be somehow optimal by complying with several, sometimes antagonist, requirements:
  - the time to travel from one station to another has to be minimal,
  - the train speed has to be lower than speed limits,
  - the train speed has to be lower than its braking curve, taking into account the minimum train braking capability,
  - train acceleration/deceleration has to be kept within bounds, ensuring a comfortable travel to passengers.
  Such an acceleration profile is given in Fig. 2.
- **a model of the train.** Reacting to the acceleration/braking of the driver, this model includes technical characteristics like tractive effort/speed diagrams, load, length, adhesion factor, and power systems. It also takes into account track gradients (Fig. 3) that make the computation of the train dynamics more complicated [2]:

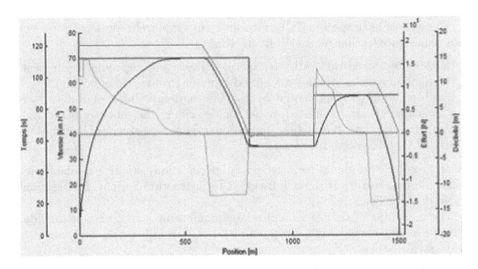

Fig. 2. An example of speed profile. X axis represents the train position, red curve is breaking curve, blue curve is speed limit, black curve is train speed, beige curve is train acceleration. (Color figure online)

- positive gradient slows down the train and reduces travel performances,
- negative gradient has to be taken into account for the safety braking curves in relation with the minimal braking capabilities,
- bathtub curve gradient combines both effects. In case of a train at standstill in such a place, an oscillation movement could be observed.

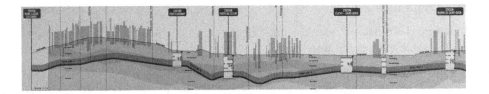

Fig. 3. Paris Metro line 14 tunnel depth.

The wheel-rail interface is also a complex domain to model [1,15]. Wheel slipping occurs when tractive effort exceeds adhesive weight whereas sliding occurs when braking effort exceeds adhesive weight. In both the situations, it is the adhesive weight playing the most important role. When tractive effort is more than adhesive weight, difference in power accelerates the wheel which results into grinding action on the rail. In the similar manner, when braking effort exceeds the adhesive weight, extra braking force prevents its rotation but with continuation of linear motion which results rubbing of wheel at one location on the circumference and called development of wheel flat.

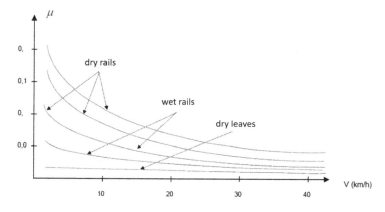

Fig. 4. Maximum actionable adhesion in function of speed and rail state.

Both these conditions create unsafe situation. Weather and environmental conditions, including dry leaves, play a vital role in reducing adhesion. Slipping and sliding have a dramatic impact on the safety:

- braking distances may be greater than expected, leading to a potential collision with a train.
- train position is deduced from a number of inputs sources (beacons, odometer, GPS). In a tunnel, the position between two beacons is estimated with the rotation of the wheels - sliding may bias the precision of the position and lead to a collision if the train is ahead of its estimated position.

Many other aspects, not listed here, have an impact on the behaviour of the train. For example, strong wind (Mistral wind in Provence) implies a speed restriction because of important windward grip (strong side wind may lead to train rollover [18]).

3.4 Timetables

With several trains being operated on a line, a timetable specifies where each train is located at given times over a certain period and is often presented as a graphical space-time diagram (Fig. 5). That the timetable is feasible means that it should be free of conflicts between trains and satisfy certain functional constraints given by the railway system, such as the track capacity resulting from the physical infrastructure and the signalling system.

The timetable stores information for each train at each station, including arrival and departure times, minimal stop time, and connections to other trains. It can be computed from the static model (routes) and from the dynamic model.

Simulation tools (like OpenTrack or SafeCap) could be used to evaluate timetables by introducing random delays. Predefined trains run according to the timetable on a railway network. During the simulation, train movements are calculated under the constraints of the signalling system and timetable.

Traffic is:

- cyclic (or not): all train services are operated with some fixed interval time
- homogeneous (or not): trains have the same profile (speed, running time, stop patterns).
- passengers traffic or freight traffic or mixed.

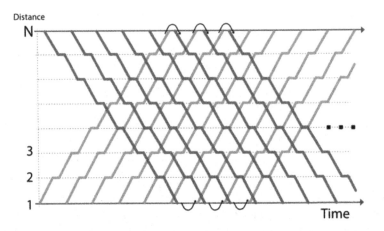

Fig. 5. Diagram of a single route timetable [20]

After a simulation run, train graphs, occupation diagrams and statistics are used for assessment. In particular, the headway between two successive trains is used to identify critical block sections. Simulation may be used to:

- compute real-time optimum strategies for traffic flow,
- explore the design space by modifying the track plan and the signalling parameters,
- minimise energy usage: when employing rheostatic braking, a train could provide energy to the network that could be used by another close accelerating train.

In [8], the automation of a large part of the ETCS rail track planning process is addressed by the algorithmic sequencing of formalized planning rules based on the knowledge and some best practices obtained from experienced track planners.

Simulation may also be used to assess compliance to standards. For example, the ERSA traffic simulator implements the ERTMS principles[1] that are explained in 700 pages (Fig. 6).

---

[1] https://www.era.europa.eu/content/set-specifications-3-etc.s-b3-r2-gsm-r-b1_en.

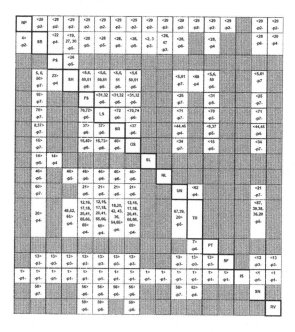

Fig. 6. Transitions between ERTMS driving modes (matrix 17 × 17 !). White cells represent conditions and priorities for feasible transitions. Priorities enable avoiding conflict between simultaneously actionable transitions.

4   Modelling Safety

Models are also developed and used to ensure safety.

4.1   Automatic Pilot - Braking

The automatic train protection (ATP for the metro) is a system on-board the train which continually checks that the speed of a train is compatible with the permitted speed allowed by signalling, including automatic stop at certain signal aspects.

If it is not, ATP activates an emergency brake to stop the train. The braking curve is calculated based on the track topology (including gradient), the distance to go to the next red signal (including a safety margin), the guaranteed train braking capability and the estimated train localisation (Sect. 3.3).

Around 30% of the automatic metros ATP specification are modelled with the B language (Fig. 7). Their implementation are proved [3] to be correct refinements (no contradiction wrt specification). The model is huge, representing more than 50,000 lines of specification. The overall model requires to mathematically demonstrate 23,000 proof obligations to ensure its correctness.

```
variables : (types &
    properties &
    properties_train &

(loc_trainLocated = TRUE =>
    0 <= loc_locationUncertainty
    & kine_kineInvalid = FALSE
    & loc_train_track /= {}
    & first(loc_train_track) = loc_ext2Block |-> oppositeDirection(loc_ext2Dir)
    & !ii.(ii : 1..size(loc_train_track)-1 => loc_train_track(ii) : dom(sidb_nextBlock))
    & !ii.(ii : 1..size(loc_train_track)-1 => sidb_nextBlock (loc_train_track(ii)) = loc_
    & #aa.(aa : 1..size(loc_train_track) & prj1(t_block,t_direction)(loc_train_track(aa))

    & loc_rearBlock = { c_cabin1 |-> loc_ext2Block, c_cabin2 |-> loc_ext1Block, c_none |-
    & (loc_rearBlock = c_block_init
        =>loc_rearDir=c_up)
    & ( not (loc_rearBlock = c_block_init)
        => loc_rearDir   = { c_cabin1 |-> oppositeDirection(loc_ext2Dir), c_cabin2 |-> c
    & loc_rearAbs    = { c_cabin1 |-> loc_ext2Abs, c_cabin2 |-> loc_ext1Abs, c_none |-> 0
    & loc_frontBlock = { c_cabin1 |-> loc_ext1Block, c_cabin2 |-> loc_ext2Block, c_none |
    & loc_frontDir   = { c_cabin1 |-> loc_ext1Dir, c_cabin2 |-> loc_ext2Dir, c_none |-> c
    & loc_frontAbs   = { c_cabin1 |-> loc_ext1Abs, c_cabin2 |-> loc_ext2Abs, c_none |-> s
    ))
```

Fig. 7. Top-level specification of an ATP main loop (excerpt) written in B. For each cycle, the software has to verify all conditions to either enable a permissive behaviour or stop the train.

4.2   Estimating Maintenance Periods

The rail integrity is a critical subject for train control as well as for maintenance strategies. Over all the possible rail flaws, a broken rail is obviously the most sensitive point. Typically, flaws are detected with special ultrasound monitoring trains and with unusual noise reports from drivers.

Two facts have a strong influence on the availability and safety of the railway system:

– the occurrence of critical defects of infrastructure subsystems,
– false alarms for instance triggered by monitoring devices designed for the defect detection.

For these two points, the railway operators need a degradation model of the rail and, as accurate as possible, an estimated rate of good detection of defects by their measuring devices. Then, various maintenance strategies can be simulated and their impact on the broken rail monitoring process can be completely estimated. In [4], dynamic Bayesian networks theory are introduced for the rail degradation and for the broken rail monitoring process model. The objective is keep (or improve) the ability to detect flaws when automating metros (the driver's feedback is not available anymore).

4.3   Formal Data Validation

Data validation consists in the verification and validation of the static data (Sect. 3.2) against railways signalling rules (that are specific to every country or even each company in a single country), on rolling stock features (constant or variable train size or configuration) and operating conditions. By data validation, we mean the validation of the parameters (i.e. constants) that determine a specific behaviour of a software/system over a wide range of possible sets of values. Microsoft Excel defines data validation in terms of type checking: a cell may contain a date, an integer, a string or a floating point number. In our case, the data to validate are not only scalar but also represent more complex structures like graphs. A metro line is seen as a graph, made of connected tracks with distributed signals and switches implementing signalling rules. Graphs are encoded through a large number of tables.

```
FOR
        sig
WHERE
        sig : sys_sud_er::Signal &
        sig : dom(sys_sud_er::Signal__dptId) &
        sig : dom(ic::sys_sud_er::signal_geopoint) &
        ic::sys_sud_er::signal_geopoint(sig) : ic::sys_sud_er::zone_GPZone
(sys_sud_er::IXL_Core__singleZone(ixl))
THEN
        VERIFY
                sys_sud_er::Signal__dptId(sig) : ran(sys_sud_er::IXL_Core__signal(ixl))
        MESSAGE
                «The signal %1 belongs to IXL_Core %2 territory but is not referenced
                among its signals.»
                ARG sys_sud_er::Signal__name(sig) TYPE STRING
                ARG sys_sud_er::IXL_Core__name(ixl) TYPE STRING
        ENDVERIFY
ENDFOR
```

Fig. 8. Example of verification rule. Signals belonging to an interlocking territory are searched (clause WHERE); such signals have to be linked to this interlocking (clause VERIFY). If not, an error message is displayed for each faulty signal found (clause MESSAGE).

Formal data validation consists in:

- formalising the verification rules,
- formally proving that the data to verify comply with the formal rules.

In [14], rules are formalised with the B language (Fig. 8) and the proof is performed with the ProB model checker. Formal data validation has been applied to complete metro lines/main lines interlocking systems, demonstrating its applicability to large systems. In [17], configuration rules for interlocking are specified by temporal logic formulas interpreted on Kripke structure representations of the interlocking configuration.

4.4   Proving Interlocking (Model-Checking, Installation-Based)

An interlocking is the safety-critical system that controls the movement of trains in a station and between adjacent stations. The interlocking monitors the status of the objects in the railway yard and allows or denies the routing of trains in accordance with the railway safety and operational regulations that are generic for the region or country where the interlocking is located. Verification of correctness of control tables has always been a central issue for formal methods practitioners, and the literature counts the application of several techniques to the problem. It is a well known fact that interlocking systems, due to their inherent complexity related to the high number of variables involved, are not amenable to automatic verification, typically incurring in state space explosion problems. Model-checking [10,11] has been exercised with considerable success for specific implementation and up to a certain complexity measured by a number of managed Boolean equations.

4.5   Modelling Design Reasoning

A railway system is often huge and very difficult to assess as structural modelling is not able to scale up properly. For example, a RER A regional train simulator modelling all track-side equipment (including wires, relays, etc.) contains more than 2,000,000 variables and requires seven computer to simulate simplified traffic scenarios on the central sector of the line. In [16], structural formal modelling is applied to an existing interlocking specification, but the results are a single error ("well known" by the customer) and an Event-B model refined 15 times, unreadable/unusable by the recipients.

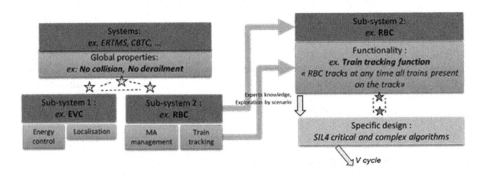

Fig. 9. The complete picture of the formal approach for safe systems.

A different formal methodology was then invented [6,19] where the design reasoning is modelled and proved against properties, based on assumptions admitted by all experts. Figure 9 below illustrates its different stages, which can be called "the ideal formal world" and which makes it possible to obtain a system that is guaranteed to be zero-defect:

- The left side of the diagram represents the "formal proof of correct interoperability". The aim is to ensure that if the individual sub-systems making up the overall solution are implemented in accordance with their specifications, then the safety of the overall system is guaranteed. This proof enables the entity responsible for the integrated system to ensure that there are no hidden safety bugs in the subsystem breakdown.

- The right side of the schema could be named "formal proof of correct design". It is a question of guaranteeing that a given implementation is designed in such a way that the safety expectations expressed in the specifications are effectively met.

The by-product of this methodology is a book, written in natural language, providing an irrefutable mathematical demonstration that the various subsystems meet the expected refined properties [7].

5 Convergence and Relevance

The previous sections show that many railway activities are now subject to modelling. The complete picture of the situation is difficult to obtain as many of them are not publicly disclosed, for various reasons (competitiveness, secrecy, insufficient maturity, etc.) or are more a marketing by-product unable to survive the demonstration/prototyping phase.

Several initiatives to combine/associate theses modelling activities have been launched in order to address larger engineering problems or new paradigms like AI, hybrid modelling[2], and model-in-the-loop. Among them, we may notice:

- MegaM@RT[3] project, with the analysis of traces at execution time by comparison with system-level models (search for patterns, AI)
- Shift2Rail[4] improved train localisation with the formal modelling of the forthcoming Moving Block specification and the fusion of diverse data (GPS, odometer, kinematics, digital maps) to get rid of most track-side signalling.
- Simulating ERTMS Hybrid level 3 specification [12], a novel approach between ETCS level 2 fixed blocks and full moving blocks. Figure 10 shows the formal B model being executed in real-time, along with a visualisation of the model's state: over 40 issues were identified.
- SNCF Réseau[5] is developing a digital mock-up of its network to provide valuable input for scheduling predictive maintenance operations, foresee behaviour, train teams and test-drive strategic solutions.
- Alstom[6] develops a rail network digital twin for railway yard design and predictive fleet maintenance based on AnyLogic.

---

[2] The combination of continuous and discrete models to associate a logic controller to the physics of a controlled system described with differential equations.

[3] https://megamart2-ecsel.eu/.

[4] Call for Project 2R-OC-IP2-01-2020.

[5] https://www.sncf-reseau.com/en/entreprise/newsroom/sujet/the-digital-twin.

[6] https://www.anylogic.com/digital-twin-of-rail-network-for-train-fleet-maintenance-decision-support/.

Fig. 10. Formal B model of Hybrid Level 3 Principles running in real-time.

- On-going autonomous train projects[7] are integrating AI for decision and diverse sensors for detection, while ensuring a human remote control in case of unexpected situation.

Besides the fact of using state-of-the-art techniques, how relevant the concept of digital twin is in the railways? Due to the different domains, timescales, and objectives[8] covered by the modelling activities listed above, having a digital twin of a whole railway system does not seem much adequate.

A digital twin would probably find a more suitable usage for a restricted domain/timescale/objective combination like training simulation or validation test bench[9]. More precise results are expected with the integration of additional modelling dimensions. However tool/model integration costs are a high barrier as there are many tools, specific to a line/model/plant, for which source code/(design, interface) documentation is often hardly available. The combination of these tools/models, developed separately, would induce extra effort to validate their semantic and pragmatic consistency, especially if used for safety certification. Moreover developing new tools/models for legacy systems already in exploitation requires a sound justification (exploitation/maintenance costs saving, solving design issues uncovered lately).

---

[7] https://tech.sncf.com/dossier/train-autonome/.

[8] For example, respectively functional vs safety, seconds for slipping vs thousands years for rail maintenance, and development vs certification.

[9] SNCF test bench BATIR enabling the real-time functional simulation, including HiL, of full high speed trains to validate embedded software.

Digital twin is probably more adequate to address newer systems (new baseline) or new themes like:

- ERTMS: its evolving specification and the lack of feedback (compared to historical national signalling which have been designed over decades/century), difficult to deploy[10] and enabling the late discovery of errors [12].
- Cyber security: critical transportation infrastructure is facing increasing security risks given that many systems are (going to be) connected to the Internet, while related standards are as of today being written (hence not ready for deployment). In particular, joint security and safety modelling are closely related and are good candidates to populate a digital twin.
- Terrorism: At the highest level, there is a clear need for the combination of models from different transportation systems[11], to take into account multi-modalities, especially with respect to the terrorist risk and the way independent transportation infrastructures will manage security.
- Autonomy: automating trains requires to consider more aspects than for automated metros, as the environment is more complex with more elements, interfaces, and interactions. The variety of scenarios and situations met requires precise models of the system and its environment to ensure AI consistency.

6   Conclusion and Perspectives

Railways are heavy modelling providers and users. Most models are:

- separate;
- have different natures and objectives: logic, physical world, performances, safety, etc.
- have different subjects: infrastructure, rolling stocks, environment;
- used for different activities (specification, development, validation, qualification/certification, exploitation/maintenance);

The on-going tendency is to support more engineering activities with modelling or cross-modelling (either by combining modelling to obtain an augmented one, or by exercising modelling with the support of another one). For example, slipping/sliding physical modelling provides outputs (i.e. tables) for the estimation of the train localisation precision, but is not included into train traffic simulation per se.

However it seems unreasonable to imagine a model of a complete railway system (a metro line) shared among different stakeholders, as the range of uses is quite large and the systems considered made of many equipment/subsystems/parts.

Applications to new themes (AI for autonomy, cyber security, terrorist risks, etc.) might constitute a suitable entry point for digital twins in the railways.

---

[10] "Bring in the disruptors to drive rail innovation", Stuart Calvert, Digital Rail, TransCityRail North conference, London, 06/10/2017.

[11] H2020 Call SU-INFRA-01-2020: Prevention, detection, response and mitigation of combined physical and cyber security threats to critical infrastructure in Europe.

References

1. Alacoque, J.C., Chapas, P.: Traction ferroviaire adhérence par commande d'effort. Techniques de l'ingénieur Infrastructure ferroviaire et matériel roulant base documentaire : TIB576DUO. (ref. article : d5535) (2005). https://www.techniques-ingenieur.fr/base-documentaire/ingenierie-des-transports-th14/infrastructure-ferroviaire-et-materiel-roulant-42576210/traction-ferroviaire-d5535/, fre

2. Banach, R.: Issues in automated urban train control: 'tackling' the rugby club problem. In: Butler, M., Raschke, A., Hoang, T.S., Reichl, K. (eds.) ABZ 2018. LNCS, vol. 10817, pp. 171–186. Springer, Cham (2018). https://doi.org/10.1007/978-3-319-91271-4_12

3. Behm, P., Benoit, P., Faivre, A., Meynadier, J.-M.: Météor: a successful application of B in a large project. In: Wing, J.M., Woodcock, J., Davies, J. (eds.) FM 1999. LNCS, vol. 1708, pp. 369–387. Springer, Heidelberg (1999). https://doi.org/10.1007/3-540-48119-2_22

4. Bouillot, L.: Dynamic bayesian networks modelling maintenance strategies: prevention of broken rails. In: WCCR 2008, vol. 2008, Seoul, South Korea (2008)

5. Ciszewski, T., Kornaszewski, M., Nowakowski, W.: RailML application for description of railway interlocking systems, vol. 19, pp. 373–377, December 2018

6. Comptier, M., Déharbe, D., Perez, J., Mussat, L., Pierre, T., Sabatier, D.: Safety analysis of a CBTC system: a rigorous approach with event-B. In: Fantechi, A., Lecomte, T., Romanovsky, A. (eds.) RSSRail 2017. LNCS, vol. 10598, pp. 148–159. Springer, Cham (2017). https://doi.org/10.1007/978-3-319-68499-4_10

7. Comptier, M., Leuschel, M., Mejia, L.-F., Perez, J.M., Mutz, M.: Property-based modelling and validation of a CBTC zone controller in event-B. In: Collart-Dutilleul, S., Lecomte, T., Romanovsky, A. (eds.) RSSRail 2019. LNCS, vol. 11495, pp. 202–212. Springer, Cham (2019). https://doi.org/10.1007/978-3-030-18744-6_13

8. Dillmann, S., Hähnle, R.: Automated planning of ETCS tracks. In: Collart-Dutilleul, S., Lecomte, T., Romanovsky, A. (eds.) RSSRail 2019. LNCS, vol. 11495, pp. 79–90. Springer, Cham (2019). https://doi.org/10.1007/978-3-030-18744-6_5

9. Ferrari, A., et al.: Survey on formal methods and tools in railways: the ASTRail approach. In: Collart-Dutilleul, S., Lecomte, T., Romanovsky, A. (eds.) RSSRail 2019. LNCS, vol. 11495, pp. 226–241. Springer, Cham (2019). https://doi.org/10.1007/978-3-030-18744-6_15

10. Ferrari, A., Magnani, G., Grasso, D., Fantechi, A.: Model checking interlocking control tables. In: Schnieder, A., Tarnai, G. (eds.) FORMS/FORMAT 2010, pp. 107–115. Springer, Heidedlberg (2011). https://doi.org/10.1007/978-3-642-14261-1_11

11. Halchin, A., Feliachi, A., Singh, N.K., Aït-Ameur, Y., Ordioni, J.: B-PERFect - Applying the PERF approach to B based system developments. In: Fantechi, A., Lecomte, T., Romanovsky, A. (eds.) RSSRail 2017. LNCS, vol. 10598, pp. 160–172. Springer, Cham (2017). https://doi.org/10.1007/978-3-319-68499-4_11, https://hal.archives-ouvertes.fr/hal-02451007

12. Hansen, D., et al.: Validation and real-life demonstration of ETCS hybrid level 3 principles using a formal B model. Int. J. Softw. Tools Technol. Transf. **22**, 315–332 (2020)

13. Hlubuček, A.: Railtopomodel and RailML 3 in overall context. In: Acta Polytechnica CTU Proceedings, vol. 11, p. 16, August 2017

14. Lecomte, T., Mottin, E.: Formal data validation in the railways. In: Safety Critical Symposium, Brighton, UK (2016)
15. Malvezzi, M., Pugi, L., Papini, S., Rindi, A., Toni, P.: Identification of a wheel-rail adhesion coefficient from experimental data during braking tests. Proc. Inst. Mech. Eng. Part F J. Rail Rapid Transit **227**, 128–139 (2013)
16. Metayer, C., Clabaut, M.: DIR 41 case study. In: Börger, E., Butler, M., Bowen, J.P., Boca, P. (eds.) ABZ 2008. LNCS, vol. 5238, pp. 357–373. Springer, Heidelberg (2008). https://doi.org/10.1007/978-3-540-87603-8_44
17. Peleska, J., Krafczyk, N., Haxthausen, A.E., Pinger, R.: Efficient data validation for geographical interlocking systems. In: Collart-Dutilleul, S., Lecomte, T., Romanovsky, A. (eds.) RSSRail 2019. LNCS, vol. 11495, pp. 142–158. Springer, Cham (2019). https://doi.org/10.1007/978-3-030-18744-6_9
18. Quost, X.: Modélisation de l'effet du vent sur les trains à grande vitesse. Ph.D. thesis, Ecole Centrale de Lyon (2005)
19. Sabatier, D.: Using formal proof and B method at system level for industrial projects. In: Lecomte, T., Pinger, R., Romanovsky, A. (eds.) RSSRail 2016. LNCS, vol. 9707, pp. 20–31. Springer, Cham (2016). https://doi.org/10.1007/978-3-319-33951-1_2
20. Wikipedia Contributors: Fundamentals of transportation/timetabling and scheduling – wikibooks (2020). https://en.wikibooks.org/wiki/Fundamentals_of_Transportation/Timetabling_and_Scheduling. Accessed 05 June 2020
21. Wikipedia Contributors: Programmable logic controller – Wikipedia, the free encyclopedia (2020). https://en.wikipedia.org/wiki/Programmable_logic_controller. Accessed 08 May 2020

Engineering a Digital Twin for Manual Assembling

Alexandru Matei(✉) 🆔, Nicolae-Adrian Țocu 🆔, Constantin-Bălă Zamfirescu(✉) 🆔, Arpad Gellert 🆔, and Mihai Neghină 🆔

Lucian Blaga University of Sibiu, Victoriei Blvd. 10, 550024 Sibiu, Romania
{alex.matei,nicolae.tocu,constantin.zamfirescu,arpad.gellert,
mihai.neghina}@ulbsibiu.ro

Abstract. The paper synthesizes our preliminary work on developing a digital twin, with learning capabilities, for a system that includes cyber, physical, and social components. The system is an industrial workstation for manual assembly tasks that uses several machine learning models implemented as microservices in a hybrid architecture, a combination between the orchestrated and the event stream approaches. These models have either similar objectives but context-dependent performance, or matching functionalities when the results are fused to support real-life decisions. Some of the models are descriptive but easy to transform in inductive models with extra tuning effort, while others are purely inductive, requiring intrinsic connection with the real world.

Keywords: Manual assembling · Digital twin · Virtual simulation · Machine learning

1 Introduction

Due to their flexibility, human operators are pervasive in many factories where full automation is either unfeasible or too costly. Manual assembling is one of the manufacturing operations where humans are still playing the major role. Therefore, in the last decade there has been an increased interest from both academia and industry to develop intelligent assistance systems to support the assembling process. These systems are complex cyber-physical-social systems, with extended sensing capabilities of a working environment with physical, cyber, and human components. They should be able to recognize the product components and human features and actions, to learn patterns and correlate human operator contexts with the assembly states of a product, to assist in the correct product assembly by recommending the next step or by detecting the wrong ones, to train the human operator and so on.

The main challenge in the engineering of such systems is the complexity of integrating several sensors, with their own control capabilities, in a specific socio-technical context. The straightforward way to integrate these models is a virtual reality (VR) environment, enabling the creation of an artificial world for the manual assembling. The users are immersed in this artificial world with limited behavioral capacity, disconnected

T. Margaria and B. Steffen (Eds.): ISoLA 2020, LNCS 12479, pp. 140–152, 2021.
https://doi.org/10.1007/978-3-030-83723-5_10

from the real system. Over the years, this technology proved to be sufficient to address specific issues in many domains, but we are currently at a point where we need models to control the real systems which are not suitable for the artificial system. Consequently, this integration cannot be achieved completely in a digital way and requires perpetual correlations with the real world.

In contrast to VR, the Digital Twin (DT) concept emphasizes control models for the real system and not for the virtual ones. DT is a natural evolution of the Decision Support System concept which connects the models developed in the design phase with the IoT technology. In this way the problem-solving capabilities become an order of magnitude faster, with the additional capability to synchronize the models with reality. Therefore, the combination of DT and VR is used in many industrial applications, from simple monitoring tasks of an industrial equipment [1] to more complex tasks like fine-tuning the interactions of an operator with a robotic arm [2].

To faithfully reflect the real system along its entire life-cycle, a DT should exhibit some key characteristics [3]: 1) the ability to inspect the system at multiple levels, from system level to system of systems level; 2) the ability to transform, combine and establish equivalence between models; 3) the ability to integrate, add or replace models and the ability to describe the closeness to the physical system. Moreover, a DT needs to integrate the human's data and related context, either to assess the working conditions of humans in a factory [4] or to investigate the task allocation problem in human-robot collaborations [5]. Note that these desiderata are the key concerns in developing multi-model co-simulations as well.

The paper synthesizes the preliminary development of a DT with learning capabilities for a manual assembly workstation. Section 2 introduces the adopted architectural concept to engineer the DT. The underlying technologies and the microservices that are developed to provide the DT functionalities are described in Sect. 3. These services employ several machine learning models which are discussed in Sect. 4. Most of these models are descriptive but can easily be converted into inductive models with extra tuning effort. The last section highlights the current research and conclusions.

2   Assembly Workstation Digital Twin Concept

In the manufacturing industry, the implementation of a DT is following several methods that lack a common understanding, development methods and technological framework. The main concern in designing the assembly workstation is to maximize the reuse of control assets for both systems: physical and virtual. In this case, the DT will be a controller for both the physical and the virtual system that has predictive and adaptive capabilities. By following the guidelines presented in [6] to describe the DT concept, the main features for the manual assembly DT are the following:

- **Physical Entity** is the physical assembly workstation: a table frame with adjustable height for ergonomic use. The tabletop is a large smart tablet where the instructions are given to the user, either visually, audio or a combination of both. In case of heavy pieces that could potentially damage the screen of the tablet, an alternative would be to use a hard tabletop with a separate screen and a speaker.

- **Virtual Entity** is the VR application, which contains the virtual 3D model of the product together with the 3D model of the physical assembly workstation.
- **Physical Environment** is represented by the assembled modules on the assembly workstation and the human operator who is doing the assembly.
- **Virtual Environment** includes different VR rooms for specific needs, such as: simulation, tutorial, operator manual assembly training, product presentation, etc. The virtual environment is designed for a specific need. The link between the physical and virtual entities is made in the DT Scene.
- **State** composed of the variables needed to replicate in the virtual world the states of the following: physical entity (i.e. table height), physical environment (i.e. 3D position and orientation of the objects, assembly status), and human operator (i.e. emotion, eye tracking, skeleton model). In addition, the states of the control unit (i.e. the instructions that are presented) are considered as well. All these variables belong to a certain range that define the required levels of fidelity (e.g. high-fidelity for the physical entity, and medium to high fidelity for the physical environment).
- **Synchronization** presumes the bidirectional connections between the physical and virtual system together with the *twinning rate*. The *physical-to-virtual connection* is realized with various devices to acquire data about the current state of the physical objects (object types and their position with an RGB depth camera) and human operator (facial expressions and body movement with an additional camera, emotion detection with GSR sensors and/or voice recognition, intentional stance and attention with eye tracking glasses). All this data is transmitted to the VR application. The *virtual-to-physical connection* is restricted in the current implementation to the height adjustment for the physical table from the VR application. An assembly process restart or reset command from VR is possible only with the help of an external mediator who will manually rearrange the assembly parts on the physical table for correspondence with the VR scenarios. The *twinning rate* is 1 state update per second. Partial state updates can be made more frequently depending on the update frequency of each sensor.
- **Physical Processes** consist in guiding the human operator to assemble a product. The human operator must follow step by step instructions presented by the system.
- **Virtual Processes** are used for optimization, simulation, supervision, analysis, and improvement of the decision algorithms.

Note that the physical and virtual processes reflect intentions of the decision-makers, such as support human workers either for manual assembly training or real-time operation. They need to be sufficiently connected to the operational reality and complete to allow the execution of either in the physical or in the virtual space. Figure 1 depicts the main modules that are needed to control the physical or virtual assembly workstation. As mentioned, the main concern in designing the DT was to maximize the reuse of control assets for both systems (physical and virtual) while allowing early testing of the manual assembly training processes and algorithm, improving them side by side with the physical entity.

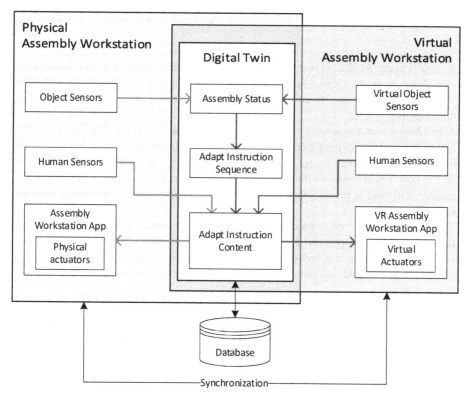

Fig. 1. The DT concept for the assembly workstation

The *Physical Assembly Workstation* has sensors to measure the physical system and environment, and actuators that are used by the Virtual Assembly Workstation to change the physical environment. The *Assembly Workstation Application* module is used to provide audio, video or written instructions to the user, highlight the assembly parts and control the physical actuators of the system. There are two types of sensors:

- *Object Sensors* are aimed at the objects that are assembled on the physical workstation. These sensors can be video cameras, depth cameras, lidars, etc. Another way is to use smart products or product tracing techniques. The data stream of these sensors will be used by the *Assembly Status* module.
- *Human Sensors* are used to detect changes in the user's emotion and intentions, where it is looking, height, and other characteristics. These sensors include video cameras, depth cameras, Galvanic Skin Response sensors, eye tracking sensors, etc.

The control elements shared between the physical and virtual assembly workstations are:

- *Assembly Status* module is responsible for identifying the current state of the assembly using input from the *Object Sensors* module. Based on that state, it must decide if it is a valid or invalid one. In other words, it detects if the user is making mistakes in the assembly process.
- *Adapt Instruction Sequence* module receives inputs from the *Assembly Status* module and recommends the next step that should be done in the assembly process. If the human operator is making mistakes, this module will repeat the current instruction and if not, it will move to the next one. When moving to the next instruction, the module will have to provide the optimal instruction from the available list of feasible ones.
- *Adapt Instruction Content* module decides on how to present the current instruction for a certain human operator. The instruction should be personalized by choosing the communication form (i.e. video, audio, text, or a combination of those). It should also decide the timing and amount of information given to the human operator.

In the case of the *Virtual Assembly Workstation*, all the data that is acquired in the *Physical Assembly Workstation* using *Object Sensors* will be available directly from the VR application through the SDK, without the need of additional sensors or equipment. We will consider this functionality of the SDK as virtual sensors – named *Virtual Object Sensors* in Fig. 1. Some of the user's information is also available using the VR SDK but this requires the VR equipment which will be considered as part of the *Human Sensors* in this case for the *Virtual Assembly Workstation*. There are some exceptions in the case of *Human Sensors* of the *Virtual Assembly Workstation* where some parameters cannot be extracted because the user's face is obstructed by the VR headset. The same sensors from the physical workstation could monitor the human operator and send the data to the VR application. However, these sensors are hard to use from the virtual side. Also, under some circumstances, their usage from the virtual side is unnecessary because the virtual environment is a controlled environment where most of the information is easily available in the software. Next, a correspondence between the sensors used to capture the physical environment and the ones used for the virtual environment is presented in Table 1.

The *database* is used to store the assemblies done on either the physical or the virtual assembly workstation for a later analysis and verification through replay. Using the recorded assembly processes, it is possible to continuously improve the Machine Learning (ML) algorithms of the system, especially the *Adapt Instruction Sequence* and *Adapt Instruction Content* modules.

Using the real time *synchronization* between the *Physical* and *Virtual Assembly Stations*, additional functionalities can be enabled: a trainer from VR can supervise the trainee from real medium using the DT or vice versa, remote operator manual assembly training, real-time manual assembly training analysis, etc. In the end, the *Virtual Assembly Station* is not acting only as a simulator, but also as a product for real-time visualization and analysis or testing new functionalities using real-time sensor input from the physical environment.

Table 1. Sensor correspondence

Behavior/Measurement	Physical station	Virtual station
Determine user's body characteristics: movement, skeleton data, height	Azure Kinect	Software-based using the existing VR equipment: headset, controllers, and trackers
Eye tracking and user intention	Tobii Pro Glasses 2	HTC Vive Pro Eye Series
Tracking the objects that are being assembled	RGB depth camera	Software-based as the position of all parts is always known in the virtual environment
Detection of the user's emotional state	Video camera, Microphone, GSR sensors	Face based is not possible, Microphone, GSR sensors

3 Implementation Issues

The concept of the physical workstation is presented in [7]. The software architecture of the system is based on a hybrid microservices architecture, a combination between orchestrated and event stream approaches. Having a hybrid architecture, allows for a greater flexibility in the development of the microservices and their interaction. The microservices are developed using gRPC[1], an open-source remote procedure call (RPC) framework. For monitoring, control, discovery, and health checking of the microservices we are using Consul[2], an open-source platform. The types of services that are currently available on the assembly workstation:

- *Physical Assembly Station:*

- **Table Height Adjustment** – interface that allows control of the physical table height.

- *Object Data:*

- **Object Detection** – allows identification of known objects in an image. Depending on the assembly scenario, a customized detection algorithm is needed for each object that is assembled. For a basic and fast detection, a bounding box algorithm like YOLO [8] might be enough but for a greater, pixel-level accuracy at the expense of speed, an instance segmentation algorithm like Mask R-CNN [9] should be used. In our implementation we opted for using a YOLO artificial neural network that was trained on demo objects.
- **Object Position** – allows identification of the XYZ position of the detected objects in a depth image based on the output of the Object Detection service.

---

[1] https://grpc.io/.

[2] https://www.consul.io/.

- **Object Segmentation** – allows the further segmentation of the detected object(s). It is used to extract 2D orientation and pixel-level segmentation of the detected objects. This is achieved using traditional image processing methods like: Otsu binarization, edge detection, contour detection, contour fill, etc.

- *Human Data:*

- **User Characteristics** – used to extract user information like height, age, gender. In [10] is presented the approach for this step of extracting these human characteristics.
- **User emotion detection based on voice** – uses a phase vocoder together with an artificial neural network. The method was trained and validated using the RAVDESS database [11] (Ryerson Audio-Visual Database of Emotional Speech and Song). Details about the approach can be found in [12].
- **User emotion based on facial expression** – is a microservice that is based on an input image with the user's face, identifies face landmarks. Based on the face landmarks and the distance between them, seven possible emotions can be predicted using an artificial neural network. The seven detected emotion are: angry, disgust, fear, happy, sad, surprise and neutral.
- **User Intention** – This microservice is using the eye tracking data to predict what the user wants to assembly next. The video feed together is feed into the Object Detection microservices and based on the gaze location it can be inferred if the user is looking at an object. Currently, the algorithm behind this microservice that will determine user fixation on an object or confusion if the user is looking around is under development.

- *Assembly Instruction Data:*

- **Correct Assembly** – used to determine if user follows the assembly steps correctly. This microservice, based on the object spatial position, orientation, and segmentation from Object Segmentation microservice can determine whether the pieces are assembled correctly or not.
- **Next Assembly Step** – used to provide the next suitable instruction based on the previous instruction. For this microservice, several types of predictors were tested, like two-level prediction table, Markov predictors, prediction by partial matching and long-term short memory artificial neural networks. Details about the implemented predictors can be found in [13, 14] and [15].
- **Adapt Assembly Step** – used to adapt the next instruction based of several factors: user state, mistakes made, assembly state, etc. This microservice is currently under development.

- *Other microservices:*

- **Publish-Subscribe** – allows for a pub-sub communication/event stream-based alternative to direct RPC calls (orchestrated) between microservices.
- **Video Streaming** – this microservice allows viewing the stream of any video source (including screen) connected to the assembly station. To reduce the bandwidth, the video is H264 encoded on the server side using the Windows Media Foundation SDK.

The DT of the physical assembly workstation is an adapted VR simulation. The VR simulator was developed in Unity 3D and it is compatible with Oculus Rift and HTC Vive headsets. The compatibility problem was easily solved using the VRTK Toolkit. This toolkit is a collection of scripts and prefabs made for Unity and VR. Using VRTK and Steam VR we could use the same classes and events to access the controller's apps from both hardware. The VR simulator is further detailed in [16]. In Fig. 2 the physical assembly workstation and its virtual representation in the VR application are shown.

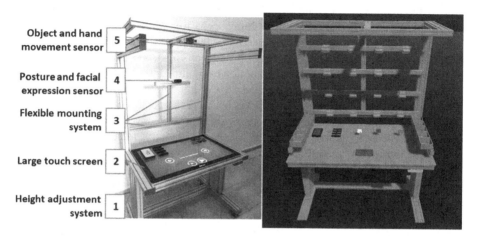

Object and hand movement sensor — 5

Posture and facial expression sensor — 4

Flexible mounting system — 3

Large touch screen — 2

Height adjustment system — 1

Fig. 2. Physical prototype [15] and its DT

4 Machine Learning Capabilities

As described in the previous section, the DT for assembly workstation combines multiple ML models developed during the design process. There are three broad categories employed in the current developments: 1) human emotion recognition, 2) context predictors for the assembling sequences, and 3) traditional image processing methods for object recognition. In the following sections the first two categories are discussed, whereas the third uses classical image processing algorithm with no need for data to improve their object recognition capability in real-time.

4.1 Human Emotions

Human emotions are known to play a significant role in human behavior and are an essential source of data for improving and adapting human interaction. There are multiple ways of recognizing human emotions, through facial expressions in [17] and [18], speech in [19] and [20], or biometric signals in [21] and [22]. For both the audio (speech) and video (face) channels, the detection of human emotions involves a pre-processing and feature extraction stage and a classification stage. The main features isolated in the audio channel are spectral, the Mel-frequency cepstral coefficients, although other time-based features such as short-term energy, zero-crossing and cross-correlation coefficients for pitch detection are additionally used. The pre-processing of the still images from the video channel revolves around the face detection and the extraction of discriminative features from salient face regions, as well as the history of those features from recent frames. For both the audio and video channel, the classifier chosen is an artificial neural network (ANN). Although there are many approaches, ANNs have been shown to be the most promising of artificial intelligence (AI) techniques, having good results in general pattern recognition tasks.

In the case of the biometric signals, only the galvanic skin response (GSR) is measured, as the heart rate reactions are relatively slow and persist for a long time (considering the general manual assembly training scenario), while EEG sensors are a lot less practical for an assembly workstation. Unlike the audio and image methods, which attempt full emotion identification, the GSR processing consists of adaptive filtering and peak detection, mainly used to identify emotion excitation. However, this approach has the big drawback of not being able to detect the explicit emotion, as the GSR peak can be triggered both by positive (e.g. happy) and negative (e.g. fear) emotions.

Each human emotion investigation channel has its strengths and weaknesses: face caption and GSR are continuous, whereas speech is voluntary; in contrast, the lack of speech inflexions despite emotions is less common than poker-face expressions, while physiological responses to emotions are almost never controlled; audio and video data can be gathered at a distance, whereas GSR, EEG and other biometric measurements require equipping the user. The combination of the methods thus offers a better chance of correctly identifying the true mix of emotions for the observed user and thus provides better data for the workstation to adapt and improve the instructions and feedback provided during the manual assembly training.

ANN methods for detecting human emotions are descriptive models trained on large sets of audio and image (or video) data. However, given the opportunity, they are easily transformed into inductive models through continuous training and refinement of the network weights based on data acquired during the operation. The assembly workstation offers the opportunity of observing the same user during multiple operations, thus enabling both the general refinement and the adaptation to the particularities of the user. In contrast, the GSR peak detection is implicitly an inductive model, adapting its filtering and thresholds to the user to compensate for variability of the physiological responses from human to human.

Although not an emotion, confusion of the user is another important state of mind that, if identified correctly, would greatly improve the performance of the assembling instructions. For the detection of this state, data from all channels may be combined with information from gaze-tracking glasses to provide valuable insights in the human state of mind.

As human emotions are personal, and represent internal biological states, questions about data privacy and ethics arise. Regarding this issue, the ANNs presented are trained on datasets that are freely available in the public domain. Also, the inferred emotional state of the user is used only momentarily by the software application and is not stored anywhere by the system.

4.2 Context-Based Predictors for the Assembly Sequences

In our previous works [13, 14] and [15] we investigated different models for context predictors, such us two-level prediction table, Markov predictors, prediction by partial matching and even long short-term memory artificial neural networks. These models have the same objective of providing adaptive assembly assistance by dynamically adapting the assembling process to the human operator's actual condition, his/her general characteristics, preferences, and behaviors in assembling products. These models are using a context-based predictor to recommend the next assembly step based on the current state of both: the semi-product, and the worker.

Being pre-trained with a set of rules extracted from a dataset of product assembly sequences we can consider them to be descriptive. The two-level context-based predictor from [13] is able to reproduce the assembly step which was last seen after a certain context, whereas the Markov predictors from [14] and [15] can provide multiple choices for the next assembly step, in their descending probability order. All these models can be enhanced with run-time training. Thus, after the pre-training, during the exploitation of the predictors, they can be updated after each assembly step. We expect that with run-time learning, the predictor can cover a higher number of situations.

In the case of the Markov predictors presented in [14], the next state probabilities for a given context are estimated using the state occurrence frequencies in that certain context. Currently, since only a limited pre-training stage is applied, these frequencies are maintained as simple counters. When a prediction is to be made for a given context, the state having the maximum counter can be provided as the most probable next state. If we extend the prediction mechanism with run-time learning, some of these counters can increase a lot in time, reaching very high magnitudes, while others can remain on low levels. Therefore, saturating counters would be more appropriate. The saturating counters, whose magnitude is limited, can adapt faster to changes in the behavior of a certain human operator, and can easily adapt also to different users. Obviously, this fast adaptation could be assured by increasing the saturating counter associated to the correct next state and by decrementing the saturating counters corresponding to wrong states, after each assembly step.

We are currently developing a prediction algorithm based on pre-trained Hidden Markov Models (HMM). That prediction scheme can be easily adapted for run-time learning by periodically adjusting the HMM on a certain window of assembly steps. Another predictor which is currently in evaluation is a Long Short-Term Memory (LSTM). It is pre-trained through a certain number of epochs. We intend to analyze the influence of a possible run-time learning over the LSTM's prediction accuracy. However, since the optimal number of epochs in the pre-training stage is 5000, we expect a slower adaptation capability for the LSTM by run-time learning with respect to the above-mentioned Markov and HMM prediction schemes.

The experiments with these models revealed that:

- If the dataset is strictly restricted to the assembly behavior of the human operator there is no significant difference if the dataset used to pre-train the ML models is generated either from physical or virtual assembly workstation. This finding may significantly speed up the pre-training of ML models.

- There will be always a tradeoff between adaptability and prediction accuracy among alternative ML models. Some works well with a large pre-training dataset, but they have slower adaptability to real-time data coming from the physical system. Therefore, choosing the optimal model depends very much on the contextual use (i.e. products diversity, assembling complexity in terms of number of sequential steps and alternative choices, etc.).
- The ML models developed to predict the assembly behavior trained with data from the virtual workspace has limited applicability. We have found strong correlations between the assembling performance of some processes with the operators' psychomotor capabilities, such as the gender, if he/she is wearing glasses, tiredness, height, etc. While it is clear that the data coming from the real space are limited due to lack of high volume of data and slower generation of data, models developed for the virtual space cannot cope with the entire spectrum of real-life data as a result of limited sensorial capabilities. Consequently, left-over parts that should be considered by the DT in extending the descriptive models into inductive ones will always remain.

5   Conclusions and Future Work

The paper synthetized the preliminary developments of a DT for a manual assembly workstation. This cyber-physical-social system employs several ML models implemented as microservices in a hybrid architecture, a combination between the orchestrated and the event stream approaches. For a fast and intuitive integration of different ML models a VR application have been twinned with the physical workstation. In addition, it was used to generate datasets to pre-train the ML models. These models analyzed in this paper have either similar objectives but context-dependent performance (i.e. context-based predictors for the assembly sequence), or matching functionalities when the results are fused to support real-life decisions (i.e. detection of human emotions). Some of the models are descriptive but easy to transform in inductive models with extra tuning effort, while others are purely inductive requiring intrinsic connection with the real world.

These results will be further exploited on at least two directions. Firstly, the prediction models investigated to suggest the next assembly step can be easily reverted and used to simulate the assembly process of a human operator. The lack of a reliable model for the cognitive behavior of a human operator in assembly tasks was the main concern in not building at design time a co-simulation. The models discussed in the previous section will be further used in a co-simulation to reproduce the user's behavior. This will increase the speed for an extended design-space exploration when new microservices will be added. Moreover, coupled with specific real-time user data (i.e. gender, if he/she is wearing glasses, tiredness, height, etc.) there is the potential to have personalized design-space exploration capabilities for various assembly tasks, limiting substantially the combinatorial complexity arising from the interactions of multiple models. Secondly, all the ML models reported in the paper were pre-trained with datasets obtained from laboratory experiments with students. Real-life experiments with human operators from industry are envisaged. These experiments will provide a better insight on how to employ the alternative models in different contexts.

Acknowledgements. This work is supported through the DiFiCIL project (contract no. 69/08.09.2016, ID P_37_771, web: http://dificil.grants.ulbsibiu.ro), co-funded by ERDF through the Competitiveness Operational Programme 2014–2020.

References

1. Schroeder, G., et al.: Visualising the digital twin using web services and augmented reality. In: IEEE 14th International Conference on Industrial Informatics (INDIN), Poitiers, pp. 522–527 (2016)
2. Havard, V., Jeanne, B., Lacomblez, M., Baudry, D.: Digital twin and virtual reality: a co-simulation environment for design and assessment of industrial workstations. Prod. Manuf. Res. 7(1), 472–489 (2019)
3. Schleich, B., Anwer, N., Mathieu, L., Wartzack, S.: Shaping the digital twin for design and production engineering. CIRP Ann. Manuf. Technol. 66(1), 141–144 (2017)
4. Lu, Y., Liu, C., Wang, K.I.-K., Huang, H., Xu, X.: Digital twin-driven smart manufacturing: connotation, reference model, applications and research issues. Robot. Comput. Int. Manuf. 61, 101837 (2020)
5. Bilberg, A., Malik, A.A.: Digital twin driven human-robot collaborative assembly. CIRP Ann. Manuf. Technol. 68(1), 499–502 (2019)
6. Jones, D., Snider, C., Nassehi, A., Yon, J., Hicks, B.: Characterising the digital twin a systematic literature review. CIRP J. Manuf. Sci. Technol. 29(A), 36–52 (2020)
7. Pîrvu, B.C.: Conceptual overview of an anthropocentric training station for manual operations in production. In: Balkan Region Conference on Engineering and Business Education, vol. 1, no. 1, pp. 362–368 (2019)
8. Redmon, J., Divvala, S., Girshick, R., Farhadi, A.: You only look once: unified, real-time object detection. In: 2016 IEEE Conference on Computer Vision and Pattern Recognition (CVPR), Las Vegas, NV, pp. 779–788. IEEE (2016)
9. He, K., Gkioxari, G., Dollár, P., Girshick, R.: Mask R-CNN. In: 2017 IEEE International Conference on Computer Vision (ICCV), Venice, Italy, pp. 2980–2988. IEEE (2017)
10. Cruceat, A.M., Matei, A., Pîrvu, B.C., Butean, A.: Extracting human features to enhance the user experience on a training station for manual operations. Int. J. User Syst. Interaction 12(1), 54–66 (2019)
11. Livingstone, S.R., Russo, F.A.: The Ryerson audio-visual database of emotional speech and song (RAVDESS): a dynamic, multimodal set of facial and vocal expressions in North American English. PLoS ONE 13(5), e0196391 (2018)
12. Govoreanu, V.C., Neghină, M.: Speech emotion recognition method using time-stretching in the preprocessing phase and artificial neural network classifiers. In: 2020 IEEE 16th International Conference on Intelligent Computer Communication and Processing (ICCP), Cluj-Napoca, Romania, pp. 69–74. IEEE (2020)
13. Gellert, A., Zamfirescu, C.B.: Using two-level context-based predictors for assembly assistance in smart factories. In: 8th International Conference on Computers Communications and Control, Oradea, Romania (2020)
14. Gellert, A., Zamfirescu, C.B.: Assembly support systems using Markov predictors in smart factories. In: 20th Open Conference of the IFIP WG 8.3 on Decision Support, Wrocław, Poland (2020)
15. Gellert, A., Precup, S.A., Pirvu, B.C., Zamfirescu, C.B.: Prediction-based assembly assistance system. In: 25th International Conference on Emerging Technologies and Factory Automation, Vienna, Austria (2020)

16. Țocu, N.A., Gellert, A., Ștefan, I.R., Nițescu, T.M., Luca, G.A.: The impact of virtual reality simulators in manufacturing industry. In: 12th International Conference on Education and New Learning Technologies (2020)
17. Dudul, S.V., Kharat, G.U.: Emotion recognition from facial expression using neural networks. In: 2008 Conference on Human System Interactions, Krakow, pp. 422–427. IEEE (2008)
18. Khanal, S.R., Barroso, J., Lopes, N., Sampaio, J., Filipe, V.: Performance analysis of Microsoft's and Google's emotion recognition API using pose-invariant faces. In: DSAI 2018: Proceedings of the 8th International Conference on Software Development and Technologies for Enhancing Accessibility and Fighting Info-Exclusion, Thessaloniki, Greece, pp. 172–178. ACM (2018)
19. Tóth, S.L., Sztahó, D., Vicsi, K.: Speech emotion perception by human and machine. In: Esposito, A., Bourbakis, N.G., Avouris, N., Hatzilygeroudis, I. (eds.) Verbal and Nonverbal Features of Human-Human and Human-Machine Interaction. LNCS (LNAI), vol. 5042, pp. 213–224. Springer, Heidelberg (2008). https://doi.org/10.1007/978-3-540-70872-8_16
20. Sezgin, M.C., Gunsel, B., Kurt, G.K.: Perceptual audio features for emotion detection. EURASIP J. Audio Speech Music Process. **2012**(1), 1–21 (2012). https://doi.org/10.1186/1687-4722-2012-16
21. Tarnowski, P., Kołodziej, M., Majkowski, A., Rak, R.J.: Combined analysis of GSR and EEG signals for emotion recognition. In: 2018 International Interdisciplinary PhD Workshop (IIPhDW), Swinoujście, pp. 137–141. IEEE (2018)
22. Wu, G., Liu, G., Hao, M.: The analysis of emotion recognition from GSR based on PSO. In: 2010 International Symposium on Intelligence Information Processing and Trusted Computing, Huanggang, pp. 360–363. IEEE (2010)

Towards Digital Twins for Knowledge-Driven Construction Progress and Predictive Safety Analysis on a Construction Site

Beidi Li[1(✉)], Rasmus O. Nielsen[1(✉)], Karsten W. Johansen[1(✉)], Jochen Teizer[2(✉)], Peter Gorm Larsen[1(✉)], and Carl Schultz[1(✉)]

[1] DIGIT, Department of Electrical and Computer Engineering, Aarhus University, Aarhus, Denmark
{beidi.li,pgl,cschultz}@ece.au.dk
[2] DIGIT, Department of Civil and Architecture Engineering, Aarhus University, Aarhus, Denmark
teizer@cae.au.dk

Abstract. Civil engineering has only recently started the digitalisation journey by standardising around Building Information Models (BIMs). In the process of construction a dimension of time is added in what is called 4D BIM and this can serve as the basis for a digital twin. It is predicted that such a digital twin can enhance the overall overview of status of the construction of a new building by means of different types of sensors, and interpreting these in relation to a BIM. In the construction phase there are rules and regulations targeting the safety of the different kinds of construction workers at the construction site. In this paper we provide a vision of how digital twins can assist with spotting potential violations of the constraints stated by the rules and regulations, and empirically evaluate a proof-of-concept software tool on a large scale, real-world 4D BIM.

1 Introduction

All project stakeholders that facilitate design, planning, construction and operation play a vital role in achieving project objectives for cost, schedule and quality. However, few recognise that design and planning can play a critical role for the safety, health and well-being of construction workers, maintenance staff or users during an entire project lifecycle. Although significant research has been undertaken in occupational construction safety, health and well-being, human-assisted software tools for detection and prevention of hazards embedded in construction schedules hardly exist in practice.

In light of this, we advocate Digital Twins as a technological framework for providing a unifying platform for enhanced construction safety that can be used to:

- integrate real-time sensor data from the construction sight (the "physical" twin) into a formal *model* of a construction site (the "digital" twin, in the form of 4D Building Information Model (BIM), Sect. 2);

© Springer Nature Switzerland AG 2021
T. Margaria and B. Steffen (Eds.): ISoLA 2020, LNCS 12479, pp. 153–174, 2021.
https://doi.org/10.1007/978-3-030-83723-5_11

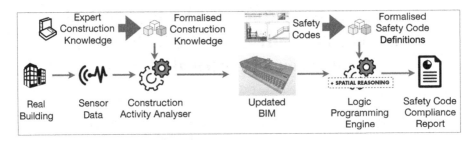

Fig. 1. Workflow pipeline for updating a 4D BIM with realtime sensor data, and automatic safety code compliance analysis. Thin grey arrows represent automatic data flows (inputs/outputs) between software components, or from sensors detecting the environment. Large blue arrows represent manual (human) *knowledge engineer* activities in formalising expert domain knowledge and natural language safety codes. The "digital" twin is the BIM (bottom middle). The "physical" twin is the real, partially constructed building (bottom left). The compliance report is delivered to construction project managers for decision support.

- facilitate *predictive* safety analysis of a construction site (Sects. 5–6).

These two roles of digital twins in construction are illustrated in the conceptual workflow pipeline in Fig. 1, centred around BIM of a building under construction. BIMs are an object oriented formal representation of buildings, including classes such as Door, Wall, Slab etc. In *construction planning*, 4D BIM is used to model how a BIM is planned to be erected in a series of discrete time steps, i.e. a 4D BIM is equivalent to a sequence of partially constructed BIMs that represent the building under construction.

In the first proposed application of digital twins, the 4D BIM is automatically updated based on sensor data, knowledge about construction activities in general, and background knowledge about the project at hand, which is formalised and used to interpret sensor data into construction activities and events. Having accurate information about progress and the current state of the partially-constructed building is critical for effective and timely safety analysis at each stage of the construction process. In Sect. 2 we present our initial results on automatically assessing construction progress and updating BIMs accordingly.

In the second application of digital twins, official standard safety codes that are currently complied with (by law) are formalised and checked against the BIM to identify hazards and recommend mitigation strategies. To keep our methodology concrete, we specifically focus on the German construction safety codes BG Bau [1].

We seek to consolidate and formalise expert knowledge on construction management into a new, semantically rich domain model of construction site *safety* called SafeConDM [20,23,24,34], that can be exploited for enhanced predictive analysis with 4D BIM. Importantly, 4D BIMs are often incomplete in that the designer has omitted certain key pieces of information (e.g. the particular order in which roof panels will be installed) that are necessary to assess whether a safety code is complied with or not.

This motivates the role of **default reasoning** in safety analysis, so that we might assume certain details that are missing from an incomplete BIM, and **hypothetical reasoning** that supports queries such as: *"Suppose a particular safety code is violated, can we fill in the missing information in such a way that would result in this violation?"*. In Sects. 5 – 6 we present our initial results in digital twins for safety analysis.

Thus, our proposed digital twin framework for safety analysis before, and during construction, consists of the following key components:

- a semantically rich domain model of different features in a 4D BIM (such as leading edges and other refining semantic categories that further distinguish different types of leading edge);
- a knowledge base of formal rules that can take a 4D BIM, analyse it, and augment it with these new concepts, injected as new, special kinds of "objects" in the model based approach on the concept of spatial artefacts;
- a reasoning engine that can take hypothetical statements about safety violations and identify construction sequences that result in such dangerous violation while still being consistent with construction plan information that is available.

1.1 Related Work

The particular research niche that our work resides in, with respect to employing BIMs in the context of digital twins is: (a) safety analysis (b) during the construction stage of a building's lifecycle. Thus far there has been relatively little attention given to automated safety analysis via 4D BIMs as the "digital" twin, and the construction site as the "physical" twin.

Digital Twins have their origins in the concept of *Mirror Worlds* by Gelernter [17], where the *digital* version of some real product or system is used for prediction: simulating "what if" scenarios and reasoning about properties of the digital model to infer properties of the real-world counterpart. Digital twin technology is not yet being fully utilised within the building and construction sector [9,21]. The primary role of digital *building* twins thus far is employed during the building operation phase (e.g. [25]), not during construction (corresponding with 4D BIM), in order to monitor and optimise building performance e.g. energy reduction [43], sustainability and waste reduction [3,32], building state degradation [11,21].

Methods have been developed for automated construction *progress* monitoring based on interpreting images, videos, laser scans, e.g.[18,19], and comparing 4D BIM "as-planned" vs "as-built" through point clouds constructed from images [10,42]. These approaches are compatible with our framework for utilising digital twins in construction safety analysis, where the digital twin platform unifies various technologies centred around a 4D BIM. The primary distinction here is that we emphasise the primary goal of *safety*, and situate sensor data interpretation within a framework of abductive (spatial) reasoning, with an emphasis on rich semantic models of experience and behaviour [4,7,14,37]. This leverages *expert knowledge*, *inference*, and *project-specific knowledge* in the form of the planned construction schedule so that, ideally, different kinds of sensors can be used to infer progress (enabling accurate safety analysis during construction) that are relatively inexpensive and simple to deploy, to complement video and laser scanning approaches.

Automated *building* code compliance has been the focus of numerous research efforts [8,12,13]. Popular commercial systems such as the Solibri Model Checker[1] primarily support *clash detection* analysis between physical components and provide a form of rule checking. The rules are parameterised and can be configured (e.g. combined, deactivated, etc.), although completely new rules cannot be defined by a user e.g. for implementing the B100 construction safety code [35,38]. Moreover, the underlying algorithms for determining spatial relations that systems such as Solibri implement (such as nearest spaces) are subject to numerical instabilities, and are impossible to directly verify and modify due to being proprietary and closed. The approach we are developing incorporates real arithmetic constraint solving (i.e. not only floating point) to overcome such limitations [22,24].

2 Automatic Construction Progress Analysis

In this first phase we aim to automatically infer progress of the construction plan and update the 4D BIM accordingly based on sensor data collected from the construction site. We cannot directly 'sense' task completion, i.e. there is no such device as a 'wall exists' sensor, and thus we use sensor data, such as worker location tracking, to infer the *plausbility* of work being done. This application of digital twins corresponds to the workflow illustrated in the left part of the workflow in Fig. 1.

We adopt the common approach of decomposing so-called 'high level' construction tasks into a hierarchy of subtasks that can be more reliably reasoned about based on sensor data (e.g., [47]). For example, erecting brick pillars may consist of the following subtasks:

- cutting bricks at the saw machine;
- moving bricks from the saw machine to the pillar zone; and
- laying the bricks in the pillar zone.

Given sensor data collected from the construction site, our system needs to infer such subtasks that are consistent with this sensor data in real time, and subsequently qualitatively assess task completion. For example, given a timestamped series of georeferenced locations associated with a particular worker (e.g., tracked Ultra Wideband (UWB) tags attached to personal protective equipment (PPE)) our system may infer that the worker has moved from region A to job site B where they remained for some time, and then moved back to region A. Moreover, given the time spent at job site B our system may infer progress on task X assigned to the worker that can only be undertaken using a particular machine at worksite B.

---

[1] www.solibri.com.

Such inferences are only plausible, tentative explanations of the data: if it was indeed the case that the worker undertook these activities then we would expect the sensor readings that we did in fact observe. However, many other scenarios would also result in these sensor readings - what if the PPE with the tags were accidentally swapped between workers? Given this new information our system would need to be able to revise its previous inferences. This kind of explanation-based hypothetical reasoning is a form of *abduction* (in contrast to deduction in which inferences are never retracted). The challenge in abductive reasoning is to efficiently produce a select few useful hypotheses that are justified by the data, out of the enormous multitude of hypotheses that are also consistent with the data available.

2.1 Explaining Sensor Data via Abductive Reasoning

Consider the fundamental equation of inference [28]:

$$BK \wedge H \models Obs$$

In our framework based on logic programming, Background Knowledge (BK) is a set of *IF-THEN* rules between propositions, and facts that we know to hold in the current setting such as the 4D BIM of the construction project, the up-to-date worker roster, current time of day, construction project plan and task schedules, etc. For example, a number of work areas have been identified in the construction site illustrated in Fig. 2, represented as polygonal regions.

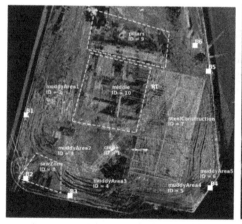 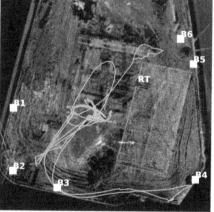

Fig. 2. *Left:* Semantically meaningful work areas represented as polygons on a construction site. *Right:* Worker trajectory data (cyan lines) captured via UWB sensors are directly converted into symbolic facts asserting the time intervals during which the worker was located in particular work areas.

Observations (*Obs*) are represented as symbolic facts, derived directly from sensor data. For example, we convert detailed 2D trajectory data (Fig. 2, right) into discrete symbolic facts that assert the time intervals during which a given worker is located in a given work area, as defined in Fig. 2 (left).

Hypotheses (*H*) are tentative facts that, when combined with BK, entail the observations. For example, the hypothesis that worker W performed the subtask of *"cutting bricks at the saw machine"* during time interval T entails that the worker was located in the same area where the saw machine is located (the *"sawZone"*), and that the duration of time they spent in that area is above a plausible threshold (e.g. more than five minutes), to distinguish workers that are instead only passing through that area.

Deduction is the process of inferring Obs given H and BK. Abduction [40] is the process of inferring H given BK and Obs, such that background knowledge alone is not enough to explain the observations ($BK \not\models Obs$), the hypothesis is not inconsistent with background knowledge ($BK \wedge H \not\models false$) and the hypothesis is sufficient to explain the observations together with background knowledge. Our abductive reasoning module is implemented using Answer Set Programming (ASP) [16,26].

2.2   Answer Set Programming (ASP)

ASP is a declarative logic programming language that is used to represent and reason about semantic information in a given application domain (such as 4D BIM and safety) in the form of facts and rules, and has an in-built search engine for finding models (combinations of deduced facts) that follow from the given premises. In the context of logic programming, the rules in BK that provide the basis for abductive reasoning are a set of Horn clauses of the form: $h \leftarrow b_1, \ldots, b_n$, where proposition h is true (the rule head) if propositions $b_1, \ldots, b_n$ are all true (the rule body). We represent a 4D BIM in ASP as ASP facts, background knowledge about construction activities are formalized as ASP rules, and valid hypothetical explanations are encoded as ASP models discovered by the ASP search engine. In ASP syntax, rules are denoted as follows (read as "IF $b_1, \ldots, b_n$ are true THEN h must be true):

    h :- b1, ..., bn.

An ASP fact h is a rule of the form: $h \leftarrow true$. An integrity constraint that forbids $b_1 \wedge \cdots \wedge b_n$ is a rule of the form: $false \leftarrow b_1, \ldots, b_n$. A *weak constraint* is a default integrity constraint that intuitively states that: prefer models that satisfy the constraint. Weak constraints provide a means to find optimal models that minimise the number of violated weak constraints. Specifically, for each weak constraint that is violated in a given model, the model is assigned a penalty p, assigned to a so-called term tuple t.[2] ASP then searches for models that minimise the sum of penalties. In ASP syntax, weak constraints with penalty w and term tuple t are denoted as:

    :~ b1, ..., bn. [w, t]

---

[2] The role of the term tuple can be understood as follows: when a weak constraint is violated, a term tuple is added to the model and assigned the penalty, rather than the weak constraint itself. This provides a mechanism to relate weak constraints. We will not elaborate on the details of term tuples here, and instead refer the reader to ASP documentation [15].

ASP supports *choice rules*: given propositions $h_1, \ldots, h_m$ a choice rule is used to specify that zero or more of those propositions can be true in a model. This is generalised so that at least i and at most j of the propositions must appear in each model. In ASP syntax choice rules are denoted as:

```
i {h1; ...; hm} j :- b1, ..., bn.
```

Finally, unlike another well known logic programming language Prolog (the predecessor of ASP), ASP operates in a 3-valued logic setting: propositions in a model can be *true*, *false*, and *neither* (which can be interpreted as *unknown* depending on the application context). The proposition $-p$ denotes that "p is false" in classic propositional logic. A model can not contain both p and $-p$, which is defined as a logical contradiction, whereas models can omit both p and $-p$ (i.e. which, as mentioned, can be interpreted as "p is unknown"). The operator "*not p*" is satisfied if p is not in the model, i.e. the model either contains $-p$ or neither p nor $-p$. Similarly, "*not $-p$*" is satisfied if $-p$ is not in the model, i.e. the model either contains p or neither p nor $-p$.

2.3   Abductive Reasoning Using Answer Set Programming

We implement abduction in ASP by adapting the approach presented in [30]. Observations $o_1, \ldots, o_n$ derived from sensor data (also referred to as *evidence*) are implemented as ASP facts:

```
holds(o_1).
...
holds(o_n).
```

Each hypothetical predicate p in H (called an *abducible*) is implemented as an ASP choice rule:

```
{hypothesis(p)}.
```

This choice rule means that every hypothesis can either be made or not (i.e. the abducible is either asserted to hold, or remain unknown). Given n hypotheses then the corresponding set of choice rules yields at most 2^n complete explanations (models), i.e. the set of models is a subset of every combination of hypotheses. We rank these models by preferring models that propose hypotheses over those that do not (as also argued in [30]), i.e. we use ASP to derive rich interpretations of the construction scenario that are consistent with the data.

Such an "optimistic" set of hypotheses corresponds to an upper bound on construction progress where observations are used to justify the largest number of hypotheses about work progress. We implement this in ASP using weak constraints [30]:

```
:~ hypothesis(p). [1, p]
```

The knowledge that hypothesis p entails observation o (or other consequent propositions) is implemented as an ASP rule:

```
expected(o) :- hypothesis(p).
```

If multiple observations $o_1, \ldots, o_k$ are entailed, then this is implemented as choice rules requiring all k propositions to be in the model:

```
k{expected(o_1),...,expected(o_k)}k :- hypothesis(p).
```

Every expected observation inferred from a hypothesis must be *corroborated* by evidence. This is implemented as an ASP integrity constraint asserting that a model is inconsistent if it contains an *expected* observation that was not observed from sensor data:

```
:- expected(o), not holds(o).
```

3   From Physical Twin to Digital Twin: The Framework and Workflow

This section details the three modules in our construction progress framework. In this first iteration of our framework, sensor data from the construction site consists of Real-Time Locating System (RTLS)-data of human workers and on-site heavy vehicles. We opted for Ultra Wideband (UWB)-based localization as the means of capturing trajectory in this first iteration, due to UWB being relatively uncomplicated to install, operate and maintain. In comparison to GPS, UWB requires more effort and time to install and configure, however it also provides up to an order of magnitude improved location tracking accuracy. Tags are configured to run at an update rate between 1–60 Hz, and are attached to human workers and heavy vehicles moving on the construction site. It is assumed that these subjects do not exceed a speed threshold of 7 km/h during typical construction site activities.

3.1   Three Framework Modules

These modules are responsible for collecting and preparing trajectory data collected from workers on a construction site that is ultimately used to determine construction project progress, which in turn is used to update the 4D BIM digital twin to reflect the reality on the construction site.

Module 1 is responsible for data preparation (Fig. 3). This consists of preprocessing RTLS trajectory data in a continuous stream-fashion, and for preparing the original as-planned 4D BIM once at the start up of the digital twin platform.

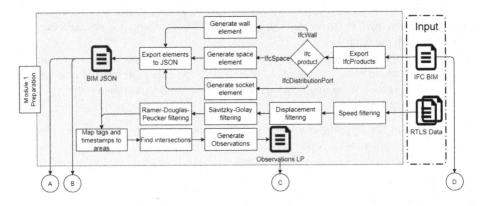

Fig. 3. Workflow diagram of Module 1 for data preparation.

Preprocessing RTLS (UWB) Data. Firstly, adjacent data points that exceed a threshold *speed* limit of 7 km/h for human workers and heavy vehicles are filtered away, removing noisy data spikes. Next, line smoothing is applied to more accurately capture human movement patterns, specifically via Savitzky–Golay filter which fits polynomial functions to sliding windows of data points [33]. Finally, redundant data points that are within a collinearity threshold ϵ are removed via the Ramer-Douglas-Peucker algorithm [31], i.e. curve decimation up to a threshold Hausdorff distance.

4D BIM. The open Industry Foundation Classes (IFC) BIM standard has been adopted in our framework. Building elements (members of the class *IfcProduct*) with properties such as their location and orientation are converted into JSON format for interoperability between modules. Five temporal scheduling properties are added to each product: the planned- and actual- start date, and end date, and the *status* which is the digital twin property that is updated from construction site sensor data. Status represents the stage of construction of the product, taking the values of either *built*, *possibly built*, and *not built*.

Observations. Symbolic terms representing semantic observations during specified time intervals are generated by combining processed trajectory data with the 4D BIM. The following initial set of observations in our framework were derived iteratively through pilot studies on real construction case data, and through rounds of dialogue with construction expert and co-author Jochen Teizer:

- proximity to a building element: "worker is *near* a particular element";
- work-zone occupancy: "worker is *in* a particular work zone";
- qualitative changes in speed: "worker movement is *faster/slower/stopped*";
- qualitative changes in height: "worker position is *lower/higher*";
- paths clashing with building elements: "worker moved *through* as-planned product", used as evidence that the given element has not yet been constructed;
- paths avoiding building elements: "worker moved *around* as-planned product", used as evidence that the given element has now been constructed.

Module 2 is responsible for inferring construction progress (Fig. 4), as described in Sects. 2.1–2.3. Module 3 is responsible for updating the 4D BIM digital twin based on inferences made about construction progress (Fig. 5). Inferences on construction progress formatted in JSON are parsed back into the IFC BIM format, annotating *as-planned* products (not yet physical) as *as-built* products according to the updated status properties, or marking zones around *possibly built* products where construction is (hypothetically) inferred to be underway.

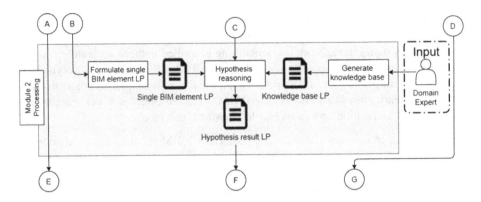

Fig. 4. Workflow diagram of Module 2 for hypothesis generation of construction progress.

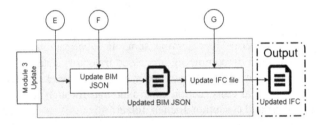

Fig. 5. Workflow diagram of Module 3 for updating the 4D BIM digit twin.

4   Functional Demonstration with Trajectory Data from a Construction Site

This section presents a prototype implementation of the system, applied to a real construction case in which RTLS trajectory data was collected from workers. The purpose is to demonstrate feasibility of our framework on real data, with respect to reliably updating a 4D BIM (i.e. the digital twin of the construction environment) within a practical amount of time.

Our prototype system used in this functional demonstration generates hypotheses based on trajectory data, an extract of which is presented in Fig. 2 (right). Six hours worth of work time on a construction site was recorded as as Ultra Wideband (UWB) localization data tracking 32 tags (where each tag roughly corresponds to one worker). Trajectory data was preprocessed to:

- eliminate clear instances of noise where spatial locations were recorded to jump erratically beyond a threshold distance *epsilon* within a single timestep, and
- to reduce the number of geo-referenced time points without changing the interpretation of construction activities; the UWB system ran 60 Hz, generating far more data points than needed to effectively track the workers.

Data was then converted into *holds/1* symbolic observations over time intervals asserting the area that the tag was in, *inArea/3*, and whether the tag was moving or stopped, *movement/2*. For example, an extract of facts is listed as follows:

```
holds(inArea(tag50e,1,interval(0,5692))).
holds(inArea(tag50e,10,interval(5692,5706))).
holds(inArea(tag50e,1,interval(5706,5712))).
holds(inArea(tag50e,10,interval(5712,5719))).
...
```

Intervals from the observations are used to discretise the time periods over which hypotheses are made:

```
interval(T1,T2)  :- holds(inArea(_,_,interval(T1,T2))).
```

We implemented three subtasks to demonstrate a proof of concept of our abduction approach:

- `working saw`: worker is located in the area with the saw for a duration more than a threshold amount of time (e.g. 2 min);
- `laying bricks`: worker is located in the area where pillars are being constructed for a duration more than a threshold amount of time (e.g. 2 min);
- `moving bricks`: worker spends some duration of time at the saw location (where bricks are cut and prepared), and later arrives and spends some time at the pillar location, without stopping in any other area in between.

We implement these abducible hypotheses in ASP as follows (where predicate "h" is used to represent "hypothesis" for brevity):

```
{h(working_saw(Tag, Area, at(T1,T2)))} :-
  tag(Tag), saw(Area), interval(T1,T2).

{h(laying_bricks(Tag, Area, at(T1,T2)))} :-
  tag(Tag), pillars(Area), interval(T1,T2).

{h(moving_bricks(Tag, Area, at(T1,T3)))} :-
                  tag(Tag), pillars(Area), interval(T1,T2),
interval(T3,T4),
  T2 - T1 > 5, T4 - T3 > 5.
```

Domain constraints on hypotheses are implemented as ASP integrity constraints. For example, the following constraint forbids the hypothesis that working at the saw takes less than 5 units of time:

```
  :- h(working_saw(_,_, at(T1,T2))), T2 - T1 < 5.
```

Models that propose hypotheses are preferred, implemented as weak constraints, e.g. the following weak constraint applies for the *working saw* hypothesis:

```
:~ tag(Tag), interval(T1,T2),
 not h(working_saw(Tag, 3, at(T1,T2))).
 [1,h(working_saw(Tag, 3, at(T1,T2)))]
```

Expected consequences of hypotheses are implemented as ASP rules, e.g. the hypothesis that the worker assigned to the UWB tag *Tag* is working at the saw from time t_1 to t_2 entails the expected observation that the tag is located at the saw area during this period:

```
expected(inArea(Tag,Area,interval(T1,T2)))  :-
  h(working_saw(Tag, Area, at(T1,T2))).
```

The following is an example of a hypothesis that entails multiple expected observations, including the *negation* of observations. It states that *moving bricks* entails being located at the saw area during the period t_1 to t_2, not stopping until time t_3, and arriving at the pillar location during the period t_3 to t_4:

```
3{ expected(inArea(Tag,SawArea,interval(T1,T2)));
   expected(inArea(Tag,PillarArea,interval(T3,T4)));
  -expected(movement(Tag,stopped,interval(T2,T3)))
} :-
  h(moving_bricks(Tag,PillarArea, at(T1,T4))),
  pillars(PillarArea), saw(SawArea),
  interval(T1,T2), interval(T3,T4), T2 <= T3.
```

Finally, expected observations entailed from hypotheses must be corroborated by observation evidence, implemented as ASP integrity constraints, e.g.:

```
:- expected(inArea(Tag,Area,interval(T1,T2))),
     not holds(inArea(Tag,Area,interval(T1,T2))).
```

Similarly, expecting the *negation* of observations during time period t_1 to t_4 is implemented as an ASP integrity constraint that forbids evidential observations appearing during this period between time points t_2 and t_3 such that $t_1 < t_2$ and $t_3 < t_4$, for example:

```
:- -expected(movement(Tag,Motion,interval(T1,T4))),
   holds(movement(Tag,Motion,interval(T2,T3))),
   T1 < T2, T3 < T4.
```

We ran our system with the above rules on the trajectory data illustrated in Fig. 2 (right). The data was preprocessed into 133 *holds/1* facts (symbolic observations). Our system found an optimal interpretation in 0.28 seconds (generating 6 prior sub-optimal models) that maximised the number of corroborated hypotheses that explain the observations, totalling 46 hypotheses in the model. The optimal model had a penalty score of 1147, meaning that 1147 potential hypotheses were rejected (either they could not be corroborated or they otherwise contradicted other hypotheses in the same model).

In total, 87 observations were not directly explained by any hypothesis (out of the 133 observations). Importantly, we do not aim to explain the maximum number of observations. Instead, our focus is on (a) ensuring that every presented hypothesis has a solid, plausible foundation in observed evidence, and (b) maximising the number of such generated hypotheses. More observations would be explained with the inclusion of additional rules representing activities such as *lunch breaks, moving through an area,* and so on. Based on the interpretation, the total amount of (hypothesised) work time can be summed up as a qualitative estimate of progress on erecting the pillars, which in turn is used to update progress on the 4D BIM.

As the execution completed within less than 1 s, this demonstration suggests that our framework for generating optimal, plausible interpretations operates fast enough to run in real-time on real-world construction site data.

5   From Manual to Automatic Safety Analysis

Safety and health of workers is among the top priorities in construction. Thus, concerning high-impact safety analysis, approximately 1/3 of all fatalities are due to falls from a dangerous height and thus falls are the largest category of causes of fatalities, out of the four major categories of fatal accidents [2]. Construction safety codes identify situations where such hazards arise, and dictate mitigation measures that must be employed to prevent accidents. For example, Fig. 6 illustrates the preventative German construction safety reg-

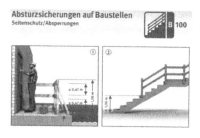

Fig. 6. Example of safety regulation for fall prevention [1]

ulation B100 for prevention [1]. The code states that a guard rail must be installed at a leading edge if a worker could fall more than 2m, or a covering if the drop is a hole in the platform greater than 9m².

To detect and prevent, for example, a fall-from-height hazard and apply a protective guardrail system, in an ideal case, a designer would design-out the hazard (so it does not appear during construction or later in mainte-nance). In reality, a safety engineer *manually* identifies the hazard locations on paper-based drawings (e.g. colours in Fig. 7 indicate types and locations where protective equipment needs to be installed) or substitutes unsafe construc-tion methods with a safer method (e.g., instead

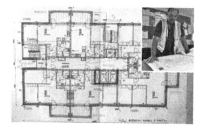

Fig. 7. Manual hazard identification and mitigation.

of workers using ladders that can tilt, workers should apply a scissor lift platform). While Prevention through Design (PtD) concepts have been practiced for many years [41], most of the existing risk mitigation approaches are done *manually*, and are thus prone to error or not performed at the right time [39]. We aim to automate this safety analysis on 4D BIMs that are being updated in real time.

5.1   Formalising Safety Building Codes for Automatic Safety Analysis

Research on Job Hazard Analysis (JHA) [44] and safety rule checking [27,36,45,46] that can *automatically* detect and resolve known hazards embedded in individual work activities have been introduced. However, there is still a wide gap in standardisation of safety concepts and software tools and a lack of strong demand from project owners and contractors. An extensible, intuitive to apply, integrated suite of safety analysis software tools for construction is currently still missing.

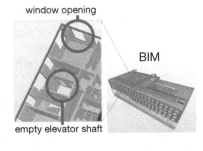

Fig. 8. Example violations of the B100 safety code on fall hazards in the given 4D BIM.

For example, given a BIM we seek to develop tools that can identify hazards that are defined in (natural language) safety codes. Figure 8 illustrates a BIM with two hazards highlighted that are described by the B100 code.

Our approach has been developed based on previous research in ontological and logic-based approaches to Construction Safety including [44,46]. To illustrate this we integrate our approach into a broader existing ontological framework for construction safety. Figure 9 illustrates the Construction Safety Ontology by Zhang, Boukamp and Teizer [44] extended with new (abstract) classes: spatial artefact and hazard space [34]. The authors distinguish the following three modelling layers: (1) Construction Product Model: building products and relations, such as doors, walls, storeys, slabs, and so on; (2) Construction Process Model: the construction plan including resources (equipment, materials, labour); (3) Construction Safety Model: construction safety knowledge (potential hazards, regulations, mitigating steps).

We define pertinent spatial artefacts [6] that capture semantic information about regions of empty space based on construction site activities, and human perception and behaviour (movement, visibility, falling spaces, activity, etc.). Similarly, we model hazards as spatial artefacts whose existence and (geometric) definition is often a simple expression involving topological relations and Boolean operations between regions (intersection, union, offset etc.), i.e. the *algorithm* for hazard detection is often as simple as clash detection. Spatial artefacts are modelled on the same ontological level as any other object in the product model, i.e. they inherit from the abstract class Product.

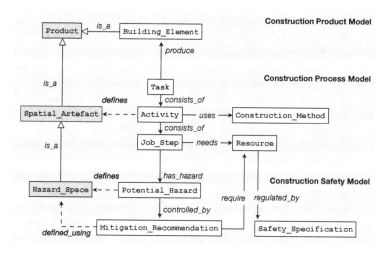

Fig. 9. Construction Safety Ontology from [44] extended with spatial artefacts to create Safe-ConDM [34] (magenta boxes are our extension).

5.2 The Shape of Meaningful "Empty Spaces" in Construction Safety

To explain the concept of *spatial artefacts*, a simple scenario is illustrated in Fig. 10 consisting of a worker, an excavator, and a job site, and a relevant safety code hazard definition is that: *"a worker is located too close to a heavy vehicle while occupied with an activity"*. In order to formalise this hazard, consider the *empty space* around the excavator that it needs to move through to carry out its function; we may refer to this special region of empty space as the excavator's *operational space* (Fig. 10). Similarly, there is a region of empty space around the job site within which the worker needs to be located in order to carry out their task, i.e. the *functional space* of the job site. These two semantically rich regions of empty space can be treated as objects in the BIM, and used to formalise the hazard: *"The intersection between the operational space of the excavator and the functional space of the job site"*.

These are examples of spatial arte-facts, a concept that was pioneered by Bhatt et al. in the context of architec-tural analysis [5,6]: regions of empty space that are rich with perceptual-locomotive semantics. Spatial artefacts "elevate" these semantically meaning-ful regions of empty space to become first-class objects, on the same onto-logical level as doors, walls, slabs, etc. Concretely, in a BIM such as IFC, spa-tial artefacts form an abstract class that is a subclass of IfcSpace. Consider the

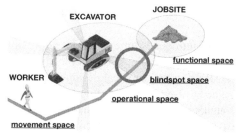

Fig. 10. Construction scenario augmented with spatial artefacts that provides a suitable concep-tual language to formalise safety codes.

previously discussed natural language code about a specific fall hazard: *"A platform that has a leading edge to a drop of more than 2m must be secured by a guardrail."*

We define a new spatial artefact called *Fall Space*, parametrically defined as: the region in which a person will fall by at least height a "dangerous distance" parameter i.e. in the German code example the parameter is set to 2m. The dangerous platform edges can now be precisely, formally defined as: *"where Movement spaces horizontally meet (touch) a Fall Space"*. An example illustrating fall spaces is presented in Fig. 11; the building cross-section is taken from the study from [29].

This formalisation based on spatial artefacts is (a) very faithful to the original natural language code (semantics only), (b) easy to understand and verify (transparent); (c) directly applies to different contexts without changing the declarative statement that formalises the code, i.e. the geometry of Fall Space is customised according to the project and context, whereas the concept 'dangerous edge' as defined above does not need to change. Importantly, this provides a uniform approach for modelling a large range of human-centred concepts (movement, visibility, performing tasks etc.) that can seamlessly be integrated within a BIM, and are effective "building blocks" for formalising a broad range of hazards in a clear and transparent way.

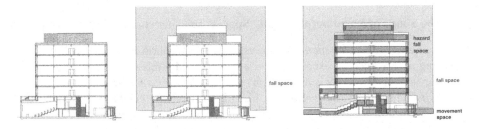

Fig. 11. Building cross section (left) [29] augmented with fall spaces (orange regions), movement spaces of workers (pink regions), and hazardous leading edges (red regions) defined as the intersection of fall spaces with movement spaces. (Color figure online)

6   Reasoning About Safety in 4D BIM Construction Plans

4D BIM introduces time to model a (possibly incomplete) construction plan. We formalise 4D BIM using ASP, specifically, we encode temporal information of a 4D BIM in ASP using two predicates, *construct/2* and *next/2*. Each element can optionally be assigned to a symbolic time point *construct/2*. The set of time points form a partial order through an intransitive relation *next/2*: given time points t_i, t_j then the interpretation of $next(t_i, t_j)$ is that t_j occurs directly after t_i such that there does not exist time point t_k where $next(t_i, t_k)$ and $next(t_k, t_j)$. Importantly, time points can branch (defining the partial order), e.g. given time points t_i, t_j, t_k and relations $next(t_i, t_j)$, $next(t_i, t_k)$ then the following two alternative time point sequences are consistent with the partial order: $<t_i, t_j, t_k>$ and $<t_i, t_k, t_j>$. The temporal relation *before/2* between time points is the transitive closure of *next/2*. Finally, 4D BIMs express temporal dependencies between elements: *dependency/2* between two BIM elements A, B means that element A must be constructed before B.

The following ASP rule states that, for all movement spaces that meet flush (touch horizontally) with a fall space, deduce a fall hazard space object. Its geometric representation is the intersection of the movement with the fall space offset by a given threshold e.g. 0.2 m in this example.

```
define_fall_hazard_space_(Id, RepFallHazard) :-
    movement_space(M), representation(M, RepM),
    fall_space(F),      representation(F, RepF),
    meets_flush(RepM, RepF),
    unique_guid(Id),
    OffsetRepF = @offset(RepF, 0.2),
    RepFallHazard = @intersection(RepM, OffsetRepF).

fall_hazard_space(Id) :- define_fall_hazard_space_(Id, _).

representation(Id, RepFallHazard) :-
    define_fall_hazard_space_(Id, RepFallHazard).
```

Similarly, movement spaces are created as the volume 2m directly on top of slabs, geometrically subtracted by 3D regions occupied by walls, columns and other movement obstacles. Fall spaces are the volume of space between the top surface of each object, and the next surface directly above (or the "sky") with the lower 2m subtracted. For this first prototype we simplified the calculation of movement spaces as the top surface of slabs subtracted by movement obstacles (columns and walls with voids where windows and doors will be placed), and we simplified fall spaces by taking a 2D bounding box of the site on each building storey (i.e. level by level) and subtracting the slabs on that storey.

6.1 Functional Demonstration of Safety Analysis

We have developed a second prototype system that applies the safety code B100 to a 4D BIM. In this section we present a functional demonstration of this second prototype on a real BIM to illustrate the effectiveness of our approach in implementing a safety code, and its practicality with respect to runtime performance. Our case study deals with Navitas (Fig. 13), a large multi-story multi-purpose building in Aarhus, Denmark. We extract the first floor from the BIM model and identify 1 slab, 102 walls, and 43 columns.

At time point 1, we identify 14 movement spaces, each demarcated by floor-intersecting obstacles (walls and columns), and derive 10 fall hazard spaces on the leading edge of the lower slab. At time point 2, the previous leading edge is connected to a middle slab, thus previous fall hazards disappear. We identify new walls and columns that are supported by the middle slab and union them with previous movement obstacles. We derive 12 new fall hazard spaces that are present on the boundaries of the slabs (where a worker could fall from the edge), or along

Fig. 12. The Navitas BIM used in the demonstration.

the holes in the slabs (where a worker could fall onto a open space). At time point 3, all slabs are constructed. We derive 15 fall hazard spaces, that must be guarded by safety rails or covering depending on their shape (Fig. 12).

Table 1 presents the number of spatial artefacts derived at time point 1, 2, 3 and runtime statistics. Figure 13 shows fall hazard spaces at each time point. Navitas has 707 building objects with an average number of 55 vertices (which we estimate to be small to medium in terms of typical real-world BIM size). IfcConvert[3] was used to generate 3D meshes from the BIM, taking 19.0 s. Our ASP program with spatial optimisations run with the *clingo* ASP solver derives a total of 94 spatial artefacts at time point 3 in an average of 0.24 s.

As the derivation of spatial artefacts (which constitutes safety compliance checking) completes within less than 1 s, it is fast enough to be used in practice where BIM updates are expected approximately once every few minutes (at most). This is significantly faster, semantically richer, and more numerically stable than previous fall hazard detection software systems, that instead opt for a *point-test sampling* strategy to determine dangerous leading edges [27].

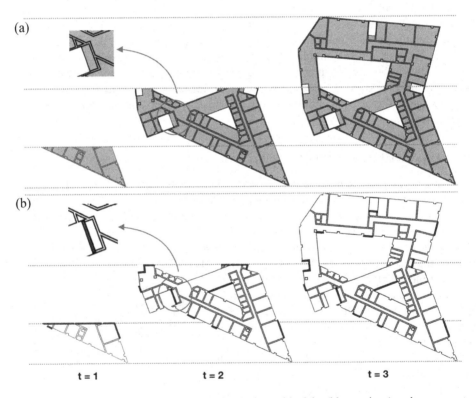

Fig. 13. a) Top-down view of the first floor in Navitas with slabs (blue regions) and movement obstacles (red regions); b) Fall hazards spaces (green regions, bottom row) (Colour figure online)

---

[3] http://www.ifcopenshell.org/.

Table 1. BIM statistics and runtime for safety compliance analysis, including deriving all spatial artefacts for the Navitas case study.

BIM objects	Time point	Fall spaces	Movement spaces	Fall hazard spaces	*clingo* Runtime (seconds)
707	$t = 1$	2	14	10	0.238
	$t = 2$	4	52	12	0.242
	$t = 3$	8	71	15	0.244

7 Concluding Remarks and Future Work

In this paper we proposed a digital twin framework for construction progress and safety analysis. Firstly, to update 4D BIMs in real time based on sensor data collected from a construction site we employ abductive reasoning via ASP to generate plausible hypotheses about construction site activities, corroborated by the sensor data. These hypotheses are then used as a qualitative measure of construction progress which is used to update the 4D BIM.

Secondly, to formalise natural language construction safety codes we use spatial artefacts, and develop a new kind of spatial artefact referred to as *fall spaces*. We demonstrated our approach with a prototypical implementation that formalises the German safety code B100, that we apply to a real BIM of the Navitas building in Denmark. Results show that the system identifies hazardous leading edges as defined in B100, and is practical in scaling to large BIMs, taking less than 1 s per time step of the 4D BIM.

Although the work presented here has not yet been deployed in a digital twin context we are convinced that this will be a reality in the coming years inside two new H2020 projects called BIM2Twin and COGITO. The time constraints in the building industry may only give sensor inputs on a daily basis but it would be sufficient to be able to flag potential hazards that could occur on a construction site. Thus a digital twin could be a proactive way of dealing with safety on a construction site which, for example, would encourage the application of protective guardrail systems at the right point of time in the process.

Acknowledgments. The authors gratefully acknowledge the Independent Research Fund Denmark for their financial support of the project "Intelligent Software Healing Environments" (DFF FTP1). We acknowledge the European Union for funding the BIM2TWIN (Grant agreement ID: 958398) and COGITO (Grant agreement ID: 958310) projects related to digital twins in a building context and the Poul Due Jensen Foundation for their funding for basic research in relation with digital twins.

References

1. Bau, B.G.: Absturzsicherungen auf Baustellen (2019). https://www.bgbau.de/fileadmin/Medien-Objekte/Medien/Bausteine/b_100/b_100.pdf. Accessed 28 Feb 2020
2. OSHA: Commonly used statistics (2019). www.osha.gov/data/commonstats. Accessed 28 Feb 2020

3. Akbarieh, A., Jayasinghe, L.B., Waldmann, D., Teferle, F.N.: BIM-based end-of-lifecycle decision making and digital deconstruction: literature review. Sustainability **12**(7), 2670 (2020)

4. Bhatt, M.: Reasoning about space, actions, and change: a paradigm for applications of spatial reasoning. In: Qualitative Spatio-Temporal Representation and Reasoning: Trends and Future Directions, pp. 284–320. IGI Global (2012)

5. Bhatt, M., Hois, J., Kutz, O.: Ontological modelling of form and function for architectural design. Appl. Ontol. **7**(3), 233–267 (2012)

6. Bhatt, M., Schultz, C., Huang, M.: The shape of empty space: human-centred cognitive foundations in computing for spatial design. In: 2012 IEEE Symposium on Visual Languages and Human-Centric Computing (VL/HCC), pp. 33–40. IEEE (2012)

7. Bhatt, M., Wallgrun, J.O.: Geospatial narratives and their spatio-temporal dynamics: commonsense reasoning for high-level analyses in geographic information systems. ISPRS Int. J. Geo Inf. **3**(1), 166–205 (2014)

8. Bloch, T., Sacks, R.: Clustering information types for semantic enrichment of building information models to support automated code compliance checking. J. Comput. Civ. Eng. **34**(6), 04020040 (2020)

9. Boje, C., Guerriero, A., Kubicki, S., Rezgui, Y.: Towards a semantic construction digital twin: directions for future research. Autom. Construct. **114**, 103179 (2020)

10. Braun, A., Tuttas, S., Borrmann, A., Stilla, U.: A concept for automated construction progress monitoring using BIM-based geometric constraints and photogrammetric point clouds. ITcon **20**(8), 68–79 (2015)

11. Deo, D., Esterman Jr., M., Thorn, B.K.: A methodology to quantify Cumulative Damage Function (CuDF) for integration into an object-oriented Life Cycle Assessment (LCA). In: International Design Engineering Technical Conferences and Computers and Information in Engineering Conference, vol. 58165, p. V004T05A033. American Society of Mechanical Engineers (2017)

12. Dimyadi, J., Amor, R.: Automated building code compliance checking-where is it at. In: Proceedings of CIB WBC, vol. 6, p. 1 (2013)

13. Dimyadi, J., Clifton, C., Spearpoint, M., Amor, R.: Regulatory knowledge encoding guidelines for automated compliance audit of building engineering design. In: Computing in Civil and Building Engineering, pp. 536–543. ASCE (2014)

14. Dubba, K., Bhatt, M., Dylla, F., Hogg, D.C., Cohn, A.G.: Interleaved inductive-abductive reasoning for learning complex event models. In: Muggleton, S.H., Tamaddoni-Nezhad, A., Lisi, F.A. (eds.) ILP 2011. LNCS (LNAI), vol. 7207, pp. 113–129. Springer, Heidelberg (2012). https://doi.org/10.1007/978-3-642-31951-8_14

15. Gebser, M., Kaminski, R., Kaufmann, B., Ostrowski, M., Schaub, T., Wanko, P.: Theory solving made easy with Clingo 5. In: Technical Communications of the 32nd International Conference on Logic Programming (ICLP 2016). Schloss Dagstuhl-Leibniz-Zentrum fuer Informatik (2016)

16. Gebser, M., Kaufmann, B., Neumann, A., Schaub, T.: *clasp*: a conflict-driven answer set solver. In: Baral, C., Brewka, G., Schlipf, J. (eds.) LPNMR 2007. LNCS (LNAI), vol. 4483, pp. 260–265. Springer, Heidelberg (2007). https://doi.org/10.1007/978-3-540-72200-7_23

17. Gelernter, D.: Mirror Worlds: Or: the Day Software Puts the Universe in a Shoebox... How It Will Happen and What It Will Mean. Oxford University Press, Oxford (1993)

18. Golparvar-Fard, M., Bohn, J., Teizer, J., Savarese, S., Peña-Mora, F.: Evaluation of image-based modeling and laser scanning accuracy for emerging automated performance monitoring techniques. Autom. Construct. **20**(8), 1143–1155 (2011)

19. Golparvar-Fard, M., Peña-Mora, F., Savarese, S.: D4AR-A 4-dimensional augmented reality model for automating construction progress monitoring data collection, processing and communication. J. Inf. Technol. Construct. **14**(13), 129–153 (2009)

20. Johansen, K.W., Nielsen, R.O., Schultz, C., Teizer, J.: Non-monotonic reasoning for automated progress analysis of construction operations. In: 20th International Conference on Construction Applications of Virtual Reality (CONVR 2020), pp. 292–303 (2020)
21. Khajavi, S.H., Motlagh, N.H., Jaribion, A., Werner, L.C., Holmström, J.: Digital twin: vision, benefits, boundaries, and creation for buildings. IEEE Access **7**, 147406–147419 (2019)
22. Li, B., Bhatt, M., Schultz, C.: lambdaProlog (QS): functional spatial reasoning in higher order logic programming (short paper). In: 14th International Conference on Spatial Information Theory (COSIT 2019). Schloss Dagstuhl-Leibniz-Zentrum fuer Informatik (2019)
23. Li, B., Schultz, C., Melzner, J., Golovina, O., Teizer, J.: Safe and lean location-based construction scheduling. In: 37th International Symposium on Automation and Robotics in Construction (ISARC 2020), pp. 1409–1416 (2020)
24. Li, B., Teizer, J., Schultz, C.: Non-monotonic spatial reasoning for safety analysis in construction. In: Proceedings of the 22nd International Symposium on Principles and Practice of Declarative Programming, pp. 1–12 (2020)
25. Lu, Q., Xie, X., Parlikad, A.K., Schooling, J.M., Konstantinou, E.: Moving from building information models to digital twins for operation and maintenance. Proc. Inst. Civ. Eng. Smart Infrastruct. Construct. 1–11 (2020)
26. Marek, V.W., Truszczyński, M.: Stable models and an alternative logic programming paradigm. In: Apt, K.R., Marek, V.W., Truszczynski, M., Warren, D.S. (eds.) The Logic Programming Paradigm, pp. 375–398. Springer, Heidelberg (1999). https://doi.org/10.1007/978-3-642-60085-2_17
27. Melzner, J., Zhang, S., Teizer, J., Bargstädt, H.J.: A case study on automated safety compliance checking to assist fall protection design and planning in building information models. Construc. Manage. Econ. **31**(6), 661–674 (2013)
28. Michalski, R.S.: Inferential theory of learning as a conceptual basis for multistrategy learning. Mach. Learn. **11**(2–3), 111–151 (1993)
29. Migda, W., Szczepański, M., Lasowicz, N., Jakubczyk-Gałczyńska, A., Jankowski, R.: Non-linear analysis of inter-story pounding between wood-framed buildings during ground motion. Geosciences **9**(12), 488 (2019)
30. Perri, S., Scarcello, F., Leone, N.: Abductive logic programs with penalization: semantics, complexity and implementation. Theory Pract. Logic Program. **5**(1–2), 123 (2005)
31. Ramer, U.: An iterative procedure for the polygonal approximation of plane curves. Comput. Graph. Image Process. **1**(3), 244–256 (1972)
32. Rocca, R., Rosa, P., Sassanelli, C., Fumagalli, L., Terzi, S.: Integrating virtual reality and digital twin in circular economy practices: a laboratory application case. Sustainability **12**(6), 2286 (2020)
33. Savitzky, A., Golay, M.J.: Smoothing and differentiation of data by simplified least squares procedures. Anal. Chem. **36**(8), 1627–1639 (1964)
34. Schultz, C., Li, B., Teizer, J.: Towards a unifying domain model of construction safety: SafeConDM. In: 27th International Workshop On Intelligent Computing In Engineering (EG-ICE) (2020)
35. Schwabe, K., König, M., Teizer, J.: BIM applications of rule-based checking in construction site layout planning tasks. In: ISARC. Proceedings of the International Symposium on Automation and Robotics in Construction, vol. 33, p. 1. IAARC Publications (2016)
36. Schwabe, K., Teizer, J., König, M.: Applying rule-based model-checking to construction site layout planning tasks. Autom. Construct. **97**, 205–219 (2019)
37. Suchan, J., Bhatt, M., Walega, P., Schultz, C.: Visual explanation by high-level abduction: on answer-set programming driven reasoning about moving objects. In: 32nd AAAI Conference on Artificial Intelligence (AAAI 2018), New Orleans, USA, 2–7 February 2018, pp. 1965–1972. AAAI Press (2018)

38. Sydora, C., Stroulia, E.: Towards rule-based model checking of building information models. In: ISARC. Proceedings of the International Symposium on Automation and Robotics in Construction, vol. 36, pp. 1327–1333. IAARC Publications (2019)
39. Teizer, J.: Right-time vs real-time pro-active construction safety and health system architecture. Construction Innovation (2016)
40. Thagard, P., Shelley, C.: Abductive reasoning: logic, visual thinking, and coherence. In: Dalla Chiara, M.L., Doets, K., Mundici, D., van Benthem, J. (eds.) Logic and scientific methods, pp. 413–427. Springer, Dordrecht (1997). https://doi.org/10.1007/978-94-017-0487-8_22
41. Toole, T.M., Gambatese, J.A., Abowitz, D.A.: Owners' role in facilitating prevention through design. J. Prof. Issues Eng. Educ. Pract. **143**(1), 04016012 (2017)
42. Tuttas, S., Braun, A., Borrmann, A., Stilla, U.: Acquisition and consecutive registration of photogrammetric point clouds for construction progress monitoring using a 4D BIM. PFG J. Photogram. Remote Sens. Geoinf. Sci. **85**(1), 3–15 (2017)
43. Vering, C., Mehrfeld, P., Nürenberg, M., Coakly, D., Lauster, M., Müller, D.: Unlocking potentials of building energy systems' operational efficiency: application of digital twin design for HVAC systems. In: 16th International Building Performance Simulation Association (IBPSA) (2019)
44. Zhang, S., Boukamp, F., Teizer, J.: Ontology-based semantic modeling of construction safety knowledge: towards automated safety planning for job hazard analysis (JHA). Autom. Construct. **52**, 29–41 (2015)
45. Zhang, S., Sulankivi, K., Kiviniemi, M., Romo, I., Eastman, C.M., Teizer, J.: BIM-based fall hazard identification and prevention in construction safety planning. Saf. Sci. **72**, 31–45 (2015)
46. Zhang, S., Teizer, J., Lee, J.K., Eastman, C.M., Venugopal, M.: Building information modeling (BIM) and safety: automatic safety checking of construction models and schedules. Autom. Construct. **29**, 183–195 (2013)
47. Zoliner, R., Pardowitz, M., Knoop, S., Dillmann, R.: Towards cognitive robots: building hierarchical task representations of manipulations from human demonstration. In: Proceedings of the 2005 IEEE International Conference On Robotics and Automation, pp. 1535–1540. IEEE (2005)

Software Verification Tools

Software Verification Tools
(Track Introduction)

Markus Schordan[1]🆔, Dirk Beyer[2]🆔, and Irena Bojanova[3]🆔

[1] Lawrence Livermore National Laboratory, CA, USA
[2] LMU Munich, Germany
[3] National Institute of Standards and Technology, MD, USA

Abstract. This ISoLA track is concerned with methods for the evaluation and comparison of analysis and verification techniques: we discuss conservative static-analysis and verification tools, as well as discuss and evaluate state-of-the-art approaches. As developers of conservative static-analysis tools aim at reducing the false-alarm rate, developers of verification tools aim at reducing the resource consumption when verifying program properties, that is, within a shorter period of time and with lower memory requirements, but still provide a definitive answer whether a program satisfies a specification or not, avoiding to report false alarms.

Keywords: Static analysis · Software verification · False-alarm rate · Tool Competition · Formal Methods · Verification Tools

1   Introduction

An existing static analysis in a compiler is always a good basis for a software-analysis tool implementation, and in recent years there has been an increasing effort in providing more open and flexible compiler technology for advanced static analysis. The Clang analyzer[4], based on Clang, has been available several years, and an alternative analysis can also be performed at the LLVM-IR level. This technology has been integrated with several tools in recent years with growing interest. It has created an active community in the Clang/LLVM community, offering several tutorials in an attempt to make it easier for developers to start utilizing static analysis in software projects. Recently, starting with the release of GCC 10, there has been also a lot of activity in the GCC community with positive reactions from various groups, about the new static analysis in GCC [1, 14, 15]. Companies such as Google started also building their own static-analysis tools in recent years [16]. They evaluated their tools with respect to how much users benefit from using the tool, and indeed for tools in practice, this is the ultimate challenge to meet.

In addition to more accessible compiler infrastructures, over the last few years, competitions and challenges have played an increasingly important role in the formal-methods community. In 2019, the TOOLympics brought together

---

[4] https://clang-analyzer.llvm.org

© Springer Nature Switzerland AG 2021
T. Margaria and B. Steffen (Eds.): ISoLA 2020, LNCS 12479, pp. 177–181, 2021.
https://doi.org/10.1007/978-3-030-83723-5_12

16 different competitions of formal-methods tools [3]. The competitions have quite different competition formats, ranging from fully automated to interactive evaluations, from collected and maintained benchmark sets to yearly generated benchmark sets, and from objective scoring schemas to voting-based rankings, to assess who or which tool provided the best-quality results. Also the target languages and program representations greatly differ.

The International Competition on Software Verification (SV-COMP) [4] is fully automated, where participants submit a verification tool and each verification tool is evaluated on the benchmark suite SV-Benchmarks (https://github.com/sosy-lab/sv-benchmarks), comprising thousands of C programs divided into various categories. A number of correctness properties are specified for each program. The properties include the absence of assertion violations, memory-safety errors, concurrency bugs, and program termination. The programs, properties, and expected results are all provided to the participants beforehand. SV-COMP requires that the verification tools give a reason for their verdict, that is, it is not sufficient to return an answer true or false, but tools must supplement the answer with a verification witness [5, 6, 7], which can be used to validate the verification result or understand the reason for violation or correctness.

In contrast, in the annual RERS Challenge [11, 12] new benchmarks are synthesized every year from specifications. Each RERS problem presents a reactive system and a set of properties of that system. (That is, one RERS problem induces a set of verification tasks.) Like other competitions, RERS has also added tracks over the years, since 2012, and consists now of 4 tracks, separated into two sequential and parallel categories where each one is again split into two tracks, one for reachability analysis and one for the verification of properties specified in linear temporal logic. All sequential programs are available in two languages, C and Java. The parallel verification tasks are provided as a parallel system of (rooted) labeled transition systems (LTS) that communicate via synchronized transitions. In RERS only the results are submitted, but not the tools themselves. This is possible because resources are not controlled and new benchmarks are generated every year and the correct answers are not known to the participants.

One crucial aspect of detected errors is how they are reported, what terminology is used to describe them, and in general how people can speak about them and agree on bug fixes. The Bugs Framework (BF) [8] is one attempt to provide a proper terminology for this purpose. It organizes software weaknesses (bugs) into distinct classes, such as Memory Allocation, Injection, and Encryption. With BF, software-testing tools could produce more precise reports. With BF, practitioners and researchers could more accurately and clearly (a) describe problems in software and discuss the classes of bugs that tools report, and (b) explain what kinds of vulnerabilities the proposed mitigation techniques prevent. Each BF class has an accurate and precise definition and comprises (i) a level (high or low) that identifies the fault as language-related or semantic, (ii) attributes that identify the software fault, (iii) causes of the fault, (iv) consequences the fault could lead to, and (v) sites in code where the fault might occur. Those concerned with software quality, the reliability of programs and digital systems, or cyber-security, might be able to make more rapid progress by more clearly labeling the results of errors in software using BF. Those responsible for designing, operating, and maintaining computer clusters can communicate more exactly about threats, attacks, patches, and exposures.

2   Contributions with Published Papers in the Track

This year, four papers dealing with different aspects of evaluating, comparing, and combining software-verification tools were accepted for this track.

In *Benchmarking Open-Source Static Analyzers for Security Testing for C* [10], Christoph Gentsch, Rohan Krishnamurthy, and Thomas S. Heinze present an in-depth evaluation of static-analysis security testing (SAST) tools. They evaluate eleven static-analysis tools for the C programming language on the Juliet test suite and six tools on the Wireshark application.

In *Verification of Liveness and Safety Properties of Behavioral Programs using BPjs* [2], Michael Bar-Sinai and Gera Weiss present an approach and a tool suite for the specification and verification of safety and liveness properties. Liveness properties are defined using so called "hot states", in which scenarios are allowed to stay for a finite time, but not forever. Safety properties are defined using assertions. They define liveness violations with regards to specific program components and describe an approach for validating the absence of such violations. The proposed approach is supported by BPjs, an open-source tool suite developed by the authors.

In *On Correctness, Precision, and Performance in Quantitative Verification: QComp 2020 Competition Report* [9], Carlos E. Budde, Arndt Hartmanns, Michaela Klauck, Jan Kretinsky, David Parker, Tim Quatmann, Andrea Turrini, and Zhen Zhang present a detailed report of the QComp Competition 2020. QComp evaluates tools for quantitative verification. These tools compute probabilities, expected rewards, or steady-state values for formal models of stochastic and timed systems. The paper reports on experimental evaluations of trade-offs between precision and achieved performance. The trade-offs are necessary because exact results often cannot be determined efficiently for such systems, and most tools use floating-point arithmetic in iterative algorithms to approximate the quantity of interest. In 2020, nine tools participated in the competition. They gave rise to a performance evaluation in five tracks with varying correctness criteria, which are presented and explained in detail in the report.

In *Every Component Matters: Generating Parallel Verification Benchmarks with Hardness Guarantees* [13], Marc Jasper, Maximilian Schlüter, David Schmidt, and Bernhard Steffen present an approach for generating hard verification problems for concurrent systems. In some areas of verification, there is only a limited amount of benchmark verification tasks available and there is a need for more verification tasks. The new contribution of this paper is to consider concurrent systems and make sure that for analyzing the generated system, one cannot simply ignore (abstract away) one of the components. Rather, the approach gives certain guarantees that all components must be analyzed. This approach nicely complements existing methods and can be helpful for closing gaps in benchmark sets by automatically generating new problems.

3   Conclusion

The evaluation of conservative static-analysis and verification tools has become an important aspect in the development of secure software and quality assurance in software development in general. In this track, the publications give insights into the state-of-the-art of conservative static-analysis tools [10], into a specific verification technique for safety and liveness properties [2], into the competition QComp 2020, reporting about several experimental evaluations of trade-offs between precision and performance with varying correctness criteria [9], and into an approach to generate hard verification tasks for the verification of concurrent systems [13]. All four publications have in common that software tools aid developers in better understanding the various aspects of program correctness and performance, and are contributions of researchers in advancing the state-of-the-art of software-verification technology.

Acknowledgments

This work was partially performed under the auspices of the U.S. Department of Energy by Lawrence Livermore National Laboratory under Contract DE-AC52-07NA27344, Lawrence Livermore National Security, LLC. IM release number LLNL-CONF-814571, and was partially funded by the Deutsche Forschungsgemeinschaft (DFG) – 418257054 (Coop).

Disclaimer

Certain trade names and company products are mentioned in the text or identified. In no case does such identification imply recommendation or endorsement by the National Institute of Standards and Technology (NIST), nor that they are necessarily the best available for the purpose.

References

1. Bahena, V.R.: Major improvements in GCC 10.1 (2020), https://clearlinux.org/blogs-news/major-improvements-gcc-101, (urldate: 2020-07-27)
2. Bar-Sinai, M., Weiss, G.: Verification of liveness and safety properties of behavioral programs using BPjs. In: Proc. ISoLA 2020, LNCS. Springer (2021). https://doi.org/10.1007/978-3-030-83723-5_14
3. Bartocci, E., Beyer, D., Black, P.E., Fedyukovich, G., Garavel, H., Hartmanns, A., Huisman, M., Kordon, F., Nagele, J., Sighireanu, M., Steffen, B., Suda, M., Sutcliffe, G., Weber, T., Yamada, A.: TOOLympics 2019: An overview of competitions in formal methods. In: Proc. TACAS (3). pp. 3–24. LNCS 11429, Springer (2019). https://doi.org/10.1007/978-3-030-17502-3_1

4. Beyer, D.: Software verification: 10th comparative evaluation (SV-COMP 2021). In: Proc. TACAS (2). pp. 401–422. LNCS 12652, Springer (2021). https://doi.org/10.1007/978-3-030-72013-1_24

5. Beyer, D., Dangl, M., Dietsch, D., Heizmann, M.: Correctness witnesses: Exchanging verification results between verifiers. In: Proc. FSE. pp. 326–337. ACM (2016). https://doi.org/10.1145/2950290.2950351

6. Beyer, D., Dangl, M., Dietsch, D., Heizmann, M., Stahlbauer, A.: Witness validation and stepwise testification across software verifiers. In: Proc. FSE. pp. 721–733. ACM (2015). https://doi.org/10.1145/2786805.2786867

7. Beyer, D., Dangl, M., Lemberger, T., Tautschnig, M.: Tests from witnesses: Execution-based validation of verification results. In: Proc. TAP. pp. 3–23. LNCS 10889, Springer (2018). https://doi.org/10.1007/978-3-319-92994-1_1

8. Bojanova, I., Black, P.E., Yesha, Y., Wu, Y.: The bugs framework (BF): A structured approach to express bugs. In: Proc. QRS. pp. 175–182 (2016). https://doi.org/10.1109/QRS.2016.29

9. Budde, C.E., Hartmanns, A., Klauck, M., Kretinsky, J., Parker, D., Quatmann, T., Turrini, A., Zhang, Z.: On correctness, precision, and performance in quantitative verification - QComp 2020 competition report. In: Proc. ISoLA 2020, LNCS. Springer (2021). https://doi.org/10.1007/978-3-030-83723-5_15

10. Gentsch, C., Krishnamurthy, R., Heinze, T.S.: Benchmarking open-source static analyzers for security testing for C. In: Proc. ISoLA 2020, LNCS. Springer (2021). https://doi.org/10.1007/978-3-030-83723-5_13

11. Howar, F., Isberner, M., Merten, M., Steffen, B., Beyer, D., Păsăreanu, C.S.: Rigorous examination of reactive systems. International Journal on Software Tools for Technology Transfer 16(5), 457–464 (2014). https://doi.org/10.1007/s10009-014-0337-y

12. Jasper, M., Fecke, M., Steffen, B., Schordan, M., Meijer, J., Pol, J.v.d., Howar, F., Siegel, S.F.: The RERS 2017 challenge and workshop (invited paper). In: Proc. SPIN. pp. 11–20. SPIN 2017, ACM (2017). https://doi.org/10.1145/3092282.3098206

13. Jasper, M., Schlüter, M., Schmidt, D., Steffen, B.: Every component matters: Generating parallel verification benchmarks with hardness guarantees. In: Proc. ISoLA 2020, LNCS. Springer (2021). https://doi.org/10.1007/978-3-030-83723-5_16

14. Malcolm, D.: Static analysis in GCC 10 (2020), https://developers.redhat.com/blog/2020/03/26/static-analysis-in-gcc-10, (urldate: 2020-03-26)

15. Nichols, S.: GCC 10 gets security bug trap. And look what just fell into it: OpenSSL and a prod-of-death flaw in servers and apps (2020), https://www.theregister.com/2020/04/23/gcc_openssl_vulnerability, (urldate: 2020-04-23)

16. Sadowski, C., Aftandilian, E., Eagle, A., Miller-Cushon, L., Jaspan, C.: Lessons from building static analysis tools at Google. Commun. ACM 61(4), 58–66 (Mar 2018). https://doi.org/10.1145/3188720

Benchmarking Open-Source Static Analyzers for Security Testing for C

Christoph Gentsch$^{(\boxtimes)}$, Rohan Krishnamurthy$^{(\boxtimes)}$, and Thomas S. Heinze$^{(\boxtimes)}$

German Aerospace Center (DLR), Institute of Data Science, Jena, Germany
{`christoph.gentsch,rohan.krishnamurthy,thomas.heinze`}`@dlr.de`

Abstract. As the number of available static analysis security testing (SAST) tools grows, the more difficult it becomes for developers to decide which tool(s) to use. We report on our evaluation of 11 open-source general-purpose SAST tools for the C programming language on the SARD Juliet Test Suite and of six tools on the Wireshark software. In line with the previous work, we find that there is no single superior tool, though sound tools performed the best on the Juliet test cases.

1 Introduction

In recent years, the market for *static analysis security testing (SAST) tools* has expanded, since software security increasingly becomes a concern and draws more and more attention. As a result, there exists a variety of tools, whether commercial or open-source, which claim more or less to do a "security analysis". Some of these tools are basically simple syntax checkers, which apply context-insensitive pattern matching to check program source code for compliance to a certain standard or best practices. As these tools certainly can help in improving code style and security to some extent, it is though questionable, how good they are at finding, e.g., deep nested memory errors or concurrency problems. Then there are more sophisticated, semantic analyzers, which focus on finding bugs and vulnerabilities instead of compliance checking, but make no claims on the complete absence of vulnerabilities or run-time errors. Last, there are sound semantic analyzers, which rely for example on abstract interpretation or reasoning on program behavior using Hoare logic, and promise to make strong guarantees. What this means in practice may vary, depending on the addressed use case. Most sound tools try to guarantee the absence of vulnerabilities by over-approximating program behavior and thus accept that some of the reported warnings are false positives – e.g., for the authors of *Frama-C*, soundness means to "aim at being correct, that is, never to remain silent for a location in the source code where an error can happen at run-time"[1]. Other sound tools in contrast aim at reducing the burden from developers to scroll through numerous

---

[1] cf. Frama-C website (https://www.frama-c.com).

T. Margaria and B. Steffen (Eds.): ISoLA 2020, LNCS 12479, pp. 182–198, 2021.
https://doi.org/10.1007/978-3-030-83723-5_13

reported warnings and try to reduce the number of false positives. The authors of *Infer* thus state: "soundness" does not translate to 'no bugs are missed' [3].

As the variety of tools and techniques can be confusing for a developer, it is apparent that an evaluation of their abilities is desirable. The objective of our paper is to conduct such an evaluation and, in particular, to measure to which extent open-source SAST tools are capable of finding vulnerabilities in C code. The focus on C has several reasons: C is still one of the most important programming languages around. Approximately one third of the packages of Debian Linux are written in C. In the field of (in-)security, C also stands out: A small fraction of C programs is responsible for 50% of all vulnerabilities in Debian Linux (cf. Sect. 3). There exist several tools for analyzing C code and datasets with C code to analyze. The *SARD Juliet Test Suite* [5] provides a state-of-the-art benchmarking dataset for SAST tools and is also the basis for our evaluation. The limitation to open-source tools comes from our requirement to have for anyone reproducible results and avoid problems with *DeWitt clauses*, as used in license agreements of commercial tools [12]. As open-source developers usually use open-source tools themselves, this is also a test of the ability of the open-source community to facilitate secure software development.

The question we want to answer is: *If I, as a software developer, use this tool, what can I expect of the security of my code?* In this light, a SAST tool can also be seen as a kind of "insurance" for the developer: "*If I run this tool, my code is mostly secure*". Apparently, this proposition only holds if the used tool is able to identify most types of defects which threaten security. Thus, we need a benchmark which reflects the most common vulnerabilities, weighted for their observed frequency, or "prevalence", and test every tool on it. We therefore also focus on general-purpose SAST tools for C, which address a wide-spread spectrum of software vulnerabilities. For this reason, we have also deliberately chosen to mostly exclude verification technology, and with the exception of three tools, excluded software verifiers from our evaluation. Apparently, including more tools in the evaluation, for example software verifiers, would allow for drawing a more extensive picture. We however believe that our study can be a valuable building block in creating this bigger picture on the state-of-the-art of SAST tools for C. Thus, the contributions of the paper can be summarized as follows:

- We evaluated 11 open-source general-purpose static analysis security testing tools for C on the *Juliet Test Suite* and report on the tools' accuracy.
- We analyzed the prevalence of vulnerability patterns in the *Juliet Test Suite* and in *Debian Linux*, as a representative for production software.
- We conducted a trial of the six most promising SAST tools on *Wireshark v1.8* and report on the tools' recall in finding real vulnerabilities.

The rest of the paper is structured as follows: In Sect. 2 we review related work and discuss the challenges when evaluating SAST tools for C. An investigation on the prevalence of C-related vulnerabilities for the Debian Linux distribution is presented in Sect. 3. Based upon this, we introduce the evaluation methodology and dataset in Sect. 4 and present the results in Sect. 5. Threats of validity are discussed in Sect. 6 and, eventually, Sect. 7 concludes the paper.

2   Previous Work on Benchmarking SAST Tools for C

Several authors have analyzed the effectiveness of SAST tools in finding vulnerabilities in C code. Chatzieleftheriou and Katzaros [4] tested four open-source tools and two commercial tools using their own test suite of C programs, covering 30 vulnerability patterns selected from the *Common Weakness Enumeration (CWE)*[2] catalogue and the *CERT C Secure Coding Standard* [13]. The test suite included "bad" code, representing real vulnerabilities, and "good" code, representing spurious findings if reported by a SAST tool, for each vulnerability pattern and thus allowed to assess the tools effectiveness in terms of precision and recall. They found the two commercial tools to rank best, achieving a F-Score of 0.85, closely followed by the open-source tools *Frama-C* (0.8) and *UNO* (0.7). *CppCheck* and *Splint* ranked at the lower end (<0.6). The same test suite was used later in [10] to compare the tools *Splint*, *CppCheck*, *Frama-C*, *Infer* and *Clang*. *Clang* and *Frama-C* lead again with a F-Score > 0.9, followed by *Infer* (0.88) and *CppCheck* (0.78). The good scores may indicate that the test suite is now too outdated to give a good measure for comparison of SAST tools.

The *SARD Juliet Test Suite* for C/C++ was first published in 2011 and last updated in 2017 [5, 11]. The test suite covers more than 100 different CWE's in 64k test cases. Similar to Chatzieleftheriou and Katzaros [4], each test case has a "bad" and a "good" function, together with the labels for the tested CWE. As half of the test cases thus consists of "bad" functions, this implies that the measured precision is only a precision for 50% prevalence – which means, there is a 50% chance for a SAST tool to just *guess* the right location. To address this, the authors suggested another metric in [11], the discrimination rate, wherein the findings counted as true positive only if a tool reported the "bad" function, but not the "good" function. Note that the type of error (CWE) also has to match with the CWE associated to the test case. As this is a feasible procedure in theory, the practical application is not as straightforward, especially when testing open-source tools. Those tools often do not report CWE's, or just report some abstract CWE class, whereas the *Juliet Test Suite* asks for specific CWE variants. One solution to this is proposed by Goseva-Popstojanova and Perhinschi [6], who also used the *Juliet Test Suite* for benchmarking three anonymous commercial tools. They carried out a fuzzy matching of vulnerabilities by matching CWE's that are closely related in the CWE hierarchy. This approach though does not help in all cases. Consider the following example from the *Juliet Test Suite*[3]:

---

[2] https://cwe.mitre.org/.

[3] File `CWE195_Signed_to_Unsigned_Conversion_Error__negative_malloc_18.c`.

Listing 1.1. Example code from the Juliet Test Suite for C/C++

```
1  data = -1;
2  if (data < 100)
3  {
4          char * dataBuffer = (char *)malloc(data);
5  ...
```

Here, a SAST tool could report *CWE-686* (function call with incorrect argument type) at line 5, since *malloc* expects unsigned integers. Otherwise, a *CWE-131* (incorrect calculation of buffer size) would also be correct. The *Juliet Test Suite* however expects *CWE-195* (signed To unsigned conversion error). The complexity of the CWE hierarchy is causing these issues. With more than 800 weaknesses, it is very fine-grained and in addition offers more than 30 different views, which change the relation between CWE's. In this jungle, choosing the correct CWE is hard for test suite designers and tool developers.

For a pragmatic approach, one could, instead of matching CWE's, sophistically design the test cases in a way that only one type of vulnerability can be identified at a specific location. This approach was taken by Shiraishi et al. [14] and lead to the *ITC Benchmark*. This test suite has the advantage of being more easy to comprehend, as there is no need to check the location of a vulnerability and no CWE mapping has to be done. However, the tests are rather easy such that static analysis tools can achieve up to perfect results on this benchmark in case of some defect patterns [14]. As a result, comparing tools above this cutoff is infeasible. Other issues regarding the *ITC Benchmark* include the inclusion of unintended defects in the test cases, wrong and/or missing vulnerability markers and the selection of types of defects in the test cases, which is not representative [7]. Besides, the *ITC Benchmark* has been designed with respect to safety tools such that tests for security-related defects and flaws concerning input validation, path traversal, or code injection are completely missing. The benchmark is though used in [1] to compare open-source SAST for C. According to the results, *Clang* and *Frama-C* are leading the field, closely followed by *CppCheck*.

While the *Juliet Test Suite* was primarily designed for evaluating the effectiveness of commercial SAST tools and benchmarking results are therefore presented anonymously [5], Lu et al. [9] report on a more recent comparison of open-source SAST tools and one commercial tool. They used the *Juliet Test Suite*, but left the method for evaluating the tools findings and measuring precision and recall unspecified. Despite the included commercial tool, the best F-Scores were reached by *CppCheck* (0.34), *Frama-C* (0.3), and *Clang* (0.3). We also acknowledge the existence of benchmarks for the evaluation of static analysis tools for C without a focus on security testing. As an example, the *SV-Benchmark* [2][4] provides an up-to-date collection of verification tasks to evaluate the effectiveness and efficiency of fully automatic software verifiers for C. An overhaul of SAST tool testing datasets, like the *Juliet Test Suite*, using insights gained from these benchmarks seems a promising item for future work.

---

[4] https://github.com/sosy-lab/sv-benchmarks.

3   Prevalence of C-Related Vulnerability Patterns

To investigate which C-related flaws cause the most vulnerabilities found in production software, and therefore should be included in a test suite for benchmarking SAST tools, we analyzed vulnerabilities and vulnerability patterns reported for the Debian Linux distribution[5]. Debian comes with thousands of software packages, ranging from desktop applications like OpenOffice or Firefox to web servers like Apache or shells like bash, which makes it a representative example for production software. As a first step, we downloaded all software packages from the stable Debian release when conducting our research, i.e., *Debian 9 "Stretch"*. We then gathered reported vulnerabilities for the packages, as listed by means of *Common Vulnerabilities and Exposures (CVE)* in the packages' change-log files. CVE's are vulnerabilities, which were reported to the public CVE database[6].

Table 1. Statistics on Debian vulnerabilities

Packages total:	24,438
Packages containing CVE's:	1,327
Packages with C as main language:	8,132
Packages with C as main language containing CVE's:	838
CVE's since 1988 (not only Debian):	103,193
CVE's in the Debian packages:	10,472
CVE's in all C packages:	5,639
⊘ CVE's per package:	0.4
⊘ CVE's per C-package:	0.7

As can be seen in Table 1, we found 10k CVE's reporting vulnerabilities for all Debian software packages. Note that this accounts for approx. 10% of all CVE's ever reported since 1988. Considering only the Debian packages with C as the main language, we found that 10% of those packages contain 50% of all CVE's reported for the Debian packages. The average count of CVE's in a C package is consequently higher than the overall average of CVE's per package.

Combining the gathered CVE data with data from the *National Vulnerability Database (NVD)*[7] allowed us to map individual CVE's to vulnerability patterns, i.e., CWE's, and weight them with their severity scores. This way, we were able to analyze which types of vulnerabilities were found in those Debian packages, whose main language is C. To gain an impression of the current situation, we only considered CVE's as reported in the years 2017–2018. Table 2 presents the Top-10 CWE's for C packages, according to the summed up NVD severity scores. Apparently, the "buffer overflow" is still the leading flaw in C

---

[5] https://www.debian.org.

[6] https://cve.mitre.org.

[7] https://nvd.nist.org.

Table 2. Top-10 vulnerabilities in Debian packages with C as main language

Common Weakness ID	Percentage
CWE-119 (Improper Restriction of [..] the Bounds of a Memory Buffer)	32.1%
CWE-20 (Improper Input Validation)	10.5%
CWE-125 (Out-of-bounds Read)	10.0%
CWE-399 (Resource Management Errors)	8.1%
CWE-190 (Integer Overflow or Wraparound)	6.1%
CWE-476 (NULL Pointer Dereference)	5.0%
CWE-787 (Out-of-bounds Write)	4.3%
CWE-284 (Improper Access Control)	3.6%
CWE-264 (Permissions, Privileges, and Access Controls)	3.8%
CWE-416 (Use After Free)	3.6%

programs, followed by several other memory-related vulnerabilities. To provide a more comprehensive overview, we also mapped the C-related CWE's to the clusters of the *Software Fault Patterns (SFP)* view of the CWE hierarchy[8].

Table 3. Top SFP clusters found in Debian packages with C as main language

Cluster	Percentage
Memory access	49.3%
Resource management	12.8%
Tainted input	10.7%
Risky values	6.8%

As shown in Table 3, the top fault cluster is memory access with a fraction of approx. 50% of all found vulnerabilities. Members of this cluster are vulnerabilities like, e.g., faulty buffer access, faulty pointer use, improper NULL termination. The second-severe fault cluster resource management with a fraction of 12% includes vulnerabilities like use after free or missing release of file handles. Tainted input with approx. 10% is related to missing sanitization of data from user input. Finally, risky values consists of vulnerabilities related to integer overflow, incorrect type conversions or divides by zero. Note that this result is on par with the findings by other research [8]. Altogether, it seems like most vulnerabilities come from implementation errors which have been in the focus of static analysis tools for many years. In the following, we report on our evaluation of the capabilities of SAST tools finding these errors.

---

[8] https://cwe.mitre.org/data/definitions/888.html.

4   SAST Tool Evaluation Method

4.1   Tested Open-Source SAST Tools

The open-source SAST tools for C which we included in our evaluation are shown in Table 4. We included general-purpose static analysis tools for security testing, but deliberately decided to omit pure linters, e.g., *Lint, cpplint*, and model checkers, e.g., *Blast, CPAchecker*. A more exhaustive analysis, also taking into account these kinds of tools, is an open item for future work. Also, we did not include tools which are not maintained anymore, like *Splint, RATS*, or *ITS4*. Besides, three sound SAST tools have been tested: *Infer, IKOS*, and *Frama-C*. The latter was already evaluated on the *Juliet Test Suite* in [5], but in a separate category for sound tools, which makes it difficult to compare with the other tools. For all tools, we chose the latest stable version in Ubuntu 18.04 LTS in an virtualization environment with disk size of 150 GB and 16 GB of RAM under Intel i7-6600U CPU @ 2.60 GHz with 2 cores when conducting our research. Since we were interested in the tools' recall and precision and not in their resource usage, we did not implement resource control for the benchmarking.

Table 4. In our study evaluated static analysis tools

Tool	Version	Reference
AdLint	3.2	http://adlint.sourceforge.net
Clang-Tidy	4.0	http://clang.llvm.org/extra/clang-tidy/index.html
Clang Scan-Build	4.0	http://clang-analyzer.llvm.org/scan-build.html
CppCheck	1.72	http://cppcheck.sourceforge.net
Flawfinder	1.31	http://dwheeler.com/flawfinder
Frama-C Eva	17	http://frama-c.com
IKOS	2.0	http://github.com/NASA-SW-VnV/ikos
Infer	0.15	http://fbinfer.com
OCLint	0.13.1	http://oclint.org
Pscan	1.2-9	http://deployingradius.com/pscan
Sparse	0.5.0	http://sparse.wiki.kernel.org/index.php/

4.2   Evaluation Datasets

As discussed in the report of the *Static Analysis Tool Exposition (SATE) V* [5], the ideal benchmarking dataset should be representative of real, production code, have large amounts of test data to yield statistical significance, and have a known ground truth. Three types of datasets can thus be used:

Synthetic Test Suites. A synthetic test suite includes generated code with limited complexity and precisely placed vulnerabilities and defects in it. For the C/C++ track of *SATE V*, this is covered by the *Juliet Test Suite 1.3 for C/C++*. The *Juliet Test Suite* was developed specifically for assessing the capabilities of SAST tools and contains 64,099 test cases in 100k files. The suite covers more than 100 different weaknesses, including all major software fault patterns and satisfies the requirements of having ground truth and statistical significance. Therefore, precision and recall metrics are applicable. In Table 5, the distribution of software fault pattern clusters is shown. As can be seen, the top clusters are comparable to the ones we found in our preliminary investigation of common C fault patterns for Debian packages in Sect. 3.

Table 5. Top SFP clusters in the Juliet Test Suite 1.3 for C/C++

SFP cluster	Percentage
Memory access	31.4%
Resource management	6.4%
Tainted input	12.1%
Risky values	32.6%

Production Software. Production software offers realism and statistical significance, due to the large number of warnings issued by tools. Production software however suffers from the lack of ground truth, since we can not be sure about all the defects it may contain. Findings thus need to be reviewed manually for correctness and for evaluating the precision of the tools; recall cannot be calculated at all. All this makes this kind of data inappropriate for automated evaluation.

Software with CVE's. Real production software with publicly reported vulnerabilities from the *Common Vulnerabilities and Exposures (CVE)* database, which forms a prime source of known defects in production software. On the one-hand side, they are unfortunately still too few to achieve statistical significance for measuring tools' precision. On the other-hand side, the high realism regarding code and the vulnerabilities is an advantage.

In our research, we have primarily used the *Juliet Test Suite 1.3 for C/C++* and additionally conducted a trial on the *Wireshark v1.8* software with 83 known CVE's. For the *Juliet Test Suite*, we though used a subset since we are focusing on C programs on Linux, therefore skipping C++ and Win32 test cases, and we used a single-file test setup, thus omitting multi-module-test cases.

4.3   Evaluation Procedure for Synthetic Test Cases

As pointed out in Sect. 2, benchmarking SAST tools using the *Juliet Test Suite* is not straightforward, since vulnerabilities as reported by the tools need be mapped to the CWE's associated to test cases. This can introduce a bias. Consider for example a tool output like "memory error", mapping this result to CWE-119, or to CWE-120, or to CWE-125 makes a difference for evaluating the recall of the tool and so the overall measured tool performance. This gets even more problematic with respect to the many possible views in the CWE hierarchy. Due to this, we decided for a different approach. Under the assumption, that the probability of a tool reporting a defect at the exact location but for another defect type is very low, we matched reported defects and test case CWE's solely based upon the defect location, thus ignoring the reported defect type.

In more detail, we run the tools on the dataset file by file, and log the tool reports. The test cases for a specific CWE are thus not compiled into one application, as also possible with the *Juliet Test Suite*, but rather analyzed separately. The tool reports are collected in a database for further processing. A tool's findings are compared with the *Juliet Test Suite* manifest files, specifying the exact defect location for a test case by file and line number. If there is match between a tool's finding and a test case with respect to the reported location, we count that as a true positive. If a tool reports another location, we count that as false positive. All non-reported locations are treated as either true or false negatives, according to whether the test case represents "good" or "bad" code. Note that we in this way assume, that the totality of condition negative equates to the lines of code of all test cases. This is in contrast to the original procedure, where the totality of condition negative equates to the sum of test cases. In our case, the probabilities for gaining a true positive or a true negative are though supposed to be more realistic, compared to the 50:50 chance for the default *Juliet Test Suite* procedure [5]. Although, this comes at the cost of penalizing tools which report the right error on a different location, and otherwise rewards tools, which report all locations with a wrong defect type. Using the counts of true/false positives/negatives, the tools' precision, recall and *Matthews correlation coefficient (MCC)* are calculated. We chose MCC in favor of the F-Score, because the former also rewards a higher number of true negatives in contrast to the latter. This penalizes very noisy tools which report every location. The MCC is in general suggested when dealing with imbalanced datasets, as is often the case for vulnerabilities. Measures like accuracy and F-Score do not reflect this imbalance properly. The used metrics, i.e., precision, recall, MCC, are defined as follows:

$$Precision = \frac{TP}{TP + FP}$$

$$Recall = \frac{TP}{TP + FN}$$

$$MCC = \frac{TP \times TN - FP \times FN}{\sqrt{(TP + FP)(TP + FN)(TN + FP)(TN + FN)}}$$

with TP denoting the number of true positives, TN the number of true negatives, FP the number of false positives, and FN the number of false negatives.

4.4   Trial on Production Software

For our trial on production software with real CVE's, we only used the most promising tools as evaluated in the first experiment. In general, this part was more difficult to carry out, for several reasons:

- As first tests showed, it was not feasible to analyze the whole *Wireshark* software at once using the sound analyzers like *Frama-C* and *IKOS*. Both tools have the option to analyze single modules, using an alternative entry point for the file to be analyzed. This however causes issues in finding a suitable entry point among all functions in the module. We approached this by calculating the call graphs of all modules and choosing the roots as entry points. We in this way though still miss inter-module defects.
- Except for *CppCheck* and *Flawfinder*, all tools required include files and pre-processor definitions of the sources under test. For *Wireshark*, we created a JSON compilation database, where each source file had an entry for its definitions and dependencies. All tools supported this compilation database except *AdLint* and therefore *AdLint* was excluded from the trial.
- Similar to the *Juliet Test Suite*, we used a file-by-file test setup, collecting the tools' reports in a database. We also imported the CVE data into the database. The CVE data did not only contain the defect, but also other information, which required us to manually review the matched findings to ensure that only true positives are counted. Due to the number of findings reported by the tools, we only measured the tools' recall, but not the precision.

5   Results and Discussion

In this section, we present the results of our evaluation. A replication package is available online[9]. In the evaluation, we were mainly interested in the five following research questions, which will be discussed in the following:

- *What is the effect of the tools' severity threshold parameter on the tools' precision and recall?*
- *Are there differences in the tools' sensitivity with respect to specific vulnerability patterns?*
- *What is the overall tools' accuracy on the Juliet Test Suite?*
- *Are one tool's findings subsumed by another tool's findings, i.e., do the tools' findings overlap?*
- *What is the tools' precision on the Wireshark production software?*

5.1   Effect of Severity Thresholds

The SAST tools *Flawfinder, Clang-Tidy, IKOS*, and *OCLINT* support a severity threshold parameter, i.e., a minimum severity level upon which found vulnerabilities are reported by the respective tool. In Fig. 1, the influence on the tools'

---

[9] https://github.com/RohanKrishnamurthy/sastevaluation

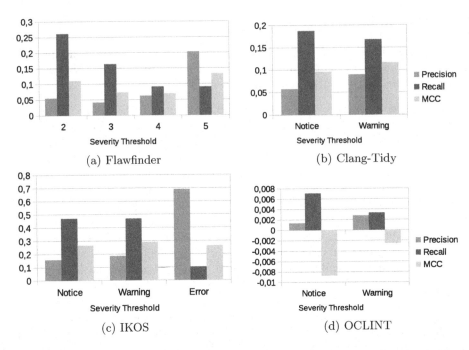

Fig. 1. Vulnerability detection metrics with respect to chosen severity threshold

precision, recall, and MCC are shown for the *Juliet Test Suite*. As can be seen, with increasing severity thresholds, most tools also showed an increase in their precision, while their recall decreased. This is partly as expected, as *IKOS* for example considers an *Error* to be a runtime error, while a *Warning* is either considered a runtime error for certain executions or a statement where the tool is not powerful enough to prove the absence of errors. For other tools, like *Flawfinder*, this is a rather coincidental, though beneficial, effect, as the severity associated to a vulnerability is determined by its assumed security risk. Overall the accuracy, as measured by *MCC*, did not change substantially. Note that the preference for high recall or precision also depends on the use case, i.e., a tool for proving the absence of vulnerabilities should aim at high recall, while a vulnerability detector should aim at high precision. Due to this, we have chosen the *Warning*-level as minimum severity in all further experiments. For *Flawfinder* we chose the highest level (5) to achieve optimal accuracy.

5.2 Tools' Recall on SFP Clusters

Next, we were interested in whether some tools provided a better sensitivity for vulnerabilities of certain types of vulnerabilities. In Fig. 2, we show the recall of the 11 SAST tools on the top four SFP clusters, as introduced in Sect. 3. Apparently, the sound tools *Frama-C* and *IKOS* excel particularly for the clusters memory access and risky values, while having only an average recall for

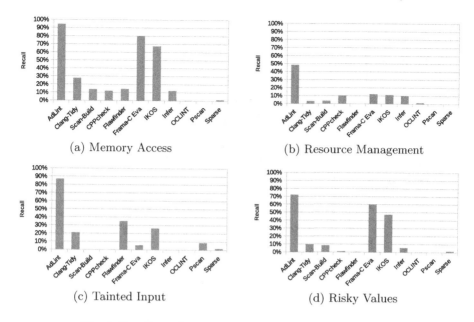

Fig. 2. Recall on the Juliet Test Suite for top SFP clusters

vulnerabilities related to resource management and tainted input. In general, with the exception of *AdLint*, none of the tools covers all the clusters with the same sensitivity. Furthermore, some tools only provide a good sensitivity for vulnerabilities of a certain type, such as *Pscan* for the cluster tainted input. For an explanation of the good recall of *AdLint*, see the following section.

5.3 Overall SAST Tool Accuracy

In Fig. 3, we present the measured precision, recall, and MCCs for all 11 tested SAST tools on the *Juliet Test Suite*. Apparently, there are differences in the tools' accuracy. With respect to recall, some of the tools found nearly nothing (*OCLINT*), while others found more than 50% of all tested vulnerabilities (*AdLint, Frama-C*). Regarding precision, there are tools where almost every second finding is a true positive (*Pscan*), and others, where a developer would have to go through hundred of findings to have only one true positive (*OCLINT*). In particular two tools show a gap between precision and recall. *PScan* seems to be highly specialized on certain types of vulnerabilities and therefore has only a low recall but a high precision in that, what it finds. The tool *AdLint* shows a good recall, but this comes at the cost of a bad precision. In fact, *AdLint* produced warnings for about 1/8 of the test suite, resulting in 800k warnings in total. Note that a tool reporting just every line of code as vulnerability gains 100% recall. Finally, we can observe, that the different characteristics of precision and recall lead to nearly aligned MCCs for some tools. Thus, the accuracy of *AdLint, Clang-Tidy, CppCheck*, and *Flawfinder* are almost on par, while the sound tools

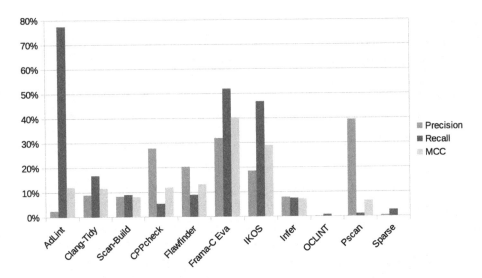

Fig. 3. Precision, recall and MCC metrics on the Juliet Test Suite

Frama-C and *IKOS* are outstanding. This result is in line with the findings in related work [1, 4, 9, 10], in which *Frama-C* ranked similarly. We have though no comparison for *IKOS*, as it was not included in those evaluations. Other tools with reported good accuracy were *Clang* and *CppCheck*. We can confirm a high precision of *CppCheck* and a fair recall of *Clang* in our experiments.

5.4 SAST Tool Overlap

We have also analyzed, if vulnerabilities reported by one tool are reported by another tool as well. Basically, we were asking if there exists one superior tool or if, instead, it makes sense to use more than one SAST tool. In Table 6, we denote the measured overlap of the vulnerabilities reported for the *Juliet Test Suite* for the four tools with the most findings, i.e., *Clang-Tidy*, *Flawfinder*, *Frama-C*, and *IKOS* and several other tools. For example, *Clang-Tidy* found 75.6% of the vulnerabilities that were also reported by *Clang Scan-Build* and *Flawfinder* found all of the vulnerabilities found by *Pscan*. This last example may indicate, that in some cases, using one SAST would make the use of another SAST tool redundant. However, considering *Flawfinder* and *Pscan*, note that the latter tool provides better precision than the former one and therefore still may the option of choice. In general, we can observe that there exists no one single superior open-source SAST tool for the C programming language.

5.5 Trial on Production Software

The results for the trial of the six tools *Clang-Tidy*, *CppCheck*, *Flawfinder*, *Frama-C*, *Infer*, and *IKOS* on the *Wireshark v1.8* production software are shown

Table 6. Overlap of reported vulnerabilities for subset of tested SAST tools

	Clang-Tidy	CppCheck	Infer	Pscan	Scan-Build	Frama-C
Clang-Tidy		47.5%	40.2%	0.0%	75.6%	20.5%
Flawfinder	9.5%	6.4%	1.7%	100.0%	1.5%	4.3%
Frama-C	20.5%	38.0%	13.2%	0.0%	16.5%	
IKOS	17.5%	36.6%	12.7%	50.0%	8.9%	57.9%

in Table 7. As mentioned in Sect. 4, we decided to only measure the tools' recall but not precision, due to the rather large number of reported warnings which would need to be checked manually for being true or false positives otherwise. It is apparent, that all of the six tools have much more difficulties in finding real vulnerabilities in production software, compared to finding vulnerabilities in the synthetic *Juliet Test Suite*. Altogether, only 17 out of the 83 CVE's included in the *Wireshark v1.8* dataset [5] were found. That is even more surprising, as most of the CVE's are related to the SFP cluster memory access, which is supported by most of the tools. Except for a large fraction of CVE's related to infinite loops, vulnerabilities which are out of the tools' scope, like wrong API usage, did not play a substantial role. There was also no overlap, each tool reported different vulnerabilities. *CppCheck* and *Infer* surprisingly did not find any of the CVE's. *IKOS* produced so many warnings because of unknown side effects of included code, that we removed it from the trial. Also, the other sound tool *Frama-C* did not perform as good as on the synthetic data.

Table 7. Recall results for the SARD-94 test cases (*Wireshark v1.8*)

Tool	Findings	TP	Recall
Clang-Tidy	1,733	1	1.2%
CppCheck	74	0	0.0%
Flawfinder	2,256	9	10.8%
Frama-C	10,273	7	8.4%
Infer	3,022	0	0.0%
IKOS	48,130	-	-

6 Threats to Validity

In this section, we discuss the threats to the validity for our research.

Tool Selection. First to mention, a bias is introduced through the selection of SAST tools. Since we did not consider commercial tools and mostly excluded verification technology, we can not provide a complete picture of the capabilities of SAST tools. Nonetheless, we believe that we have covered a substantial selection of mature and maintained general-purpose open-source SAST tools for C. Another threat relates to the chosen version for the tools. Since we used the latest stable version available for Ubuntu 18.04 LTS, some versions are already outdated. This is especially true for the Clang-tools, which we tested for their version 4. This is a general problem, as many tools are continuously updated and improved. Establishing a ongoing SAST tools benchmark facility with automated evaluation and reporting could help to cope with this problem.

Test Cases. Since our focus has been to benchmark open-source SAST tools, which often did not support the Windows Platform, we omitted the Windows test cases from the *Juliet Test Suite*. Also, since not all tools fully support C++ code, we omitted all C++ test cases. Note that this is no serious flaw of our evaluation, but should be considered before one draws any conclusions on the the tools for Windows-targeted code and/or C++. Also, as already mentioned, the realism of synthetic test code as used in the *Juliet Test Suite* is not high, and does probably not reflect the accuracy of the tools on production code. There is no easy solution for this, due to the trade-off when benchmarking SAST tools between realism and statistical significance and/or unknown ground truth.

Tool Coverage. We have chosen to test all 11 open-source SAST tools on all test cases – regardless of the respective vulnerability pattern. Our results may therefore differ from other benchmarks. For instance, in the *SAMATE evaluation* [5], they used a special measure called applicable recall, where the supposed tools' coverage on vulnerability patterns is taken into account, which therefore enhances the recall significantly. We have decided against such a measure, in order to make the results more comparable and provide a comprehensible result.

Procedure. As discussed in Sect. 4, our method of counting true positives using the vulnerabilities' locations is based on the assumption that it is unlikely, that a SAST tool would report the correct location with a wrong vulnerability. A very noisy tool that reports almost every line of code as erroneous thus achieves low precision but high recall, since we do not check if the tool reports the expected vulnerability types. Averaging precision and recall by the F-Score, such a tool would gain a reasonable ranking. To compensate for this, we use the MCC instead of the F-Score. Our approach also penalizes tools, which report the expected vulnerabilities at a different code location, and tools, which find other defects than the expected ones. This is problematic for tools like *Frama-C* and *IKOS*, as they halt analysis after finding a defect, and may thus explain their unexpected low precision of under 50% in the evaluation as well as their low recall for vulnerability patterns related to memory access and risky values. As mentioned in Sect. 2, *Frama-C* and *IKOS* may report another type of defect for a test case of the *Juliet Test Suite* and subsequently stop analysis for this test case, thus missing the expected defect. However, these are general problems and known issues of the *Juliet Test Suite*.

7   Conclusion

In this paper, we have reported on our evaluation of 11 open-source SAST tools for the C programming language using synthetic test cases of the *SARD Juliet Test Suite 1.3 for C/C++* and the *Wireshark v1.8* production software with real CVE's. Starting with a preliminary investigation on fault patterns and vulnerabilities in the Debian Linux distribution, we found that half of all vulnerabilities are coding errors related to memory management, followed by errors related to resource management, tainted input, and risky values. We therefore decided to use the *Juliet Test Suite* as a dataset for our evaluation, as it covers these weaknesses with a similar weighting. We confirmed findings of previous work on benchmarking SAST tools for C, using other test suites and evaluation procedures. For example, we can confirm that no superior tool among the evaluated 11 open-source SAST tools for C exists and the tools accuracy in detecting real vulnerabilities in production software still leaves much room for improvement. We also found that *Frama-C* is the best among the evaluated tools, even though it is not specifically focused on security. Another sound tool *IKOS*, which has not yet been evaluated on the *Juliet Test Suite* before, performed similar and ranks second in our benchmark. While our evaluation considered the tools' performance over all SFP clusters, a more selective analysis taking only into account a tool's asserted vulnerability types is a prospect of future work.

Future benchmarks would as well benefit from a new or overhauled test suite, which addresses the known problems we have also identified, like the absence of unintended defects and vulnerabilities or better test annotations for matching reported with expected vulnerabilities. It would be of general interest to develop a benchmark suite as open standard, where tool developers and security experts can join to promote realistic SAST tool benchmarking. To cope with the rapid outdating of benchmarks and tools, establishing a regular and an automated evaluation of SAST tools, e.g., analog to similar efforts in the software verification community [2], would be a valuable contribution. Including more SAST tools in the evaluation, in particular software verifiers, which we deliberately choose to exclude from our evaluation, would also allow for drawing a more extensive picture. However, we believe that our study can be a valuable building block in creating this bigger picture on the state-of-the-art of SAST tools for C.

References

1. Arusoaie, A., Ciobâcă, Ş., Craciun, V., Gavrilut, D., Lucanu, D.: A comparison of open-source static analysis tools for vulnerability detection in C/C++ code. In: SYNASC, pp. 161–168. IEEE Computer Society (2017)
2. Beyer, D.: Advances in automatic software verification: SV-COMP 2020. TACAS 2020. LNCS, vol. 12079, pp. 347–367. Springer, Cham (2020). https://doi.org/10. 1007/978-3-030-45237-7_21

3. Calcagno, C., et al. : Moving fast with software verification. In: Havelund, K., Holzmann, G., Joshi, R. (eds.) NFM 2015. LNCS, vol. 9058, pp. 3–11. Springer, Cham (2015). https://doi.org/10.1007/978-3-319-17524-9_1

4. Chatzieleftheriou, G., Katsaros, P.: Test-driving static analysis tools in search of C code vulnerabilities. In: COMPSAC Workshops 2011, pp. 96–103. IEEE Computer Society (2011)

5. Delaitre, A., Stivalet, B., Black, P.E., Okun, V., Ribeiro, A., Cohen, T.S.: Sate V report: ten years of static analysis tool expositions. Tech. Rep. NIST-SP-500-326, NIST (2018). https://doi.org/10.6028/NIST.SP.500-326

6. Goseva-Popstojanova, K., Perhinschi, A.: On the capability of static code analysis to detect security vulnerabilities. Inf. Softw. Technol. **68**, 18–33 (2015)

7. Herter, J., Kästner, D., Mallon, C., Wilhelm, R.: Benchmarking static code analyzers. Reliab. Eng. Syst. Saf. **188**, 336–346 (2019)

8. Kuhn, R., Raunak, M.S., Kacker, R.: Can reducing faults prevent vulnerabilities? IEEE Comput. **51**(7), 82–85 (2018)

9. Lu, B., Dong, W., Yin, L., Zhang, L.: Evaluating and integrating diverse bug finders for effective program analysis. In: Bu, L., Xiong, Y. (eds.) SATE 2018. LNCS, vol. 11293, pp. 51–67. Springer, Cham (2018). https://doi.org/10.1007/978-3-030-04272-1_4

10. Moerman, J., Smetsers, S., Schoolderman, M.: Evaluating the performance of open source static analysis tools. Bachelor thesis, Radboud University, The Netherlands, p. 24 (2018)

11. NAS-CAS: On analyzing static analysis tools. Technical report, National Security Agency Center for Assured Software (2017), https://media.blackhat.com/bh-us-11/Willis/BH_US_11_WillisBritton_Analyzing_Static_Analysis_Tools_WP.pdf

12. Prause, C., Gerlich, R., Gerlich, R.: Evaluating automated software verification tools. In: ICST 2018, pp. 343–353. IEEE Computer Society (2018)

13. Seacord, R.C.: The CERT® C Coding Standard, Second Edition: 98 Rules for Developing Safe, Reliable, and Secure Systems, 2nd edn. Addison-Wesley Professional (2014)

14. Shiraishi, S., Mohan, V., Marimuthu, H.: Test suites for benchmarks of static analysis tools. In: ISSRE Workshops 2015, pp. 12–15. IEEE Computer Society (2015)

Verification of Liveness and Safety Properties of Behavioral Programs Using BPjs

Michael Bar-Sinai$^{(\boxtimes)}$ and Gera Weiss

Ben-Gurion University of the Negev, Be'er-Sheva, Israel
`barsinam@post.bgu.ac.il`

Abstract. This paper presents semantics, syntax, and tools for specification and verification of safety and liveness properties of behavioral programs. Verification is performed directly on program code, by traversing its transition system. Liveness properties are defined using "hot states", in which scenarios are allowed to stay for a finite time, but not forever. Safety properties are defined using assertions which allow labeling program states as having violations, and by analyzing program states for deadlocks detection. The paper defines liveness violations with regards to specific program components and describes an approach for validating the absence of such violations is a system. The proposed approach is supported by BPjs, an open-source tool suite developed by the authors.

Keywords: Behavioral programming · Model-based software engineering · Formal methods · Tools

1 Introduction

Behavioral programming (BP, [17,18]) is a paradigm for designing reactive systems focused on allowing formal executable specifications of reactive systems that are fully aligned with the requirement documents. In this paper we discuss a variant of BP, called BPjs [2,9], where a specification is given as a collection of small fragments of JavaScript code, each describing an independent thread of required system behaviour. These fragments are interwoven at runtime using a simple protocol.

Ideally, when using BP, there is a module in the model per paragraph in the document [12]. So far, however, BP was limited to describing safety properties (properties that can be violated in a finite length of time), thus not allowing direct modelling of liveness properties (properties whose violation requires an infinite length of time). This work proposes an extension to the BP formal model, allowing it to represent liveness requirements as well. Similar to the original version, the extended BP model is executable and formally analyzable using the BPjs tool. We describe an updated version of BPjs that integrates the new capabilities with all existing features of the tool.

© Springer Nature Switzerland AG 2021
T. Margaria and B. Steffen (Eds.): ISoLA 2020, LNCS 12479, pp. 199–215, 2021.
https://doi.org/10.1007/978-3-030-83723-5_14

The main contributions of this paper are: An updated formal definition for BP, which supports liveness properties using a concept called *hot synchronization*; A distinction between types of liveness violations, based on the set of b-threads that remain forever hot; An algorithm for verifying liveness and safety properties of BP-based programs, supported by a reusable tool; And a discussion of a case where phrasing safety requirements using liveness terms allows for a higher-level description of what requirements were violated.

The rest of this paper is organized as follows. Section 2 presents the extended formal BP model. Section 3 presents and discusses applications of the updated model in an MBSE setting, using BPjs. Section 4 evaluates the updated BPjs version. Section 5 looks at related work, and Sect. 6 concludes.

2   Problem Formulation

We begin with a mathematical formulation of the problem addressed in this paper, based on the model of behavioral programs presented in [17]. We then present the verification problems this paper focuses on. Our proposed model describes a system from a specification, using product of labelled transition systems. Below, we use the mathematical model formalized in this section as the foundation for the proposed programming and analysis tools.

Recall that a labeled transition system is defined as a quadruple $\langle S, E, \rightarrow, init \rangle$, where S is a set of states, E is a set of events, $\rightarrow$ is a transition relation contained in $(S \times E) \times S$, and $init \in S$ is the initial state [21]. The runs of such a transition system are sequences of the form $s_0 \xrightarrow{e_1} s_1 \xrightarrow{e_2} \ldots \xrightarrow{e_i} s_i \ldots$ where $s_0 = init$, and $\forall i \in \mathbb{N}$, $s_i \in S$, $e_i \in E$, and $s_{i-1} \xrightarrow{e_i} s_i \in \rightarrow$.

The key concepts of behavioral programming, as presented in [17], is the behavioral thread, or b-thread. A b-thread is a component in a system that can request, wait-for, and block events. The semantics for these operators are: (1) *Requesting an event* means proposing that said event be triggered, and asking to be notified when this happens; (2) *Waiting for an event* means asking to be notified if said event is triggered, but not proposing it be; (3) *Blocking an event* means forbidding the triggering of said event, vetoing requests of other b-threads. When a b-thread submits a request/wait-for/block statement, it is said to reach a *synchronization point*. When it reaches such point, the b-thread is paused until an event it requested or waited-for is triggered. B-threads do not interact directly – they communicate only through this event-based, synchronization protocol.

We propose an extension to the above definition in two ways: (1) We allow b-threads to explicitly specify the events they wait for; (2) We add a specification of a labeling function that marks states as hot, cold or being in violation. The first addition is technical, the waited-for events were specified via the transitions system in [17] and we allow explicit specification in order to allow natural translation to code (a more direct compliance with the syntax and semantics of BPjs). The second addition is more substantial as it allows formal specification of liveness and safety properties, as will be discussed shortly.

Definition 1 (B-thread). *A tuple* $\langle S, E, \rightarrow, init, R, W, B, LBL \rangle$ *where* $\langle S, E,$ $\rightarrow, init \rangle$ *forms a labeled transition system,* $R \colon S \rightarrow 2^E$ *maps a state s to a set of events requested by the b-thread when in s,* $W \colon S \rightarrow 2^E$ *maps a state s to a set of events waited-for by the b-thread when in s,* $B \colon S \rightarrow 2^E$ *maps a state s to a set of events blocked by the b-thread when in s.* $LBL \colon S \rightarrow$ $\{HOT, COLD, VIOLATION\}$ *is a labeling function that indicates if the b-thread considers a state as hot, cold, or a violation.*

The main design goal of this model is to independently represent individual aspects of a system using b-threads. Then, using the request, wait-for, and block idioms, b-threads can be combined to represent a complex system behavior. The runs of a set of b-threads (a b-program) are defined as in [17], adding only the requirement to respect the new wait-for specification:

Definition 2 (B-program). *Runs of a* $\{\langle S_i, E_i, \rightarrow_i, init_i, R_i, W_i, B_i,$ $LBL_i \rangle\}_{i=1}^n$ *set of b-threads, are the runs of the labeled transition system* $\langle S, E, \rightarrow$ $, init \rangle$, *where* $S = S_1 \times \cdots \times S_n$, $E = \bigcup_{i=1}^n E_i$, $init = \langle init_1, \ldots, init_n \rangle$, *and* $\rightarrow$ *includes a transition*

$$\langle s_1, \ldots, s_n \rangle \xrightarrow{e} \langle s'_1, \ldots, s'_n \rangle$$

if and only if

$$e \in \bigcup_{i=1}^n R_i(s_i) \bigwedge e \notin \bigcup_{i=1}^n B_i(s_i)$$

and, for all $i = 1, \ldots, n$,

$$\left(e \in R_i(s_i) \cup W_i(s_i) \Rightarrow s_i \xrightarrow{e} s'_i\right) \wedge \left(e \notin R_i(s_i) \cup W_i(s_i) \Rightarrow s_i = s'_i\right).$$

Depending on the order in which events are selected from the set of requested and non-blocked events, there may be more than a single run of a given b-program. The main addition this paper makes to the formal model is using the labeling function added to the b-threads for categorizing the runs of a system. This categorization enables better alignment of code with system requirements, and improved tool support for model driven engineering, as we will elaborate later.

The main new notion that we add is the concept of "hot" runs that, as the name suggests, takes after the seminal work of Damm & Harel [11]. The adjustment of the term to our context is given in the following definition:

Definition 3 (Hot run). *An infinite run* $\langle s_1^{(0)}, \ldots, s_n^{(0)} \rangle \xrightarrow{e_1} \langle s_1^{(1)}, \ldots, s_n^{(1)} \rangle \xrightarrow{e_2}$ $\cdots$ *of a b-program* $\{\langle S_i, E_i, \rightarrow_i, init_i, R_i, W_i, B_i, LBL_i \rangle\}_{i=1}^n$ *is hot with respect to a set of b-thread indices* $H \subseteq \{1, \ldots, n\}$ *if there exists* $t_0 \geq 0$ *such that* $\forall t \geq t_0, \exists i \in H$ *s.t.* $LBL_i(s_i^{(t)}) = HOT$. *A finite run of length t is hot with respect to H if the last state of the run satisfies* $\exists i \in H$ *s.t.* $LBL_i(s_i^{(t)}) = HOT$ *(called hot termination condition).*

The set H in the above definition can be a singleton, in which case we say that the run contains a "hot b-thread" violation, or the whole system in which case we say that the run contains a "hot system" violation. The idea is that a set of states is marked as "hot" if b-threads can stay in them for a while, but it is a violation to stay in them forever. For example, a mutual exclusion protocol may allow a task to wait for the critical section for a while, but not forever (as this is considered "starvation"). The set H is usually a singleton in which case a single b-thread is responsible for a single type of hotness. This definition allows for sets that contain more than one b-thread, to support rare cases where a specification of a certain type of hotness is better defined using multiple b-threads.

The motivation for introducing the notion of hotness to BP is that without it, in some natural cases, it may not be possible to represent individual requirements using individual b-threads. This is a significant addition since the ability to align code with requirements is one of the main "claim-to-fame"s of BP. Consider, for example, the following requirements:

- A run must contain 10 A's.
- A run must contain 10 B's.
- A run must not contain two B's in a row.

A direct translation to BP, without using HOT states, is:

- $BT_1 = \langle S, E, \rightarrow, init, R, W, B, LBL \rangle$ where $S = \{s_0, \ldots, s_{10}\}$, $E = \{A\}$, $\rightarrow = \{\langle s_i, A, s_{i+1} \rangle : i < 10\}$, $init = \{s_0\}$, $R = \{s_0, \ldots, s_9 \mapsto \{A\}, s_{10} \mapsto \emptyset\}$, $W = B = \{s \mapsto \emptyset : s \in S\}$, and $LBL = \{s \mapsto COLD : s \in S\}$.
- $BT_2 = \langle S, E, \rightarrow, init, R, W, B, LBL \rangle$ where $S = \{s_0, \ldots, s_{10}\}$, $E = \{B\}$, $\rightarrow = \{\langle s_i, B, s_{i+1} \rangle : i < 10\}$, $init = \{s_0\}$, $R = \{s_0, \ldots, s_9 \mapsto \{B\}, s_{10} \mapsto \emptyset\}$, $W = B = \{s \mapsto \emptyset : s \in S\}$, and $LBL = \{s \mapsto COLD : s \in S\}$.
- $BT_3 = \langle S, E, \rightarrow, init, R, W, B, LBL \rangle$ where $S = \{s_0, s_1\}$, $E = \{A, B\}$, $\rightarrow = \{\langle s_0, B, s_1 \rangle, \langle s_0, A, s_0 \rangle, \langle s_1, A, s_0 \rangle\}$, $init = \{s_0\}$, $R = \{s \mapsto \emptyset : s \in S\}$, $W = \{s \mapsto \{A, B\} : s \in S\}$, $B = \{s_0 \mapsto \emptyset, s_1 \mapsto \{B\}\}$, and $LBL = \{s \mapsto COLD : s \in S\}$.

This model violates the second requirement, as it contains runs such as $\langle s_0, s_0, s_0 \rangle \xrightarrow{A} \langle s_1, s_0, s_0 \rangle \xrightarrow{A} \cdots \xrightarrow{A} \langle s_9, s_0, s_0 \rangle \xrightarrow{B} \langle s_9, s_1, s_1 \rangle$. The reason is that, without HOT states, a b-program can only enforce safety properties while the requirement to have at least ten A's is a liveness property. To solve this, with our new addition to the syntax, one can declare the states $s_0, \ldots, s_9$ as HOT and make said run hot.

Another type of problematic runs that we consider in this paper are runs that lead to direct violation:

Definition 4 (Violation). *A run* $\langle s_1^{(0)}, \ldots, s_n^{(0)} \rangle \xrightarrow{e_1} \langle s_1^{(1)}, \ldots, s_n^{(1)} \rangle \xrightarrow{e_2} \cdots$ *of a b-program* $\langle \{S_i, E_i, \rightarrow_i, init_i, R_i, W_i, B_i, LBL_i\}_{i=1}^n \rangle$ *contains a violation if there is a* $t_0 > 0$ *such that* $\bigvee_{i=1}^m LBL_i(s_i^{(t)}) = VIOLATION$.

This is a more standard type of error that has been studied before, e.g., in [15]. We include it in this paper in order to show how the proposed types of analyses integrate and complement existing ones.

3   Model Driven Engineering with BP

We now apply the extended BP model proposed in Sect. 2 to a model-driven engineering context [25]. We describe a software controller for a pancake batter mixer, whose control decisions are made by a model, implemented by a b-program. Model decisions – events triggered by said b-program – are executed by an actuation layer, implemented using traditional code.

Pancake batter is made of two mixtures: dry (flour, baking soda, salt), and wet (eggs, buttermilk). Our batter mixer has two computer-controlled containers, one for each type of mixture. When the mixer's b-program triggers an ADD_DRY event, its actuation layer releases a part of dry mixture into the mixing bowl. When its b-program triggers an ADD_WET event, its actuation layer releases a part of wet mixture.

B-programs in this paper are written using BPjs [9], an open-source tool suite for execution and analysis of b-programs[1]. BPjs is a Java library that can be embedded in traditional Java programs using a engine/listener pattern: The host program executes a b-program by loading it into a runtime engine and registering a listener on it. The host sends data to a b-program by enqueueing events into its external event queue. For example, if a b-program needs to respond to engine status, the host can read the status, wrap it in an event object, and enqueue that event in the b-program's external event queue. B-program verification is done in a similar manner, but using an analysis engine instead of a runtime one.

BPjs uses direct program analysis: transition between two b-program states is performed using program execution, with no model transformations. During analysis, when it arrives at a new b-program state, BPjs stores that state, and visits all next possible states by selecting each event requested and not blocked at said state. During this traversal, the model checker searches for violating nodes or paths[2]. BPjs allows developers to specify what violations are searched for. BPjs users can add custom inspections by implementing a Java interface.

We begin with a naïve b-program for preparing basic batter (Listing 1.1). To prepare batter for 5 pancakes, the mixer is required to add 5 doses of each mixture. These requirements are represented by the b-program's two b-threads. These b-threads do not wait-for or block each other's events. Thus, there are no constraints over the order in which mixtures are added.

3.1   Conforming with Safety Properties

Unconstrained addition order may cause the batter to become very thick or very thin, for example when a single wet dose is followed by many dry ones. Extreme batter viscosities may harm the mixer's engine – making it run too fast or to

---

[1] Code shown in this section is available in the code appendix [3].

[2] For this technically complex feat, BPjs relies in part on the Mozilla Rhino JavaScript engine [24]. For the work presented here, we expanded BPjs to support hot synchronization points, among other improvements. This work included code donations to Mozilla Rhino itself.

Listing 1.1. Naive b-program for preparing batter for 5 pancakes. Consists of two b-threads, each requesting the addition of 5 doses of mixture. B-threads are added by invoking `bp.registerBThread`. B-threads enter a synchronization point by invoking `bp.sync`, passing it events they request, wait-for, and block.

```
1  var DOSE_COUNT=5;
2  bp.registerBThread("AddDries", function(){
3    for ( var i=0; i<DOSE_COUNT; i++ ) {
4      bp.sync({request:ADD_DRY});
5  }});
6  bp.registerBThread("AddWets", function(){
7    for ( var i=0; i<DOSE_COUNT; i++ ) {
8      bp.sync({request:ADD_WET});
9  }});
```

exert too much effort. Thus, we add a safety requirement: *batter viscosity should be constrained within given bounds*. To this end, we add the `ViscosityMeter` b-thread (Listing 1.2, lines 7–14), which publishes batter viscosity via a `Viscosity` event.

First, let us verify that the naïve controller may violate the bounded viscosity requirement. For this, we add b-thread that waits-for viscosity events, and asserts that their data is within bounds (Listing 1.2, 29–33). Indeed, when analyzing the controller b-program, BPjs finds a violating run were viscosity exceeds its required bounds[3].

It is possible to keep batter viscosity within its required bounds by blocking addition events before they cause the batter to become too thick or too thin. B-thread `RangeArbiter` (Listing 1.2, 16–27) presents one possible implementation: it keeps track of batter viscosity by waiting for `Viscosity` events. When batter viscosity index nears a certain threshold, it blocks events that would take it over that threshold. E.g. when batter viscosity reaches 2, it blocks `ADD_DRY`.

`RangeArbiter` makes the controller b-program *correct by construction* with regards to the batter viscosity bounds requirement, ostensibly making assertions redundant. However, assertions are useful for numerous reasons.

First, not all safety requirements can be conformed with by construction – a b-program can only block its internal events. It makes no sense to block, e.g., an external event reporting that a mixer's engine overheats. During verification, it is common to add b-threads that simulate the b-program's environment, as well as b-threads asserting the relations between the verified b-program and its environment. For example, a b-thread can assert that after the engine sends an overheating alert event, the controller b-program must initiate an emergency shutdown.

---

[3] See code appendix [3] for code and execution instructions.

Listing 1.2. B-threads keeping track, constraining, and verifying batter viscosity. Lines 1-5 define constants and event sets used by the b-threads that follow. B-thread `ViscosityMeter` publishes current batter viscosity after each addition event. When publishing viscosity, this b-thread must block all addition events, to prevent the published value from becoming stale. B-thread `RangeArbiter` restricts batter viscosity to a given range by waiting for viscosity events, and blocking addition events. This type of restriction avoids over-specification by restricting event selection only when said events will cause a requirement volation. Lastly, b-thread `ViscosityVerification` formally implements the textual requirement "batter viscosity has to be between -3 and 3". This is a typical *requirement b-thread*, as it does not interfere with the core b-program's events, and is directly aligned with the requirement it validates.

```
1  const VISCOSITY_BOUND=2;
2  const ADDITION_EVENTS = [ADD_DRY, ADD_WET];
3  const VISCOSITY_EVENTS = bp.EventSet("Viscosity", function(e){
4    return e.name.contains("Viscosity");
5  });
6
7  bp.registerBThread("ViscosityMeter", function(){
8    let vsc=0;
9    while ( true ) {
10     let evt = bp.sync({waitFor:ADDITION_EVENTS});
11     if ( evt.equals(ADD_DRY) ) vsc++;
12     if ( evt.equals(ADD_WET) ) vsc--;
13     bp.sync({request:bp.Event("Viscosity",vsc), block:ADDITION_EVENTS});
14  }});
15
16 bp.registerBThread("RangeArbiter", function(){
17   while ( true ) {
18     let viscosityEvent = bp.sync({waitFor:VISCOSITY_EVENTS});
19     let viscosity = viscosityEvent.data;
20     let toBlock;
21     if ( Math.abs(viscosity) >= VISCOSITY_BOUND ) {
22       toBlock = (viscosity>0) ? ADD_DRY : ADD_WET;
23     } else {
24       toBlock = bp.none;
25     }
26     let evt = bp.sync({waitFor:ADDITION_EVENTS, block:toBlock});
27  }});
28
29 bp.registerBThread("ViscosityVerification", function(){
30   while ( true ) {
31     let evt = bp.sync({waitFor:VISCOSITY_EVENTS});
32     bp.ASSERT(Math.abs(evt.data)<=VISCOSITY_BOUND, "Viscosity violation");
33  }});
```

Second, assertions may be used to state required properties in a declarative way. Consider the code for `RangeArbiter` (Listing 1.2, 16–27), responsible for maintaining batter viscosity within bounds. This code is statefull and procedural, and as such prone to errors such as replacing `>=` with `>`. These error can be detected during verification, by a b-thread that waits for `Viscosity` events and asserts that $|viscosity| < 3$.

Last, assertions may be useful at runtime, where a failed assertion causes the b-program to halt. This can be viewed a as a form of safety monitoring, or *runtime verification* [1]. Should this happen, BPjs informs the host program about the failed b-program assertion, allowing the host to drop to a "safe mode", or attempt recovery.

Listing 1.3. B-threads controlling and verifying blueberry addition. B-thread `Blueberries` requests an `ADD_BLUEBERRIES` event which, when selected, causes the actuation layer to add blueberries to the pancake batter. B-threads `EnoughBatter` and `BatterThinEnough` prevent blueberry addition where there is not enough batter, or when the batter is too thick. B-thread `EventuallyAddBlueberries` ensures that, eventually, blueberries are added.

```
bp.registerBThread("Blueberries", function(){
  bp.sync({request:ADD_BLUEBERRIES});
});

bp.registerBThread("EnoughBatter", function(){
  bp.sync({waitFor:ADDITION_EVENTS, block:ADD_BLUEBERRIES});
  bp.sync({waitFor:ADDITION_EVENTS, block:ADD_BLUEBERRIES});
  bp.sync({waitFor:ADDITION_EVENTS, block:ADD_BLUEBERRIES});
});
bp.registerBThread("BatterThinEnough", function(){
  var toBlock=bp.none;
  while ( true ) {
    var viscosityEvt=bp.sync({waitFor:VISCOSITY_EVENTS, block:toBlock});
    toBlock=(viscosityEvt.data>=0) ? BLUEBERRIES:bp.none;
}});

bp.registerBThread("EventuallyAddBlueberries", function(){
  bp.hot(true).sync({waitFor:BLUEBERRIES});
});
```

3.2   Deadlock Detection

A b-program is deadlocked at a state s, when s contains requested events, and they are all blocked (for other definitions, see Sect. 5). In these cases, no b-thread can advance, even though some request to. As event blocking is a central to the BP paradigm, deadlocks are a concern developers have to keep in mind; Formal analysis for deadlock detection is an important tool in a b-programmer's toolbox.

To demonstrate a deadlock, let us consider an upgrade to our batter mixer: support for blueberry pancakes. This requires adding a b-thread requesting a new event – `ADD_BLUEBERRIES` – whose semantics are similar to those of `ADD_WET` and `ADD_DRY`. To reduce the amount of blueberries bursting, we additionally require that (a) there is enough batter in the mixing bowl when blueberries are added, and (b) that batter is relatively thin. Listing 1.3 contains b-threads for adding blueberries, and for timing their addition.

Adding blueberry support to our controller b-program may cause it to deadlock. Specifically, in runs where batter thickness is always non-negative, the b-program will arrive at a situation where the `Blueberries` b-thread requests to add blueberries, `BatterThinEnough` blocks their addition, and the mixture adding b-threads (Listing 1.1) have terminated. Thus, the controller program cannot advance, event though some b-threads request to.

Assertions cannot be used to detect deadlocks, because assertions are made by b-threads, which are locked in place. Hence, deadlock detection has to be done at the b-program level. BPjs can detect and report these cases as it traverses a b-program's state-space. Deadlock reports include the involved b-threads, their role in the detected deadlock (requestors or blockers), and the event trace leading up to the deadlock (see Fig. 1 left).

Deadlocks and Hot Terminations. Recall that a hot termination occurs when a b-program terminates while one or more of its b-threads are hot (Definition 3). Hot synchronization points are intended to specify liveness requirements, which of course do not constrain finite runs, such as those that end in a deadlock. However, describing requirements using liveness terms may allow a verification process to detect what requirements are being violated at a higher level.

Consider the above blueberry batter b-program, composed with the b-thread EventuallyAddBlueberries from Listing 1.3. This new b-thread consists of a single declarative statement, stating that blueberries should eventually be added to the batter. It does not affect the controller's behavior, as it does not request or block any events – only waits for a blueberry addition event. When a hot-termination of this b-thread is detected during verification, the verifier is able to report that the requirement to eventually add blueberries was violated.

Hot termination analysis may offer a significant improvement over deadlock analysis, which provides a low-level explanation of how things went wrong ("event e requested by t_1 and blocked by t_2"), but misses the higher-level picture of *what* went wrong. Here, it is not incorrect to say that the ADD_BLUEBERRIES event was requested and blocked and that the b-program as a whole could not advance. But a better, closer to the requirements phrasing of the problem would be "we requested blueberries but they were never added". Indeed, a hot termination analysis of the controller reports that EventuallyAddBlueberries can be hot when the controller terminates, and does not look into the technicalities of how this violation comes to be. Figure 1 compares the two report types.

To intuit why hot terminations are better phrased as liveness violations, trivially extend finite runs to infinite ones as follows: Let r be a finite b-program run $s_0 \xrightarrow{e_0} s_1 \xrightarrow{e_1} \ldots \xrightarrow{e_{n-1}} s_n$. Extend it to an infinite run by adding a self loop at s_n, using a trivial event τ. Now, r becomes the hot b-thread run: $s_0 \xrightarrow{e_0} \ldots \xrightarrow{e_{n-1}} s_n \xrightarrow{\tau} s_n \xrightarrow{\tau} s_n \ldots$. The generated cycle violates the requirement violated by the original hot termination, but does so as a "proper" liveness violation, in an infinite run in which an event should happen, but never does.

Hot-termination analysis allows developers to declare that a certain event should be triggered, without specifying who requests it. This is important for BP-based systems, where programs are composed of multiple b-threads. As such, they are prone to mis-configurations (e.g. omissions of program parts). In cases where the missing parts are those responsible for requesting an essential event, adding a b-thread that hot-waits for that event ensures mis-configured programs will not pass verification.

```
Inspections:                              Inspections:
* Failed Assertions                       * Hot B-Program Cycles
* Hot B-Program Cycles                     * Hot Terminations
* Hot Terminations                        * Hot B-Program Cycles
* Deadlocks
Starting verification                     Starting verification
- truncated -                             - truncated -
Verification completed.                   Verification completed.
Found Violation:                          Found Violation:
Deadlock: [BEvent name:ADD_BLUEBERRIES]   Hot Termination - The following b-
requested by:{Blueberries} blocked by:    threads were hot when the b-program
{BatterThinEnough}                        ended: EventuallyAddBlueberries
Counter example trace:                    Counter example trace:
[BEvent name:ADD_WET]                     [BEvent name:ADD_WET]
[BEvent name:Viscosity data:-1.0]         [BEvent name:Viscosity data:-1.0]
[BEvent name:ADD_WET]                     [BEvent name:ADD_WET]
[BEvent name:Viscosity data:-2.0]         [BEvent name:Viscosity data:-2.0]
[BEvent name:ADD_DRY]                     [BEvent name:ADD_DRY]
- truncated -                             - truncated -
```

Fig. 1. Two verification reports of the same issue: a run terminates without adding blueberries to the batter. The report to the left treats the issue as a deadlock, providing a low-level explanation of how the b-program has deadlocked. The report to the right treats the issue as a *hot termination*, and provides a higher level explanation of which requirement was violated.

3.3   Liveness Requirements

We now turn to definition and analysis of liveness requirements in b-programs, using the proposed hot synchronization concept. Baier and Katoen [5], define liveness properties as applying to infinite runs only. A typical liveness property would be "eventually X happens" or "Y happens infinitely often". We begin by presenting a b-program whose runs are infinite, and thus can be constrained by liveness requirements. Then, we discuss various requirements and hot runs of said b-program.

Consider an industrial pancake batter mixer. It repeatedly prepares batter for a pancake batch, releases it (presumably to an automated pan, left for future work) and then prepares batter for the next batch. The server code, part of which appears in Listing 1.4, builds on the code in Listing 1.1. Mixture addition loops are wrapped in infinite loops, and are followed by a wait for a RELEASE event. A newly added b-thread releases the batter when the bowl contains enough of it.

Hot B-Thread Run: Industrial Blueberry Pancakes. We begin by requiring our industrial mixer to add blueberries to the batter *infinitely often* (LTL: □◇ADD_BLUEBERRIES). To this end, we add the blueberry addition and requirement b-threads to its controller (Listing 1.3). These b-threads are modified to support repetitive execution, by wrapping their code in an infinite loop.

Listing 1.4. Parts of the pancake server code. Mixture-adding b-threads run in an infinite loop where they add the required amount of doses to the mixer bowl, and then wait for the batter to be released. A `Releaser` b-thread is responsible for releasing the batter, when the batter amount reaches a set threshold. For brevity, some definitions and b-threads were omitted. Full code is available at [3]

```
 1  const RELEASE = bp.Event("RELEASE_BATTER");
 2
 3  bp.registerBThread("Dry", function(){
 4      while ( true ) {
 5          for ( var i=0; i<DOSE_COUNT; i++ ){
 6              bp.sync({request:ADD_DRY});
 7          }
 8          bp.sync({waitFor:RELEASE});
 9  });
10
11  bp.registerBThread("Releaser", function(){
12      var doseCount = 0;
13      while ( true ) {
14          bp.sync({waitFor:ADDITION_EVENTS});
15          doseCount++;
16          if ( doseCount === (DOSE_COUNT*2) ) {
17              bp.sync({request:RELEASE, block:ADDITION_EVENTS});
18              doseCount=0;
19  }}});
```

Because of the requirement that the batter is thin enough when blueberries are added, certain mixture addition orders prevent blueberries from being added infinitely often (a situation similar to that described in Subsection 3.2). In such runs, where blueberries are added a finite number of times, the iterative variant of the `EventuallyAddBlueberries` b-thread eventually becomes always hot, making the run a *hot run*. BPjs can detect these runs and provide execution traces which allows developers to fix the b-program[4].

Hot System Run: Industrial Blueberry-Kale Pancakes. Our final mixer variant prepares healthy pancake batter, containing equal amounts of blueberries and kale. To this end, we define the `ADD_EXTRAS` event, which holds two data fields: amount of blueberries that should be added, and amount kale that should be added. Two new b-threads—one for each ingredient—monitor the amount of added extras, and issue requests to ensure the amounts are eventually balanced. Listing 1.5 contains selected part of the code. Both b-threads request addition of their respective ingredient using hot synchronization statements, stating that the ingredient portion *must* be added eventually.

Consider a case where, during a run of a blueberry-kale mixer controller, half a dose of kale is added to the batter. The two adder b-threads start adding blueberries and kale to the mix, but cannot balance the kale/blueberry ratio, as they add a single ingredient dose each time. The b-program is trapped in a hot run, where the extras bias forever changes from 0.5 to −0.5 and back.

---

[4] Sample execution logs are available at [3].

Listing 1.5. Code for balancing the amount of blueberries and kale in our proposed blueberry-kale pancake batter maker. The `BlueberryAdder` and `KaleAdder` b-threads monitor the blueberry/kale bias of the batter, and request events to correct it, when it goes out of balance. Requests are done using `bp.hot(true).sync`, to signal that the ingredients must eventually be added. Some code omitted for brevity.

```
function addExtrasEvent( blueberries, kales ) {
  return bp.Event("ADD_EXTRAS", {
    blueberries:blueberries,
    kales:kales
  });
}
var ADD_EXTRAS = bp.EventSet("sADD_EXTRAS", function(e){
  return e.name.equals("ADD_EXTRAS");
});

bp.registerBThread( "KaleAdder", function(){
  var fruitBias=0;
  while (true) {
    var evt = null;
    if ( fruitBias > 0 ) {
      evt = bp.hot(true).sync({request:addExtrasEvent(1,0),
                               waitFor:ADD_EXTRAS});
    } else {
      evt = bp.sync({waitFor:ADD_EXTRAS});
    }
    fruitBias = fruitBias+evt.data.blueberries-evt.data.kales;
}});
bp.registerBThread( "BlueberryAdder", function(){...});
```

As described here, a b-program hot system run is a bug. However, one can think of similar cases where a b-program hot system run is desirable. One example is a traffic lights system, where a round-robin queue of the lights must keep progressing forever.

4 Evaluation

This section evaluates BPjs' performance both as a model analysis tool, and as an execution engine. The b-program used was a simulation of a robot moving in a house, where it has to avoid traps and walls, and cannot stay in areas marked as "hot" forever [6]. Each measurement was repeated 10 times and averaged.

To evaluate BPjs as a runtime engine, we measured the time required for a robot to perform 1000 moves in a house simulation program[5]. For this test, we removed the trap cell, to ensure that runs were not terminated prematurely. We repeated the experiment with a range of floor plan sizes, and compared the results against a similar b-program executed using BPJ, the Java BP runtime library introduced in [17]. The results show that BPJ is about 5 times faster than BPjs (see Table 1). This is to be expected, as Java is a compiled language whilst

---

[5] Measurements were taken on a 2.9 GHz Intel Core i9 MacBook Pro with 32 GB RAM, of which 16 GB was allocated to Java. The JVM used was OpenJDK 18.9 (Java 11).

Table 1. Average time required for a robot to take 1000 steps in a house simulation (milliseconds). Measurements were taken using OpenJDK 18.9 (Java 11), on a 2.9 GHz MacBook Pro with 16 GB of RAM (out of 32) allocated to Java. Each measurement was repeated 10 times.

Floor size	B-threads	BPJ (msec)	BPjs (msec)
5×5	25	65.2 $\pm$6	238.4 $\pm$72
10×10	100	89.6 $\pm$12	403.5 $\pm$74
20×20	400	189.4 $\pm$17	1,094.7 $\pm$91
50×50	2,500	2031.2 $\pm$20	8,461.3 $\pm$102
100×100	10,000	*Out of memory*	12,605.7 $\pm$110

JavaScript is interpreted. Moreover, due to technical restrictions, BPjs cannot use runtime optimizations during execution. However, because BPjs can run multiple b-threads using the same OS thread, it can execute b-programs with a larger concurrent b-thread count. When running a simulation for a 100×100 floor plan (containing 10,000 b-threads), BPJ exhausted its 16 GB memory allowance, while BPjs was able to run the program to completion.

To evaluate the performance of BPjs as an analysis engine, we measured the time required to fully traverse the state space of the house simulation b-program. This metric is used, since it provides an upper bound for detecting both liveness and safety violations. We used different floor plan sizes, and a hash-based visited state store[6] (see Table 2). We used two Java virtual machines: OpenJDK, and the more advanced GraalVM[7]. While the latter was consistently faster, the speed increase was not dramatic.

Table 2. Average time required for BPjs to fully traverse the state space of a b-program simulating a robot moving in a house. Measurements were taken using OpenJDK 18.9 and GraalVM 20ce, on a 2.9 GHz MacBook Pro with 32 GB of RAM. 16 GB were allocated to the JVMs. Each measurement was repeated 10 times. *sd*: Standard Deviation

Floor size	OpenJDK18.9		GraalVM	
	time (msec)	sd	time (msec)	sd
5×5	290.2	45	233.1	58
10×10	544.3	34	535.7	20
20×20	1,531.1	12	1,510.7	34
50×50	10,810.5	179	9,966.7	194
100×100	66,703.5	1,769	64,152.6	1,231

---

[6] BPjs visited state store is pluggable; other state stores exist as well.
[7] https://www.graalvm.org.

To compare BPjs' verification performance against other verification alternatives, we implemented a similar program, using a modified version of BPJ [7], verifying it with NASA's JavaPathFinder (JPF) [19]. BPJ, which does not use pluggable design, needed to be modified in order to support a random-based event selection strategy. JPF is a modular Java virtual machine, aimed at program analysis and verification. We used the core JPF system, which verifies a program by running all of its possible thread interleaving combinations, and enumerating the overall random decision points. Thus, JPF's view of a b-program's state space is much larger than that of a BP engine: A BP engine only counts synchronization points as states, whereas JPF looks at thread interleaving options. Not surprisingly, the JPF verification process took much longer, taking 85 s to verify a 1×1 floor plan (containing 3 b-threads), visiting 438,568 states. While trying to verify a 2×2 floor plan (6 b-threads), JPF ran out of memory after 8:31 min[8]. JPF is a mature and active product, used here as a common reference point; other Java verification tools exist (see, e.g., [10]).

We explored two other alternatives for verification, and found both not viable. BPMC, a model checker based on BPJ [15], does not support Java versions later than Java 5, last updated at 2009. Thus, we no longer consider it a practical tool. Our attempts to verify BPjs using JPF failed for technical reasons, as JPF does not support some of the Java constructs used by BPjs.

5   Related Work

The work presented here draws its main concept—a *hot* state that a program must eventually leave—from Live Sequence Charts (LSC) [11,16]. LSC is a form of scenario-based programming that extends Message Sequence Charts. Under LSC, when a lifeline arrives at a location where it sends a *hot* message, that message must eventually be passed, or the run is marked as violating the specification. BP and LSC are both scenario-based [13], but differ significantly: LSC models conversations between objects, while BP models synchronized behaviors.

LSC additionally defines the notion of a *cut*—the current location of each of the chart's lifelines during chart execution. If any of these locations are hot, the cut is considered hot as well. LSC considers exiting a chart while its cut is hot as a violation. The hot termination concept presented here is the BP equivalent of that requirement.

LSC specifications can be verified through translation to LTL or to automatons [22]. In [8], Marron and the authors offer a way of translating LSC to BPjs programs for execution. Drawing on that translation and the hot synchronization concept presented here, LSCs can be verified through transformation to BP.

---

[8] Measurements were taken on a 2.9 GHz Intel Core i9 MacBook Pro with 32 GB RAM, of which 16 GB was allocated to Java. We used Java 8 (1.8.0_201), as JPF was not able to run on Java 11.

BPmc [15] is the first model checker for b-programs. While it was the first work to deliver on the promise of BP as a verifiable model, it is limited to safety properties, and does not support some recent BP features, such as dynamic b-thread additions and pluggable event selection strategies. The paper presenting BPmc also sketched a methodology for verifying liveness properties by detecting hot cycles in a b-program state-space. The work presented here builds on this sketch, and broadens it with an updated formal model for BP, an elaborated notion of hot run (respective to a group of b-threads), the hot termination concept, and support for the modern BP feature set.

BPmc and BPjs detect deadlocks in the same way, but differ on their interpretation of a state with no requested events: BPmc regards it as a deadlock, as it is a state with no successors. BPjs, on the other hand, does not regard it as a deadlock, since no b-thread is blocked. This distinction only holds for safety properties—if a b-program gets to a state where no events are requested but at least one b-thread is hot, BPjs will declare this a liveness violation. Furthermore, BPjs' pluggable architecture allows adding a BPJ-style deadlock detection easily.

BPC is a behavioral programming library for C++, presented by Katz and Harel in [14]. It supports indirect verification through translation of programs to SPIN [20], a popular verification system.

To the best of out knowledge, this paper is the first to present a formal model of BP which allows representation and verification of liveness properties, the first to offer a tool for direct verification of liveness properties of b-programs, the first to present the concept of hot runs respective of a group of b-threads, and the first to present the *hot termination* concept into the context of BP.

BPjs was used as a model execution engine in an MBSE design by Greenyer, Sadon, Marron, and the authors for controlling an autonomous rover, as a solution for a design challenge published by MODELS18 [13]. Sadon, Elyasaf, and the authors used BPjs in a similar manner to create an on-board controller for a satellite [2].

Another system that combines traditional programming with formal modeling is Umple [23]. It does so by adding UML concepts to mainstream languages. A developer can define relations between classes using UML notation, and have Umple generate the required code when the model is realized. For modeling dynamic system behavior, Umple uses UML Statecharts. These charts can be analyzed at the model level, using execution scenarios [4]. However, Umple is UML-based, and does not support BP concepts directly.

6 Conclusion

This paper proposes an extension to the BP formal model, enabling expression and verification of both safety and liveness properties. Liveness violations are detected by marking b-threads as *hot* at certain synchronization points, and searching for hot cycles in the verified b-program's transition system. Safety violations are detected by marking specific program states as having a violation, or by detecting deadlocks. The paper presents the concept of a hot run with respect to a group of b-threads, and identifies two specific cases: *hot b-thread runs*, which are always a violation of a liveness property, and *hot system runs*, which may or may not be a violation. Additionally, the paper defines *hot termination*—a case where phrasing a safety requirement using liveness terms allows model checkers to identify requirements violated by finite runs at a higher abstraction level than a safety phrasing would allow.

References

1. Runtime Verification Conference Website (2001–2019). http://www.runtime-verification.org/
2. A scenario based on-board software and testing environment for satellites. In: Proceedings of the 59th Israel Annual Conference on Aerospace Sciences (2019)
3. Appendix, Code: Verification of Liveness and Safety Properties of Behavioral Programs Using BPjs. Zenodo, July 2020. https://doi.org/10.5281/zenodo.3967250
4. Aljamaan, H., Garzon, M., Lethbridge, T.: UmpleRun: a dynamic analysis tool for textually modeled state machines using umple. In: EXE@MoDELS, pp. 16–20 (2015)
5. Baier, C., Katoen, J.P.: Principles of Model Checking. MIT Press, Cambridge (2008)
6. Bar-Sinai, M.: BP visual running examples code repository (2019). https://github.com/bthink-bgu/VisualRunningExamples
7. Bar-Sinai, M., Weiss, G.: Code Appendix for "BPjs - A Behavioral Programming Tool Suite" (2018). https://github.com/michbarsinai/BPjs-SCP-OSP_CodeAppendix
8. Bar-Sinai, M., Weiss, G., Marron, A.: Defining semantic variations of diagrammatic languages using behavioral programming and queries. In: EXE@MoDELS (2016)
9. Bar-Sinai, M., Weiss, G., Shmuel, R.: BPjs: an extensible, open infrastructure for behavioral programming research. In: Proceedings of the 21st ACM/IEEE International Conference on Model Driven Engineering Languages and Systems: Companion Proceedings, MODELS 2018, Copenhagen, Denmark, 14–19 October 2018, pp. 59–60 (2018). https://doi.org/10.1145/3270112.3270126
10. Beyer, D.: Advances in automatic software verification: SV-COMP 2020. In: TACAS 2020. LNCS, vol. 12079, pp. 347–367. Springer, Cham (2020). https://doi.org/10.1007/978-3-030-45237-7_21
11. Damm, W., Harel, D.: LSCs: breathing life into message sequence charts. Formal Methods Syst. Des. **19**(1), 45–80 (2001). https://doi.org/10.1023/A:1011227529550
12. Gordon, M., Marron, A., Meerbaum-Salant, O.: Spaghetti for the main course?: observations on the naturalness of scenario-based programming. In: Proceedings of the 17th ACM Annual Conference on Innovation and Technology in Computer Science Education (ITiCSE 2012). ACM, New York (2012). https://doi.org/10.1145/2325296.2325346

13. Greenyer, J., Bar-Sinai, M., Weiss, G., Sadon, A., Marron, A.: Modeling and pro-
    gramming a leader-follower challenge problem with scenario-based tools. In: Hebig,
    R., Berger, T. (eds.) Proceedings of MODELS 2018 Workshops: ModComp, MRT,
    OCL, FlexMDE, EXE, COMMitMDE, MDETools, GEMOC, MORSE, MDE4IoT,
    MDEbug, MoDeVVa, ME, MULTI, HuFaMo, AMMoRe, PAINS co-located with
    ACM/IEEE 21st International Conference on Model Driven Engineering Lan-
    guages and Systems (MODELS 2018), Copenhagen, Denmark, 14 October 2018.
    CEUR Workshop Proceedings, vol. 2245, pp. 376–385. CEUR-WS.org (2018).
    http://ceur-ws.org/Vol-2245/mdetools_paper_8.pdf
14. Harel, D., Katz, G.: Scaling-up behavioral programming: steps from basic principles
    to application architectures. In: Proceedings of the 4th International Workshop on
    Programming Based on Actors Agents & Decentralized Control, pp. 95–108. ACM
    (2014)
15. Harel, D., Lampert, R., Marron, A., Weiss, G.: Model-checking behavioral pro-
    grams. In: Proceedings of 11th International Conference on Embedded Software
    (EMSOFT), pp. 279–288 (2011)
16. Harel, D., Marelly, R.: Come, Let's Play: Scenario-Based Programming Using LSCs
    and the Play-Engine. Springer, Heidelberg (2003). https://doi.org/10.1007/978-3-
    642-19029-2
17. Harel, D., Marron, A., Weiss, G.: Programming coordinated behavior in Java. In:
    D'Hondt, T. (ed.) ECOOP 2010. LNCS, vol. 6183, pp. 250–274. Springer, Heidel-
    berg (2010). https://doi.org/10.1007/978-3-642-14107-2_12
18. Harel, D., Marron, A., Weiss, G.: Behavioral programming. Comm. ACM 55(7)
    (2012)
19. Havelund, K., Pressburger, T.: Model checking Java programs using Java
    PathFinder. Int. J. Softw. Tools Technol. Transfer 2(4), 366–381 (2000). https://
    doi.org/10.1007/s100090050043
20. Holzmann, G.J.: The model checker SPIN. IEEE Trans. Softw. Eng. 23(5), 279–295
    (1997). https://doi.org/10.1109/32.588521
21. Keller, R.M.: Formal verification of parallel programs. Commun. ACM 19(7), 371–
    384 (1976). https://doi.org/10.1145/360248.360251
22. Klose, J., Toben, T., Westphal, B., Wittke, H.: Check it out: on the efficient formal
    verification of live sequence charts. In: Ball, T., Jones, R.B. (eds.) CAV 2006.
    LNCS, vol. 4144, pp. 219–233. Springer, Heidelberg (2006). https://doi.org/10.
    1007/11817963_22
23. Lethbridge, T.C., Mussbacher, G., Forward, A., Badreddin, O.: Teaching UML
    using umple: applying model-oriented programming in the classroom. In: 2011 24th
    IEEE-CS Conference on Software Engineering Education and Training (CSEE T),
    pp. 421–428, May 2011. https://doi.org/10.1109/CSEET.2011.5876118
24. Mozilla, individual contributors: The Mozilla Rhino JavaScript Engine (2019).
    https://mozilla.org/rhino
25. Rodrigues da Silva, A.: Model-driven engineering. Comput. Lang. Syst. Struct.
    43(C), 139–155 (2015). https://doi.org/10.1016/j.cl.2015.06.001

On Correctness, Precision, and Performance in Quantitative Verification
QComp 2020 Competition Report

Carlos E. Budde[1], Arnd Hartmanns[1](✉), Michaela Klauck[2],
Jan Křetínský[3], David Parker[4], Tim Quatmann[5],
Andrea Turrini[6,7], and Zhen Zhang[8]

[1] University of Twente, Enschede, The Netherlands
a.hartmanns@utwente.nl
[2] Saarland University, Saarland Informatics Campus, Saarbrücken, Germany
[3] Technical University of Munich, Munich, Germany
[4] University of Birmingham, Birmingham, UK
[5] RWTH Aachen University, Aachen, Germany
[6] State Key Laboratory of Computer Science, Institute of Software,
Chinese Academy of Sciences, Beijing, China
[7] Institute of Intelligent Software, Guangzhou, Guangzhou, China
[8] Utah State University, Logan, UT, USA

Abstract. Quantitative verification tools compute probabilities, expected rewards, or steady-state values for formal models of stochastic and timed systems. Exact results often cannot be obtained efficiently, so most tools use floating-point arithmetic in iterative algorithms that approximate the quantity of interest. Correctness is thus defined by the desired precision and determines performance. In this paper, we report on the experimental evaluation of these trade-offs performed in QComp 2020: the second friendly competition of tools for the analysis of quantitative formal models. We survey the precision guarantees—ranging from exact rational results to statistical confidence statements—offered by the nine participating tools. They gave rise to a performance evaluation using five tracks with varying correctness criteria, of which we present the results.

1 Introduction

Quantitative formal models feature probabilistic choices, real-time aspects, or continuous dynamics. They are used to study safety, dependability, or performance aspects of e.g. randomised algorithms, network protocols, biological

The authors are listed alphabetically. This work was supported by DFG grant 389792660 as part of TRR 248 (CPEC), DFG grant 383882557 (SUV), ERC Advanced Grant 787914 (FRAPPANT), ERC Advanced Grant 834115 (FUN2MODEL), ERC Advanced Grant 695614 (POWVER), the Guangdong Science and Technology Department (grant no. 2018B010107004), the National Natural Science Foundation of China (grant nos. 61761136011, 61532019, 61836005), National Science Foundation grant CCF-1856733, NWO project 15474 (SEQUOIA), and NWO VENI grant no. 639.021.754.

T. Margaria and B. Steffen (Eds.): ISoLA 2020, LNCS 12479, pp. 216–241, 2021.
https://doi.org/10.1007/978-3-030-83723-5_15

processes, or cyber-physical systems [1,58]. Probabilistic models need dedicated numeric algorithms to compute or approximate rational or real-valued probabilities, expected values, or long-run averages. In this paper, we focus on tools for the analysis of probabilistic formal models w.r.t. such quantitative properties.

Over the past two decades, a variety of algorithms have been devised for this purpose. Most of them can roughly be categorised as variants of *probabilistic model checking* (PMC) [9] and *statistical model checking* (SMC) [2], with *probabilistic planning* closely related to the former. In PMC, the model's state space is explored—partially or exhaustively—to obtain an in-memory representation of the model's underlying semantics, which is typically a Markov chain or some extension thereof. The value of interest can then be computed using numeric algorithms such as value iteration. PMC is thus subject to the state space explosion problem, limiting its ability to be applied to very large case studies. SMC, on the other hand, relies on Monte Carlo simulation—generating random runs through the model's semantics—to statistically estimate the value of interest. It does not need to store states other than the current and next one during run generation, and thus avoids state space explosion entirely. However, when faced with a rare event—e.g. when trying to estimate a reachability probability on the order of 10^{-9} with a suitable error of, say, 10^{-10}—the number of runs needed explodes. Furthermore, nondeterminism—controllable or adversarial unquantified choices, such as in Markov decision processes (MDP) [78]—turn the estimation problem into an optimisation problem, which SMC cannot directly handle. Probabilistic planning is similar to PMC, but crucially employs heuristics to try to avoid exploring the entire state space. Its focus is on *finding strategies* in MDP, i.e. the choices that lead to the maximum reward, whereas PMC traditionally *computes values* (e.g. expected rewards) and checks complex logical formulas.

With new algorithms come new tools: first academic prototypes, which may over time develop into extensive collections of algorithms or tools targeting various problems and use cases. In 2019, the first competition of tools for the analysis of quantitative formal methods, QComp 2019 [46], took place. Using selected benchmarks from the quantitative verification benchmark set (QVBS) [58], all of which are available in the tool-independent JANI model interchange format [19], it compared nine tools—ranging from general-purpose probabilistic model checkers to specialised SMC tools for rare events in dynamic fault trees—in terms of performance, versatility, and usability. A major concern that surfaced during the setup of QComp 2019 was that quantitative verification tools return *numbers*—and most of them use inexact methods to obtain these numbers, relying on floating-point arithmetic and iterative algorithms that only approximate the true values. Additionally, the long-time standard algorithm used by PMC tools, value iteration, is known to be unsound [43]; and SMC tools can only deliver statistical guarantees that allow them to produce incorrect results with a certain probability (typically $\leq 5\%$ of the time). Thus, while we on the one hand should demand verification tools to always deliver correct verdicts, correctness in quantitative verification cannot effectively be achieved without admitting *some* error. The best we can do, then, is to accompany results with precise statements about *how* correct they are guaranteed to be.

In this paper, we report on QComp 2020, the second edition of this competition. We focus on the issue of correctness of results, in particular on the trade-off between strength of correctness guarantees and analysis performance. After an overview of the types of formalisms and properties considered by QComp 2020 in Sect. 2, we thus expand on this in Sect. 3. Subsequently, in Sect. 4, we describe the tools that participated in the competition, noting in particular which kinds of correctness guarantees each tool can provide. Finally, we describe in Sect. 5 the setup of the QComp 2020 performance evaluation, and present its outcomes.

2   Languages, Formalisms, and Properties

Formal models are specified in *modelling languages*: graphical or textual notations designed for human users to compactly describe complex systems. They are equipped with a semantics in terms of a mathematical *formalism* that provides the basis for various analysis algorithms. Models are accompanied by *properties* that specify a quantity of interest related to a set of behaviours of the model.

Modelling Languages. QComp 2020 draws its benchmarks from the QVBS, which currently consists of 78 different models, many of them parametrised to scale from small to large state spaces, with a set of properties associated to each model. Every model is available in JANI, a JSON-based format designed as an intermediate representation that bridges tools and that other modelling languages can be transformed into, as well as in its "original" modelling language. The models used for QComp 2020 were originally specified in the GALILEO format [86] for fault trees, the GREATSPN format [4] for generalised stochastic Petri nets, the process algebra-based high-level modelling language MODEST [47], the PGCL specification for probabilistic programs [40], PPDDL for probabilistic planning domains [89], and the guarded-command PRISM language [68].

Formalisms. Most modelling languages or higher-level formalisms map to some extension of automata, i.e. graphs of states (that may contain relevant structure) connected by transitions (possibly with several annotations). The benchmarks of QComp 2020 have a semantics in terms of discrete- and continuous-time Markov chains (**DTMC** and **CTMC**, respectively), which provide finite-support probabilistic choices and, in CTMC, stochastic delays that follow exponential distributions; Markov decision processes (**MDP**), which extend DTMC with nondeterministic choices; Markov automata (**MA**) [35], which combine CTMC and MDP in a compositional way; and probabilistic timed automata (**PTA**) [71], which marry MDP and timed automata [3], thus providing probabilistic choices together with nondeterministic continuous real-time behaviour.

Properties. For QComp 2020's performance evaluation, we consider basic types of quantitative properties only. This is to ensure that, for every property, we have more than one tool able to compute its value. In particular, we include unbounded probabilistic reachability ("what is the—maximum or minimum, in case of models with nondeterminism—probability to eventually reach a given set of goal states"), or P-type properties for short; bounded probabilistic reachability

(P-type properties with the additional requirement of reaching the states before some quantity exceeds a specified bound, in particular time for Pt-type and an accumulated reward for Pr-type properties, both summarised as type Pb); expected accumulated rewards until a given set of states is reached, or E-type properties, including bounded variants (type Eb); and long-run average rewards for CTMC and MA (type S, with the special case of steady-state probabilities).

Beyond QComp. Many other quantitative modelling languages not yet represented in the QVBS exist such as UPPAAL's XML format [13] or those supported by MÖBIUS [26]. The formalisms of QComp are part of a larger family tree of quantitative automata-based formalisms as shown in the previous competition report [46, Fig. 1]. They are all 1- or 1.5-player games; a future QComp may expand to games with more players that capture competitive behaviour towards conflicting goals as tool support for stochastic games expands. From our basic properties, logics can be constructed that allow the expression of *nested* quantitative requirements, e.g. that with probability 1, we must reach a state within n transitions from which the probability of eventually reaching an unsafe state is $< 10^{-9}$. Examples are CSL [10] for CTMC, PTCTL [71] for PTA, and rPATL [25] for stochastic games. Of further interest are *multi-objective* trade-offs [36], which query for Pareto-optimal strategies balancing multiple goals.

3   Correctness and Precision

We now describe the challenges and trade-offs in evaluating and ensuring the correctness of quantitative analysis results, and how QComp 2020 addresses them.

3.1   Correctness Challenges

Unsound Algorithms. For a long time, the standard algorithm for PMC was value iteration (VI). It associates a value to each state that approximates the local value of the quantity of interest (e.g. the probability to reach the goal from that state), then iteratively improves those values. VI converges towards the true correct values, but may never reach them. However, it also lacks an effective criterion to determine whether the current value is within some ε-interval around the true value. Tools thus used the standard relative-error criterion: if $v_i(s)$ is the value for state s in iteration i, then they stopped as soon as $\max_s |v_i(s) - v_{i-1}(s)| \leq \alpha \cdot v_i(s)$. However, this does not guarantee $|v_i(s) - v_{true}(s)| \leq \alpha \cdot v_{true}(s)$, where $v_{true}(s)$ is the (unknown) correct value [43]. QComp 2019 allowed the use of VI in this way. Since the benchmark problems and associated results were known, every tool could have chosen to use, for every benchmark instance, the highest α that produces a result satisfying the QComp 2019 correctness criterion of a relative error with $\varepsilon = 10^{-3}$, achieving correctness at optimal VI performance. This would unrealistically over-tweak tools for the competition in a way that no user would be able to do themselves, not knowing the true value on their own model a priori. As a workaround, all participants agreed to use

$\alpha = 10^{-6}$, which is the default setting of the PRISM model checker, for VI. Although this levelled the playing field for tools using VI, it puts other tools that only implement slower algorithms guaranteeing the required error bound at a disadvantage: they were essentially penalised for producing correct results.

Statistical Errors. Those participants that use SMC are unaffected by the VI problem. However, they cannot satisfy the correctness criterion of always ensuring at most an error of relative $\varepsilon = 10^{-3}$ at all: SMC tools estimate the value of interest using random sampling. As such, there is always a chance that the samples happen to be so bad that the result is more than ε off. A typical guarantee is that $\mathbb{P}(|v - v_{true}| > \varepsilon) < \delta$ for $\delta = 0.05$, i.e. one in twenty results may be incorrect. Similar guarantees can be established for the relative error, though fewer statistically correct methods exist for that case. To check whether a tool statistically satisfies the QComp 2019 correctness criterion in such a way would require a statistical test involving many repeated tool executions for each benchmark instance, which is not feasible in a small-scale competition like QComp.

3.2 Correct Algorithms

Since the unsoundness of VI came to the attention of the PMC community, several extensions appeared that compute *intervals* of values v_l and v_u guaranteed to be lower and upper bounds on the true values, respectively. Then a sound relative-error criterion is to stop when $v_u(s_0) - v_l(s_0) \leq \varepsilon \cdot v_l(s_0)$. The algorithms mainly differ in how the upper values are computed. The first was *interval iteration* [11,44], originally proposed in 2014 [43] concurrently with a learning-based approach [15] that uses the same idea. *Sound value iteration* [80] and most recently *optimistic value iteration* [56] are newer variants with improved performance. Implementations use (double-precision) floating-point arithmetic since the smaller and smaller increments from iteration to iteration do not play well with using unlimited-precision rational numbers. Thus we may still get incorrect approximations due to floating-point imprecisions and error accumulation.

It is possible to obtain exact rational results for some formalism and property type combinations. The algorithms that do so, for example rational search [12] or the topological approaches implemented in STORM (see Sect. 4), are usually much slower and less scalable to large models than the approximative approaches, though. Most of these may also be implemented using floating-point arithmetic, sacrificing unconditional correctness to gain some performance; the only errors caused by such implementations are then due to floating-point imprecisions.

3.3 Correctness in QComp 2020

As a *verification* competition, QComp should in principle not allow tools to deliver incorrect results. However, as we saw above, correctness comes in various forms, and comparing all tools under the least commonly achievable form is unfair. For QComp 2020, we thus adopted five tracks whose requirements match the different kinds of guarantees provided by the various available approaches:

Table 1. Tool capabilities overview (with changes compared to QComp 2019 marked)

Tool	GALILEO	GREATSPN	JANI	MODEST	PGCL	PPDDL	PRISM	DTMC			CTMC				MDP			MA				PTA		
								P	Pr	E	P	Pt	E	S	P	Pr	E	P	Pt	E	S	P	Pt	E
DFTRES	✓	✓						+			+	✓	+	✓				+	✓	+	✓			
ePMC		✓						✓	✓		✓	✓	✓	✓	✓		✓							
MCSTA			✓	✓				✓	✓	✓	✓	✓	✓	+	✓	✓	✓	✓	✓	✓	+	✓	✓	✓
MODES			✓	✓				✓	✓	✓	✓	✓	✓	+	✓	✓	✓	✓	✓	✓	+	✓	✓	✓
MFPL			✓	✓											+			+						
PRISM					✓	✓	✓	✓	✓	✓	✓	✓	✓	✓	✓	✓	✓					✓	✓	✓
PET					✓	✓		✓							✓									
STAMINA								+			+													
STORM	✓	✓	✓				✓	✓	✓	✓	✓	✓	✓	✓	✓	✓	✓	✓	✓	✓	✓	✓	✓	✓

correct results must match the rational true value, if known, i.e. $\varepsilon = 0$.

floating-point correct results must come from an algorithm that would produce an exact result, except that it may use floating-point arithmetic; correctness is checked w.r.t. $\varepsilon = 10^{-14}$ as an approximation of `double`'s precision.

ε-correct results must *always* be correct up to $\varepsilon = 10^{-6}$; this track matches with the guarantees provided by sound variants of VI.

probably ε-correct results must be correct up to $\varepsilon = 5 \cdot 10^{-2}$ with probability 0.95; this requirement can be satisfied by SMC tools, thus also the higher ε.

often ε-correct results must be correct up to $\varepsilon = 10^{-3}$, but we allow algorithms that do not *always* deliver such precision; thus VI can be used here.

often ε-correct results (10'): instead of being asked to deliver a fixed-precision result, every tool has 10 min to obtain as precise a value as possible.

All ε-correctness checks are for relative error; the often ε-correct track mirrors the QComp 2019 requirements. Tools participate in one and all less restrictive tracks.

4 Participating Tools

Nine tools participated in QComp 2020. Compared to the previous edition, Probabilistic Fast Downward dropped out, and STAMINA is a new entrant. Table 1 shows the modelling languages, formalisms, and property types supported by all tools. Checkmarks indicate capabilities that were already present as of QComp 2019; plus signs highlight new capabilities. Smaller checkmarks or plus signs indicate limited support as explained below.

In the following, we give a brief description of each tool, with more detailed information on the algorithms it uses to achieve the requirements of the different tracks. Table 2 shows the tracks that each tool participates in. For every benchmark instance, tools could provide a default and a specific command line; see Sect. 5 for a detailed explanation of this distinction.

Table 2. Participation of tools in QComp 2020 tracks

track	DFTRES	ePMC	mcsta	modes	MFPL	Prism	PET	Stamina	Storm
correct	—	—	—	—	—	—	—	—	✓
floating-p.	—	—	✓	—	—	—	—	—	✓
ε-correct	—	—	✓	—	—	✓	✓	—	✓
probably ε	✓	—	✓	✓	—	✓	✓	✓	✓
often ε	✓	✓	✓	✓	✓	✓	✓	✓	✓
often ε (10')	✓	—	✓	✓	✓	—	✓	✓	✓

DFTRES [83], the *dynamic fault tree rare event simulator*, is a statistical model checker for dynamic fault trees (DFT) that uses the Path-ZVA algorithm [81] for rare event simulation. Implemented in Java, it works on Linux, macOS, and Windows. It is free and open source, available at github.com/utwente-fmt/DFTRES.

By default, DFTRES uses DFTCALC [5] to parse the GALILEO format, with extensions such as repairs and inspections [82]. DFTRES supports Galileo DFT and a subset of JANI with DTMC, CTMC, and MA semantics. In MA, nondeterminism must be spurious, i.e. different choices must result in the same measures. DFTRES implements statistical estimation of system reliability, availability, and mean time to failure (covering subsets of P-, Pt-, S-, and E-type properties). Simulations run in parallel on all available processor cores, resulting in near-linear speedup on multi-core systems. Each thread can run importance sampling, e.g. forcing [73] and Path-ZVA, allowing for efficient analysis of rare event behaviour in a modest amount of memory. Path-ZVA is optimised for S properties, but also supports probabilistic reachability. Since it performs a statistical analysis, the guarantees that DFTRES provides—confidence-interval estimates with nominal real-value coverage—match with the probably ε-correct track. Accordingly, it also participates in the often ε-correct track, including the 10-minute variant, without any specific parameters or optimisations for its more relaxed requirements.

The current version of DFTRES is 1.0.1. Since its participation in QComp 2019, it gained support for DTMC and some optimisations: First, the automata in parallel composition are *reduced*: if the composition of two automata will have fewer than 256 states (overapproximated as the product of the individual state space sizes), the automata are replaced by their composition, which is minimised modulo weak bisimulation. Second, the *don't-care optimisation* removes transitions once they can no longer affect observable behaviour. For instance, if one child of a DFT OR gate fails, transitions from the other children are pruned. Finally, for Pt properties—where high-performance cycles cannot be collapsed—a new basic importance sampling scheme boosts runs leaving the cycle.

ePMC (formerly iscasMC [51]) is mainly written in Java, with some performance-critical parts in C. It runs on 64-bit Linux, Mac OS, and Windows. It is available open-source at github.com/ISCAS-PMC/ePMC. It supports the PRISM language and JANI as input; DTMC, CTMC, MDP, and stochastic games as formalisms; and PCTL* and reward-based properties. ePMC targets extensibility: it consists of a small core while plugins provide the ability to parse models, model-check properties of certain types, perform graph-based analyses, or integrate BDD packages [34]. In this way, EPMC can easily be extended for special purposes or experiments without affecting the stability of other parts. EPMC focuses on complex linear-time properties [50] and stochastic parity games [52]. It has been extended to support multi-objective model checking [48] and bisimulation minimisation [49] for interval MDP. It also has experimental support for parametric Markov models [39,74]. Specialised branches model check quantum Markov chains [37] and epistemic properties of multi-agent systems [38]. However, EPMC so far only implements VI for QComp's formalisms and property types, and thus only participates in the often ε-correct track (but not its 10-minute variant, since it cannot return partial results on early termination).

MCSTA is the MODEST TOOLSET's [53] explicit-state probabilistic model checker. The toolset is centred around the MODEST modelling language, but also supports JANI. It is implemented in C# and works on 64-bit Linux, macOS, and Windows. Currently at version 3.1, it is freely available at modestchecker.net.

MCSTA provides state-of-the-art PMC algorithms for MDP and MA [21]. It also supports PTA (as MDP via digital clocks [70]) as well as DTMC and CTMC (as special cases of MDP and MA, respectively), but does not provide specialised higher-performance algorithms for these submodels. The distinguishing features of MCSTA are its disk-based exploration and analysis [54], which allows checking large unstructured models by making use of secondary storage like hard disks and solid-state drives, and its comprehensive support for MA. MCSTA participates in the floating-point correct track by attempting to run VI until a (floating-point) fixpoint is reached (not approximated) for P- and E-type properties, and by using state elimination [45] for Pb properties on DTMC, MDP, and PTA. In the ε-correct and probably ε-correct tracks, it uses optimistic value iteration, switching to VI for the often ε-correct track.

Since its participation in QComp 2019, interval iteration for E-type properties, sound value iteration, and optimistic value iteration were implemented in MCSTA, considerably improving support for ε-correct results. State-of-the-art algorithms for the analysis of MA were added [21], providing the switch-step algorithm [20] for Pt properties as an alternative to Unif+, and adding support for long-run average rewards (S-type properties). Finally, the essential states reduction [29] brings significant speedups for some models at minimal overhead.

MODES [18] is the MODEST TOOLSET's statistical model checker. As a sibling of MCSTA, it supports the same platforms and modelling languages. By default, MODES rejects models with nondeterminism—since that cannot be simulated—and thus supports DTMC and CTMC. To efficiently estimate rare event probabilities, MODES provides rare event simulation methods based on importance splitting [16], with a high degree of automation [17]. It implements lightweight scheduler sampling (LSS) [72] to bring SMC to nondeterministic models like MDP, MA [28], and PTA [27,59]. LSS chooses m random schedulers resolving the nondeterminism and performs an SMC analysis on the DTMC or CTMC induced by each. Its key insight is how to represent a scheduler in just 32 bits. It needs an adapted statistical evaluation that takes the repeated tests into account. However, since LSS can only provide upper/lower bounds on minimum/maximum probabilities or rewards with no guaranteed error, and the best choice of m is highly model-dependent, MODES only uses LSS to check MDP, MA, and PTA in the 10-minute variant of the often ε-correct track, sampling as many schedulers as possible within the time limit. In the regular probably ε-correct and often ε-correct tracks, MODES only considers DTMC and CTMC. It does not use rare event simulation in the competition. The main addition to MODES since QComp 2019 is support for S-type properties.

Modest FRET-π LRTDP (MFPL) implements *probabilistic planning* for quantitative formal models, motivated by earlier performance comparisons of using planning algorithms for model checking [64,65]. Built upon the MODEST TOOLSET in C#, it supports the same input languages as MCSTA and MODES and runs on the same platforms. It is freely available at dgit.cs.uni-saarland.de.

Probabilistic planning uses MDP heuristic search to try to avoid state space explosion by computing values only for a small fraction of the states, just enough for the given property and precision. The algorithms are usually designed for maximum reachability and maximum expected rewards, and assume a specific class of MDP. To apply them to QComp's general MDP problems, they need to be wrapped in FRET iterations [66,85]. MFPL uses the FRET-π [85] variant of FRET together with the LRTDP [14] heuristic search optimisation of value iteration. Compared to the version used in QComp 2019, which calculated maximum reachability probabilities only, it has been extended with support for minimum and maximum P- and E-type properties. Because MFPL's core is based on VI, it takes part in the often ε-correct track and its 10-minute variant only.

PET is the *partial exploration tool*: an explicit-state model checker for unbounded reachability in discrete-time models. Implemented in Java, it works cross-platform. It uses PRISM as a library for model parsing and exploration, and hence handles PRISM language models, with migration to JANI planned.

PET only partially explores a model's state space, focusing computation on "important" areas [15]: states that are rarely reached can be omitted from the computation if one is only interested in an approximate solution. For each state in the system, the algorithm stores sound upper and lower bounds. It repeatedly samples paths (like in simulation) and back-propagates the bounds on the paths' states as in interval iteration, until convergence, with proper treatment of end components. PET can thus participate in the ε-correct track and all tracks with weaker requirements. Its performance depends on the structure of the model: on some, the PET approach is orders of magnitude faster than standard interval iteration; on the other hand, it is inherently ill-suited for e.g. strongly connected models like restarting mutual exclusion protocols. PET supports (unbounded) P-type properties on MDP, DTMC, and CTMC, plus step-bounded reachability on MDP and DTMC. Truly continuous-time dynamics (such as Pt properties for MA) are not handled yet due to the technical subtleties of such an extension [6].

Since QComp 2019, PET was extended by an SMC module [8] that uses the same basic idea to solve problems where the transition dynamics are not known, and thus have to be learnt. It however is not a competitor to the other tools in QComp since it intentionally ignores information present in the models. Other branches of PET support stochastic games [63] and mean-payoff/S-type properties on DTMC and MDP [7], which, however, are not part of QComp.

PRISM [68] is a general-purpose probabilistic model checker with support for a wide range of formalisms and property types. It has been actively developed for 20 years; the first formal release was in 2001. It is implemented in C++ and Java, runs cross-platform, and is open-source, available at prismmodelchecker.org.

PRISM supports DTMC, CTMC, MDP, and PTA models specified in the guarded command-based PRISM language. It focuses on the ε-correct and often ε-correct tracks. For the former, Markov chains and MDP are solved using interval iteration; for the latter, iterative numerical methods are used for Markov chains and VI for MDP. Bounded properties are always (except on PTA) solved using iterative numerical methods (for DTMC and MDP) or uniformisation (for CTMC), which provide guaranteed error bounds. PTA are solved using stochastic-game abstraction refinement [67]. PRISM participates in the probably ε-correct track using the same algorithms as for ε-correct results (thus guaranteeing the requested error with probability 1). While PRISM includes an SMC engine, which would more closely match the requirements of the probably ε-correct track, that engine only provides absolute error bounds, not relative ones as required in QComp. PRISM does not provide a mechanism for delivering partial results when terminated early, thus it does not participate in the 10-minute often ε-correct variant. PRISM incorporates simple heuristics to choose appropriate solution methods based on the type and size of the model and the property being checked; these are mostly used for the specific invocations. In particular, PRISM automatically switches to its MTBDD engine for very large models, with a lower threshold for QComp since the larger models here (as in the PRISM benchmark suite [69], from which many of them derive) are more likely to perform well with symbolic approaches than might be expected in typical verification scenarios.

PRISM participates in QComp 2020 with its current public release, version 4.6. Since the previous edition of the competition, most development on PRISM focused on support for models (e.g. stochastic games) or properties (e.g. automata-based specifications) which are not yet part of QComp.

STAMINA [76], the *stochastic approximate model checker for infinite-state analysis*, was created in early 2019 with a focus on complex synthetic biological network models. It supports CTMC written in the PRISM language and upper-bounded transient CSL properties. Implemented in Java, it runs on Linux and macOS. STAMINA iteratively performs state space expansion and calls PRISM to perform CTMC analysis. Based on the truncation method [77], STAMINA uses property-guided pruning [76] to reduce large and possibly infinite-state CTMC models to finite state representations. Truncation assumes that the probability mass concentrates on a small number of states, and does not distribute

Table 3. Overview of algorithms used by STORM

formalism	prop.	(floating-point) correct	(probably) ε-correct	often ε-correct
DTMC, CTMC	P, E	LU-factorisation	optimistic value iter.	gmres
MDP, MA	P, E	policy iter.	optimistic value iter.	value iteration
DTMC, CTMC	S	LU-factorisation	value iteration	gmres
MDP, MA	S	Linear programming	value iteration	value iteration
DTMC, MDP	Pb, Eb	Matrix-vector mult. (steps), sequential approach (rewards)		
CTMC	Pb, Eb	–	uniformisation	uniformisation
MA	Pb	–	Unif+	Unif+

uniformly as time progresses. Therefore, STAMINA only participates for CTMC with Pt-type properties. Its approach delivers upper and lower bounds on the probabilities being approximated, the difference representing the states that are cut off. STAMINA thus participated in the probably ε-correct and often ε-correct tracks.

Motivated by addressing large and infinite-state probabilistic models, STAMINA does not require a user to manually bound variables in a PRISM model. Its runtime advantage starts to manifest as the state space size grows, as evidenced in [76]. However, QComp only includes three PRISM-language CTMC benchmark instances with Pt properties, and in particular no infinite-state models, meaning that STAMINA cannot show its strengths in the competition.

STORM [32] is a probabilistic model checker that supports many modelling languages including JANI, the PRISM language, DFT, and generalised stochastic Petri nets. Markov models can be built and checked using explicit and decision diagram-based representations. STORM's modular design, efficient C++ core, and extensive Python API yield a powerful toolbox for PMC, parameter synthesis, counterexample generation, fault tree analysis, and many other purposes. STORM has been in active development since 2012. It runs on Linux and macOS, and is open source, available at stormchecker.org.

STORM supports DTMC, CTMC, MDP, and MA. Some PTA models can be checked after converting them to MDP using the MODEST TOOLSET to apply digital clocks [70]. STORM participates in all tracks of QComp 2020. An overview of the algorithms used for each combination of track, formalism, and property type is given in Table 3. For P- and E-type properties, STORM divides the model into strongly connected sub-models that can then be solved individually with the method indicated in the first two rows of Table 3. For the correct track, numbers are represented as infinite-precision rationals. LU-factorisation solves linear equation systems exactly; it is performed within Eigen. Gmres is a fast numerical solution method for systems of linear equations implemented in Gmm++. VI for S-type properties on CTMC and MA [23] provides sound precision guarantees. STORM can also check such properties in MDP and MA exactly by solving a linear program [42] using z3 [75]. Reward-bounded properties are solved using a sequential approach [45,55] that avoids an expensive unfolding of the model.

Time-bounded properties on CTMC are solved via uniformisation following Fox and Glynn [61]. Unif+ [22,41] extends uniformisation to MA. Time-bounded properties for CTMC and MA cannot be solved exactly. DFT without repairs are solved with methods that exploit the fault tree structure [87].

Compared to the version used in QComp 2019, STORM now applies optimistic value iteration for ε-correct P- and E-type properties. The implementation of Unif+ [22,41] has been revamped and now supports relative precision requirements. Model construction has been improved, including support for symbolic MA. Upon timeouts, Storm now reports the best result known so far. The Python interface has been extended and the command line interface streamlined. While experts can still select specific analysis engines, first-time users now benefit from an automatic engine choice: using features of the input JANI model, such as the number of parallel automata or the average variable range, a decision tree predicts the most appropriate model checking approach. To avoid over-fitting, the automatic choice currently only selects among four alternatives: *sparse* (explicit-state), *hybrid* (BDD-based exploration, but explicit data structures for numeric computations), *exact* (like sparse, but using rational arithmetic), and *symbbisim* (like hybrid, but additionally applying symbolic bisimulation minimisation).

STORM implements many alternatives to the aforementioned algorithms. For example, optimistic value iteration can be replaced by interval iteration or sound value iteration. STORM can synthesise high-level counterexamples [30] useful for synthesis loops [24]. In multi-objective model checking, STORM computes Pareto fronts for multi-objective MDP [55] and MA [79] under general and more restricted strategies [33]. Parametric model checking is supported by techniques to (i) compute closed-form solution functions, (ii) divide the parameter space into satisfying and rejecting regions, and (iii) analyse and exploit monotonicities [84]. STORM serves as the backend for the parameter synthesis tool PROPh-ESY [31,62]. STORMPY provides a simple Python interface to STORM's underlying data structures, algorithms, and engines which enables rapid prototyping. More details on these and other features of STORM are given in [60].

5 Performance Evaluation

To evaluate the performance of the participating tools, they were executed on benchmark *instances*—a model, fixed values for the model's parameters, and a property—taken from the QVBS. QComp 2020 used the same set of 100 instances as QComp 2019. We also ran the performance evaluation on the same system: a standard desktop with an Intel Core i7-920 CPU and 12 GB of RAM running 64-bit Ubuntu Linux 18.04. Tools were given 30 min wall-clock time per instance. We can thus compare the current and previous results in the often ε-correct track. We again allowed every tool to submit two command lines per instance—one running the tool in a default configuration, the other being allowed to use instance-specific parameters to tweak for maximum performance. However, we relaxed the requirements for the default invocations: they need not run the tool in its default configuration (modulo any parameters necessary to achieve the track's correctness requirements), but could instead use the parameters that the tool's authors would *today recommend as defaults* for the given combination of formalism and property type. This is because a tool's default settings may be considered part of its interface, which authors may not want to change for compatibility reasons, even though they would implement different defaults today. This slightly reduces the ability to compare with QComp 2019. The ability to submit specific invocations was not used by all tools, and overall only made a significant difference for STORM, and a noticeable but smaller difference for PRISM. In the remainder of this section, we thus mostly show the performance of the default runs. As STORM was the only tool that participated in the correct track, we do not show performance comparison results for this track. Similarly, we found that the model checkers were able to obtain exact results on almost all instances within the time limit of the 10-minute often ε-correct track, rendering our intended comparison of the achieved relative error useless.

On STORM's Automatic Engine Choice. STORM can now automatically select a specific configuration for each benchmark instance, and its authors recommend doing so by default. This, however, would render QComp's distinction between default and specific invocations somewhat pointless. While QComp participants agree that such automatic self-configuration is necessary to improve the usability of quantitative verification tools as they gain more and more analysis engines, algorithms, and parameters, it was not expected to appear in tools for QComp 2020. We will thus drop the default/specific distinction for future competitions. For QComp 2020, we adopted the following pragmatic approach: STORM uses its automatic engine choice by default, and does not use specific invocations. However, this configuration runs *hors concours* for the individual tool comparisons in Sect. 5.2. In addition to STORM, we also evaluate "STORM-static" (abbreviated ST.-static): the same version of STORM, but without automatic engine choice. It thus uses today's recommended defaults for the default invocations, and hand-tweaked command lines for the specific comparison. STORM-static *is* included in *all* comparisons. Section 5.1 and the bottom-middle plot in Fig. 8 show the drastic performance gains achieved by the automatic engine selection.

Incorrect Results. For most—but not all—instances, we have *reference results* obtained via exact algorithms, or reference intervals obtained via sound algorithms using a low ε. Where available, we use these to establish whether a tool delivers an incorrect result. Note that some incorrect results may go undetected because no reference value is available. In all but the often ε-correct and probably ε-correct tracks, tools shall not deliver incorrect results. In the probably ε-correct track, we should expect no more than 5% of a tool's results to be incorrect.

In the correct track, STORM did not deliver any incorrect results. In the floating-point correct track, MCSTA delivered 9, STORM-static 7, and STORM 3 incorrect results. In particular, MCSTA terminated on several cyclic models where VI was not expected to reach a fixpoint, indicating that the termination was entirely due to rounding in floating-point computations. In the ε-correct track, MCSTA, PET, PRISM, and STORM only returned correct results, with STORM-static having just one incorrect result in its default invocations. In the

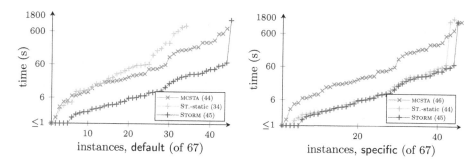

Fig. 1. Quantile plots for the floating-point correct track

probably ε-correct track, where some incorrect results are allowed, one was delivered by each of STORM-static, PRISM, and STAMINA. As tools switched to unsound algorithms for the often ε-correct track, more incorrect results were delivered; see the respective plots in Sect. 5.2 for an indication of their numbers per tool.

5.1 Quantile Plots

We first look at selected subsets of tools via *quantile plots*. We usually only consider the instances supported by *all* of the tools shown in the plot; this is to avoid unsupported instances having the same visual effect as timeouts and errors. For example, for Fig. 1, the intersection of what MCSTA and STORM support contained $n = 67$ instances (shown as "of n" in the x-axis label). The plots' legends indicate the number of correctly solved benchmarks for each tool in parenthesis (i.e. where no timeouts or error occurred and the result was correct). A point $\langle x, y \rangle$ on the line of a tool in this type of plot signifies that the *individual* runtime for the x-th fastest instance as solved by the tool was y seconds.

By ordering instances independently for each tool, quantile plots only allow a comparison of the *total* performance of tools over the included instances. In particular, cases where e.g. a tool is slower overall, but manages to solve some hard instances much faster than any other, will not be visible in a quantile plot. We thus exclude the specialised tools, whose the entire purpose is to solve *some hard* instances better than anyone else, from most of the quantile plots we show.

floating-point correct. The quantile plots in Fig. 1 show that MCSTA's ad-hoc "just try VI" approach to get floating-point correct results turned out to be rather competitive. STORM-static more often timed out and delivered four more incorrect results. The automatic engine selection moves STORM into a class of its own. As the right-hand side of Fig. 1 shows, its performance is only nearly matched by the hand-optimised configurations of the same tool.

ε-correct. In Fig. 2, we compare the general-purpose tools that participated in the ε-correct track. Since PRISM only supports models in the PRISM language, the plots only range over 43 instances; the intersection of what MCSTA and

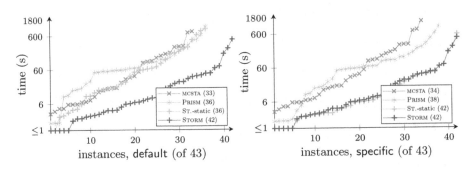

Fig. 2. Quantile plots for the ε-correct track

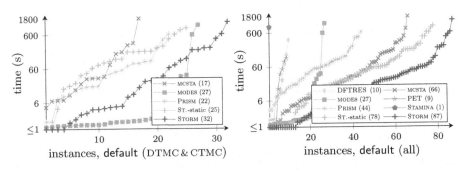

Fig. 3. Quantile plots for the probably ε-correct track

STORM support covers 86 instances. We see that MCSTA, PRISM, and STORM-static perform similarly with default settings. Once it can make use of its wide range of different engines and algorithms, however, STORM cannot be matched.

probably ε-correct. Once statistical model checkers can join in, the competition becomes more diverse. If we plot the results of the probably ε-correct track for the general-purpose tools, the overall relationships remain the same as in Fig. 2, thus we do not show these plots. Instead, we restrict to DTMC and CTMC. Then, we can make a useful comparison that includes MODES, as shown on the left-hand side of Fig. 3. We see that MODES is drastically faster than the model checkers in most cases, needing just a few seconds for more than 20 of the instances. Its runtime only rises significantly when confronted with somewhat rare events (due to the relative-error requirement), and for some complex models where computing the available transitions in itself takes significant computation time. On the right-hand side of Fig. 3, we show a quantile plot over *all* 100 instances and *all* tools in the track. This mainly shows how many instances each tool supports *and* solves, but does not do justice to the specialised tools.

often ε-correct. All QComp 2020 participants compete in the often ε-correct track, including in particular the fourth general-purpose model checker, ePMC. We show the results in Fig. 4, limited to default results since few tools supplied and gained from specific invocations. The top two plots in Fig. 4 can be compared

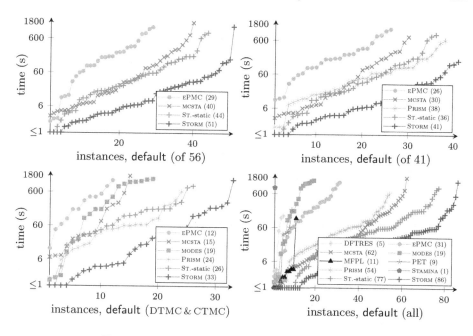

Fig. 4. Quantile plots for the often ε-correct track

with QComp 2019 [46, Fig. 2] modulo the relaxed definition of default settings, while the bottom two plots correspond to Fig. 3. In particular, we see that SMC in the form of MODES is no longer competitive given the much increased precision requirement of $\varepsilon = 10^{-3}$. This confirms the results of earlier comparisons between PMC- and SMC-based methods in different settings [88].

5.2 Scatter Plots

We next show scatter plots that compare the performance of each tool over all individual instances to the best-performing other tool for each instance, using default invocations only. A point $\langle x, y \rangle$ states that the runtime of the plot's tool on one instance was x seconds while the best runtime on the same instance among all other tools *except* STORM *with automatic engine selection*[1] was y seconds. Thus points above the solid diagonal line indicate instances where the plot's tool was the fastest; it was more than ten times faster than any other tool on points above the dotted line. Points on the "TO", "ERR" and "INC" lines indicate instances where the plot's tool encountered a timeout, reported an error (such as running out of memory), or returned an incorrect result, respectively. Points on the "n/a" line indicate instances that none of the other tools was able to solve. These plots provide more detailed information than the quantile plots

---

[1] STORM, on the other hand, is not compared with STORM-static, thus its "wins n" numbers, marked *, are not part of the same sum as those of the other tools.

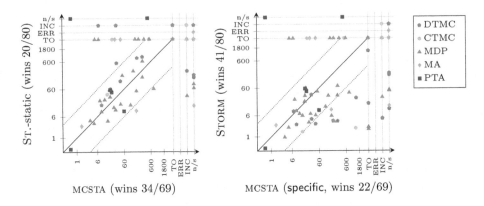

Fig. 5. Scatter plots for the floating-point correct track

since they compare the performance on individual instances, and also include instances outside of the intersections of what is supported by multiple tools. For example, the right-hand plot of Fig. 5 shows that MCSTA manages to be faster than STORM on a few instances whereas Fig. 1 looked like MCSTA is always slower.

floating-point correct. Figure 5 compares MCSTA to STORM-static and STORM using floating-point correct algorithms. The "n/s" lines indicate instances not supported by the other tool. STORM behaves nearly like STORM-static in specific mode, which is why we show STORM on the right-hand side. Both tools solve several instances where the other fails with a timeout; in the default case, performance is similar when we exclude timeouts. As mentioned, MCSTA's approach surprisingly worked, usually correctly, on models where it was not expected to terminate. In summary, the two tools' very different approaches appear complementary, together being able to solve many more instances than each on its own.

ε-correct. Data for the ε-correct track is plotted in Fig. 6. These now include useful data for PET: we see that it times out on most instances, but is the fastest of all tools on nearly half of the ones that it does solve in time. This matches the expectations for an approach highly dependent on the models' structure.

probably ε-correct. Figure 7 now includes SMC tools for the probably ε-correct track. We do not show STAMINA since it works for only three instances, out of which it solves one successfully; the current QComp benchmarks simply do not match STAMINA's purpose as discussed in Sect. 4. We now see the typical behaviour of a specialised tool for DFTRES again, with PET showing markedly improved performance relative to the other tools due to the relaxed precision requirement. MODES' ability to solve many models in almost no time is evident.

often ε-correct. Figure 8 provides the details for QComp 2020's largest track, with often ε-correct results. We omit DFTRES (it only solves two instances now, facing the same problems as MODES from the increased precision requirement),

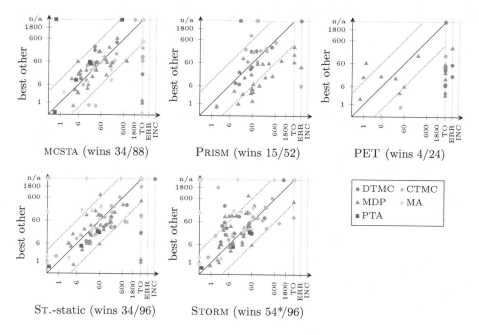

Fig. 6. Scatter plots for the ε-correct track

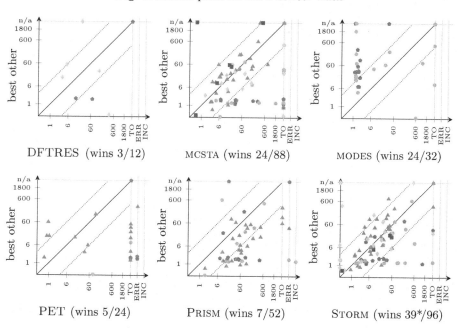

Fig. 7. Scatter plots for the probably ε-correct track

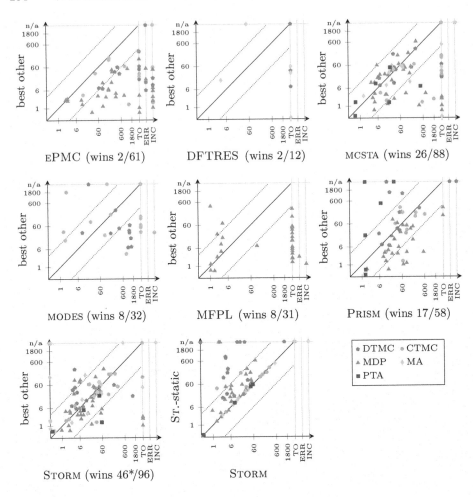

Fig. 8. Scatter plots for the often ε-correct track

PET (with the same pattern as in the probably ε-correct track at somewhat worse performance), and STAMINA (as before). These plots can be compared with QComp 2019 [46, Figs. 4–6]. The bottom-middle plot compares STORM to STORM-static (default), again highlighting the gains of automatic engine choice.

6   Conclusion

QComp 2020 conservatively extended QComp 2019, focusing on the critical field of problems and performance trade-offs around the correctness and precision of results in quantitative verification. The different tools provide different ranges of guarantees, from exact rational results to no sure guarantees at all in the often ε-correct track. Overall, STORM with its new automatic engine selection dominates the competition. As the first significantly self-configuring model checker in

QComp, it advances the usability of PMC tools but also poses challenges to competition design. Still, once we look more deeply into the results—e.g. via scatter plots—we see that *each* tool contributes to solving the QComp benchmark set, and several specialised tools successfully occupy clearly defined niches.

QComp 2020 did not evaluate usability: aside from STORM's improved automation, little has changed, with still only PRISM providing a graphical user interface. In particular, we learned from the previous competition that a usability evaluation needs clear and widely agreed-upon criteria to be useful, and plan to create such a usability scorecard for a future edition of QComp. More tools now venture into stochastic games, opening a direction to expand QComp.

Roles of Authors and Acknowledgments. Arnd Hartmanns and Michaela Klauck organised QComp 2020. Carlos E. Budde submitted DFTRES; the tool's main developer is Enno Ruijters. Andrea Turrini submitted ePMC; its main developer is Ernst Moritz Hahn. Arnd Hartmanns develops and submitted MCSTA and MODES; Yuliya Butkova added many new MA model checking algorithms to MCSTA. Michaela Klauck develops and submitted MODEST FRET-π LRTDP. Jan Křetínský submitted PET; it is developed by Pranav Ashok, Tobias Meggendorfer, and Maximilian Weininger. David Parker submitted PRISM with support from Joachim Klein. Tim Quatmann submitted STORM; it is co-developed by Christian Hensel, Sebastian Junges, Joost-Pieter Katoen, Jip Spel, Matthias Volk, and many others. Zhen Zhang submitted STAMINA; it is developed by Thakur Neupane, Brett Jepsen, Riley Roberts, and Zhen Zhang.

Data Availability. The tools used and data generated in the performance evaluation are archived at qcomp.org and DOI 10.5281/zenodo.3965313 [57].

References

1. Abate, A., et al.: ARCH-COMP19 category report: stochastic modelling. In: ARCH. EPiC Series in Computing, vol. 61, pp. 62–102. EasyChair (2019). https://doi.org/10.29007/f2vb
2. Agha, G., Palmskog, K.: A survey of statistical model checking. ACM Trans. Model. Comput. Simul. **28**(1), 6:1–6:39 (2018). https://doi.org/10.1145/3158668
3. Alur, R., Dill, D.L.: A theory of timed automata. Theoret. Comput. Sci. **126**(2), 183–235 (1994). https://doi.org/10.1016/0304-3975(94)90010-8
4. Amparore, E.G., Balbo, G., Beccuti, M., Donatelli, S., Franceschinis, G.: 30 years of GreatSPN. In: Fiondella, L., Puliafito, A. (eds.) Principles of Performance and Reliability Modeling and Evaluation, pp. 227–254. Springer, Cham (2016). https://doi.org/10.1007/978-3-319-30599-8_9
5. Arnold, F., Belinfante, A., Van der Berg, F., Guck, D., Stoelinga, M.: DFTCALC: a tool for efficient fault tree analysis. In: Bitsch, F., Guiochet, J., Kaâniche, M. (eds.) SAFECOMP 2013. LNCS, vol. 8153, pp. 293–301. Springer, Heidelberg (2013). https://doi.org/10.1007/978-3-642-40793-2_27
6. Ashok, P., Butkova, Y., Hermanns, H., Křetínský, J.: Continuous-time Markov decisions based on partial exploration. In: Lahiri, S.K., Wang, C. (eds.) ATVA 2018. LNCS, vol. 11138, pp. 317–334. Springer, Cham (2018). https://doi.org/10.1007/978-3-030-01090-4_19

7. Ashok, P., Chatterjee, K., Daca, P., Křetínský, J., Meggendorfer, T.: Value iteration for long-run average reward in Markov decision processes. In: Majumdar, R., Kunčak, V. (eds.) CAV 2017. LNCS, vol. 10426, pp. 201–221. Springer, Cham (2017). https://doi.org/10.1007/978-3-319-63387-9_10

8. Ashok, P., Křetínský, J., Weininger, M.: PAC statistical model checking for Markov decision processes and stochastic games. In: Dillig, I., Tasiran, S. (eds.) CAV 2019. LNCS, vol. 11561, pp. 497–519. Springer, Cham (2019). https://doi.org/10.1007/978-3-030-25540-4_29

9. Baier, C., de Alfaro, L., Forejt, V., Kwiatkowska, M.: Model checking probabilistic systems. In: Handbook of Model Checking, pp. 963–999. Springer, Cham (2018). https://doi.org/10.1007/978-3-319-10575-8_28

10. Baier, C., Katoen, J.-P., Hermanns, H.: Approximative symbolic model checking of continuous-time Markov chains. In: Baeten, J.C.M., Mauw, S. (eds.) CONCUR 1999. LNCS, vol. 1664, pp. 146–161. Springer, Heidelberg (1999). https://doi.org/10.1007/3-540-48320-9_12

11. Baier, C., Klein, J., Leuschner, L., Parker, D., Wunderlich, S.: Ensuring the reliability of your model checker: interval iteration for Markov decision processes. In: Majumdar, R., Kunčak, V. (eds.) CAV 2017. LNCS, vol. 10426, pp. 160–180. Springer, Cham (2017). https://doi.org/10.1007/978-3-319-63387-9_8

12. Bauer, M.S., Mathur, U., Chadha, R., Sistla, A.P., Viswanathan, M.: Exact quantitative probabilistic model checking through rational search. In: FMCAD, pp. 92–99. IEEE (2017). https://doi.org/10.23919/FMCAD.2017.8102246

13. Behrmann, G., et al.: UPPAAL 4.0. In: QEST, pp. 125–126. IEEE Computer Society (2006). https://doi.org/10.1109/QEST.2006.59

14. Bonet, B., Geffner, H.: Labeled RTDP: improving the convergence of real-time dynamic programming. In: ICAPS, pp. 12–21. AAAI Press (2003)

15. Brázdil, T., et al.: Verification of Markov decision processes using learning algorithms. In: Cassez, F., Raskin, J.-F. (eds.) ATVA 2014. LNCS, vol. 8837, pp. 98–114. Springer, Cham (2014). https://doi.org/10.1007/978-3-319-11936-6_8

16. Budde, C.E., D'Argenio, P.R., Hartmanns, A.: Better automated importance splitting for transient rare events. In: Larsen, K.G., Sokolsky, O., Wang, J. (eds.) SETTA 2017. LNCS, vol. 10606, pp. 42–58. Springer, Cham (2017). https://doi.org/10.1007/978-3-319-69483-2_3

17. Budde, C.E., D'Argenio, P.R., Hartmanns, A.: Automated compositional importance splitting. Sci. Comput. Program. **174**, 90–108 (2019). https://doi.org/10.1016/j.scico.2019.01.006

18. Budde, C.E., D'Argenio, P.R., Hartmanns, A., Sedwards, S.: An efficient statistical model checker for nondeterminism and rare events. STTT (2020, to appear)

19. Budde, C.E., Dehnert, C., Hahn, E.M., Hartmanns, A., Junges, S., Turrini, A.: JANI: quantitative model and tool interaction. In: Legay, A., Margaria, T. (eds.) TACAS 2017. LNCS, vol. 10206, pp. 151–168. Springer, Heidelberg (2017). https://doi.org/10.1007/978-3-662-54580-5_9

20. Butkova, Y., Fox, G.: Optimal time-bounded reachability analysis for concurrent systems. In: Vojnar, T., Zhang, L. (eds.) TACAS 2019. LNCS, vol. 11428, pp. 191–208. Springer, Cham (2019). https://doi.org/10.1007/978-3-030-17465-1_11

21. Butkova, Y., Hartmanns, A., Hermanns, H.: A Modest approach to modelling and checking Markov automata. In: Parker, D., Wolf, V. (eds.) QEST 2019. LNCS, vol. 11785, pp. 52–69. Springer, Cham (2019). https://doi.org/10.1007/978-3-030-30281-8_4

22. Butkova, Y., Hatefi, H., Hermanns, H., Krčál, J.: Optimal continuous time Markov decisions. In: Finkbeiner, B., Pu, G., Zhang, L. (eds.) ATVA 2015. LNCS, vol. 9364, pp. 166–182. Springer, Cham (2015). https://doi.org/10.1007/978-3-319-24953-7_12

23. Butkova, Y., Wimmer, R., Hermanns, H.: Long-run rewards for Markov automata. In: Legay, A., Margaria, T. (eds.) TACAS 2017. LNCS, vol. 10206, pp. 188–203. Springer, Heidelberg (2017). https://doi.org/10.1007/978-3-662-54580-5_11

24. Češka, M., Hensel, C., Junges, S., Katoen, J.-P.: Counterexample-driven synthesis for probabilistic program sketches. In: ter Beek, M.H., McIver, A., Oliveira, J.N. (eds.) FM 2019. LNCS, vol. 11800, pp. 101–120. Springer, Cham (2019). https://doi.org/10.1007/978-3-030-30942-8_8

25. Chen, T., Forejt, V., Kwiatkowska, M.Z., Parker, D., Simaitis, A.: Automatic verification of competitive stochastic systems. Formal Methods Syst. Des. **43**(1), 61–92 (2013). https://doi.org/10.1007/s10703-013-0183-7

26. Courtney, T., Gaonkar, S., Keefe, K., Rozier, E., Sanders, W.H.: Möbius 2.3: an extensible tool for dependability, security, and performance evaluation of large and complex system models. In: DSN, pp. 353–358. IEEE Computer Society (2009). https://doi.org/10.1109/DSN.2009.5270318

27. D'Argenio, P.R., Hartmanns, A., Legay, A., Sedwards, S.: Statistical approximation of optimal schedulers for probabilistic timed automata. In: Ábrahám, E., Huisman, M. (eds.) IFM 2016. LNCS, vol. 9681, pp. 99–114. Springer, Cham (2016). https://doi.org/10.1007/978-3-319-33693-0_7

28. D'Argenio, P.R., Hartmanns, A., Sedwards, S.: Lightweight statistical model checking in nondeterministic continuous time. In: Margaria, T., Steffen, B. (eds.) ISoLA 2018. LNCS, vol. 11245, pp. 336–353. Springer, Cham (2018). https://doi.org/10.1007/978-3-030-03421-4_22

29. D'Argenio, P.R., Jeannet, B., Jensen, H.E., Larsen, K.G.: Reduction and refinement strategies for probabilistic analysis. In: Hermanns, H., Segala, R. (eds.) PAPM-PROBMIV 2002. LNCS, vol. 2399, pp. 57–76. Springer, Heidelberg (2002). https://doi.org/10.1007/3-540-45605-8_5

30. Dehnert, C., Jansen, N., Wimmer, R., Ábrahám, E., Katoen, J.-P.: Fast debugging of PRISM models. In: Cassez, F., Raskin, J.-F. (eds.) ATVA 2014. LNCS, vol. 8837, pp. 146–162. Springer, Cham (2014). https://doi.org/10.1007/978-3-319-11936-6_11

31. Dehnert, C., et al.: PROPhESY: a PRObabilistic ParamEter SYnthesis tool. In: Kroening, D., Păsăreanu, C.S. (eds.) CAV 2015. LNCS, vol. 9206, pp. 214–231. Springer, Cham (2015). https://doi.org/10.1007/978-3-319-21690-4_13

32. Dehnert, C., Junges, S., Katoen, J.P., Volk, M.: A Storm is coming: a modern probabilistic model checker. In: CAV. LNCS, vol. 10427, pp. 592–600. Springer (2017). https://doi.org/10.1007/978-3-319-63390-9_31

33. Delgrange, F., Katoen, J.-P., Quatmann, T., Randour, M.: Simple strategies in multi-objective MDPs. In: TACAS 2020. LNCS, vol. 12078, pp. 346–364. Springer, Cham (2020). https://doi.org/10.1007/978-3-030-45190-5_19

34. van Dijk, T., et al.: A comparative study of BDD packages for probabilistic symbolic model checking. In: Li, X., Liu, Z., Yi, W. (eds.) SETTA 2015. LNCS, vol. 9409, pp. 35–51. Springer, Cham (2015). https://doi.org/10.1007/978-3-319-25942-0_3

35. Eisentraut, C., Hermanns, H., Zhang, L.: On probabilistic automata in continuous time. In: LICS, pp. 342–351. IEEE Computer Society (2010). https://doi.org/10.1109/LICS.2010.41

36. Etessami, K., Kwiatkowska, M.Z., Vardi, M.Y., Yannakakis, M.: Multi-objective model checking of Markov decision processes. Logic. Methods Comput. Sci. **4**(4) (2008). https://doi.org/10.2168/LMCS-4(4:8)2008

37. Feng, Y., Hahn, E.M., Turrini, A., Ying, S.: Model checking omega-regular properties for quantum Markov chains. In: CONCUR. LIPIcs, vol. 85, pp. 35:1–35:16. Schloss Dagstuhl - Leibniz-Zentrum für Informatik (2017). https://doi.org/10.4230/LIPIcs.CONCUR.2017.35

38. Fu, C., Turrini, A., Huang, X., Song, L., Feng, Y., Zhang, L.: Model checking probabilistic epistemic logic for probabilistic multiagent systems. In: IJCAI, pp. 4757–4763. ijcai.org (2018). https://doi.org/10.24963/ijcai.2018/661

39. Gainer, P., Hahn, E.M., Schewe, S.: Accelerated model checking of parametric Markov chains. In: Lahiri, S.K., Wang, C. (eds.) ATVA 2018. LNCS, vol. 11138, pp. 300–316. Springer, Cham (2018). https://doi.org/10.1007/978-3-030-01090-4_18

40. Gordon, A.D., Henzinger, T.A., Nori, A.V., Rajamani, S.K.: Probabilistic programming. In: FOSE, pp. 167–181. ACM (2014). https://doi.org/10.1145/2593882.2593900

41. Gros, T.P.: Markov automata taken by Storm. Master's thesis, Saarland University, Germany (2018)

42. Guck, D., Hatefi, H., Hermanns, H., Katoen, J.-P., Timmer, M.: Modelling, reduction and analysis of Markov automata. In: Joshi, K., Siegle, M., Stoelinga, M., D'Argenio, P.R. (eds.) QEST 2013. LNCS, vol. 8054, pp. 55–71. Springer, Heidelberg (2013). https://doi.org/10.1007/978-3-642-40196-1_5

43. Haddad, S., Monmege, B.: Reachability in MDPs: refining convergence of value iteration. In: Ouaknine, J., Potapov, I., Worrell, J. (eds.) RP 2014. LNCS, vol. 8762, pp. 125–137. Springer, Cham (2014). https://doi.org/10.1007/978-3-319-11439-2_10

44. Haddad, S., Monmege, B.: Interval iteration algorithm for MDPs and IMDPs. Theoret. Comput. Sci. **735**, 111–131 (2018). https://doi.org/10.1016/j.tcs.2016.12.003

45. Hahn, E.M., Hartmanns, A.: A comparison of time- and reward-bounded probabilistic model checking techniques. In: Fränzle, M., Kapur, D., Zhan, N. (eds.) SETTA 2016. LNCS, vol. 9984, pp. 85–100. Springer, Cham (2016). https://doi.org/10.1007/978-3-319-47677-3_6

46. Hahn, E.M., et al.: The 2019 comparison of tools for the analysis of quantitative formal models. In: Beyer, D., Huisman, M., Kordon, F., Steffen, B. (eds.) TACAS 2019. LNCS, vol. 11429, pp. 69–92. Springer, Cham (2019). https://doi.org/10.1007/978-3-030-17502-3_5

47. Hahn, E.M., Hartmanns, A., Hermanns, H., Katoen, J.P.: A compositional modelling and analysis framework for stochastic hybrid systems. Formal Methods Syst. Des. **43**(2), 191–232 (2013). https://doi.org/10.1007/s10703-012-0167-z

48. Hahn, E.M., Hashemi, V., Hermanns, H., Lahijanian, M., Turrini, A.: Multi-objective robust strategy synthesis for interval Markov decision processes. In: Bertrand, N., Bortolussi, L. (eds.) QEST 2017. LNCS, vol. 10503, pp. 207–223. Springer, Cham (2017). https://doi.org/10.1007/978-3-319-66335-7_13

49. Hahn, E.M., Hashemi, V., Hermanns, H., Turrini, A.: Exploiting robust optimization for interval probabilistic bisimulation. In: Agha, G., Van Houdt, B. (eds.) QEST 2016. LNCS, vol. 9826, pp. 55–71. Springer, Cham (2016). https://doi.org/10.1007/978-3-319-43425-4_4

50. Hahn, E.M., Li, G., Schewe, S., Zhang, L.: Lazy determinisation for quantitative model checking. CoRR abs/1311.2928 (2013). arxiv.org/abs/1311.2928

51. Hahn, E.M., Li, Y., Schewe, S., Turrini, A., Zhang, L.: ISCASMC: a web-based probabilistic model checker. In: Jones, C., Pihlajasaari, P., Sun, J. (eds.) FM 2014. LNCS, vol. 8442, pp. 312–317. Springer, Cham (2014). https://doi.org/10.1007/978-3-319-06410-9_22

52. Hahn, E.M., Schewe, S., Turrini, A., Zhang, L.: A simple algorithm for solving qualitative probabilistic parity games. In: Chaudhuri, S., Farzan, A. (eds.) CAV 2016. LNCS, vol. 9780, pp. 291–311. Springer, Cham (2016). https://doi.org/10.1007/978-3-319-41540-6_16

53. Hartmanns, A., Hermanns, H.: The Modest Toolset: an integrated environment for quantitative modelling and verification. In: Ábrahám, E., Havelund, K. (eds.) TACAS 2014. LNCS, vol. 8413, pp. 593–598. Springer, Heidelberg (2014). https://doi.org/10.1007/978-3-642-54862-8_51

54. Hartmanns, A., Hermanns, H.: Explicit model checking of very large MDP using partitioning and secondary storage. In: Finkbeiner, B., Pu, G., Zhang, L. (eds.) ATVA 2015. LNCS, vol. 9364, pp. 131–147. Springer, Cham (2015). https://doi.org/10.1007/978-3-319-24953-7_10

55. Hartmanns, A., Junges, S., Katoen, J.-P., Quatmann, T.: Multi-cost bounded reachability in MDP. In: Beyer, D., Huisman, M. (eds.) TACAS 2018. LNCS, vol. 10806, pp. 320–339. Springer, Cham (2018). https://doi.org/10.1007/978-3-319-89963-3_19

56. Hartmanns, A., Kaminski, B.L.: Optimistic value iteration. In: Lahiri, S.K., Wang, C. (eds.) CAV 2020. LNCS, vol. 12225, pp. 488–511. Springer, Cham (2020). https://doi.org/10.1007/978-3-030-53291-8_26

57. Hartmanns, A., Klauck, M.: The 2020 comparison of tools for the analysis of quantitative formal models: results and reproduction. Zenodo (2020). https://doi.org/10.5281/zenodo.3965313

58. Hartmanns, A., Klauck, M., Parker, D., Quatmann, T., Ruijters, E.: The quantitative verification benchmark set. In: Vojnar, T., Zhang, L. (eds.) TACAS 2019. LNCS, vol. 11427, pp. 344–350. Springer, Cham (2019). https://doi.org/10.1007/978-3-030-17462-0_20

59. Hartmanns, A., Sedwards, S., D'Argenio, P.R.: Efficient simulation-based verification of probabilistic timed automata. In: Winter Simulation Conference, pp. 1419–1430. IEEE (2017). https://doi.org/10.1109/WSC.2017.8247885

60. Hensel, C., Junges, S., Katoen, J.P., Quatmann, T., Volk, M.: The probabilistic model checker Storm. CoRR abs/2002.07080 (2020). arxiv.org/abs/2002.07080

61. Jansen, D.N.: Understanding Fox and Glynn's "Computing Poisson probabilities". CTIT technical report series (2011)

62. Junges, S., et al.: Parameter synthesis for Markov models. CoRR abs/1903.07993 (2019). arxiv.org/abs/1903.07993

63. Kelmendi, E., Krämer, J., Křetínský, J., Weininger, M.: Value iteration for simple stochastic games: stopping criterion and learning algorithm. In: Chockler, H., Weissenbacher, G. (eds.) CAV 2018. LNCS, vol. 10981, pp. 623–642. Springer, Cham (2018). https://doi.org/10.1007/978-3-319-96145-3_36

64. Klauck, M., Steinmetz, M., Hoffmann, J., Hermanns, H.: Compiling probabilistic model checking into prob. planning. In: ICAPS, pp. 150–154. AAAI Press (2018)

65. Klauck, M., Steinmetz, M., Hoffmann, J., Hermanns, H.: Bridging the gap between probabilistic model checking and probabilistic planning: survey, compilations, and empirical comparison. J. Artif. Intell. Res. 68, 247–310 (2020). https://doi.org/10.1613/jair.1.11595

66. Kolobov, A., Mausam, Weld, D.S., Geffner, H.: Heuristic search for generalized stochastic shortest path MDPs. In: ICAPS. AAAI Press (2011)

67. Kwiatkowska, M., Norman, G., Parker, D.: Stochastic games for verification of probabilistic timed automata. In: Ouaknine, J., Vaandrager, F.W. (eds.) FORMATS 2009. LNCS, vol. 5813, pp. 212–227. Springer, Heidelberg (2009). https://doi.org/10.1007/978-3-642-04368-0_17

68. Kwiatkowska, M., Norman, G., Parker, D.: PRISM 4.0: verification of probabilistic real-time systems. In: Gopalakrishnan, G., Qadeer, S. (eds.) CAV 2011. LNCS, vol. 6806, pp. 585–591. Springer, Heidelberg (2011). https://doi.org/10.1007/978-3-642-22110-1_47

69. Kwiatkowska, M.Z., Norman, G., Parker, D.: The PRISM benchmark suite. In: QEST, pp. 203–204. IEEE Computer Society (2012). https://doi.org/10.1109/QEST.2012.14

70. Kwiatkowska, M.Z., Norman, G., Parker, D., Sproston, J.: Performance analysis of probabilistic timed automata using digital clocks. Formal Methods Syst. Des. **29**(1), 33–78 (2006). https://doi.org/10.1007/s10703-006-0005-2

71. Kwiatkowska, M.Z., Norman, G., Segala, R., Sproston, J.: Automatic verification of real-time systems with discrete probability distributions. Theoret. Comput. Sci. **282**(1), 101–150 (2002). https://doi.org/10.1016/S0304-3975(01)00046-9

72. Legay, A., Sedwards, S., Traonouez, L.-M.: Scalable verification of Markov decision processes. In: Canal, C., Idani, A. (eds.) SEFM 2014. LNCS, vol. 8938, pp. 350–362. Springer, Cham (2015). https://doi.org/10.1007/978-3-319-15201-1_23

73. Lewis, E., Böhm, F.: Monte Carlo simulation of Markov unreliability models. Nucl. Eng. Design **77**(1), 49–62 (1984). https://doi.org/10.1016/0029-5493(84)90060-8

74. Li, Y., Liu, W., Turrini, A., Hahn, E.M., Zhang, L.: An efficient synthesis algorithm for parametric Markov chains against linear time properties. CoRR abs/1605.04400 (2016)

75. de Moura, L., Bjørner, N.: Z3: an efficient SMT solver. In: Ramakrishnan, C.R., Rehof, J. (eds.) TACAS 2008. LNCS, vol. 4963, pp. 337–340. Springer, Heidelberg (2008). https://doi.org/10.1007/978-3-540-78800-3_24

76. Neupane, T., Myers, C.J., Madsen, C., Zheng, H., Zhang, Z.: STAMINA: STochastic Approximate Model-checker for INfinite-state Analysis. In: Dillig, I., Tasiran, S. (eds.) CAV 2019. LNCS, vol. 11561, pp. 540–549. Springer, Cham (2019). https://doi.org/10.1007/978-3-030-25540-4_31

77. Neupane, T., Zhang, Z., Madsen, C., Zheng, H., Myers, C.J.: Approximation techniques for stochastic analysis of biological systems. In: Liò, P., Zuliani, P. (eds.) Automated Reasoning for Systems Biology and Medicine. CB, vol. 30, pp. 327–348. Springer, Cham (2019). https://doi.org/10.1007/978-3-030-17297-8_12

78. Puterman, M.L.: Markov Decision Processes: Discrete Stochastic Dynamic Programming. Wiley Series in Probability and Statistics, Wiley (1994). https://doi.org/10.1002/9780470316887

79. Quatmann, T., Junges, S., Katoen, J.-P.: Markov automata with multiple objectives. In: Majumdar, R., Kunčak, V. (eds.) CAV 2017. LNCS, vol. 10426, pp. 140–159. Springer, Cham (2017). https://doi.org/10.1007/978-3-319-63387-9_7

80. Quatmann, T., Katoen, J.-P.: Sound value iteration. In: Chockler, H., Weissenbacher, G. (eds.) CAV 2018. LNCS, vol. 10981, pp. 643–661. Springer, Cham (2018). https://doi.org/10.1007/978-3-319-96145-3_37

81. Reijsbergen, D., de Boer, P.T., Scheinhardt, W.R.W., Juneja, S.: Path-ZVA: general, efficient, and automated importance sampling for highly reliable Markovian systems. ACM Trans. Model. Comput. Simul. **28**(3), 22:1–22:25 (2018). https://doi.org/10.1145/3161569

82. Ruijters, E., et al.: FFORT: a benchmark suite for fault tree analysis. In: ESREL (2019). https://doi.org/10.3850/978-981-11-2724-3_0641-cd

83. Ruijters, E., Reijsbergen, D., de Boer, P.T., Stoelinga, M.: Rare event simulation for dynamic fault trees. Reliab. Eng. Syst. Saf. **186**, 220–231 (2019). https://doi.org/10.1016/j.ress.2019.02.004

84. Spel, J., Junges, S., Katoen, J.-P.: Are parametric Markov chains monotonic? In: Chen, Y.-F., Cheng, C.-H., Esparza, J. (eds.) ATVA 2019. LNCS, vol. 11781, pp. 479–496. Springer, Cham (2019). https://doi.org/10.1007/978-3-030-31784-3_28

85. Steinmetz, M., Hoffmann, J., Buffet, O.: Goal probability analysis in probabilistic planning: exploring and enhancing the state of the art. J. Artif. Intell. Res. **57**, 229–271 (2016). https://doi.org/10.1613/jair.5153

86. Sullivan, K.J., Dugan, J.B., Coppit, D.: The Galileo fault tree analysis tool. In: FTCS, pp. 232–235. IEEE Computer Society (1999). https://doi.org/10.1109/FTCS.1999.781056

87. Volk, M., Junges, S., Katoen, J.P.: Fast dynamic fault tree analysis by model checking techniques. IEEE Trans. Ind. Informatics **14**(1), 370–379 (2018). https://doi.org/10.1109/TII.2017.2710316

88. Younes, H.L.S., Kwiatkowska, M.Z., Norman, G., Parker, D.: Numerical vs. statistical probabilistic model checking. Int. J. Softw. Tools Technol. Transf. **8**(3), 216–228 (2006). https://doi.org/10.1007/s10009-005-0187-8

89. Younes, H.L.S., Littman, M.L., Weissman, D., Asmuth, J.: The first probabilistic track of the International Planning Competition. J. Artif. Intell. Res. **24**, 851–887 (2005). https://doi.org/10.1613/jair.1880

Every Component Matters: Generating Parallel Verification Benchmarks with Hardness Guarantees

Marc Jasper[✉], Maximilian Schlüter, David Schmidt, and Bernhard Steffen[✉]

TU Dortmund University, Dortmund, Germany
{marc.jasper,maximilian.schlueter,david3.schmidt,
bernhard.steffen}@tu-dortmund.de

Abstract. In this paper, we show how to automatically generate *hard* verification tasks in order to support events like the Model Checking Contest or the Rigorous Examination of Reactive Systems Challenge with tailored benchmark problems for analyzing the validity of linear-time properties in parallel systems. Characteristic of the generated benchmarks are two hardness guarantees: (i) every parallel component is relevant and (ii) the state space of the analyzed system is *exponential* in the number of its parallel components. Generated benchmarks can be made available, e.g., as Promela code or Petri nets.

Keywords: Benchmark generation · Program verification · Temporal logics · LTL · Model checking · Property preservation · Modal transition systems · Modal contracts · Alphabet extension

1 Introduction

Automated verification has seen a number of success stories in the last decades, like the verification of medical device transmission protocols [10], industrial call-processing software [6], or the autonomous behavior of the Curiosity rover [5]. The treatment of realistic parallel systems is, however, still in its infancy. The development of corresponding verification tools is an area of very active research, which is increasingly supported by competitions and challenges such as the Model Checking Contest (MCC) [20] that aim at revealing the strengths and weaknesses of state-of-the-art tools. One of the major challenges of such competitions is the preparation of adequate benchmark problems. Ideally, they should be of realistic size and have interesting yet known properties, a combination that is hard to achieve. Traditionally, MCC focuses on realistic benchmarks and uses majority voting during its property evaluation, while the Rigorous Examination of Reactive Systems (RERS) Challenge [14] uses automatically generated benchmarks with properties that are guaranteed by construction. RERS argues for practicality by referring to the increasing importance of requirement-driven/generative programming [14,15].

In this paper, we extend the results of our previous work [29] to not only ensure that benchmarks are large, but also *hard* in the following sense:

© Springer Nature Switzerland AG 2021
T. Margaria and B. Steffen (Eds.): ISoLA 2020, LNCS 12479, pp. 242–263, 2021.
https://doi.org/10.1007/978-3-030-83723-5_16

i. no component can be neglected during the analysis and
ii. the number of reachable states of the considered parallel system is *exponential* in the number of its parallel components.

Key to our approach is the construction of a complex 'context' that constrains the behavior of an initial system.

On the one hand, the first item listed above guarantees that a task is not trivial because one cannot simply abstract from parallel components while still correctly solving a given task. A trivial modification to our approach allows to freely adjust how many parallel components are required for correctly verifying or refuting a given temporal property, hence we can arbitrarily scale the relevance of the constructed parallel context. For simplicity, this paper focuses on the case where all parallel components are required to solve a task.

On the other hand, the second of the above-listed items ensures that there exist sufficient parallel interleavings to confront analyzers with what is commonly referred to as state explosion, thus avoiding the generation of tasks that can fit into modern computer memory.

Technically, the verification tasks $V(L, \varphi)$ discussed in this paper consist of a parallel composition L of labeled transition systems and a linear-time temporal logic property φ. We do not address the subsequent code generation phase here which allows to produce, e.g., Promela code [8,13] or (Nested-Unit) Petri nets [7,16,25,28].

Fundamental to our construction are *modal contracts* [29], a specific type of assume-guarantee contracts [2–4,11,26] that allow to decompose a component into two new components such that temporal properties are preserved. Modal contracts have been used successfully to generate large model checking tasks based on the known dining philosophers problem [18], for weak bisimulation checking tasks [30], and also for tasks based on branching-time properties [17].

In this paper, we provide a constructive method for achieving our hardness results which have already been stated in [29]. The first of the following two steps, namely the construction of an initial contract, has already been treated in [19]. Thus, we focus on the second step that iteratively decomposes this initial contract into a larger parallel composition.

Initial Contract Construction. Given a linear-time property φ, construct an initial system M that (1) violates φ and (2) has a *counterexample handle* for φ, i.e., a transition that is part of every counterexample trace. The construction of such an M, as well as the subsequent construction of a corresponding *initial contract* is detailed in [19,29].

Please note that for a verification task to which "False" is the correct answer[1]—named negative verification task in the following—the initial contract guarantees that both components need to synchronize in order to traverse the handle. In contrast, for a verification task with correct answer "True"—named positive verification task throughout this paper—the initial contract ensures that one component prohibits such synchronization and thereby disables the handle.

---

[1] This means that property φ does not hold in the final task.

Iterative Decomposition. This decomposition process refines the contract and alphabet extension-based approach of [29] by *propagating dependencies* from contract to contract via counterexample handles. These handles are the key to guaranteeing our notion that φ is *sensitive* to the constructed parallel composition, i.e., the relevance of each component of the latter.

For negative verification tasks, we construct a *decomposition tree* and take its leaves as the generated composition. This composition *enables* a counterexample for φ, however abstracting from any leaf *disables* all such violation witnesses.[2]

Dually, our construction of a positive verification task is based on a *decomposition chain* that *disables* all counterexamples for φ in a way such that abstracting from any element of the final composition *enables* a potentially feasible counterexample. Figure 1 sketches such a disabling chain.

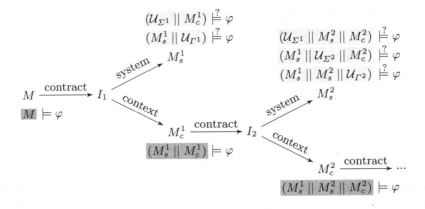

Fig. 1. Dependency propagation during contract-based decompositions. A satisfied property cannot be verified if one abstracts from an entire component [29].

After some preliminaries in Sect. 2, Sect. 3 formally introduces our notion of hardness. Subsequently, Sects. 4 and 5 present our core contributions, the construction of hard negative verification tasks and hard positive verification tasks, respectively, before we close in Sect. 6 with our conclusions and directions for future work.

2   Preliminaries

Every verification task whose construction is explained in this paper consists of a parallel composition of labeled transition systems (LTSs) and a linear temporal logic (LTL) property. As an intermediate model structure during this construction, we employ modal transition systems (MTSs) [23], a generalization of LTSs

---

[2] To be precise, the information of whether or not such violation witnesses exist is lost during abstraction.

that feature a refinement relation which preserves temporal properties such as LTL formulas.

2.1 Modal Transition Systems

Modal transition systems [23] allow to distinguish between behavior that must be feasible and behavior that may be feasible.

Definition 1 (Modal Transition System). *Let S be a set of states and Σ an alphabet of action symbols. $M = (S, s_0, \Sigma, \dashrightarrow, \longrightarrow)$ is called a (rooted) modal transition system (MTS) with root $s_0 \in S$ iff the following condition holds:*

$$\longrightarrow \; \subseteq \; \dashrightarrow \; \subseteq \; (S \times \Sigma \times S)$$

Elements of $\dashrightarrow$ are called may transitions and those of $\longrightarrow$ must transitions. We use the notations $s \overset{a}{\dashrightarrow} s'$ and $s \overset{a}{\longrightarrow} s'$ to denote transitions $(s, a, s') \in \dashrightarrow$ and $(s, a, s') \in \longrightarrow$, respectively. We further define the operator $\Sigma(M) := \Sigma$ to access the alphabet of M and overload it to access labels of transitions, i.e., $\Sigma(s \overset{a}{\dashrightarrow} s') := a$ for any $t \in \dashrightarrow$ and $\Sigma(T) := \bigcup_{t \in T}\{\Sigma(t)\}$ for any $T \subseteq \dashrightarrow$.[3]

Definition 2 (Path, Transition Precedence, and Reachability). *Given an MTS $(S, s_0, \Sigma, \dashrightarrow, \longrightarrow)$, a* path *is a sequence $\pi = s_0 \overset{a_1}{\dashrightarrow} s_1 \overset{a_2}{\dashrightarrow} s_2 \cdots$ of transitions that starts in s_0 with i ranging from 0 to either a positive integer or infinity. We use set notation to refer to the transitions of a path, e.g. $s_0 \overset{a_1}{\dashrightarrow} s_1 \in \pi$. The word w induced by the label sequence $a_1 a_2 \ldots$ is denoted as $w(\pi)$.*

For a path π, the relation $<_\pi \; \subseteq \pi \times \pi$ is defined such that $t <_\pi t'$ holds iff $t' \in \pi$ implies that t precedes t' on π. A state $s \in S$ is reachable *iff a path exists that ends in s.*

An MTS can be seen as an extension of a traditional (rooted) labeled transition system (LTS), which allows the following definition:

Definition 3 (Labeled Transition Systems). *A labeled transition system (LTS) is an MTS $M = (S, s_0, \Sigma, \dashrightarrow, \longrightarrow)$ with $\dashrightarrow \; = \; \longrightarrow$. We thus join components four and five in case of LTSs.*

The following notion of refinement allows one to regard certain LTSs as implementations of MTSs [23].

Definition 4 (MTS Refinement)
Let $M_1 = (S_1, s_0^1, \Sigma, \dashrightarrow_1, \longrightarrow_1)$, $M_2 = (S_2, s_0^2, \Sigma, \dashrightarrow_2, \longrightarrow_2)$ be MTSs. A relation $\lesssim \; \subseteq (S_1 \times S_2)$ is called a refinement *iff the following hold for all $(p, q) \in \lesssim$:*

$$1.) \; \forall p \overset{a}{\dashrightarrow}_1 p', \; \exists q \overset{a}{\dashrightarrow}_2 q' : p' \lesssim q'$$

$$2.) \; \forall q \overset{a}{\longrightarrow}_2 q', \; \exists p \overset{a}{\longrightarrow}_1 p' : p' \lesssim q'$$

M_1 *refines* M_2, *written as $M_1 \lesssim M_2$, iff there exists a refinement $\lesssim$ with $s_0^1 \lesssim s_0^2$.*

---

[3] Note that $\Sigma(M) = \Sigma(\dashrightarrow)$ is not guaranteed in general.

For the model checking of LTL properties, the maximal and minimal languages defined by an MTS M are important:

Definition 5 (Minimal and Maximal Language). *The language $\mathcal{L}(L)$ of words in an LTS L equals the label sequences of all paths in L. Infinite words in a language $\mathcal{L}$ are denoted by $\mathcal{L}^\omega$. Given an MTS $M = (S, s_0, \Sigma, \dashrightarrow, \longrightarrow)$,*

1. *$\mathcal{L}_\perp(M) := \mathcal{L}((S, s_0, \Sigma, \longrightarrow))$ is called the minimal language and*
2. *$\mathcal{L}_\top(M) := \mathcal{L}((S, s_0, \Sigma, \dashrightarrow))$ the maximal language*

of M, respectively. This definition propagates to subsets of infinite words. For a word w from some language $\mathcal{L}$, $\Sigma(w)$ denotes the set of symbols that occur in w.

Obviously, we have $\mathcal{L}_\perp(M) \subseteq \mathcal{L}_\top(M)$ because of $\longrightarrow \, \subseteq \, \dashrightarrow$. The following observation follows directly from the definition of MTS refinement and explains why it preserves linear-time properties (see Sect. 2.4).

Proposition 1 (Preserved Languages). *Let M, M' be two MTSs such that $M' \lesssim M$. Then it holds that $\mathcal{L}_\perp(M) \subseteq \mathcal{L}_\perp(M')$ and $\mathcal{L}_\top(M') \subseteq \mathcal{L}_\top(M)$.*

2.2 Parallel Composition and Weakest Specification

Our parallel composition operator for MTSs as introduced in [29] is reminiscent of CSP [12] with synchronization of components on their common alphabets:

Definition 6 (Parallel MTS Composition). *Let $M_1 = (S_1, s_0^1, \Sigma_1, \dashrightarrow_1, \longrightarrow_1)$, $M_2 = (S_2, s_0^2, \Sigma_2, \dashrightarrow_2, \longrightarrow_2)$ be two MTSs. The parallel composition*

$$M_1 \parallel M_2 := (S_1 \times S_2, (s_0^1, s_0^2), \Sigma_1 \cup \Sigma_2, \dashrightarrow, \longrightarrow)$$

is then defined as a commutative and associative operation[4] satisfying the following operational rules where $\rightarrow$ identifies the type of transition and is once instantiated to represent may transitions and once to represent must transitions:[5]

$$\frac{p \xrightarrow{a}_1 p' \quad q \xrightarrow{a}_2 q'}{(p, q) \xrightarrow{a} (p', q')} \quad \cdot \quad \frac{p \xrightarrow{a}_1 p' \quad a \notin \Sigma_2}{(p, q) \xrightarrow{a} (p', q)}$$

It is straightforward to establish that $\parallel$ preserves refinement for both operands:

Proposition 2 (Refinement Monotonicity). *Let M, M', and M'' be MTSs. Then refinement is preserved by parallel composition:*

$$M \lesssim M' \quad \text{implies} \quad (M \parallel M'') \lesssim (M' \parallel M'')$$

---

[4] These laws are meant to hold up to graph isomorphism.
[5] Please note that every must transition is also a may transition.

Note that due to the commutativity of operator $||$, this monotonicity holds for both components of a composition.

It follows directly that parallel composition can only reduce the minimal and maximal languages of an MTS if synchronization occurs.

Proposition 3 (Orthogonal Composition). *Let M, M' be two MTS with $\Sigma(M) \cap \Sigma(M') = \emptyset$. Then we have:*

$$\mathcal{L}_\perp(M) \subseteq \mathcal{L}_\perp(M \,||\, M') \quad and \quad \mathcal{L}_\top(M) \subseteq \mathcal{L}_\top(M \,||\, M')$$

The following notion allows us to link transitions of a component MTS to transitions in a parallel composition.

Definition 7 (Transition Occurrences)
Let $M_1 = (S_1, s_0^1, \Sigma_1, \dashrightarrow_1, \longrightarrow_1)$ and $M_2 = (S_2, s_0^2, \Sigma_2, \dashrightarrow_2, \longrightarrow_2)$ be two MTSs with $M := M_1 \,||\, M_2$ and $t = p \overset{a}{\dashrightarrow}_1 p'$ a transition in M_1. Then the set

$$\{\, (p, q) \overset{a}{\dashrightarrow} (p', q') \mid \exists q, q' \in S_2 \,\}$$

of may transitions in M is denoted by $t|_M$. This definition extends naturally to sets T of transitions, i.e. $T|_M := \bigcup_{t \in T}(t|_M)$. For any set of transition T' in M, we define $t|_{T'} := t|_M \cap T'$.

Parallel components are relevant for a verification task if they cannot be abstracted to their weakest specification [24]:

Definition 8 (Weakest Modal Specification)
Let Σ be an alphabet. We call the one-state MTS $\mathcal{U}_\Sigma$ with may transitions for every $a \in \Sigma$ the weakest modal Σ-specification:

$$\mathcal{U}_\Sigma =_{def} (\{s\}, s, \Sigma, (\{s\} \times \Sigma \times \{s\}), \emptyset)$$

The following proposition follows from the semantics of parallel composition.

Proposition 4 (Unconstrained Maximal Language). *Let M be an MTS and $\mathcal{U}_\Sigma$ the weakest modal Σ-specification for some alphabet Σ. Then we have:*

$$\mathcal{L}_\top(M) \subseteq \mathcal{L}_\top(M \,||\, \mathcal{U}_\Sigma)$$

2.3   Alphabet View

Throughout this paper, we frequently inspect words that result form a projection to sub-alphabets.

Definition 9 (Alphabet View). *For a word w over Σ, we define $[w]_\Gamma$ as the word that results from skipping all symbols in w that do not exist in $\Gamma \subseteq \Sigma$. This definition extends naturally to languages.*

It is apparent that adding parallel components only reduces the language of an MTS when projected to its own alphabet.

Proposition 5 (Composition Monotonicity). *Let M, M' be two MTSs. Then the following hold:*

$$[\mathcal{L}_\perp((M \parallel M'))]_{\Sigma(M)} \subseteq \mathcal{L}_\perp(M) \ and \ [\mathcal{L}_\top((M \parallel M'))]_{\Sigma(M)} \subseteq \mathcal{L}_\top(M)$$

Moreover, we have:

Proposition 6 (Maximal-Language Monotonicity). *Let M, M', and M'' be three MTSs such that $(\Sigma(M)\backslash\Sigma(M'))\cap\Sigma(M'') = \emptyset$. Then the following holds*

$$[\mathcal{L}_\top^\omega(M')]_{\Sigma(M)} \subseteq \mathcal{L}_\top^\omega(M) \quad implies \quad [\mathcal{L}_\top^\omega(M' \parallel M'')]_{\Sigma(M \parallel M'')} \subseteq \mathcal{L}_\top^\omega(M \parallel M'')$$

The following monotonicity property is important for establishing the hardness of positive verification tasks:

Proposition 7 (Minimal-Language Monotonicity). *Let M, M', and M'' be three MTSs such that $(\Sigma(M')\backslash\Sigma(M)) \cap \Sigma(M'') = \emptyset$. Then we have:*

$$\mathcal{L}_\perp(M) \subseteq [\mathcal{L}_\perp(M')]_{\Sigma(M)} \quad implies \quad \mathcal{L}_\perp(M \parallel M'') \subseteq [\mathcal{L}_\perp(M' \parallel M'')]_{\Sigma(M \parallel M'')}$$

2.4   Linear Temporal Logic Model Checking

The following definitions specify linear temporal logic (LTL) [1,31], more precisely, action-based LTL [9,27]:

Definition 10 (Syntax of Linear Temporal Logic (LTL)). *Let Σ be an alphabet of actions and $a \in \Sigma$. The syntax of (action-based) LTL is defined using the following grammar in Backus-Naur form:*

$$\varphi ::= \top \mid a \mid \varphi \wedge \varphi \mid \neg\varphi \mid \mathbf{X}\,\varphi \mid (\varphi \, \mathbf{U} \, \varphi)$$

LTL is the set of formulas φ that can be constructed this way.

The operator $\mathbf{X}$ (or "next") describes behavior that has to hold at the next time step. A formula $(\varphi_1 \, \mathbf{U} \, \varphi_2)$ describes that φ_2 has to occur eventually and that φ_1 has to hold until φ_2 occurs in a word. The formal semantics of LTL is based on a satisfaction relation between infinite words and LTL formulas [1]:

Definition 11 (LTL Semantics). *Let Σ be an alphabet of action symbols. For any infinite word $w = a_1 a_2 \ldots \in \Sigma^\omega$ and any $i \in \mathbb{N}$, let $w_i = a_i$ be the i-th element of w and $w^i = a_i a_{i+1} \ldots$ the suffix of w starting at index i.*
The satisfaction relation $\models \subseteq (\Sigma^\omega \times \text{LTL})$ is defined as the minimal relation that adheres to the following rules for any $w \in \Sigma^\omega$ and $\varphi, \psi \in \text{LTL}$:

1. $w \models \top$
2. $w \models a$ iff $w_1 = a$
3. $w \models (\varphi \wedge \psi)$ iff $w \models \varphi$ and $w \models \psi$
4. $w \models \neg\varphi$ iff $w \not\models \varphi$
5. $w \models \mathbf{X}\,\varphi$ iff $w^1 \models \varphi$

6. $w \models (\varphi \; \mathbf{U} \; \psi)$ *iff* $\exists k \in \mathbb{N} : w^k \models \psi$ *and* $\forall i \in \mathbb{N}_{<k} : w^i \models \varphi$

The semantics *of a formula* $\varphi \in \mathrm{LTL}$ *is given by* $[\![\varphi]\!]_A := \{ w \in \Sigma^\omega \mid w \models \varphi \}$.

Common abbreviations include $\mathbf{F}\,\varphi := (\top \; \mathbf{U} \; \varphi)$ which expresses that φ will eventually become true and its dual operator $\mathbf{G}\,\varphi := \neg\mathbf{F}\,\neg\varphi$ which claims that φ is always true.

     Model checking an LTL property on an MTS means to decide which of the following three possibilities hold:

Definition 12 (Satisfaction/Violation Between MTSs and LTL). *Let* M *be an MTS and* φ *an LTL formula. Then* M *satisfies* φ *(denoted as* $M \models \varphi$*) iff:*

$$\forall w \in \mathcal{L}_\top^\omega(M) : w \models \varphi$$

Similarly, M *violates* φ *(denoted as* $M \not\models \varphi$*) iff:*

$$\exists w \in \mathcal{L}_\bot^\omega(M) : w \not\models \varphi$$

Moreover, M *is indecisive concerning* φ *(denoted as* $M \overset{?}{\models} \varphi$*) iff* M *neither satisfies nor violates* φ.

3   Hardness

In this section, we establish our central notions of hardness of a verification task.

Definition 13 (Verification Task). *A parallel composition* $L = (L_1 \|\cdots\| L_n)$ *of LTSs and a temporal property* φ *specify a verification task* $V(L, \varphi)$ *that is called* positive verification task *iff* $L \models \varphi$ *and* negative verification task *iff* $L \not\models \varphi$.

The following two definitions are significant when defining the relevance of parallel components for a verification task.

Definition 14 (Component Abstraction)
Let $M = (M_1 \|\cdots\| M_n)$ *be a parallel composition of MTSs,* $\Sigma_i = \Sigma(M_i)$ *the alphabet of the i-th component of M, and* $\mathcal{U}_{\Sigma_i}$ *the weakest modal Σ_i-specification (see Definition 8). Then we call the parallel MTS composition*

$$\alpha(M, i) =_{def} (M_1 \|\cdots\| M_{i-1} \| \mathcal{U}_{\Sigma_i} \| M_{i+1} \|\cdots\| M_n)$$

the i-th component abstraction of M.

Definition 15 (φ-Lossy Generalization). *Let* M *be an MTS and* φ *a temporal property such that* M *either satisfies or violates* φ. *Then any MTS* M' *that is indecisive concerning* φ *is called a φ-lossy generalization of M.*

System sensitivity guarantees that all components of a parallel composition are relevant for the verification/refutation of the considered formula φ.

Definition 16 (System-Sensitive Properties). *Let* $M = (M_1 \| \cdots \| M_n)$ *be a parallel composition of MTSs and* φ *a temporal property. We call* φ M-*sensitive iff the following holds:*

$$\forall i \in 1 .. n : \alpha(M, i) \text{ is a } \varphi\text{-lossy generalization of } M$$

We obtain the parallel composition of LTSs for a verification task by means of component-wise modal refinement.

Definition 17 (LTS Component Refinement). *Let* $M = (M_1 \| \cdots \| M_n)$ *be a parallel composition of* n *MTSs. A parallel composition* $L = (L_1 \| \cdots \| L_n)$ *of* n *LTSs is called* LTS component refinement *of* M *iff* $L_i \lesssim M_i$ *holds for each* $i \in 1 .. n$.

Our approach depends on the following notion of *interruptible* temporal properties [27].

Definition 18 (Interruptible LTL Property). *Let* φ *be an LTL property over an alphabet* Σ. *Then* φ *is called* interruptible *iff for any alphabet* Σ_E *and any infinite words* $w \in \Sigma^\omega, w_E \in \Sigma_E^\omega$, *the following holds:*

$$w = [w_E]_\Sigma \text{ implies } (w \models \varphi \iff w_E \models \varphi)$$

In Sects. 4 and 5, we will show how to establish n-hard verification tasks for *interruptible* temporal properties.

Definition 19 (n-Hardness). *Let* $V(L, \varphi)$ *be a verification task such that* L *contains* n *parallel components. We call* $V(L, \varphi)$ n-*hard iff the following conditions are met:*

1. *Property* φ *is* L-*sensitive.*
2. *The expanded LTS* L *consists of at least* 2^n *distinct reachable states.*

The following two sections follow the same pattern: (1) initial contract construction followed by (2) iterative decomposition. Conceptually, these sections are dual, which is directly reflected in required correctness arguments. Guaranteeing hardness, however, turns out to be much more involved for positive verification tasks than for negative ones.

4   Negative Verification Tasks

In this section, we first sketch how to construct *initial green contracts* following the lines of [19] and [29], before we present our iterative, decomposition-based construction of hard negative verification tasks.

4.1   Initial Green Contract Construction

In order to control the validity of a property φ, we start our generation with a single MTS M_0 that features a transition which toggles the satisfaction of φ [19].

Definition 20 (CE-handle). *Let M be an MTS and φ an LTL formula such that $M \not\models \varphi$. A transition t in M is called a* counterexample handle (CE-handle) *for φ in M iff the removal of t results in $M \models \varphi$.*

Given an initial MTS with a CE-Handle, we utilize green contracts for parallel decomposition in order to obtain multiple components.

Definition 21 (Green Contract). *Let $M = (S, s_0, \Sigma, \dashrightarrow, \longrightarrow)$ be an MTS and $\Gamma \subseteq \Sigma$. The* green contract (GC) $I = (M, \Gamma)$ *specifies a set of context MTSs $\mathcal{M}_c(I)$ such that for every $M_c \in \mathcal{M}_c(I)$, we have $\Sigma(M_c) = \Gamma$ and $M \parallel M_c \lesssim M$. We define $G(I) := \{ s \xrightarrow{a} s' \mid a \in \Gamma \}$ and color transitions of $G(I)$ green.*

In the context of parallel decomposition, we refer to M as the *system* of I. Intuitively speaking, a green contract specifies a set of must transitions for which a corresponding context component always has to guarantee synchronization. We can reuse the construction presented in [29] to obtain a matching context MTS.

Proposition 8 (Green Context Construction). *Given a GC $I = (M, \Gamma)$, one can efficiently construct a context MTS M_c for I.*

By combining CE-handles and green contracts and thereby the approaches presented in [19] and [29], we obtain the starting point for our decomposition.

Definition 22 (Initial Green Contract). *Let φ be an LTL property and $M_0 = (S, s_0, \Sigma, \dashrightarrow, \longrightarrow)$ an MTS such that a CE-handle $s \xrightarrow{a} s'$ for φ in M_0 exists. Then a GC $I_0 := (M_0, \Gamma)$ with $a \in \Gamma$ is called* initial green contract *for φ based on M_0.*

Example 1. Consider MTS M_0 from Fig. 2a and the interruptible LTL property $\varphi := \mathbf{F}\,\mathbf{G}\,\neg a$. We have $M_0 \not\models \varphi$ because of the fact that the infinite path π with $w(\pi) = (abcd)^\omega$ violates φ: it satisfies its negation $\mathbf{G}\,\mathbf{F}\,a$. The single transition labeled b is a CE-handle for φ because one needs to traverse it on every infinite path π in M_0 for which $w(\pi)$ contains a.[6] Therefore, choosing $\Gamma = \{b, c\}$ yields an initial green contract $I_0 = (M_0, \Gamma)$ for φ (Fig. 2b).

Our construction can start with an arbitrary LTL property.

Theorem 1 (Initial Green Contract Construction). *We can construct an initial green contract for any LTL property φ that is not a tautology.*

This theorem holds based on the following sketch to construct an MTS with a CE-handle (see [19] for details):

---

[6] Note that other CE-handles for φ exist, for example the transition labeled a itself.

1. Synthesize a Büchi automaton B with language $\mathcal{L}(B) = [\![\varphi]\!]_A$.
2. Transform B to an MTS M of may transitions with $\mathcal{L}_{\top}^{\omega}(M) \subseteq \mathcal{L}(B)$ by cutting all non-accepting loops.
3. Choose a counterexample lasso h with $w(h) \in [\![\neg\varphi]\!]_A$.
4. Merge h into M while heuristically aiming for a long shared prefix between h and M.
5. The first transition of h after this shared prefix is then a CE-handle for φ.

Section 4.2 shows how we can iteratively decompose our initial contract such that hardness of the generated task is guaranteed.

4.2   Iterated Decomposition

Given the GCs introduced in the previous section, it is straightforward to iteratively decompose an initial MTS into arbitrarily many parallel components such that properties are preserved due to the underlying modal refinement, regardless of how the initial green contract was chosen. We will see, however, that guaranteeing hardness requires additional care.

Definition 23 (Prerequisite Contract). *Let $I = (M, \Gamma)$, $I' = (M', \Gamma')$ be two GCs. Then I' is called* prerequisite contract *of I iff the following holds for all paths π in $M \parallel M'$:*[7]

$$\forall t \in G(I)|_{\pi}, \ \exists t' \in G(I')|_{\pi} : \ t' \prec_{\pi} t$$

Example 2. Figure 2c contains three MTSs that include green transitions: these all depict GCs. The two GCs on the intermediate level of the depicted tree are prerequisite contracts of the tree's root: on any path within these prerequisite contracts, transitions labeled b and c are preceded by a green transition. Note that for each of these prerequisite contracts, the underlying MTS is structurally equivalent to its composition with the MTS that underlies the root GC.

Given Proposition 5 and the definition of parallel MTS composition (Definition 6), one can see that the precedence correspondence enforced by a prerequisite contract is preserved under composition:

Proposition 9 (Preserved Precedence). *Let $M_1 = (S, s_0, \Sigma, \dashrightarrow, \longrightarrow)$, M_2 be MTSs with $t_1, t_1' \in \dashrightarrow$. If $t_1' \prec_{\pi_1} t_1$ holds for all paths π_1 in M_1, then for any path π in $M_1 \parallel M_2$ and any $t \in t_1|_{\pi}$, there exists a $t' \in t_1'|_{\pi}$ such that $t' \prec_{\pi} t$.*

A straightforward transitivity argument now directly yields:

Corollary 1 (Precedence Transitivity)
Let $I_0 = (M_0, \Gamma_0), \ldots, I_k = (M_k, \Gamma_k)$ be $k + 1$ GCs such that for all $j \in 0 .. k$, there exists an $i \in 0 .. j - 1$ such that I_j is a prerequisite contract of I_i. Let π be any path in $M_0 \parallel M_1 \parallel \ldots \parallel M_k$. Then the following holds for all $m \in 1 .. k$:

$$\forall t \in G(I_0)|_{\pi}, \ \exists t' \in G(I_m)|_{\pi} : \ t' \prec_{\pi} t$$

---

[7] Please recall that the precedence relation $\prec_{\pi}$ has been introduced in Definition 2.

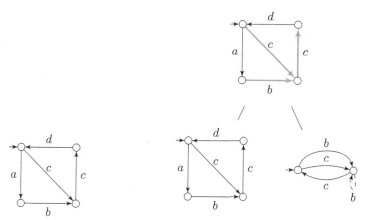

(a) MTS M_0 which is a variant of Milner's four-state cycler as shown in [28] with a CE-handle labeled b for the interruptible LTL property $\mathbf{F\,G}\,\neg a$

(b) Enabling tree based on M_0: Initial green contract I_0 for $\mathbf{F\,G}\,\neg a$ based on M_0 with its system M_0 (left child) and a corresponding context M_c^0 (right child)

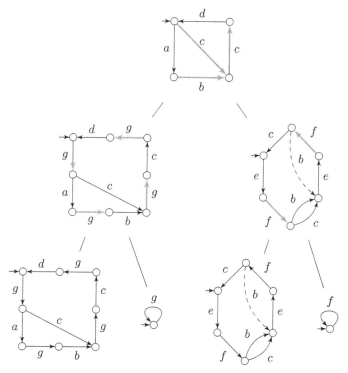

(c) Enabling tree based on M_0 after extending the alphabet of each leaf in Fig. 2b and then replacing it with a prerequisite contract of I_0 and corresponding subtree.

Fig. 2. Exemplary construction of an enabling tree

Corollary 1 implies that the set of green transitions of any prerequisite contract serves as a handle for the reachability of green transitions in the initial GC.

Corollary 2 (Green Remote Handle)
Let $I_0 = (M_0, \Gamma_0), \ldots, I_k = (M_k, \Gamma_k)$ be $k + 1$ GCs such that for all $j \in 0 \ldots k$, there exists an $i \in 0 \ldots j - 1$ such that I_j is a prerequisite contract of I_i. Further, let $M := M_0 \parallel \cdots \parallel M_k$. Then for any $m \in 0 \ldots k$, removing all transitions $G(I_m)|_{M_m}$ causes all transitions in $G(I_0)|_M$ to be unreachable in M.

The following definition of *alphabet extension* is key towards scalability in size:

Definition 24 (Alphabet Extension). *Let M, M_E be two MTSs such that $\Sigma_E := \Sigma(M_E) \setminus \Sigma(M) \neq \emptyset$. Then M_E is called Σ_E-alphabet extension of M iff the following conditions hold:*

$$\mathcal{L}_\perp^\omega(M) = [\mathcal{L}_\perp^\omega(M \parallel M_E)]_{\Sigma(M)} \text{ and } \mathcal{L}_\top^\omega(M) = [\mathcal{L}_\top^\omega(M \parallel M_E)]_{\Sigma(M)}$$

Example 3. Consider again the three GCs with their green transitions in Fig. 2c. When interpreting green transition as must transitions and thereby inspecting the underlying MTS, the two on the intermediate level are alphabet extensions of the MTS M_0 on top.

Alphabet extensions can be constructed by utilizing a scheme that we introduced previously [29]. This allows us to efficiently construct a prerequisite contract of I based on the system or any context of I.

Lemma 1 (Prerequisite Contract Construction)
Given a GC $I = (M, \Gamma)$, an $M' \in \{M\} \cup \mathcal{M}_c(I)$, and an alphabet $\Sigma_E \neq \emptyset$ disjoint from $\Sigma(M)$, one can efficiently construct

1. *a Σ_E-alphabet extension M_E of M' and*
2. *a GC $I' = ((M' \parallel M_E), \Gamma')$ with $\Gamma' \subseteq \Sigma_E$*

such that I' is a prerequisite contract of I.

Proof. Let M_E be a deterministic MTS with two states such that Σ_E leads from the start state to the second state and Γ the other way around and such that all transitions in M_E are must transitions. Then M_E is a Σ_E-alphabet extension of M' and $I' = ((M' \parallel M_E), \Sigma_E)$ is a GC.

For I' to be a prerequisite contract of I, we need to show that whenever a path π in $M \parallel M_E$ traverses some $t \in G(I)|_{M \parallel M_E}$, then it previously traversed a $t' \in G(I')|_{M \parallel M_E}$ (Definition 23). By the construction of M_E we have that for every path in M_E, transitions from Γ are always preceded by Σ_E. By Proposition 5, this property carries over to the composition $M \parallel M_E$. The result follows as $\Sigma(G(I')|_{M \parallel M_E}) \subseteq \Sigma_E$ and $\Sigma(G(I)|_{M \parallel M_E}) \subseteq \Gamma$. $\square$

Our goal is to automatically generate a set of prerequisite contracts that satisfies the condition in Corollary 2 so that we can toggle the reachability of green transitions from the initial green contract—and thereby that of the CE-handle itself. The required decomposition history can be organized as a tree.

Definition 25 (Enabling Tree). *Given an MTS M_0, a decomposition tree T based on M_0 is inductively defined by starting with the trivial tree that only contains M_0 and then iteratively replacing any leaf M in T with either*

1. *a Σ_E-alphabet extension of M such that Σ_E contains symbols not yet in T, or*
2. *a subtree with root $I = (M, \Gamma)$, a GC, and two children M and $M_c \in \mathcal{M}_C(I)$.*

The parallel composition of the leaves of T is denoted by $M(T)$. We call T enabling tree iff, except for its root, each GC I in T is a prerequisite contract of some ancestor of I.

Example 4. The sub-figures in Fig. 2 each illustrate an enabling tree based on an initial MTS M_0 (Fig. 2a). The sub-figures build upon each other based on the inductive definition of a decomposition tree.

Given the definition of an alphabet extension, the language preservation of modal refinement (Proposition 1), and the monotonicity of this preservation w.r.t. parallel MTS composition (Propositions 6 and 7), the parallel composition of the leaves of an enabling tree preserves both minimal and maximal languages.

Proposition 10 (Language Preservation of Enabling Tree). *Let T be a decomposition tree based on M_0. Then we have:*

$$\mathcal{L}_\perp(M_0) \subseteq [\mathcal{L}_\perp(M(T))]_{\Sigma(M_0)} \ \text{and} \ [\mathcal{L}_\top^\omega(M(T))]_{\Sigma(M_0)} \subseteq \mathcal{L}_\top^\omega(M_0)$$

Note that all components which share an alphabet symbol need to synchronize based on must transitions for must behavior to prevail in the corresponding composition. Combined with Corollary 2, this ensures that abstracting any leaf of an enabling tree eliminates all counterexamples from the minimal language.

Proposition 11 (Green-Based Sensitivity). *Let φ be an interruptible LTL property and T an enabling tree for some M_0 such that its root is a green initial contract for φ based on M_0. Then φ is $M(T)$-sensitive.*

Component refinement is a special form of modal refinement. Thus, the following proposition is straightforward.

Proposition 12 (Preserved Sensitivity). *Let φ be a temporal property, M a parallel composition of MTSs such that $M \not\models \varphi$, and L an LTS component refinement of M. If φ is M-sensitive, then it is also L-sensitive.*

Exponential growth of the state space of the constructed parallel compositions can be enforced as illustrated in [28]. Together with Proposition 12, this yields:

Theorem 2 (Hard Negative Verification Task). *Given an initial green contract I_0 for some interruptible LTL property φ, one can efficiently construct an n-hard negative verification task $V(L, \varphi)$.*

5   Positive Verification Tasks

In this section, we first sketch how to construct *initial modal contracts*, following the lines of [29] and [19], before we present our decomposition-based, iterative construction of hard positive verification tasks.

5.1   Initial Modal Contract Construction

For positive verification tasks, we employ modal contracts [29] in a way that the CE-handle plays a dual role compared to initial green contracts: rather than being enabled by the constructed contexts, it has to be disabled.

Definition 26 (Modal Contract). *Let $M = (S, s_0, \Sigma, \dashrightarrow, \longrightarrow)$ be an MTS, $\Gamma \subseteq \Sigma$, $R \subseteq S \times \Gamma \times S$ with $R \cap \dashrightarrow = \emptyset$, and $M_s := (S, s_0, \Sigma, \dashrightarrow \cup R, \longrightarrow \cup R)$. Then the tuple $I = (M, \Gamma, R)$ is a* modal contract (MC) *of M with communication alphabet Γ iff*

$$\mathcal{M}_C(I) := \{M_c \mid M_s \parallel M_c \precsim M \wedge \Sigma(M_c) = \Gamma\} \neq \emptyset.$$

Moreover, $G(I) := \{s \xrightarrow{a} s' \mid a \in \Gamma\}$ and we color transitions of $G(I)$ green and transitions of R red. We call $M_s(I) := M_s$ the system of I and any $M_c \in \mathcal{M}_C(I)$ a context *of I.*

Definition 27 (Initial Modal Contract). *Let φ be an LTL property and $M = (S, s_0, \Sigma, \dashrightarrow, \longrightarrow)$ an MTS such that a CE-handle $s \xrightarrow{a} s'$ for φ in M exists. Then an MC $I_0 := (M_0, \Gamma, R)$ is called* initial modal contract *for φ iff*

1. *$M_0 = (S, s_0, \Sigma, \dashrightarrow \backslash R, \longrightarrow \backslash R)$,*
2. *$s \xrightarrow{a} s' \in R$, and*
3. *$\mathcal{U}_\Sigma \parallel M_c$ is indecisive concerning φ for any context $M_c \in \mathcal{M}_C(I_0)$.*

The third condition in Definition 27 ensures that φ is $(M_s(I_0) \parallel M_c)$-sensitive. Further note that $M_s(I_0) = M$. An efficient construction of contexts was given in [29].

Proposition 13 (Modal Context Construction). *A context $M_c \in \mathcal{M}_C(I)$ of an MC $I = (M, \Gamma, R)$ can be constructed efficiently such that*

$$\mathcal{L}_\top(M_c) = (\Gamma^* \cup \Gamma^\omega) \backslash [\mathcal{L}_R]_\Gamma$$

holds where $\mathcal{L}_R$ contains all words for which a path in I exists that traverses a transition in R.

Example 5. The transition system at the top of Fig. 4 (center column) illustrates an initial modal contract I_0 for the interruptible LTL property $\varphi := \mathbf{G}\,\mathbf{F}\,a$. The red self loop labeled d at the initial state of I_0 is a CE-handle for φ in the system $M_s(I_0)$ which is depicted to the right of I_0. Below I_0 in Fig. 4, a context $M_c \in \mathcal{M}_c(I_0)$ is shown: in a composition with $M_s(I_0)$, it disables transitions that were colored red in I_0 and thus the mentioned CE-handle.

The proof that initial contracts can be constructed mostly follows the reasoning in Sect. 4.1. Note that the third condition in Definition 27 can always be satisfied by deferring communication to new symbols using alphabet extensions.

Theorem 3 (Initial Modal Contract Construction). *We can construct an initial modal contract for any LTL property φ that is not a tautology.*

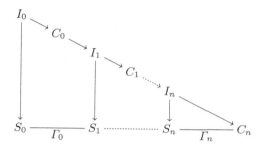

Fig. 3. Sketch of our decomposition chain for generating hard positive verification tasks. The generated composition (bottom row) consists of system components except for a final context.

5.2   Iterated Decomposition

Green transitions allow to symmetrically propagate dependencies to both system and context components in a decomposition tree. In contrast, red transitions are asymmetric: systems allow red transitions whereas contexts do not. This leads to a decomposition chain of iteratively decomposed contexts (see Fig. 3).

We actually preserve the entire minimal language of our initial system component $M_s(I_0)$—the one *with* the CE-handle—throughout our chain of constructed system components. Because the last context however disables red transitions of the initial contract, we call such a sequence of modal contracts *disabling chain*.

Definition 28 (Disabling Chain). *A sequence $C = (I_0 = (M_0, \Gamma_0, R_0), \dots, I_k = (M_k, \Gamma_k, R_k))$ of $k + 1$ MCs is called disabling chain (DC) for I_0 iff the following hold for all $j \in 1 \mathbin{..} k$:*

(a) M_j *only communicates with* M_{j-1} *and* M_{j+1} *(if existing)*
(b) $\Sigma(M_{j-1}) \cap \Sigma(M_j) = \Gamma_{j-1} \neq \emptyset$
(c) $[\mathcal{L}_\top^\omega(M_j)]_{\Gamma_{j-1}} = \mathcal{L}_\top^\omega(M_c^{j-1})$ *for some context* M_c^{j-1} *of* I_{j-1}
(d) $\mathcal{L}_\perp(M_s(I_{j-1})) \subseteq [\mathcal{L}_\perp(M_s(I_{j-1}) \,\|\, M_s(I_j))]_{\Gamma_{j-1}}$

We further define:

1. $M_s(C) := M_s(I_0) \,\|\, \cdots \,\|\, M_s(I_k)$
2. $\mathcal{M}(C) := \{M_s(C) \,\|\, M_c^k \mid M_c^k \text{ is a context of } I_k\}$

Given an initial modal contract I_0, we can automatically generate a DC of I_0 by using alphabet extensions.

Lemma 2 (DC Construction). *Given an MC I_0, one can efficiently construct a sequence $I_1, \ldots, I_k$ of MCs such that $C = (I_0, I_1, \ldots, I_k)$ is a DC.*

The proof of Lemma 2 is straightforward but tedious and therefore omitted in this exposition.

Example 6. Figure 4 illustrates the construction of a DC C with two MCs based on the initial modal contract of Example 5. Conditions (a) and (b) of Definition 28 are ensured by choosing new symbols from an alphabet extension for the second MC. Similarly, condition (c) is ensured because of the language preservation of alphabet extensions (Definition 24). The minimal language preservation in condition (d) is realized by introducing a red transition labeled f that leads to an otherwise unreachable state: this target state enables the CE-handle in the parallel composition of system components.

Given the modal refinement of MCs, the monotonicity stated in Proposition 6, and condition (c) of Definition 28, it follows that a DC does not extend the maximal language of the MTS that underlies its initial contract (see also Fig. 1).

Proposition 14 (Maximal-Language Reduction)
Let $C = ((M_0, \Gamma_0, R_0), \ldots, I_k)$ be a DC and $M \in \mathcal{M}(C)$. Then we have:

$$[\mathcal{L}_\top^\omega(M)]_{\Sigma(M_0)} \subseteq \mathcal{L}_\top^\omega(M_0)$$

Moreover, based on Proposition 7, it is easy to show:

Proposition 15 (Preservation Transitivity). *Let M, M', M'' be MTSs with $\Sigma(M) \cap \Sigma(M'') = \emptyset$. If we know that $\mathcal{L}_\perp(M) \subseteq [\mathcal{L}_\perp(M \parallel M')]_{\Sigma(M)}$ and also $\mathcal{L}_\perp(M') \subseteq [\mathcal{L}_\perp(M' \parallel M'')]_{\Sigma(M')}$, then $\mathcal{L}_\perp(M) \subseteq [\mathcal{L}_\perp(M \parallel M' \parallel M'')]_{\Sigma(M)}$.*

Because of Propositions 14 and 15, we know that a DC C as defined above preserves the minimal language of $M_s(I_0)$ in $M_s(C)$, as well as the maximal language of M_0 in any $M \in \mathcal{M}(C)$. As the red transitions in R_0 are the only difference between M_0 and $M_s(I_0)$, it immediately follows that the last context of C toggles the existence of paths that traverse some $t \in R_0$ and thus the existence of a counterexample.

Corollary 3 (Red Remote Handle). *Let $C = (I_0 = (M_0, \Gamma_0, R_0), \ldots, I_k)$ be a DC and $M \in \mathcal{M}(C)$. Further, let $w \in \mathcal{L}_\perp^\omega(M_s(I_0))$ such that for every path π in $M_s(I_0)$ with $w(\pi) = w$, it holds that $R(I_0)|_\pi \neq \emptyset$. Then*

1. $w \in [\mathcal{L}_\perp^\omega(M_s(C))]_{\Sigma(M_0)}$, *however*
2. $w \notin [\mathcal{L}_\perp^\omega(M)]_{\Sigma(M_0)}$.

This allows us to prove:

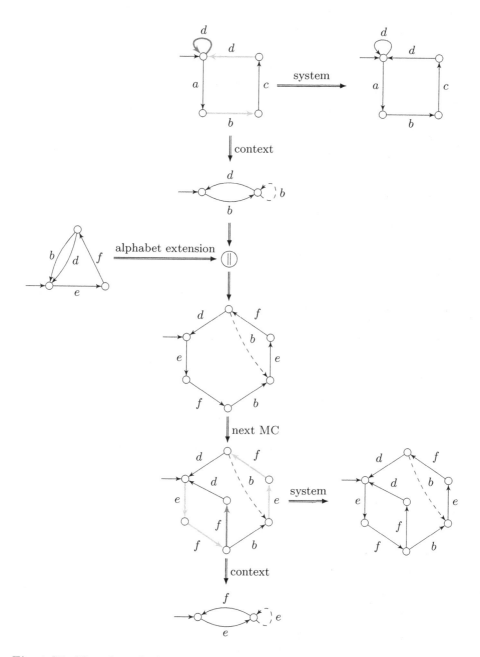

Fig. 4. Disabling chain C of an initial modal contract I_0 for the interruptible LTL property $\varphi := \mathbf{G}\,\mathbf{F}\,a$ that results in a parallel composition $M \in \mathcal{M}(C)$ of three MTSs (right column). Every LTS component refinement L of M yields a hard positive verification task $V(L, \varphi)$.

Lemma 3 (Red-based Sensitivity). *Let φ be an interruptible LTL property and $C = (I_0, \ldots, I_k)$ a DC such that I_0 is an initial modal contract for φ. Then φ is L-sensitive for any LTS component refinement L of any $M \in \mathcal{M}(C)$.*

Proof. Let φ, C satisfy the premise of Lemma 3 and $M = M_s(C) \,\|\, M_c \in \mathcal{M}(C)$. We first show that φ is M-sensitive. By construction, $R(I_0)$ contains a CE-handle and M contains $k + 2$ parallel components. Corollary 3.2 ensures that $[\mathcal{L}_\perp^\omega(M)]_{\Sigma(M_0)}$ does not contain words for which a transition in $R(I_0)$ has to be traversed, therefore M satisfies φ. In order to show that φ is M-sensitive, it remains to be proven that for any $i \in 0 \,..\, k + 2$, the component abstraction $\alpha(M, i)$ is indecisive concerning φ.

Case $i = 0$: There exists a context M_c^0 of I_0 with $\mathcal{L}_\top^\omega(M_c^0) \subseteq [\mathcal{L}_\top^\omega(M_s(I_1))]_{\Gamma_0}$ because of Definition 28(c) and the fact that the system of a modal contract only extends the maximal language of its underlying MTS. The fact that $\alpha(M, 0)$ is indecisive concerning φ thus follows from the third condition in Definition 27 and the fact that only neighboring components communicate (Definition 28(a)).

Case $i = k + 2$: Corollary 3.1 implies that $\mathcal{L}_\perp^\omega(M_s(C))$ contains a counterexample which is inherited by the maximal language of any modal generalization of $M_s(C)$, in particular by $\alpha(M, i) = M_s(C) \| U_{\Gamma_k}$ that abstracts from M_c. Thus, φ is indecisive concerning $\alpha(M, i)$.

Case $1 \le i \le k + 1$: In this case, the sub-compositions M_s^{i-1} and M_c^{i+1} defined as follows are non-empty.

$$M = \underbrace{M_s(I_0) \,\|\, \cdots \,\|\, M_s(I_{i-1})}_{M_s^{i-1}} \,\|\, M_s(I_i) \,\|\, \underbrace{M_s(I_{i+1}) \,\|\, \cdots \,\|\, M_s(I_k) \,\|\, M_c}_{M_c^{i+1}}$$

Corollary 3.1 implies that a counterexample $w \in \mathcal{L}_\perp^\omega(M_s^{i-1})$ exists based on the sub-chain of i MCs. We know that $\Sigma(M_s^{i-1}) \cap \Sigma(M_c^{i+1}) = \emptyset$ due to Definition 28(a), thus Proposition 3 ensures that $w \in \mathcal{L}_\top^\omega(M_s^{i-1} \,\|\, M_c^{i+1})$. Proposition 4 guarantees that adding the weakest specification of M_i to the composition does not reduce its maximal language, therefore $w \in \mathcal{L}_\top^\omega(\alpha(M, i))$, resulting in the fact that M is indecisive concerning φ.

As a consequence, φ is M-sensitive. Because a (component) refinement of $M_s(C)$ preserves its minimal language, such a refinement still guarantees the required existence of counterexamples. Thus, φ is L-sensitive for any LTS component refinement L of M. $\qquad\square$

As an exponential number of reachable states can again be realized via alphabet extensions as in Sect. 4, we obtain:

Theorem 4 (Hard Positive Verification Task). *Given an initial modal contract I_0 for some interruptible LTL property φ, one can efficiently construct an n-hard positive verification task $V(L, \varphi)$.*

6   Conclusion and Outlook

We have presented a new method to automatically generate hard verification tasks $V(L, \varphi)$ consisting of a *synchronous* parallel system L and an *interruptible* linear-time property φ. Key to our approach is a contract-based local decomposition of components that can be iterated to construct arbitrarily large compositions of parallel components that are all relevant for solving the generated task. By using available code generators, resulting verification tasks can be made available in Promela, DOT[8] format, or in the form of Petri Nets [16].

We are currently devising specific variants of our method to ensure that, e.g., formulas concern only actions of a single component, that various verification tasks share the same parallel system, or that the prefixes of counterexamples which need to be investigated have a minimum length [15]. Another line of future research concerns the generalization to branching-time logics.

Parts of this work have already been used to generate parallel verification benchmarks for the RERS Challenge in 2020[9] while utilizing an implementation of modal contracts in the AutomataLib[10]. We target to fully support our new approach in the next iteration of RERS. It will be particularly interesting to see how well state-of-the-art approaches to (compositional) verification—including techniques inspired by already available modal-contract-based benchmarks [21, 22, 27]—can handle our hard verification tasks.

References

1. Baier, C., Katoen, J.P., Larsen, K.G.: Principles of Model Checking. MIT Press, Cambridge (2008)
2. Bauer, S.S., et al.: Moving from specifications to contracts in component-based design. In: de Lara, J., Zisman, A. (eds.) FASE 2012. LNCS, vol. 7212, pp. 43–58. Springer, Heidelberg (2012). https://doi.org/10.1007/978-3-642-28872-2_3
.3. Benveniste, A., Caillaud, B.: Synchronous interfaces and assume/guarantee contracts. In: Aceto, L., Bacci, G., Bacci, G., Ingólfsdóttir, A., Legay, A., Mardare, R. (eds.) Models, Algorithms, Logics and Tools. LNCS, vol. 10460, pp. 233–248. Springer, Cham (2017). https://doi.org/10.1007/978-3-319-63121-9_12
4. Benveniste, A., et al.: Contracts for system design. Found. Trends Electron. Des. Autom. **12**(2–3), 124–400 (2018). https://doi.org/10.1561/1000000053
5. Cardoso, R.C., Farrell, M., Luckcuck, M., Ferrando, A., Fisher, M.: Heterogeneous verification of an autonomous curiosity rover. In: Lee, R., Jha, S., Mavridou, A., Giannakopoulou, D. (eds.) NFM 2020. LNCS, vol. 12229, pp. 353–360. Springer, Cham (2020). https://doi.org/10.1007/978-3-030-55754-6_20
6. Chandra, S., Godefroid, P., Palm, C.: Software model checking in practice: an industrial case study. In: Proceedings of the 24th International Conference on Software Engineering, ICSE 2002, pp. 431–441 (2002). https://doi.org/10.1145/581339.581393

---

[8] https://graphviz.org/doc/info/lang.html.
[9] http://www.rers-challenge.org/2020/.
[10] https://learnlib.de/projects/automatalib/. Support for modal contracts is planned to be made publicly available with the next release (0.11).

7. Garavel, H.: Nested-unit Petri nets. J. Log. Algebraic Methods Program. **104**, 60–85 (2019). https://doi.org/10.1016/j.jlamp.2018.11.005

8. Geske, M., Jasper, M., Steffen, B., Howar, F., Schordan, M., van de Pol, J.: RERS 2016: parallel and sequential benchmarks with focus on LTL verification. In: Margaria, T., Steffen, B. (eds.) ISoLA 2016. LNCS, vol. 9953, pp. 787–803. Springer, Cham (2016). https://doi.org/10.1007/978-3-319-47169-3_59

9. Giannakopoulou, D., Magee, J.: Fluent model checking for event-based systems. ACM SIGSOFT Softw. Eng. Notes **28**(5), 257–266 (2003). https://doi.org/10.1145/940071.940106

10. Goga, N., Costache, S., Moldoveanu, F.: A formal analysis of ISO/IEEE P11073-20601 standard of medical device communication. In: 3rd Annual IEEE Systems Conference, pp. 163–166 (2009). https://doi.org/10.1109/SYSTEMS.2009.4815792

11. Grumberg, O., Long, D.E.: Model checking and modular verification. ACM Trans. Program. Lang. Syst. (TOPLAS) **16**(3), 843–871 (1994). https://doi.org/10.1145/177492.177725

12. Hoare, C.A.R.: Communicating sequential processes. In: The Origin of Concurrent Programming, pp. 413–443. Springer (1978). https://doi.org/10.1145/359576.359585

13. Holzmann, G.: The SPIN Model Checker: Primer and Reference Manual, 1st edn. Addison-Wesley Professional, Boston (2011)

14. Howar, F., Isberner, M., Merten, M., Steffen, B., Beyer, D., Păsăreanu, C.: Rigorous examination of reactive systems. The RERS challenges 2012 and 2013. STTT **16**(5), 457–464 (2014). https://doi.org/10.1007/s10009-014-0337-y

15. Howar, F., Jasper, M., Mues, M., Schmidt, D., Steffen, B.: The RERS challenge: towards controllable and scalable benchmark synthesis. Int. J. Softw. Tools Technol. Transfer. (2021). https://doi.org/10.1007/s10009-021-00617-z

16. Jasper, M., et al.: The RERS 2017 challenge and workshop (invited paper). In: Proceedings of the 24th ACM SIGSOFT International SPIN Symposium on Model Checking of Software. SPIN 2017, pp. 11–20. ACM (2017). https://doi.org/10.1145/3092282.3098206

17. Jasper, M., et al.: RERS 2019: combining synthesis with real-world models. In: Beyer, D., Huisman, M., Kordon, F., Steffen, B. (eds.) TACAS 2019. LNCS, vol. 11429, pp. 101–115. Springer, Cham (2019). https://doi.org/10.1007/978-3-030-17502-3_7

18. Jasper, M., Mues, M., Schlüter, M., Steffen, B., Howar, F.: RERS 2018: CTL, LTL, and reachability. In: Margaria, T., Steffen, B. (eds.) ISoLA 2018. LNCS, vol. 11245, pp. 433–447. Springer, Cham (2018). https://doi.org/10.1007/978-3-030-03421-4_27

19. Jasper, M., Steffen, B.: Synthesizing subtle bugs with known witnesses. In: Margaria, T., Steffen, B. (eds.) ISoLA 2018. LNCS, vol. 11245, pp. 235–257. Springer, Cham (2018). https://doi.org/10.1007/978-3-030-03421-4_16

20. Kordon, F., et al.: Report on the model checking contest at Petri nets 2011. In: Jensen, K., van der Aalst, W.M., Ajmone Marsan, M., Franceschinis, G., Kleijn, J., Kristensen, L.M. (eds.) Transactions on Petri Nets and Other Models of Concurrency VI. LNCS, vol. 7400, pp. 169–196. Springer, Heidelberg (2012). https://doi.org/10.1007/978-3-642-35179-2_8

21. Lang, F., Mateescu, R., Mazzanti, F.: Compositional verification of concurrent systems by combining bisimulations. In: ter Beek, M.H., McIver, A., Oliveira, J.N. (eds.) FM 2019. LNCS, vol. 11800, pp. 196–213. Springer, Cham (2019). https://doi.org/10.1007/978-3-030-30942-8_13

22. Lang, F., Mateescu, R., Mazzanti, F.: Sharp congruences adequate with temporal logics combining weak and strong modalities. In: TACAS 2020. LNCS, vol. 12079, pp. 57–76. Springer, Cham (2020). https://doi.org/10.1007/978-3-030-45237-7_4
23. Larsen, K.G.: Modal specifications. In: Sifakis, J. (ed.) CAV 1989. LNCS, vol. 407, pp. 232–246. Springer, Heidelberg (1990). https://doi.org/10.1007/3-540-52148-8_19
24. Guldstrand Larsen, K.: Ideal specification formalism = expressivity + compositionality + decidability + testability + ... In: Baeten, J.C.M., Klop, J.W. (eds.) CONCUR 1990. LNCS, vol. 458, pp. 33–56. Springer, Heidelberg (1990). https://doi.org/10.1007/BFb0039050
25. Peterson, J.L.: Petri Net Theory and the Modeling of Systems. Prentice Hall PTR (1981)
26. Raclet, J.B., Badouel, E., Benveniste, A., Caillaud, B., Legay, A., Passerone, R.: A modal interface theory for component-based design. Fund. Inform. 108(1–2), 119–149 (2011). https://doi.org/10.3233/FI-2011-416
27. Siegel, S.F., Yan, Y.: Action-based model checking: logic, automata, and reduction. In: Lahiri, S.K., Wang, C. (eds.) CAV 2020. LNCS, vol. 12225, pp. 77–100. Springer, Cham (2020). https://doi.org/10.1007/978-3-030-53291-8_6
28. Steffen, B., Jasper, M., Meijer, J., van de Pol, J.: Property-preserving generation of tailored benchmark Petri nets. In: 2017 17th International Conference on Application of Concurrency to System Design (ACSD), pp. 1–8 (2017). https://doi.org/10.1109/ACSD.2017.24
29. Steffen, B., Jasper, M.: Property-preserving parallel decomposition. In: Aceto, L., Bacci, G., Bacci, G., Ingólfsdóttir, A., Legay, A., Mardare, R. (eds.) Models, Algorithms, Logics and Tools. LNCS, vol. 10460, pp. 125–145. Springer, Cham (2017). https://doi.org/10.1007/978-3-319-63121-9_7
30. Steffen, B., Jasper, M.: Generating hard benchmark problems for weak bisimulation. In: Bartocci, E., Cleaveland, R., Grosu, R., Sokolsky, O. (eds.) From Reactive Systems to Cyber-Physical Systems. LNCS, vol. 11500, pp. 126–145. Springer, Cham (2019). https://doi.org/10.1007/978-3-030-31514-6_8
31. Warford, J.S., Vega, D., Staley, S.M.: A calculational deductive system for linear temporal logic. ACM Comput. Surv. 53(3) (2020). https://doi.org/10.1145/3387109

Author Index

Printed in the United States
by Baker & Taylor Publisher Services